QUANTUM SCIENCE OF LOVE, HEALING, HAPPINESS, AND BLISS IN ANCIENT WISDOM

QUANTUM SCIENCE OF LOVE, HEALING, HAPPINESS, AND BLISS IN ANCIENT WISDOM

Prof. (Dr.) Jai Paul Dudeja

Delhi - 11089, India

Edition : First published in paperback in July 2021
ISBN : 978-93-90889-60-0

QUANTUM SCIENCE OF LOVE, HEALING, HAPPINESS, AND BLISS IN ANCIENT WISDOM

By : Prof. (Dr.) Jai Paul Dudeja

Price : 1500/-

Cover page & Layout
Jyoti Singh

Published by
Prakhar Goonj Publication
H-3/2, Sector - 18, Rohini, Delhi - 110089
Contact : 7982710571, 7838505899, 011-27851059
Email : prakhargoonj@gmail.com,
sinha.neelu123@gmail.com
web : prakhargoonjpublications.com

CONTENTS

PREFACE

Dear Readers,

I am extremely happy to see this book titled, **"Quantum Science of Love, Healing, Happiness, and Bliss in Ancient Wisdom"** in your hands. It is my firm belief that you have chosen to read this book with a specific aim in mind, and I assure you that you will not be disappointed.

One can divide this book into **six broad sections**: The first section (chapter 1) consists of 'Introduction'; the second section (chapters 2-5) deals with **Love** (in Hinduism, Buddhism, Sufism, and Christianity); the third section (chapters 6-9) describes the process of **Healing** (in Hinduism, Buddhism, Sufism, and Christianity); the fourth section (chapters 10-13) deals with **Happiness** (in Hinduism, Buddhism, Sufism, and Christianity); the fifth section (chapters 14-17) describes the concept of **Bliss** (in Hinduism, Buddhism, Sufism, and Christianity); and sixth and the final section on **Quantum Science** (Chapters 18-21) justifies the title of this book by correlating Quantum Science with Love, Healing, Happiness and Bliss in Ancient Wisdom.
The coverage of each of these archetypes, viz., love, healing, happiness, and bliss, in various religions: Hinduism, Buddhism, Sufism, and Christianity, will truly appeal to all the readers across the globe.

Chapter 1 titled, "Love, Healing, Happiness and Bliss: Introduction" is a must read for all those who wish to appreciate the rest of this book for introducing themselves about these archetypes in Hinduism, Buddhism, Sufism, and Christianity.

There are four chapters (2-5) on 'Love' in Section 2.

Chapter 2 titled, "Love in Hinduism" describes the concept of Love based mainly on ancient Hindu scriptures, viz,. Vedas,

Upanishads, Bhagavad Gita, and Ramayana. Likewise, **Chapter 3** titled, "Love in Buddhism" deals with the concept of love as described in ancient Buddhist wisdom. **Chapter 4** titled, "Love in Sufism" and **Chapter 5** titled, "Love in Christianity" describe this archetype of Love in Sufism and Christianity, respectively.

There are four chapters (6-9) on 'Healing' in Section 3.

Chapter 6 titled, "Healing in Hinduism" describes the concept of Healing based mainly on ancient Hindu scriptures, viz,. Vedas, Upanishads etc.. Likewise, **Chapter 7** titled, "Healing in Buddhism" deals with the concept of Healing as described in ancient Buddhist wisdom. **Chapter 8** titled, "Healing in Sufism" and **Chapter 9** titled, "Healing in Christianity" describe this archetype of Healing in Sufism and Christianity, respectively.

There are four chapters (10-13) on 'Happiness' in Section 4.

Chapter 10 titled, "Happiness in Hinduism" describes the concept of Happiness based mainly on ancient Hindu scriptures, viz,. Vedas, Upanishads etc.. Likewise, **Chapter 11** titled, "Happiness in Buddhism" deals with the concept of Happiness as described in ancient Buddhist wisdom. **Chapter 12** titled, "Happiness in Sufism" and **Chapter 13** titled, "Happiness in Christianity" describe this archetype of Happiness in Sufism and Christianity, respectively.

There are four chapters (14-17) on 'Bliss' in Section 5.

Chapter 14 titled, "Bliss in Hinduism" describes the concept of Bliss based mainly on ancient Hindu scriptures, viz,. Vedas, Upanishads etc.. Likewise, **Chapter 15** titled, "Bliss in Buddhism" deals with concept of Bliss as described in ancient Buddhist wisdom. **Chapter 16** titled, "Bliss in Sufism" and **Chapter 17** titled, "Bliss in Christianity" describe this archetype of Bliss in Sufism and Christianity, respectively.

There are four chapters (18-21) on the application of Quantum Science to these four archetypes: Love, Healing, Happiness, and Bliss in Hinduism, Buddhism, Sufism, and Christianity.

Chapter 18 titled, "Basics of Quantum Science" describes the elementary principles of Quantum Mechanics in simple, non-mathematical and layman's language. **Chapter 19** titled, "Quantum Entanglement and Connection with Souls" deals with the introduction of the phenomenon of quantum entanglement and their application to love and connected souls. Two true stories based on quantum entanglement are also given in this chapter. **Chapter 20** is titled, "Quantum Science of Mind-Body Interaction". It establishes how mind and body influence each other. Last chapter, that is **Chapter 21** titled, "Quantum Science of Love, Healing, Happiness, and Bliss" truly justifies the title of this book. It takes the help of all the concepts developed earlier in this book and give an explanation of each of the archetypes with the help of Quantum Science.

I am confident that you, as a reader, will find a lot of inspiration from this book and appreciate that many aspects of love, healing, happiness and bliss, shared with you here, were not revealed to you till now.

This author sincerely believes that a book of this nature inter-weaving all these diversified topics in Hinduism, Buddhism, Sufism, and Christianity and their correlation with Quantum Science of Love, Healing, Happiness, and Bliss, explained in the layman's language will appeal to the global readership and will go a long way in bridging the existing gap between these topics.

I would gratefully and open heartedly love to receive any encouraging/critical comments as well as feedback from my dear readers at my Email ID: drjpdudeja@gmail.com

Wishing you a happy and blissful reading,

Sincerely

2021 **Prof. (Dr.) Jai Paul Dudeja**

ACKNOWLEDGMENTS

The seeds of my interest in ‘Spirituality, based on ancient scriptures’ were sown more than seventy years ago by my revered parents, **Late (Dr.) Shanti Sawrup Dudeja and Late (Mrs.) Jai Devi Dudeja**. I, therefore, bow to them, wherever they are in the other world.

I have been very fortunate to have great teachers in ‘Quantum Science’ in my life. This knowledge enabled me to correlate my concepts of Quantum Science to various aspects of Love, Healing, Happiness and Bliss in Hinduism, Buddhism, Sufism and Christianity in this book. My heartfelt gratitude to these outstanding teachers.

Further, I have greatly benefitted in going through the books and articles referred in the ‘Bibliography’ of this Book. I gratefully acknowledge these authors for enhancing my understanding on the subject matter of this book.

Last but not the least, my greatest admiration is reserved for **Mrs. Rita Dudeja, my wife**, my best friend and my constant source of encouragement, for all my ventures and endeavours like this and many others.

2021 **Prof. (Dr.) Jai Paul Dudeja**

SECTION 1

(INTRODUCTION)

CHAPTER 1

Love, Healing, Happiness and Bliss: Introduction

1.1 What Is Love?

Love is a set of emotions and behaviours characterized by intimacy, passion, and commitment. It involves care, closeness, protectiveness, attraction, affection, and trust. Love can vary in intensity and can change over time. It is associated with a range of positive emotions, including happiness, excitement, life satisfaction, and euphoria, but at times, it can also result in negative emotions such as jealousy, possessiveness and stress.

Love encompasses a range of strong and positive emotional and mental states, from the most sublime virtue or good habit, the deepest interpersonal affection, to the simplest pleasure. An example of this range of meanings is that the love of a mother differs from the love of a spouse, which differs from the love of food. Most commonly, love refers to a feeling of strong attraction and emotional attachment.

1.1.1 Types of Love

Not all forms of love are the same, and psychologists have identified a number of different types of love that people may experience. These types of love include:

(i) Friendship: This type of love involves liking someone and sharing a certain degree of intimacy.

(ii) Infatuation: This is a form of love that often involves intense feelings of attraction without a sense of commitment; it often takes place early in a relationship.

(iii) Passionate love: This type of love is marked by intense feelings of longing and attraction; it often involves an idealization of the other person and a need to maintain constant physical closeness.

(iv) Compassionate/companionate love: This form of love is marked by trust, affection, intimacy, and commitment.

(v) Unrequited or One-sided love: This form of love happens when one person loves another who does not return those feelings.

The human kind as a whole has forgotten the true meaning of the word "love". This word has been used (and abused) so much, that, sadly, many people never really find out what the true Divine love actually is.

1.1.2 Divine Love: The most fundamental feature of Divine love is that it tends to transcend itself. In other words, it has a strong urge to overcome itself, which in turn leads to an equally strong urge for creation. That's why we say that without Divine love nothing would be created. The greatest thing a person can experience is their unity with the Divine. That's the most perfect love, the one and only kind of love every single person on this planet is looking for.

The key of spiritual development is having and experiencing Divine love. If you want to know whether you are making any progress on your spiritual path, ask yourself whether you're experiencing Divine love. But Divine love can only be realized if we've become one with the very stream of love, with the River of Universal Life. If only we could experience a piece of that love, our joy would be so great, so intense, and so all-inclusive, that we could hardly restrain it at all. The Divine love has an enormous power of attraction. But, at the same time, it's also a balancing force that brings harmony inside us, harmony with the other people around us, with Nature and with God.

Ancient Greek philosophers identified six forms of love: essentially, (i) familial love, (ii) friendly love or platonic love, (iii) romantic love, (iv) self-love, guest love, and divine love. Modern authors have distinguished further varieties of love: unrequited love, empty love, companionate love, consummate love, infatuated love, self-love, and courtly love, some of these types have been described in the earlier paras.

People can be said to love an object, principle, or goal to which they are deeply committed and greatly value. For example, compassionate outreach and volunteer workers' "love" of their cause may sometimes be born not of interpersonal love but impersonal love, and strong spiritual or political convictions. People can also "love" material objects, animals, or activities if they invest themselves in bonding or otherwise identifying with those things. Interpersonal love refers to love between human beings. It is a much more potent sentiment than a simple liking for a person. Unrequited love refers to those feelings of love that are not reciprocated. Interpersonal love is most closely associated with Interpersonal relationships. Such love might exist between family members, friends, and couples. There are also a number of psychological disorders related to love.

(i) Divine Love in Hinduism

Biological models of sex tend to view love as a mammalian drive, much like hunger or thirst. The experience of love is divided into three partly overlapping stages: lust, attraction, and attachment. Lust is the feeling of sexual desire; romantic attraction determines what partners mates find attractive and pursue, conserving time and energy by choosing; and attachment involves sharing a home, parental duties, mutual defence, and in humans involves feelings of safety and security. Three distinct neural circuitries, including neurotransmitters, and three behavioural patterns, are associated with these three romantic styles.

In Hinduism, kāma is pleasurable, sexual love, personified by the god Kamadeva. For many Hindu schools, it is the third end (Kama) in life. Kamadeva is usually accompanied by his consort Rati and his companion Vasanta, lord of the spring season. In contrast to kāma, Prema – or prem – refers to elevated love. Karuna is compassion and mercy, which impels one to help reduce the suffering of others.

Bhakti is a Sanskrit term, meaning "loving devotion to the supreme God." A person who practices bhakti is called a bhakta. Hindu writers, theologians, and philosophers have distinguished nine forms of bhakti, which can be found in the Bhagavata Purana and works by Tulsidas. The philosophical work Narada Bhakti Sutras, written by an unknown author (presumed to be Narada), distinguishes eleven forms of love. In certain Vaishnava sects within Hinduism, attaining unadulterated, unconditional and incessant love for Godhead is considered the foremost goal of life. Gaudiya Vaishnavas who worship Krishna as the Supreme Personality of Godhead and the cause of all causes consider Love for Godhead (Prema) to act in two ways: sambhoga and vipralambha (union and separation)—two opposites.

According to Hindu philosophy, anything that helps to unite all and develop pure divine love and universal brotherhood, is Dharma. According to Bhakti Yoga described in Bhagavad Gita, Bhakti is one of the chief spiritual sciences. He is wealthy indeed, who has love for the Lord.

There is no sorrow other than lack of devotion to the Lord. There is no right course except love of the devotee for the Lord. The Name, qualities and Lilas (plays) of the Lord are the chief things to be remembered. The lotus-feet of the Lord are the chief objects of meditation. The devotee drinks the nectar of Prema or divine love.

According to Sri Chaitanya, Hari's Name should always be chanted by him who must be humbler than a blade of grass (which is trodden upon); who is more patient, forbearing and charitable than a tree (which does not cry out even when it is cut down and which does not beg for water even when scorched to death, but on the contrary, offers its treasure to whosoever seeks it, bears the sun and rain itself, but protects those who take shelter under it from rain and sunshine); who, however worthy of esteem should, instead of claiming respect for himself, give respect to all (from a sense of God's immanency in all beings). He who thus takes Krishna's Name gets Divine Love (Prema).

(ii) Divine Love in Buddhism

In Buddhism, Kāma is sensuous, sexual love. It is an obstacle on the path to enlightenment, since it is selfish. Karuna is compassion and mercy, which reduces the suffering of others. It is complementary to wisdom and is necessary for enlightenment. Adveṣa and metta are benevolent love. This love is unconditional and requires considerable self-acceptance. This is quite different from ordinary love, which is usually about attachment and sex and which rarely occurs without self-interest. Instead, in Buddhism it refers to detachment and unselfish interest in others' welfare.

The Bodhisattva ideal in Mahayana Buddhism involves the complete renunciation of oneself in order to take on the burden of a suffering world. The strongest motivation one has in order to take the path of the Bodhisattva is the idea of salvation within unselfish, altruistic love for all sentient beings.

(iii) Divine Love in Sufism

One of Jala ad-Din Muhammad Rumi's important ways in relation to God-Man is "love". Man can reach God through love and achieve divine qualities. According to Islamic understanding and literature, man has been valued by God's spirit when created, and the soul of God has been given to him. Therefore, the great power that is inhabited is its spirit. With this factor, man can reach to the highest order by moving from the lowest point and raising himself, and also get the chance of accessing the divine spirit. Rumi, Hafiz and Sa'di are icons of the passion and love that the Persian culture and language present. The Persian word for love is Ishq, which is derived from Arabic language; however, it is considered by most to be too stalwart a term for interpersonal love and is more commonly substituted for "doost dashtan" ("liking"). In the Persian culture, everything is encompassed by love and all is for love, starting from loving friends and family, husbands and wives, and eventually reaching the divine love that is the ultimate goal in life. Ishq, or divine love, is the emphasis of Sufism in the Islamic tradition. Practitioners of

Sufism believe that love is a projection of the essence of God to the universe. God desires to recognize beauty, and as if one looks at a mirror to see oneself, God "looks" at himself within the dynamics of nature. Since everything is a reflection of God, the school of Sufism practices to see the beauty inside the apparently ugly. Sufism is often referred to as the religion of love.

According to Rumi (Sufism), there are 3 types of human definitions in the definitions of Mathnawi: (i) a person who is an ordinary entity, (ii)) a creative and superior person, ad (iii) a person who is defined as a species or concept. In these definitions Rumi calls the precious and superior or perfect human. A person who possesses such a characteristic will be able to grasp the relationship between himself and God in a very proper and sufficient way, to understand his duties, and to understand his spirit as a physical person. Thus, it is also the concept of what will live against both itself and society. In this context, the integrated and mature person observes only the divine love in physical and metaphysical dimensions, and defines all behaviours, thoughts and words for God's sake.

Hence, the human being is not only a kind and concept, but also saved from ordinariness. As a result, humanity and humane behaviour are exhibited in all areas of every life. According to Rumi, the person who carries the name of human is absolutely "an entity that knows, feels, and possesses some of these qualities in a number of pivotal activities aimed at his or her chosen goals. Such a person carries the name "human perfection".

(iv) Divine Love in Christianity

The Christian experience of divine love is the unconditional and gracious self-giving of God that makes possible humanity's response to its Creator. It is rooted in the New Testament declaration that "God is love" (1 John 4:16). The New Testament employs the Greek term agape to connote a meaning of love distinct from eros and philia. New Testament authors deliberately prefer agape for its connotation of a selfless— and, in the life of Christ, sacrificial—love in which the beloved is loved for her own sake, without self-interest. The identification of God with this love in 1 John 4:16 gives rise to the correlative responsibility of persons to love their neighbour—who is seen—as the test case for their love of God, who remains unseen (1 John 4:20), and thus shows that they abide in God. Agape is thus both a divine prerogative, revealed pre-eminently in the Cross and Resurrection, and the task of Christian disciples who, like Christ, love sacrificially, lose themselves in loving others, and, paradoxically but unmistakably, discover themselves in the process (Luke 17:33 and parallels).

The belief that God is love comments at once on the divine life (in se), as a trinity of personal relationships in reciprocal communion, and on God's covenantal relationship with human beings (ad extra). This is evidenced by God's creating them for covenant partnership, redeeming them from their sin and self-contraction independent of their own merit, and consummating them for beatific intimacy in the divine life.

The doctrine of the trinity underscores that the divine life is self-giving love, considering that the one God who is one substance exists in three equal and active relationships of love. Rather than tritheism, this dynamic self-differentiation suggests that the divine life is constituted by personal relationships in communion, as the Father who generates the Son (filiation); as the Son generated by the Father who loves the Father in perfect obedience; and as the Holy Spirit, who according to Augustine proceeds from the Father and Son together (spiration) and is the bond of love between them. Richard of St. Victor notably held that God was necessarily triune on the basis of the nature of love, which requires that love between two persons be perfected in their shared love for a third, thus avoiding an enclosed egoism between the two precisely in their shared love for a genuine other.

1.2 What is Healing?

Healing is a course of action of the restitution of health to an unbalanced, diseased or injured organism. The word healing comes from the old-English term *haelen*, meaning "wholeness" and often refers to the process of moving towards a desired wholeness or achievement of cohesion. Healing was correlated with themes of wholeness, narrative, and spirituality. Healing is an intervention, an outcome, and a process, and at times, all the three. It also describes an ability or power, or energy, and cleansing of grief, trouble, or evil. Additional nuances of the meaning of healing are: increased order, coherence, temporality, and balance. The concept is relevant in a wide range of disciplines, including medicine, nursing, psychology, public health, education, religion, and spirituality. Healing occurs in multiple dimensions—physical, mental, emotional, spiritual, familial (relating to or occurring in a family or its members), social, communal, and environmental. It is quite clear that healing is not synonymous with curing, which focuses on elimination of the signs and symptoms of disease. Healing occurs at multiple levels from the micro level, as in cellular wound healing, to the macro level, as in national and global healing. Healing originates from within the individual and from external sources (for example, human healers and God) or substances (for example, herbs and medicines). Perspectives on healing come from healthcare practitioners, patients, priests, gurus, rabbis, energy practitioners, spiritual healers, for people close to death, for people living with pain and other chronic illnesses, for people who have suffered abuse and neglect, and for those who have suffered hardship such as divorce, miscarriage, or death of a child.

Defining attributes are the characteristics of a healing concept that differentiate from other similar or related concepts. The healing is a holistic transformative process; it is personal; it is innate or naturally occurring; it is multidimensional; and it involves repair and recovery of mind, body, and spirit/soul. The positive, transformative process, progression, or journey does not occur in a single instant but evolves over time. The process is dynamic, emergent, and experiential. It is a journey and an experience.

1.2.1 Energy Healing

Common terms used in the field of energy healing include energy healing, energy medicine, energy therapies, laying on of hands, and spiritual healing. While there is a great deal of cross pollination within and across traditions, a useful categorization of the spectrum of energy healing includes:

• East Asian traditions, which include systems such as Reiki and qigong;

• Western professional traditions, such as TT and healing touch, often practiced by nurses;

• Bioenergy traditions, a family of healing theories and methods originating primarily in Eastern Europe; and

• Contemporary metaphysical traditions that include spiritual healers.

This diversity of practice challenges the traditional medical research process in which we are accustomed to specifying a well-defined and uniform intervention.

1.2.2 Spiritual Healing

Healing is a natural gift inherent in every human being which can be used to heal oneself as well as others. Spiritual healing opens one's heart to divine love and leads to inner awakening. Spiritual healing leads to the maintenance of health, emphasizing meditation, specific movements of the body so that the health of the individual is restored to its normal state. Modern medicine claims to restore the health of the individuals but not to heal. The role of the physicians has been transferred from being the healer to the curer of the disease. Thus, religion has taken up a massive foothold in the field of providing healing to its followers. The healing traditions is one of the chief factors which gives rise to spiritual consciousness, relaxation of the mind, curer of the diseases. Overall, one can say that the healing traditions develop the proper functioning of the body, mind and the spirit together. Even in the medical sphere, understanding the body and the mind is one of the crucial factors while analysing the patients. Healing traditions related to one's diet and healthy digestion of the consumed food involved therapeutic treatment which invariably acts as the technique of the balance of behaviour and emotions. Use of the medicinal plants also acts as vital healing strategies by which the body can be cured of the pathology it is suffering from. These traditional plants are known to be the "natural antibiotics". Therefore, the healing traditions strengthen the immune system and the homeostatic mechanism of our body.

(i) Spiritual Healing in Hinduism

There are different ways and forms by which a Hindu healer tries to heal a patient out of its pathology. These ways mainly include Ayurveda, and Yoga.

Ayurveda: The formal scientific culture of healing is known as Ayurveda. The word "Ayus" means life, vitality, health and the word "veda" mean science or knowledge. Therefore, the word "Ayurveda", in Sanskrit, means the "Science of Life". Ayurveda is the traditional Hindu science of medicine that is carried out in one form or another by 80% of people of the Indian descent. It is one of the oldest healing sciences. It originated around 5000 years ago and is referred to as by many people as the "Mother of all Healing". Ayurveda puts a great amount of emphasis on the deterrence and encouragement for the healthy maintenance of one's life by maintaining a balanced life-style with proper diet.

There are three basic types of energy identified in Ayurveda. These are vata, pitta and kapha. Vata, Pitta and Kapha are created with the amalgamation of Space, Air, Fire, Water and Earth (the five elements). It is based on the "tridosha theory of disease". There is the requirement of energy to create movements of the body fluids and nutrients so that the total body can function properly. Body, mind and consciousness works together in a flow under the umbrella of Ayurveda. Vata includes the energy associated with movements.

Thus, it is composed of Space and Air. It governs breathing, blinking of the eyes, pulse of the heart etc. Pitta implies the body's metabolic system. It is therefore, composed of Fire and Water. It governs the nutrition, body temperature, digestion. Pitta leads to the production of intelligence and understanding. Anger, jealousy and hatred can crop up if the pitta is out of one's control. Kapha includes the energy that forms the body's structure, that is, bones, and muscles. It supplies water for all the body parts. If the Kapha is in balance, it can produce life, calmness but if it is out of control, the responses like greed, attachment, envy result from it. Ayurveda doesn't put its spotlight on the diseases rather on the balances of the energies within the body. It provides description of how to treat the diseases through medicinal herbs.

Yoga: Yoga is considered to be a part of healing, spirituality and meditation. It is a philosophy of the ancient and is considered as a practice of well-being of the individuals. By doing Yoga, one can control the mind. The mind is the ultimate source from where concentration emanates. Therefore, the ability to focus and discipline the mind is the work of the yoga. Yoga may not cure an individual from any kind of diseases (for example AIDS) but it can give strength to the individual and heal his mind to bear with the consequences. There are different types of yoga, such as:

Hatha Yoga--- Hatha had its origination in India in the 15th century. It is slow-paced, gentle, and focused on breathing and meditation. It relieves stress and improves breathing along with physical exercise.

Raja Yoga---It is an inclusive of all Yogas. It emphasises on meditation and self-realization as well as the evolution of the consciousness.

Tantra Yoga---It aims at expanding consciousness. It promotes a one-pointedness and centeredness that helps us to free the consciousness from any kind of limitations.

(ii) Spiritual Healing in Buddhism

Bhaiṣajyaguru is the Buddha healing of healing and medicine in Mahāyāna Buddhism. Commonly referred to as the "Medicine Buddha", he is described as a doctor who cures suffering (Pali/ Sanskrit: dukkha/samsara) using the medicine of Buddha's teachings. Bhaiṣajyaguru's original name and title was raja (King), but Xuan Zang translated it as Tathagata (Buddha). Subsequent translations and commentaries followed Xuan Zang in describing him as a Buddha.

The **Twelve Vows** of the Medicine Buddha upon attaining Enlightenment, according to the Medicine Buddha Sutra are:

1. I vow that my body shall shine as beams of brilliant light on this infinite and boundless world, showering on all beings, getting rid of their ignorance and worries with my teachings. May all beings be like me, with a perfect status and character, upright mind and soul, and finally attaining enlightenment like the Buddha.

2. I vow that my body be like crystal, pure and flawless, radiating rays of splendid light to every corner, brightening up and enlightening all beings with wisdom. With the blessings of compassion, may all beings strengthen their spiritual power and physical energy, so that they could fulfil their dreams on the right track.

3. I vow that I shall grant by means of boundless wisdom, all beings with the inexhaustible things that they require, and relieving them from all pains and guilt resulting from materialistic desires. Although clothing, food, accommodation and transport are essentials, it should be utilized wisely as well. Besides self-consumption, the remaining should be generously shared with the community so that all could live harmoniously together.

4. I vow to lead those who have gone astray back to the path of righteousness. Let them be corrected and returned to the Buddha way for enlightenment.

5. I vow that I shall enable all sentient beings to observe precepts for spiritual purity and moral conduct. Should there be any relapse or violation, they shall be guided by repentance. Provided they sincerely regret their wrong-doings, and vow for a change with constant prayers and strong faith in the Buddha, they could receive the rays of forgiveness, recover their lost moral and purity.

6. I vow that all beings who are physically disabled or sick in all aspects be blessed with good health, both physically and mentally. All who pay homage to Buddha faithfully will be blessed.

7. I vow to relieve all pain and poverty of the very sick and poor. The sick be cured, the helpless be helped, the poor be assisted.

8. I vow to help women who are undergoing sufferings and tortures and seeking for transformation into men. By hearing my name, paying homage and praying, their wishes would be granted and ultimately attain Buddhahood.

9. I vow to free all beings from evil thought and its control. I shall lead them onto the path of light through inculcating them with righteousness and honour so that they will walk the Buddha way.

10. I vow to save prisoners who have genuinely repented and victims of natural disasters. My supreme powers will bless those who are sincere and be freed from sufferings.

11. I vow to save those who suffer from starvation and those who committed a crime to obtain food. If they hear my name and faithfully cherish it, I shall lead them to the advantages of Dharma and favour them with the best food that they may eventually lead a tranquil and happy life.

12. I vow to save those who suffer from poverty, tormented by mosquitoes and wasps day and night. If they come across my name, cherish it with sincerity and practice dharma to strengthen their merits, they will be able to achieve their wishes

(iii) Spiritual Healing in Sufism

From the Sufi point of view, “spiritual healing” is an endeavour to “clear the cloak” or “ images” that captured on the hearts of people. Profound Healing, for a Sufi, is a methodology of “refining the nafs,” or the conscience. Sufi thoughts and practices are based on the Quran, hadith and Sunnah (the recorded acts and the sacred saying of the Prophet Muhammad and also the examples from the life of the Prophet and his companions. Sufi Spiritual Healing is neither a magic nor a mysterious process but is in fact very natural instinct with which every human being is born but fails to actualize this potential power. Some enlightened people are gifted with healing ability that people recognize them as natural healer while others are given the ability of healing in transmission (as disciples in sufi order) and others through their inner calling take upon this or perform healing out of compassion. The role of Sufi Spiritual Healing is not only to cure the suffering humanity but to teach them the ways to awaken the God gifted hidden treasure. The goal of the Sufi is awakening and realization. The Islamic Terminology for healing is Shifaʿ. Muslims have a staunch belief that each word of the divine book “Quran” carries Shifaʿ, however in the holy tradition; the Prophet Muhammad mentioned the healing properties of specific verses and section (Surah) of the Quran for different remedies. The major characteristics of Sufi practitioner is the utilization of the healing properties of blessed verses of the Quran.

As a believer the followers of Islam believe that Holy Quran has been sent down on earth as a guide and cure to all human beings. The term Ruqya applied for the healing through recitation of the specific verses of the Quran or to make supplication by reciting specific words that are mentioned in the saying of the Prophet Muhammad.

Ruqya can be defined as a spiritual healing prayer in which verses from the Quran or the supplication taught by the Prophet Muhammad are practiced; hence Ruqya is a Sunnah of our beloved Prophet Muhammad.

Based on the Prophetic tradition the following are called "Ayat Al-Shifa" or Six verses of healing, used in Sufi Spiritual Healing:

1. "And God shall heal the inner heart of the believers."

2. "Mankind! There has come to you a guidance from your Lord and a healing for your hearts, and for those who believe a guidance and a mercy."

3. "There issues from within the bodies of the bee a drink of varying colours wherein is healing for mankind."

4. "And We sent down in the Quran such things that have healing and mercy for the believers."

5. "And when I am ill, it is God who cures me."

6. "And declare that the Quran is a guidance and healing for the believers."

(iv) Spiritual Healing in Christianity

Spiritual Healing or Divine healing in Christianity, in its simplest form, is a complex phenomenon. Some believers are healed through prayer, while the condition of others may deteriorate even more, regardless of prayer. Some believe that the absence of divine healing indicates a lack of faith on the part of the believer. Others see it as the result of insufficient faith on the part of the person praying. Perhaps divine healing is not a reality or, if it is, perhaps only God determines who will be healed. If that is indeed the case, does it mean that the believer' s prayer is in vain?

Some reject divine healing as fiction, lacking any basis in reality, while others recognise that there may be some truth in it. Many view the reports of divine healing as an exaggeration of what really happened. Another attitude is the acceptance of accounts of healing as facts and accurate statements, which are then perceived as reality. The issue is even further categorised, namely those with faith, those with little faith and those with no faith. The afore-mentioned issues clearly portray not only different viewpoints, but also a limited understanding of divine healing.

According to the Faith Movement, divine healing is part of God's will for the believer. The presuppositions of divine healing in the Faith Movement will be discussed and investigated so as to answer the question: Is divine healing, as propagated by the Faith Movement, not merely a metaphysical process – the result of positive thinking and confessing? Information for this article was collected by means of a literature study as well as personal experience through years of active involvement in the movement.

Divine healing is used by the majority of Christians to refer to the belief that God heals people through the power of the Holy Spirit. Divine healing means the restoring of health through the direct intervention of God. The products of such an intervention constitute miracles. This practice is often exercised by the laying on of hands.

Accounts of Jesus curing physical ailments are recorded in the four Gospels. Jesus cured the woman who had a discharge of blood for twelve years and suffered much under the physicians of the time, resulting in her financial predicament and a worsening condition. However, Jesus also endorsed the usage of medical assistance. The actions of the Good Samaritan who treated the battered man with oil and wine were portrayed as those of a physician and he was presented as a role model to the disciples.

Healing in the Old Testament

Healings took place in the Old Testament. There is the account of General Naaman, suffering from incurable leprosy, who was healed after a seven-fold dipping in the river (2 Ki 5:14). A world-renowned ruler of Babylon was struck by a disease that affected his senses and he started to live like an animal, but seven years later he fully recovered and resumed his international prominence (Dn 4:33– 34). Miriam was healed of leprosy (Nm 12:13). God even restored people to life. The Zarephath widow' s son was healed by the hand of Elijah (1 Ki 17:17– 24). Elisha raised the Shunammite' s son from the dead (2 Ki 4:18– 37) (Mayhue 1983:25).

Healing in the New Testament

Healings abound in the public ministry of Jesus Christ. At no other time in history were so many people healed. However, at the base of the many healings recorded in his ministry lie reasons that need to be considered in order to understand the healing ministry of Christ. Reasons given seem to authenticate the person of Jesus as the true Messiah, as well as his authority to forgive sins and proclaim God' s kingdom (Mt 8:17; Mt 9:6; Mt 11:2– 19; Mt 12:15– 21; Mk 2:10; Lk 5:24; Lk 7:18– 23; Jn 9:3; Jn 11:4; Jn 20:30– 31; and Ac 2:22).

During the healing ministry of Jesus, he avoided public approval and reward. He ordered his disciples rather to rejoice in the fact that their names were recorded in heaven than in the power to heal (Lk 10:20). Faith on the side of the afflicted also seemed not to have been necessary. Jesus raised Lazarus from the dead (Jn 11), as well as Jairus' daughter (Mt 9) and the widow' s son (Lk 7). It could also be assumed that when Jesus healed the multitudes, they were mostly unbelievers. At other times Jesus healed when faith was displayed by someone other than the afflicted. Jesus also healed those who had faith. Jesus healed the ten lepers who called on him (Lk 17:11– 19). Jesus' healing continued via his disciples (Mt 10:1– 15). Seventy other disciples were also ordered by Jesus to preach and heal (Lk 10:1– 16).

In conclusion, the healings that Jesus performed seemed to have served a purpose, namely to authenticate the person of Jesus as the true Messiah, as well as his authority to forgive sins and proclaim God' s kingdom. Yet, healing continued via the apostles, as can been seen in the Acts of the Apostles.

1.3 What is Happiness?

The word 'happiness' is used in various ways. In the widest sense it is an umbrella term for all that is good. In this meaning it is often used interchangeably with terms like 'well-being' or 'quality of life' and denotes both individual and social welfare. The term 'happiness' is used in the context of mental or emotional states, including positive or pleasant emotions ranging from contentment to intense joy. It is also used in the context of life satisfaction, subjective well-being, eudaimonia (state of feeling well), flourishing and well-being. Research on happiness has been conducted in a wide variety of scientific disciplines, including gerontology, social psychology and positive psychology, clinical and medical research and happiness economics. Happiness is the overall appreciation of one's life as-a-whole. Overall happiness is the degree to which an individual judges the overall quality of his/her own life-as-a-whole favourably. In other words: how much one likes the life one leads.

Philosophy of happiness is often discussed in conjunction with ethics. Traditional societies often linked happiness with morality, which was concerned with the performance in a certain kind of role in a certain kind of social life. Happiness, sometimes, is no longer defined in relation to social life, but in terms of individual psychology. Happiness, however, remains a difficult term for moral philosophy. Throughout the history of moral philosophy, there has been an oscillation between attempts to define morality in terms of consequences leading to happiness and attempts to define morality in terms that have nothing to do with happiness at all. People in countries with high cultural religiosity tend to relate their life satisfaction less to their emotional experiences than people in more secular countries.

Qualities of life

The first distinction is between chances and outcomes, that is, the difference between opportunities for a good life and the good life itself. A second difference is between outer and inner qualities of life, in other words between 'external' and 'internal' features. In the first case the quality is in the environment, in the latter it is in the individual.

Ingredients of Happiness

There are several theories of happiness in the literature that attempt to identify basic psychological elements that happiness consists of. The most notable theories include: subjective well-being, objective happiness (psychological well-being, eudemonic well-being, authentic happiness/the well-being, social-psychological prosperity/ flourishing, or the onion theory of happiness.

The subjective well-being theory argues that a happy individual experiences an abundance of positive feelings and few negative feelings – a balance that serves as the basis for the evaluation of life as very satisfactory (Diener et al. 2010. The objective happiness theory argues that broad cognitive evaluations of well-being ("Am I a happy person?") are usually biased; thus, only the quality of immediate experience (in terms of good vs bad as the indicator of utility) is a valid measure of well-being. The psychological well-being theory argues that a happy individual is characterized by several positive psychological characteristics such as autonomy, environmental mastery, or personal growth . The eudemonic well-being theory argues that a happy individual is, above all, intensely engaged in self-exploration, self-expression, and the development of their best potential with positive emotions as an additional consequence or a by-product of these pursuits. Social-psychological prosperity theory lists elements of positive functioning across diverse domains that are constitutive to a very happy life (flourishing) such as having rewarding relationships, contributing to happiness of others, or being engaged in daily activities. Happiness theories or authentic happiness theory that evolved into the well-being theory have distinguished components ("routes to happiness") that constitute the full life: pleasure and positive emotions (the pleasant life), engagement or flow (the good life), and meaning (meaningful life). In his further works, Included in this are the components of achievements (conceptualized as the pursuit of them rather than their actual accomplishment) and social relationships. Happiness is described with a three-layer structure in the onion theory with the positive attractor (the will to live) as the core, the mid-layer of general subjective wellbeing, and the outer layer of current effective experience and satisfaction with specific life domains that reflects objective life events and circumstances.

Individual Differences in Happiness

Large scale cross-cultural studies indicated that most individuals consider themselves rather happy. There are however meaningful differences in happiness that result from several factors. Research has established that individual differences of various components of happiness result mostly from: (a) genetic influences that sustain a level of well-being characteristic for a specific person (i.e., the happiness set-point), (b) intentional activity (e.g., how individuals regulate their positive emotions), and, to a lesser extent, (c) life events (e.g., marriage) and circumstances (e.g., income). Life events can cause positive and negative temporal (childbirth or widowhood, respectively) or lasting changes in well-being (marriage or disability). Personality is the main determinant of well-being due to its constant interaction with several aspects of human functioning such as life events and circumstances, emotional experience, and cognitive processing. Several personality traits have been related to happiness, e.g., extroverts experience more life satisfaction, whereas individuals high on neuroticism experience less life satisfaction. Happiness-related personality traits evolve over time, e.g., individuals become more extroverted and more emotionally stable. Noteworthy, the influence of personality on happiness can be modified via intentional behavioural efforts. For instance, when less extroverted individuals intentionally try to initiate behaviours that are typical for extroverts, they temporarily improve their well-being. Various aspects of happiness (i.e., life satisfaction or positive emotions) can be successfully enhanced intentionally via happiness interventions or positive psychological interventions. These interventions are inspired by cognitive therapy methods and increase happiness through exercises that enhance positive emotions (e.g., gratitude), cognitions (e.g., optimism), or behaviours (e.g., kind acts).

(i) Happiness in Hinduism

To secure happiness here in mortal life, Hinduism prescribes a holistic method, which takes into consideration both the material and spiritual needs of human beings. It recognizes four chief aims of human life, called purusharthas, by pursuing which human beings can experience physical, mental, and spiritual happiness. They are also called the four chief purposes (purusharthas) of existence, because they are also chosen by God (Purusha) himself for his own enjoyment. Broadly speaking, in a secular sense, they refer to the pursuit of morality, prosperity, enjoyment, and spirituality. Specifically, in a religious sense, they refer to religious and moral duty (dharma), wealth (artha), conjugal bliss (kama) and liberation (moksha).

Let us examine how they contribute to our happiness. By pursuing dharma, you enjoy name and fame, social status, and respect in society. By pursuing wealth, you enjoy the comforts of life, status in society, and the satisfaction of fulfilling your obligations to family and society. By pursuing kama (sex) you enjoy conjugal bliss, companionship with your spouse, family life, and the happiness of having children, relations, and continuation of family lineage. Finally, pursuing liberation, you can secure the ultimate happiness of being absolutely and eternally free from all obligations. For a human being, the four aims are the best means to secure happiness upon earth and lay a firm foundation for future happiness in the world of Brahman, the highest Self.

Hindu scriptures further suggest that a person has better chances of securing happiness and enjoying life if he pursues these four aims according to the four phases of human life, called ashramas, during which he has to fulfil the duties and obligations that are specific to each of them. The four phases of human life are, brahmacharya, grihastha, vanaprastha, and Sanyasa. In Brahmacharya, which corresponds to childhood and young age, a person has to study the

Vedas and learn about his duties and responsibilities (dharma), apart from the knowledge of the Self and the Supreme Self. In Grihastha, which correspond to the adult life, he has to perform his obligatory duties (dharma) and earn wealth (artha) to ensure the welfare, order and regularity of his family and society. In Vanaprastha, which correspond to the old age, he has to retire into seclusion and contemplate upon his experiential wisdom (dharma) and the ultimate purpose of human life (liberation). In Sanyasa, which correspond to the last phase of human life, he has to renounce everything, including his knowledge of the scriptures (dharma), and work for his liberation (moksha). In each of these stages it is possible to experience peace and happiness by following the injunctions specified in the scriptures. If he follows them strictly, at the end of the journey he is bound to become liberated and enter the world of bliss.

Chasing happiness upon earth by worldly means is like chasing a mirage. To escape from this predicament, one should subordinate earthly happiness to spiritual happiness and, earthly goals to spiritual goals, and aim for permanent happiness, which can be secured only when a being is completely free from all attachments, and the limitations of mortal life. True happiness of the divine kind arises not from having things or fulfilling our desires, but by restraining our minds and bodies, and becoming free from our dependence upon them. When we are free from all attachments, from the impurity of maya and desires, we return to our soul's essential nature, which is permanent bliss. Reaching this state is called liberation, which one can achieve even when one is alive upon earth.

Three types of happiness

Just as everything in creation is coloured by the gunas, our upon earth is also influenced by our predominant nature. According to the predominance of the gunas, we can identify three types of happiness.

Sattvic happiness, which arises from moral and mental purity, and from being good and doing good. This also corresponds to spiritual happiness.

Rajasic happiness, which arises from fulfilling your desires, and securing power, position, name and fame, etc. This corresponded to mental happiness.

Tamasic happiness, which arises from bodily pleasures and base desires. This corresponds to physical happiness.

While sattvic happiness is the best of the three, it does not by itself guarantee liberation or true enjoyment. All types of happiness that arise from fulfilling desires and likes and dislikes are binding and have consequences. True happiness is freedom from the compulsion to be happy, dualities, and conditionality. It should arise in one as a reflection of the soul in the pure consciousness.

(ii) Happiness in Buddhism

Happiness forms a central theme of Buddhist teachings. For ultimate freedom from suffering, the Noble Eightfold Path leads its practitioner to Nirvana, a state of everlasting peace. Ultimate happiness is only achieved by overcoming craving in all forms. More mundane forms of happiness, such as acquiring wealth and maintaining good friendships, are also recognized as worthy goals for lay people. Buddhism also encourages the generation of loving kindness and compassion, the desire for the happiness and welfare of all beings.

Sukha (means happiness, pleasure, ease, joy or bliss, in Sanskrit and Pali). Among the early scriptures, 'Sukha' is set up as a contrast to 'preya' meaning a transient pleasure, whereas the pleasure of 'Sukha' has an authentic state happiness within a being that is lasting. In the Pail Canon, the term is used in the context of describing laic pursuits, meditative absorptions, and intra-psychic phenomena.

The term is used in a general sense to refer to "well-being and happiness" (hita Sukha) in either this present life or future lives. In addition, it is a technical term associated with describing a factor of meditative absorption (jhāna) and a sensory-derived feeling (vedanā). The Buddha discusses with different lay persons "well-being and happiness" (hita Sukha) "visible in this present life" (diṭṭha-dhamma) and "pertaining to the future life" (samparāyika), as exemplified by the following suttas.

In the Anaṇa Sutta (AN 4.62), the Buddha describes the following types of happiness for a "householder partaking of sensuality" (gihinā kāma-bhoginā):

The happiness of earning (atthi-sukha) wealth by just and righteous means the happiness of using (bhoga-sukha) wealth liberally on family, friends, & on meritorious deeds;

The happiness of debt-lessness (anaṇa-sukha) be free from debts;

The happiness of blame-lessness (anavajja-sukha), to live a faultless and pure life without committing evil in thought, word, and deed.

In the Dighajānu Sutta (AN 8.54), Dighajānu approaches the Buddha and states:

"We are lay people enjoying sensuality; living crowded with spouses & children; using Kasi fabrics & sandalwood; wearing garlands, scents, & creams; handling gold & silver. May the Blessed One teach the Dhamma for those like us, for our happiness & well-being in this life, for our happiness & well-being in lives to come."

The Buddha identifies four sources that lead to well-being and happiness in the current life:

productive efforts (uṭṭhāna-sampadā) in one's livelihood, protective efforts (ārakkha-sampadā) regarding ones wealth in terms of possible theft or disaster, virtuous friendship (kalyāṇa-mittatā), and even-headed living (sama-jīvikatā), abstaining from womanizing, drunkenness, gambling and evil friendships.
In terms of well-being and happiness in the next life, the Buddha

identifies the following sources:

Faith (saddhā) in the fully enlightened Buddha; virtue (sīla), as exemplified by the Five Precepts; generosity (cāga), giving charity and alms; and, wisdom (paññā), having insight into the arising and passing of things.

(iii) Happiness in Sufism

Sufism aspires towards developing a soft, feeling, compassionate heart. Understanding through the "heart's intelligence" is superior to understanding through the intelligence of the head. Indeed, the intelligence of the heart is the only instrument that can be used to discover the ultimate truth. To Sufis, reason is limited in many ways and cannot outgrow its inherent limitations. In particular, when reason denies intuitive knowledge and "blinds the eye of the heart", it becomes the target of strong criticism from Sufism. This stands in stark contrast to the Aristotelian and contemporary western emphasis on logical reasoning as the highest human faculty, which should rule the whole personality. On this basis, happiness cannot be achieved by reason and intellect, rather happiness is pursued via intuition and mystical experience. Another important concept in Sufism is the ego (the self or the nafs). The ego is a part of our psyche that consistently leads us off the spiritual path, a part of the self which commands us to do evil. The ego can impede the actualization of the spiritual potential of the heart if not controlled by the divine aspects of the personality. To achieve authentic happiness, the ego should be actively fought against throughout life. The ultimate state of happiness for a Sufi is the annihilation of the individual self. This state refers to the destruction of the individual self to become one with the Divine Being.

(iv) Happiness in Christianity

God wants us to be happy. But what does that look like? How do we find happiness? The only way to find happiness is through Him. He created us! God knows us better than we know ourselves. Some of His ways may seem counterintuitive at first, but the verses that follow demonstrate where true contentment and joy is found—in Him!

Following are some of the verses from the Bible in support of this:

1. Romans 15:13: Now may the God of hope fill you with all joy and peace in believing, that you may abound in hope by the power of the Holy Spirit.

2. Hebrews 12:1-2: Therefore, we also, since we are surrounded by so great a cloud of witnesses, let us lay aside every weight, and the sin which so easily ensnares us, and let us run with endurance the race that is set before us, looking unto Jesus, the author and finisher of our faith, who for the joy that was set before Him endured the cross, despising the shame, and has sat down at the right hand of the throne of God.

3. James 1:2-3: My brethren, count it all joy when you fall into various trials, knowing that the testing of your faith produces patience.

4. Isaiah 9:3: You have multiplied the nation and increased its joy; they rejoice before You according to the joy of harvest, as men rejoice when they divide the spoil.

5. Proverbs 10:28: The hope of the righteous will be gladness, but the expectation of the wicked, will perish.

6. Ecclesiastes 9:7: Go, eat your bread with joy, and drink your wine with a merry heart; for God has already accepted your works. Psalm 30:5: For His anger is but for a moment, His favour is for life; weeping may endure for a night, but joy comes in the morning.

7. John 16:24: Until now you have asked nothing in My name. Ask, and you will receive, that your joy may be full.

7. Psalm 34:8: Oh, taste and see that the Lord is good; blessed

is the man who trusts in Him!

8. Proverbs 16:20: He who heeds the word wisely will find good, and whoever trusts in the LORD, happy is he.

1.4 What is Bliss?

Bliss refers to a state of ecstatic happiness, a perfect and exalted state of joy and love. It also refers to a state of contentment oblivious to any problems or suffering.

The term "bliss" is associated with the words "blithe" and "bless." Blithe refers to happiness —the person in this state is joyful and gay. Bless refers to religious consecration—especially with blood, as in the French verb "blesser," meaning to wound; it means to hallow or sanctify. The state of a person who is blessed is beatitude—the loving joy that arises from salvation.

In the secular world, the word "bliss" may be used broadly to denote any form of happiness. It is used primarily in romantic love, in which the love object is idealized as a perfect being, and the lover is in a blissful state of intense love. Romantic love prevails in the courtly love tradition of Europe, but love poems reflecting this kind of love can also be found in ancient Egypt and India, and in Chinese poems of separation and loss. Additionally, bliss may describe new love, especially the love of a new mother for her infant.

There is a lot of misunderstanding about the term Bliss. Most people think of it as a form of great and continuous happiness or joy or ecstasy. That's not exactly it. Bliss is simply very high frequency energy and our awareness of it. Yes, it feels wonderful, so the connection with enormous happiness or joy or ecstasy is understandable. But that's not what it is. There is a different quality about it.

Bliss is a natural experience of our awakening. Ramana Maharshi describes it as Sat-Chit-Ananda (Existence – Consciousness – Bliss).

When we reach the higher stages of awakening, Bliss is always here. It may not always be in the foreground of our attention but it is always felt in the background. The energy is felt and experienced in the body. It is as if every cell and molecule is vibrating at a very high frequency. It is as if the body has become an enormous tuning fork. It can be quite intense at the beginning, almost overwhelming. You can see why you may mistake this for ecstasy.

The intensity can be so strong in the beginning that you don't know if your physical body can handle it or not. But it does. There's nothing to worry about it. The body actually adjusts and changes to accommodate this higher frequency energy. And this adjustment seems to be very beneficial, healing and healthy for the body. It is almost as if it is making it younger, healthier and more flexible. And perhaps it is. If you are 67 (say) of age, you may feel that you are in your 30s.I was in my 30s.

The Body

The body appears to be lighter, weightless really, as if gravity has no effect on it. It still does of course, so this is just the experience. It may explain the experience of and belief in levitation, which you had never physically seen so far. But this experience of weightlessness does feel like this. And the body appears to be made of light and energy rather than solid matter. It appears to be glowing with light, consisting of nothing but light. There is a certain radiance about it that other people can actually see. This is often referred to as the Light Body. It is sometimes referred to as another body besides the physical body, as if there were two or more bodies, the Light Body hovering outside and around the physical body. You will experience that it is the same body, just perceived and experienced in a very different way. The physical body is the old way of experiencing the body.

Bliss is a wonderful experience and it does seem to increase with the expansion of Consciousness. More and higher frequency energy seems to be experienced. And the body quickly adjusts to this new level. Many physical changes seem to correspond with each new level. And the energy does seem to affect others as well.

When attention is placed on this energy, it can be very intense. When attention is directed otherwise, it simply continues simmering and vibrating in the background.

Happiness, Joy, Ecstasy

The connection with extreme happiness, joy or ecstasy is understandable. But that is just an interpretation of Bliss. Happiness, joy and ecstasy come and go. They are not experienced as permanent states of consciousness. And there is usually some external event that triggers them. Bliss is always experienced as being here and there is no external event to trigger it.

Bliss might be thought of more as "life-force energy". Life-force energy is always here or life would not be. And Bliss is also always here, not separate from the life itself. It is experienced in the body or through the body, but it can also be sensed everywhere.

Everything is Energy

When people say everything is energy, Bliss is the direct experience of this. Attention has turned to this energy and energy is experienced more prominently than physical matter. It is realized that all physical matter, not only this body, is pure energy. What, previous to this level of awakening, was experienced as physical matter is now experienced as energy with the appearance of physical matter to the more limited human senses of sight, hearing and touch. And even these limited senses are also directly experienced as pure energy.

Bliss appears to be fundamental to our basic nature. The question the arises to you: "What is aware of this?" that dissolves everything that is not fundamental. When asked of Bliss, "What is aware of this energy?" Instead of dissolving, the energy simply increases. That has always been a sign of a fundamental nature. The other clue is that it does not come and go. It is always here, whether attention is on it fully or not.

It is cautioned about making a big deal about Bliss, searching for it or trying to attain it as if it were some kind of spiritual reward or goal. There is a pretty reliable way of never experiencing it. Just continue doing your practices, letting go of stories and opening to the Unknown. When you are ready for it, it will simply appear. And you will realize that, although you were not aware of it previously, it was actually always here, like life-force energy or the energy that holds your body's molecules together and makes your cells function. When you are aware of it, you can call it Bliss or whatever you like.

A Taste of Bliss

Bliss is usually experienced in the later stages of awakening, but you may experience it earlier. You may have already done so. In a moment of great freedom, when for just a moment all stories have fallen away, you may notice this powerful, vibrating energy. Your mind may even first interpret it as a powerful fear, even fear of your own death. If in that moment, you can let go of this story too, let go of all stories, return to this freedom before all stories, you may experience, savour and surrender to something that has always been here without your noticing. And that will be a glorious day indeed. This realization will not come as you expect it to. Keep letting go, be diligent about all practices that help you let go and, above all, pay attention. What you are seeking has always been right here under your nose and far closer and more intimate than that.
You will eventually discover that underneath every feeling you experience, there is this same Bliss. It doesn't matter what that feeling is: fear, depression, anger, jealousy, doubt, anxiety, happiness, joy, ecstasy, even love as you now know love. Underneath all of this is Bliss. If you are able to let go of the story that supports and creates these feelings, you will find Bliss. It is always here.

(i) Bliss in Hinduism

States of bliss are described in the greatest detail in three types of Hinduism: Vedanta, Tantra, and Bhakti. In the form of Vedanta known as Advaita or nondual Vedanta, the state of bliss arises from union with Brahman —the ground of being or Ultimate Reality. When the individual self or jivatman merges with the ultimate(Supreme) Self or Paramatman, the individual merges with the universal as the drop of water flows into the sea. The resulting state of freedom and liberation is described as Satchidananda—the state of perfect truth, pure consciousness, and ultimate bliss. Satchidananda is the highest attainment of the human spirit.

In the Tantric traditions, bliss is the result of union, which occurs on multiple levels. According to the philosopher Abhinavagupta, there are seven levels of bliss (ananda): innate bliss, transformative bliss, supreme bliss, bliss of Brahman, great bliss, consciousness bliss, and bliss of the world. Among the Bengali Tantric Bauls and Sahijiyas, God is found in bliss of love, and life is the carnival of love on the playground of the earth. Love causes the Tantrika to be dazzled by the rays of divine beauty, which are like lightning in the clouds. In the West, Tantra is often associated with sexual bliss; in the Hindu tantric traditions, sexuality is only one dimension of a union that is complex and unites worlds and universes.

The states of bliss associated with love appear most strongly in the devotional or Bhakti traditions of Hinduism, in which the devotee loves the god or goddess intensely. In the Vaishnava tradition (which worships the god Vishnu), there are five traditional relational moods or bhavas of love: god as master and devotee as slave; god as friend and devotee as friend; god as child and devotee as parent; god as beloved and devotee as lover; and when both are realized as ultimately identical, sharing their identities. In the Shakta tradition of goddess worship, the bhavas are similar, except that the goddess may take on the role of the mother and the devotee that of the child.

In the Gaudiya Vaishnava school of Bengali Bhakti, the ideal state for the devotee is a blissful state of love that echoes the passion of Radha—the god Krishna' s beloved and perfect devotee, his Hladini

Shakti, or power of bliss. In her most intense state of love, which is called Mahabhava, she experiences all states of passionate love simultaneously, including sorrow at the absence of the god and joy at his presence. By sharing in Radha's love, which is ever-new, the devotee gains an eternal future in Krishna's paradise of Vrindavana. One way that the devotee may do this is to take on a female soul, even if the devotee is physically male. Whereas the Gaudiya ideal is eternal romantic love, the Bengali Shakta ideal is eternal mother-child love, and the Shakta devotee looks forward to a joyful eternal life in the arms of a blissful mother.

(ii) Bliss in Buddhism

We hear that term "The bliss of the Buddha". What does it mean? When we look at it, all we know is our own experience, and our own experience is completely infused with ignorance and afflictions. That's the meaning of the word "tainted" or "polluted" or "contaminated." When we hear of this untainted bliss: "What in the world is that?" May be that's one reason why they say it's indescribable. It's beyond our concept and it's beyond our experience but we need to have something through which we can get some idea of what it must be like.

"What will it feel like, for example, not to get angry?" And you just sit and imagine that. Anybody could say anything they want. The whole world can do everything that's wrong, because it isn't what I want and I'm not going to get angry. When I think about that, what that might feel like inside—to have not just the not getting angry, but the security that I'm not going to get angry, and not even having to fight off the anger and apply gazillions of antidotes, but just the fact that something happens and the mind doesn't even go in that direction but it instead goes in the direction of compassion—when I think of that, then that gives me some sense of how it must be to be a buddha.

That clearly isn't the Buddha's great bliss, but it gives us some sense of how being a buddha is possible and how it's different from what

I'm experiencing right now. Otherwise, it's hard for us. We think of buddha-hood and since we only know our experience we just try and think of buddha-hood as a revision of our own experience. In other words, buddha-hood is you finally get whatever you want. That's what heaven was. When you're taught as kids, heaven was you finally get everything you want, which means everybody does what you want. But that's not the point here. The point is the change in the mind.

Or you think of attachment—craving, the mind of clinging desire—and you think … that just doesn't exist in the mind. Now what would that be like? You can encounter any kind of object—you could see anything, hear anything, touch, taste, smell anything, think of anything—and your mind just remains peaceful. It doesn't go into this thing of, "WOW, I want this, how am I going to get it? Oh, I do that to get it. Can I do this to get it? But then I might lose it. And maybe it wouldn't come to me. Or it'll come to me and it'll leave me, or it wouldn't like me." All this stuff that comes because of craving. Just imagine that in any situation in your life, craving just does not come up. Just try to imagine.

This is a real good thing in our meditation, just try and imagine what would it be like not to have craving, to have your mind just be completely peaceful. These things come in, they're there, they leave, they've left. Your mind's just peaceful. Whatever comes you enjoy. Whatever doesn't come you enjoy. Your mind isn't continually trying to rearrange the duckies and get new duckies. The mind is just content. Whoever you're with, you're happy. Whatever your living situation is, you're satisfied. You just look at that. This is just some way that— it's not the buddha's great bliss—but it's some way for us to get an idea that's related to our experience of what it must be like to be a buddha.

When we're wishing that all sentient beings have the bliss of a buddha when we see them happy, we're really wishing something that's quite beyond their ordinary happy state, that is something that we've actually never experienced. Or we have experience in this way—we haven't experienced the nirvana of a buddha—but we've all had times when the anger went away, or the attachment calmed down, and that feeling of peace that comes then. Or we've had the times when we look at something and it's ordinarily something we would get angry about or attached about, and then we go, "Oh, that's ok. " Just that feeling of peace in the mind, we've all had that happen.

Based on those experiences that we have had, then we can think, "Ok, it must be something even beyond that." Where you're never even worried about craving, and attachment, and clinging, and anger and resentment, and jealousy even arising because your mind doesn't even go anywhere near those things. It's in this completely peaceful state that comes from having removed these afflictions. Just thinking like that gives us some idea of what we're aiming for when we say, "May I become a buddha for the benefit of all." And when we're saying, "May I lead all sentient beings to buddha-hood." This is the kind of thing that we want to go to and where we want to take others. This is called the state of Bliss or Buddha-hood.

(iii) Bliss in Sufism

In Islam, bliss is found in the mystical Sufi traditions. It comes through appreciation of God's beauty and mercy. Beauty and love are like body and soul, and awareness of them can transform the human soul into light and allow its ascent to the one who is Truth and Unity. God is love, lover, and beloved. The blissful conditions are earthly love ('Ishq'), in which one sacrifices all for God; the state of fana, in which the person experiences divine love-madness; and the state of baqa, the state of stable perfection before God, which balances the madness. This love is shown in the story of Laila and Majnu, in which Majnu so loved Laila that the world was transformed into her image, and he lived in blissful madness surrounded by her presence. Her image eventually became that of Allah, and Majnu's love of a human woman was transformed into love of God.

Spiritual ecstasy, induced by remembrance of God (Zikr) while hearing recitation of the Qur'an, Ahadith, or spiritual poetry, is called Wajd or "Wajad" by Sufis: it is especially cultivated among the Naqshbandi and Chishti spiritual orders. This bliss is one of the many signs of the commencement of spiritual development in the disciple and also the opening for inspirations and spiritual abilities and powers. In its purest forms, Wajad is a pure state of eternal peace. Some Sufis enjoy Wajad while listening to poetry, with or without music (Qawwali).

There are five distinct levels of Wajad described by Sufi Sheikhs in their numerous books:

1. Wajd of dervishes, which produces a rhythmic motion of the body;

2. Wajd of idealists, expressed by a thrilling sensation of the body, tears and sighs.

3. Wajd of devotees, which creates an exalted state in the physical and mental body.

4. Wajd of saints, which creates perfect calm and peace.

5. Wajd of prophets, the realization of the highest consciousness called Sidrat al-Muntaha.

One may also arrive at the state of Wajd by the favour of the murshid, and/or through the Grace of Allah.

(iv) Bliss in Christianity

In Christianity, bliss may involve such visionary experiences as being caught up in the third heaven, hearing words in paradise, undergoing transformation in Christ, and becoming a new creature. There is the bliss of exaltation and glory, being risen with Christ and sharing his divine love. In Eastern Orthodoxy, the process of deification or theosis (a transformative process whose aim is likeness to or union with God, as taught by the Eastern Orthodox Church);

which allows the person to share in the light and love and energies of the Trinity, participate in God's glory, and gain perfection through love and the fire of grace. In Catholic mysticism, the saints speak of the marriage of the human soul and the Word, the bliss that occurs through conformity of the soul in the union of divine love, and the role of soul as bride to God. Among Protestant charismatics, there is bliss in the gifts of the Holy Spirit. The goal is perfect love, with God's love communicated through the soul.

1.5 Difference between Happiness, Unhappiness, and Spiritual Bliss

1.5.1 Happiness versus unhappiness

Anukoolavedaniyam sukham. Pratikoola vedaniya dukham.
-Vatsyayana 1.1.2

Meaning: Happiness is a pleasant sensation and unhappiness is an unpleasant sensation experienced by the embodied soul through the five senses, mind and / or intellect.

Yadishtam tatsukham prahuvrdeshyam dukhamiheshyate.
-Mahabharata 12.295.27

Meaning: In this world what one feels favourable is happiness and whatever one feels like despising is unhappiness.

Yadyatpriyam yasya sukham tadahustadeva dukham pravadantyanishtam.
-Mahabharat 12.201.10

Meaning: One regards what is dear to oneself as happiness and the same thing when it is disliked, as unhappiness.

Badhanalakshanam dukham. -Nyayadardhana

Meaning: Badhana means pain. That which has the form of pain is unhappiness.

Adharmajanyam sacheta pratikoolam. – Bhashaparichcheda

Meaning: That which arises from unrighteousness (adharma) and proves to be unfavourable for living beings is itself unhappiness.

Although initially it is necessary for the sense organs to have contact with external objects for the generation of worldly happiness and unhappiness, yet man experiences them with his mind. **Spiritual happiness or sorrow is always psychological.** Finally, the experiencing of all happiness or unhappiness is dependent solely on the mind; hence it is not impossible to restrain the experiences of happiness and unhappiness with the mind. It is with this very opinion that Manu (4.160) has described the features of happiness and unhappiness differently from those following a system of philosophy founded by Sage Gautam (nyayashastra), as –

Sarvam paravasham dukham sarvamatmavasham sukham.
Etavdidyatsamanasena lakshanam sukhahdukhayoh.

Meaning: All that which is in the control of external objects is unhappiness while that which is in the control of one's mind is happiness. This is the concise feature of happiness and unhappiness.

(a) Importance

The basic sensations of happiness and unhappiness are very important to survive and gain fundamental knowledge. Even an amoeba goes away if there is any undue particle in its vicinity and it finds it unpleasant, it goes to another site where there are food particles. An infant too, reaches up to the mother's breast to taste the mother's milk. A young child runs away from fire and withdraws its foot on being pricked by a thorn. From this, one will realise that all actions of any organism are motivated by a desire to obtain happiness or to escape from unhappiness or an unpleasant event.

Happiness or unhappiness are great teachers. Difficulties and poverty teach us more than happiness and wealth respectively. Happiness and unhappiness are the reward and punishment respectively, which are bestowed upon man by nature for his progress.

(b) Signs of unhappiness

'Sadness and a downcast countenance are the effects of unhappiness.'

– Prashastapadacharya

Reaction to unhappiness:

Prayena neecha vyasaneshu magna nindanti devam kukritam na tu svaṁ.

– Mahabharat 8.91.1

Meaning: Mean people blame The Lord instead of their own bad deeds when a calamity befalls them.

(c) Inevitability of happiness and unhappiness

Worldly life is an admixture of happiness and unhappiness. For example, one feels happy when one builds a house but feels unhappy when one has to pay its taxes or repair it. One feels happy when a son is born but there is unhappiness when he is disobedient. When one's daughter gets married there is happiness but when her husband ill-treats her, one is aggrieved. In this way most people go up and down in this vast ocean of happiness and unhappiness. This body has numerous aches and pains from the time of birth till death. This combination of happiness and unhappiness is called the image of worldly life.

Sukhasyantaram dukham dukhasyanantaram sukham.
Vdyametadahi jantunam alanggahyam dinaratrivat.

Meaning: Just as the night follows the day and the day dawns after the night, unhappiness follows happiness and vice versa. This cycle is inevitable.

Confusion due to the usage of the words happiness and Spiritual Bliss with various connotations

The words happiness and Bliss are often used interchangeably in spiritual texts. That is, the meaning with which the word Bliss is used in this holy text, is happiness according to other books and vice versa. Sometimes the two are used synonymously.

Bliss is of two kinds. Bliss in the presence of objects (that obtained from eating, drinking, clothes, ornaments, etc.) is termed as happiness. Bliss in the absence of objects, is termed as spiritual.

Happiness is of three types, namely – worldly happiness, that in the subtle worlds and spiritual happiness. The first type is the happiness obtained in this world, the second is that obtained in the subtle worlds. Both these types of happiness are relative to some object. Spiritual happiness however is unrelative to an object. Since spiritual happiness is self-attained, it is considered the best type of happiness. Spiritual happiness is superior to worldly happiness and that in the subtle worlds because it is permanent and unrelated to any kind of unhappiness. This spiritual happiness is the ultimate. Such unparalleled happiness is termed as the Final Liberation (Moksha).

If in any way there is destruction of nescience, then there is separation of the supposed union of the soul and the world and the embodied soul is permanently liberated from the bondage of unhappiness. The attainment of this state itself is termed as "eternal happiness" by followers of the Sankhya Philosophy.

When one is able to lead the 'dhi' frequencies up to 'kha', that is to the hollow in the Brahmarandhra, the opening in the Sahasrara chakra, one experiences happiness. If this does not occur, there is unhappiness.

1.5.2 Difference between happiness and Spiritual Bliss

Everybody wants to be happy but very rarely you will come across a happy person. Because your happiness does not stay for long. Most of the time happiness is temporary or fleeting. One day you are happy for some good news and after few days you become sad for some other reason. So, happiness which depends upon the external circumstances cannot give you permanent happiness. If you want to have permanent happiness then find some way to be happy which is not dependent on our good luck and prosperity in life.

Happiness which is uncaused by any positive event in life is of more value. Because it is not dependent on anything. So, try to maintain a happy or content attitude towards life, even in adverse conditions. Because no one can take it from you. That happiness is also not dependent on outside circumstances which keep on changing. When you can be happy in any situation then ups and downs of life do not matter to you. Bliss is also not dependent on the outside circumstances and is higher than happiness.

Why bliss is totally different from happiness?

Bliss comes when you move from the world of duality to non-duality. In the world of duality, everything is dual and has an opposite to balance it. Life moves in duality, for example, day and night, male and female, birth and death, creation and destruction... everything is balanced by its counterpart. If there is no death in the world then the world will be too populated and its resources will be over soon. Moreover, whenever death happens everything goes back to the source, so that the energy is available for creation. Destruction is needed to have the creation. So, everything moves in circle and there are cycles of creation and destruction.... day and night...same are the case with our emotions in the dual world. Some time, we are happy, some other time we are sad, angry, jealous or loving. No emotion stays for long and our emotional state is always fluctuating. Another principle of life in the dual world is change. Everything is changing in this world. So, you cannot have an emotion all the time in the dual world.

That's why you cannot have permanent happiness in the world. but you can be permanently blissful. As bliss belongs to non-dual world where it does not have any counterpart plus the things are eternal. Bliss does not belong to the dual world. Because it does not have any counterpart. Bliss comes to us whenever we transcend the boundary of mind and goes to no-mind state.

Bliss can happen to us:

1. Whenever we are total in our actions or when we are in total let go state;

2. Or when we are totally god intoxicated;

3. Or when we have lost the feeling of 'I' or ego;

4. Or when we experience samadhi or satori or no-mind state;

5. Or any other reason by which you experience non-dual state.

Bliss is a much higher quality than happiness. Bliss is a by-product of a meditative mind or a devotee who has surrendered to the God.

Happiness is a pleasant sensation experienced by the embodied soul through the five senses, mind and/or intellect whereas Bliss is a favourable spiritual experience of the embodied soul doing spiritual practice (Jivatma) or the God realised soul (Shivatma) when the functions of the five senses, mind and intellect have ceased.

Each one of us has experienced happiness at some time or the other. Since the experience is obtained through the media of the five senses, mind and intellect one can comprehend its definition. Contrary to this, since most of us have not experienced Bliss and since many are not even aware that there may be something to experience beyond the five senses, mind and intellect, most people find it difficult to understand the definition of Bliss. Just as one person blind since birth will find it difficult to accept the fact that the world is visible or a child will not be able to understand the meaning of sexuality no matter how hard one tries to explain it, so also it is difficult to explain the meaning of Bliss. It cannot be expressed in words but has to be experienced.

SECTION 2

(LOVE)

CHAPTER 2

Love in Hinduism

The one who loves all intensely, begins perceiving in all living beings a part of himself.
He becomes a lover of all, a part and parcel of the Universal Joy.
He flows with the stream of happiness, and is enriched by each soul.

- *Yajur Veda*

2.1 Hindu scriptures

Following are the six scriptures in Hinduism:

(i) Srutis, (ii) Smritis, (iii) Itihasas, (iv) Puranas, (v) Agamas and (vi) Darsanas

2..1.1 The Srutis

(i) Vedas

The Srutis are called the Vedas, or the Amnaya. The Hindus have received their religious message through revelation, the Vedas. These are direct intuitional revelations and are held to be Apaurusheya or entirely superhuman, without any author in particular. The Veda is the glorious pride of the Hindus, nay, of the whole world!

The term Veda comes from the root Vid, to know. The word Veda means knowledge. When it is applied to scripture, it signifies a book of knowledge. The Vedas are the foundational scriptures of the Hindus. The Veda is the source of the other five sets of scriptures. The Veda is the storehouse of Indian wisdom and is a memorable glory which man can never forget till eternity.

(ii) Revealed Truths Without Beginning or End

The Vedas are the eternal truths revealed by God to the great ancient Rishis of India. The word Rishi means a seer from dris, to see. He is the Mantra-Drashta, a seer of Mantra or thought. The thought was not his own. The Rishis saw the truths or heard them. Therefore, the Vedas are what are heard (Sruti). The Rishi did not write. He did not create it out of his mind. He was the seer of thought which existed already. He was only the spiritual discoverer of the thought. He is not the inventor of the Veda.

The Vedas represent the spiritual experiences of the Rishis of yore. The Rishi is only a medium or an agent to transmit to people the intuitional experiences which he received. The truths of the Vedas are revelations. All the other religions of the world claim their authority as being delivered by special messengers of God to certain persons, but the Vedas do not owe their authority to anyone. They are themselves the authority as they are eternal, as they are the Knowledge of the Lord.

Lord Brahma, the Creator, imparted the divine knowledge to the Rishis or seers. The Rishis disseminated the knowledge. The Vedic Rishis were great realised persons who had direct intuitive perception of Brahman or the Truth. They were inspired writers. They built a simple, grand and perfect system of religion and philosophy from which the founders and teachers of all other religions have drawn their inspiration.

The Vedas are the oldest books in the library of man. The truths contained in all religions are derived from the Vedas and are ultimately traceable to the Vedas. The Vedas are the fountain-head of religion. The Vedas are the ultimate source to which all religious knowledge can be traced. Religion is of divine origin. It was revealed by God to man in the earliest times. It is embodied in the Vedas.

The Vedas are eternal. They are without beginning and end. An ignorant man may say how a book can be without beginning or end. By the Vedas, no books are meant. Vedas came out of the breath of the Lord. They are the words of God. The Vedas are not the utterances of persons. They are not the composition of any human mind. They were never written, never created. They are eternal and impersonal. The date of the Vedas has never been fixed. It can never be fixed. Vedas are eternal spiritual truths. Vedas are an embodiment of divine knowledge. The books may be destroyed, but the knowledge cannot be destroyed. Knowledge is eternal. In that sense, the Vedas are eternal.

(iii) The Four Vedas and Their Sub Divisions

The Veda is divided into four great books: the Rig-Veda, the Yajur-Veda, the Sama-Veda and the Atharva-Veda. The Yajur-Veda is again divided into two parts, the Sukla and the Krishna. The Krishna or the Taittiriya is the older book and the Sukla or the Vajasaneya is a later revelation to sage Yajnavalkya from the resplendent Sun-God.

The Rig-Veda is divided into twenty-one sections, the Yajur-Veda into one hundred and nine sections, the Sama-Veda into one thousand sections and the Atharva-Veda into fifty sections. In all, the whole Veda is thus divided into one thousand one hundred and eighty recensions.

(iv) Samhitas or hymns, Brahmanas, Aranyakas and the Upanishads

Each Veda consists of four parts: the Mantra-Samhitas or hymns, the Brahmanas or explanations of Mantras or rituals, the Aranyakas and the Upanishads. The division of the Vedas into four parts is to suit the four stages in a man's life.

The Mantra-Samhitas are hymns in praise of the Vedic God for attaining material prosperity here and happiness hereafter. They are metrical poems comprising prayers, hymns and incantations addressed to various deities, both subjective and objective. The Mantra portion of the Vedas is useful for the Brahmacharis.

The Brahmana portions guide people to perform sacrificial rites. They are prose explanations of the method of using the Mantras in the Yajna or the sacrifice. The Brahmana portion is suitable for the householders.

The Aranyakas are the forest books, the mystical sylvan texts which give philosophical interpretations of the rituals. The Aranyakas are intended for the Vanaprasthas or hermits who prepare themselves for taking Sannyasa.

The Upanishads are the most important portion of the Vedas. The Upanishads contain the essence or the knowledge portion of the Vedas. The philosophy of the Upanishads is sublime, profound, lofty and soul-stirring. The Upanishads speak of the identity of the individual soul and the Supreme Soul. They reveal the most subtle and deep spiritual truths. The Upanishads are useful for the Sannyasins.

The subject matter of the whole Veda is divided into Karma-Kanda, Upasana-Kanda and Jnana-Kanda. The Karma-Kanda or Ritualistic Section deals with various sacrifices and rituals. The Upasana-Kanda or Worship-Section deals with various kinds of worship or meditation. The Jnana-Kanda or Knowledge-Section deals with the highest knowledge of Nirguna Brahman. The Mantras and the Brahmanas constitute Karma-Kanda; the Aranyakas Upasana-Kanda; and the Upanishads Jnana-Kanda.

(v) The Mantra-Samhitas

The Rig-Veda Samhita is the grandest book of the Hindus, the oldest and the best. It is the Great Indian Bible, which no Hindu would forget to adore from the core of his heart. Its style, the language and the tone are most beautiful and mysterious. Its immortal Mantras embody the greatest truths of existence, and it is perhaps the greatest treasure in all the scriptural literature of the world. Its priest is called the Hotri.

The Yajur-Veda Samhita is mostly in prose and is meant to be used by the, Adhvaryu, the Yajur-Vedic priest, for superfluous explanations of the rites in sacrifices, supplementing the Rig-Vedic Mantras.

The Sama-Veda Samhita is mostly borrowed from the Rig-Vedic Samhita and is meant to be sung by the Udgatri, the Sama-Vedic priest, in sacrifices.

The Atharva-Veda Samhita is meant to be used by the Brahma, the Atharva-Vedic priest, to correct the mispronunciations and wrong performances that may accidentally be committed by the other three priests of the sacrifice.

(vi) The Brahmanas and the Aranyakas

There are two Brahmanas to the Rig-Veda—the Aitareya and the Sankhayana. "The Rig-Veda is the most ancient book of the world. The sacred hymns of the Brahmanas stand unparalleled in the literature of the whole world; and their preservation might well be called miraculous.

The Satapatha Brahmana belongs to the Sukla Yajur-Veda. The Krishna-Yajur-Veda has the Taittiriya and the Maitrayana Brahmanas. The Tandya or Panchavimsa, the Shadvimsa, the Chhandogya, the Adbhuta, the Arsheya and the Upanishad Brahmanas belong to the Sama-Veda. The Brahmana of the Atharva-Veda is called the Gopatha. Each of the Brahmanas has got an Aranyaka.

(vii) The Upanishads

The Upanishads are the concluding portions of the Vedas or the end of the Vedas. The teaching based on them is called Vedanta. The Upanishads are the gist and the goal of the Vedas. They form the very foundation of Hinduism.

There are as many Upanishads to each Veda as there are Sakhas, branches or recensions, that is, 21, 109, 1000 and 50, respectively to the four Vedas, the Rig-Veda, the Yajur-Veda, the Sama-Veda and the Atharva-Veda.

Different philosophers of India belonging to different schools, such as Monism, Qualified Monism, Dualism, Pure Monism, Difference-cum-non-difference, etc., have acknowledged the supreme authority of the Upanishads. They have given their own interpretations, but they have obeyed the authority. They have built their philosophy on the foundation of the Upanishads.

The most important Upanishads are Isha, Kena, Katha, Prasna, Mundaka, Mandukya, Aitareya, Taittiriya, Chhandogya, Brihadaranyaka, Kaushitaki and Svetasvatara and Maitrayani. These are supremely authoritative.

(viii) The Upa-Vedas

There are four Upa-Vedas or subsidiary Vedas, viz., the Ayurveda, the Dhanurveda, the Gandharva Veda and the Arthasastra, forming auxiliaries to the four Vedas, which mean, respectively, the science of health, the science of war, the science of music and the science of polity.

(ix) The Vedangas

There are six Angas or explanatory limbs, to the Vedas: the Siksha and Vyakarana of Panini, the Chhandas of Pingalacharya, the Nirukta of Yaska, the Jyotisha of Garga, and the Kalpas (Srauta, Grihya, Dharma and Sulba) belonging to the authorship of various Rishis.

Siksha is a knowledge of phonetics. Siksha deals with pronunciation and accent. The text of the Vedas is arranged in various forms or Pathas. The Pada-patha gives each word its separate form. The Krama-patha connects the word in pairs.

Vyakarana is Sanskrit grammar. Panini's books are most famous. Without knowledge of Vyakarana, you cannot understand the Vedas.

Chhandas is metre dealing with prosody.

Nirukta is philology or etymology.

Jyotisha is astronomy and astrology. It deals with the movements of the heavenly bodies, planets, etc., and their influence in human affairs.

Kalpa is the method of ritual. The Srauta Sutras which explain the ritual of sacrifices belong to Kalpa. The Sulba Sutras, which treat of the measurements which are necessary for laying out the sacrificial areas, also belong to Kalpa. The Grihya Sutras which concern domestic life, and the Dharma Sutras which deal with ethics, customs and laws, also belong to Kalpa.

The Pratishakhyas, Padapathas, Kramapathas, Upalekhas, Anukramanis, Daivatsamhitas, Parishishtas, Prayogas, Paddhatis, Karikas, Khilas and Vyuhas are further elaborations in the rituals of the Kalpa Sutras.

Among the Kalpa Sutras, the Asvalayana, Sankhyana and the Sambhavya belong to the Rig-Veda. The Mashaka, Latyayana, Drahyayana, Drahyayana and Khadira belong to the Sama-Veda. The Katyayana and Paraskara belong to the Sukla Yajur-Veda. The Apastamba, Hiranyakesi, Bodhayana, Bharadvaja, Manava, Vaikhanasa and the Kathaka belong to the Krishna Yajur-Veda. The Vaitana and the Kaushika belong to the Atharva-Veda.

2.1.2 The Smritis

Next in importance to the Sruti are the Smritis or secondary scriptures. These are the ancient sacred law-codes of the Hindus dealing with the Sanatana-Varnasrama-Dharma. They supplement and explain the ritualistic injunctions, called Vidhis in the Vedas. The Smriti Sastra is founded on the Sruti. The Smritis are based on the teachings of the Vedas. The Smriti stands next in authority to the Sruti. It explains and develops Dharma. It lays down the laws which regulate Hindu national, social, family and individual obligations.

The works which are expressly called Smritis are the law books, Dharma Sastras. Smriti, in a broader sense, covers all Hindu Sastras save the Vedas.

The laws for regulating Hindu society from time to time are codified in the Smritis. The Smritis have laid down definite rules and laws to guide the individuals and communities in their daily conduct and to regulate their manners and customs. The Smritis have given detailed instructions, according to the conditions of the time, to all classes of men regarding their duties in life.

The Hindu learns how he has to spend his whole life from these Smritis. The duties of Varnasrama and all ceremonies are clearly given in these books. The Smritis prescribe certain acts and prohibit some others for a Hindu, according to his birth and stage of life. The object of the Smritis is to purify the heart of man and take him gradually to the supreme abode of immortality and make him perfect and free.

These Smritis have varied from time to time. The injunctions and prohibitions of the Smritis are related to the particular social surroundings. As these surroundings and essential conditions of the Hindu society changed from time to time, new Smritis had to be compiled by the sages of different ages and different parts of India.

(i) The Celebrated Hindu Law-Givers

From time to time, a great law-giver would take his birth. He would codify the existing laws and remove those which had become obsolete. He would make some alterations, adaptations, readjustments, additions and subtractions, to suit the needs of the time and see that the way of living of the people would be in accordance with the teachings of the Veda. Of such law-givers, Manu, Yajnavalkya and Parasara are the most celebrated persons. Hindu society is founded on, and governed by, the laws made by these three great sages. The Smritis are named after them. We have Manu Smriti or Manava Dharma-Sastra (the Laws of Manu or the Institutes of Manu), Yajnavalkya Smriti and Parasara Smriti. Manu is the greatest law-giver of the race. He is the oldest law-giver as well. The Yajnavalkya Smriti follows the same general lines as the Manu Smriti and is next in importance to it. Manu Smriti and Yajnavalkya Smriti are universally accepted at the present time as authoritative works all over India. Yajnavalkya Smriti is chiefly consulted in all matters of Hindu Law. Even the Government of India are applying some of these laws.

There are eighteen main Smritis or Dharma Sastras. The most important are those of Manu, Yajnavalkya and Parasara. The other fifteen are those of Vishnu, Daksha, Samvarta, Vyasa, Harita,

Satatapa, Vasishtha, Yama, Apastamba, Gautama, Devala, Sankha-Likhita, Usana, Atri and Saunaka.

The laws of Manu are intended for the Satya Yuga, those of Yajnavalkya are for the Treta Yuga; those of Sankha and Likhita are for the Dvapara Yuga; and those of Parasara are for the Kali Yuga.

The laws and rules which are based entirely upon our social positions, time and clime, must change with the changes in society and changing conditions of time and clime. Then only the progress of the Hindu society can be ensured.

(iii) Need for a New Law-Code

It is not possible to follow some of the laws of Manu at the present time. We can follow their spirit and not the letter. Society is advancing. When it advances, it outgrows certain laws which were valid and helpful at a particular stage of its growth. Many new things which were not thought out by the old law-givers have come into existence now. It is no use insisting people to follow now those old laws which have become obsolete.

Our present society has considerably changed. A new Smriti to suit the requirements of this age is very necessary. Another sage will place before the Hindus of our days a new suitable code of laws. Time is ripe for a new Smriti. Cordial greetings to this age.

(iv) The Inner Voice of Dharma

He who is endowed with a pure heart through protracted Tapas, Japa, Kirtana, meditation and service of Guru and who has a very clear conscience, can be guided by the inner voice in matters of Dharma or duty or moral action. The inner voice that proceeds from a clean heart, filled with Sattva is, indeed, the voice of God or Soul or Antaryami or Inner Ruler. This voice is more than Smriti. It is Smriti of Smritis. Purify your heart and train yourself to hear this inner voice. Keep your ear in tune with the 'voice'.

(v) The Sruti and the Smriti

The Sruti and the Smriti are the two authoritative sources of Hinduism. Sruti literally means what is heard, and Smriti means what is remembered. Sruti is revelation and Smriti is tradition. **Upanishad is a Sruti. Bhagavad-Gita is a Smriti.**

Sruti is direct experience. Great Rishis heard the eternal truths of religion and left a record of them for the benefit of posterity. These records constitute the Vedas. Hence, Sruti is primary authority. Smriti is a recollection of that experience. Hence, it is secondary authority. The Smritis or Dharma Sastras also are books written by sages, but they are not the final authority. If there is anything in a Smriti which contradicts the Sruti, the Smriti is to be rejected.

2.1.3 The Itihasas

The Friendly Treatises and the Commanding Treatises

There are four books under this heading: The Valmiki-Ramayana, the Yogavasishtha, The Mahabharata and the Harivamsa. These embody all that is in the Vedas, but only in a simpler manner. These are called the Suhrit-Samhitas or the Friendly Treatises, while the Vedas are called the Prabhu-Samhitas or the Commanding Treatises with great authority. These works explain the great universal truths in the form of historical narratives, stories and dialogues. These are very interesting volumes and are liked by all, from the inquisitive child to the intellectual scholar.

The Itihasas give us beautiful stories of absorbing interest and importance, through which all the fundamental teachings of Hinduism are indelibly impressed on one's mind. The laws of Smritis and the principles of the Vedas are stamped firmly on the minds of the Hindus through the noble and marvellous deeds of their great national heroes. We get a clear idea of Hinduism from these sublime stories.

The common man cannot comprehend the high abstract philosophy of the Upanishads and the Brahma Sutras. Hence, the compassionate sages Valmiki and Vyasa wrote the Itihasas for the benefit of common people. The same philosophy is presented with analogies and parables in a tasteful form to the common run of mankind.

The two well-known Itihasas (histories) are the epics (Mahakavyas), Ramayana and Mahabharata. They are two very popular and useful Sastras of the Hindus. The Ramayana was written by the sage Valmiki, and the Mahabharata by Vyasa.

(i) The Ramayana

The Ramayana, the Adi-Kavya or the first epic poem, relates the story of Sri Rama, the ideal man. It is the history of the family of the solar race descended from Ikshvaku, in which was born Sri Ramachandra, the Avatara of Lord Vishnu, and his three brothers. The ideal characters like Rama, Sita, Lakshmana, Bharata and Sri Hanuman that we find in Ramayana firmly establish Hindu Dharma in our minds. The story of the birth of Rama and his brothers, their education and marriages, the exile of Sri Rama, the carrying off and recovery of Sita, his wife, the destruction of Ravana, the Rakshasa King of Lanka, and the reign of Sri Rama, are described in detail in Ramayana. How a man should behave towards his superiors, equals and inferiors, how a king ought to rule his kingdom, how a man should lead his life in this world, how he can obtain his release, freedom and perfection, may be learnt from this excellent epic. The Ramayana gives a vivid picture of Indian life. Even today our domestic, social and national ideals are copied from the noble characters in the Ramayana and the Mahabharata. The great national heroes stand even today as beacon-lights to guide and inspire the people of the whole world. The lives of Rama, Bharata and Lakshmana provide a model of fraternal affection and mutual service. Sri Hanuman stands as an ideal unique Karma Yogin. The life of Sita is regarded as the most perfect example of womanly fidelity, chastity and sweetness. The Ramayana is written in twenty-four thousand verses by Sri Valmiki.

(ii) The Mahabharata

The Mahabharata is the history of the Pandavas and the Kauravas. It gives a description of the great war, the Battle of Kurukshetra, which broke out between the Kauravas and the Pandavas who were cousins and descendants of the lunar race. The Mahabharata is an encyclopaedia of Hindu Dharma. It is rightly called the fifth Veda. There is really no theme in religion, philosophy, mysticism and polity which this great epic does not touch and expound. It contains very noble moral teachings, useful lessons of all kinds, many beautiful stories and episodes, discourses, sermons, parables and dialogues which set forth the principles of morals and metaphysics. The Pandavas obtained victory through the grace of Lord Krishna. The Mahabharata is written in one hundred thousand verses by Sri Krishnadvaipayana Vyasa.

(iii) The Bhagavad-Gita

The most important part of the Mahabharata is the Bhagavad-Gita. It is a marvellous dialogue between Lord Krishna and Arjuna on the battlefield, before the commencement of the great war. Bhagavan Sri Krishna became the charioteer of Arjuna. Sri Krishna explained the essentials of Hindu religion to Arjuna. Just as the Upanishads contain the cream of the Vedas, so does the Gita contain the cream of the Upanishads. The Upanishads are the cows. Lord Krishna is the cowherd. Arjuna is the calf. The Gita is the milk. The wise men are those who drink the milk of the Gita.

The Gita is the most precious jewel of Hindu literature. It is a universal gospel. The Gita teaches the Yoga of Synthesis. It ranks high in the religious literature of the world.

Arjuna saw before him his dear relatives and teachers in the battlefield. He fainted and refused to fight against them. Then Lord Krishna imparted knowledge of the Self to Arjuna and convinced him that it was his duty to fight regardless of consequences. Afterwards Arjuna gave up his Moha, or delusion. All his doubts were cleared. He fought against the Kauravas and achieved victory.

Knowledge of Ancient Indian History and Culture

The Mahabharata contains also the immortal discourse of Bhishma on Dharma, which he gave to Yudhishthira, when he was lying on the bed of arrows. The whole Mahabharata forms an encyclopaedia of history, morals and religion unsurpassed by any other epic in the world.

2.1.4 The Puranas

The Puranas are of the same class as the Itihasas. They have five characteristics (Pancha-Lakshana) viz., history, cosmology (with various symbolical illustrations of philosophical principles), secondary creation, genealogy of kings and of Manvantaras. All the Puranas belong to the class of Suhrit-Samhitas.

Vyasa is the compiler of the Puranas from age to age; and for this age, he is Krishnadvaipayana, the son of Parasara.

The Puranas were written to popularise the religion of the Vedas. They contain the essence of the Vedas. The aim of the Puranas is to impress on the minds of the masses the teachings of the Vedas and to generate in them devotion to God, through concrete examples, myths, stories, legends, lives of saints, kings and great men, allegories and chronicles of great historical events. The sages made use of these things to illustrate the eternal principles of religion. The Puranas were meant, not for the scholars, but for the ordinary people who could not understand high philosophy and who could not study the Vedas.

The Darsanas are very stiff. They are meant only for the learned few. The Puranas are meant for the masses with inferior intellect. Religion is taught in a very easy and interesting way through these Puranas. Even to this day, the Puranas are popular. The Puranas contain the history of remote times. They also give a description of the regions of the universe not visible to the ordinary physical eye. They are very interesting to read and are full of information of all kinds. Children hear the stories from their grandmothers. Pundits and Purohits hold Kathas in temples, on banks of rivers and in other important places. Agriculturists, labourers and bazaar people hear the stories.

(i) The Eighteen Puranas

There are eighteen main Puranas and an equal number of subsidiary Puranas or Upa-Puranas. The main Puranas are: Vishnu Purana, Naradiya Purana, Srimad Bhagavata Purana, Garuda (Suparna) Purana, Padma Purana, Varaha Purana, Brahma Purana, Brahmanda Purana, Brahma Vaivarta Purana, Markandeya Purana, Bhavishya Purana, Vamana Purana, Matsya Purana, Kurma Purana, Linga Purana, Siva Purana, Skanda Purana and Agni Purana. Of these, six are Sattvic Puranas and glorify Vishnu; six are Rajasic and glorify Brahma; six are Tamasic and they glorify Siva.

Neophytes or beginners in the spiritual Path are puzzled when they go through Siva Purana and Vishnu Purana. In Siva Purana, Lord Siva is highly eulogised and an inferior position is given to Lord Vishnu. Sometimes Vishnu is belittled. In Vishnu Purana, Lord Hari is highly eulogised and an inferior status is given to Lord Siva. Sometimes Lord Siva is belittled. This is only to increase the faith of the devotees in their particular Ishta-Devata. Lord Siva and Lord Vishnu are one.

The best among the Puranas are: the Srimad Bhagavata and the Vishnu Purana. The most popular is the Srimad Bhagavata Purana. Next comes Vishnu Purana. A portion of the Markandeya Purana is well known to all Hindus as Chandi, or Devi mahatmya. Worship of God as the Divine Mother is its theme. Chandi is read widely by the Hindus on sacred days and Navaratri (Durga Puja) days.

(ii) The Srimad Bhagavata Purana and the Ten Avataras

The Srimad Bhagavata Purana is a chronicle of the various Avataras of Lord Vishnu. There are ten Avataras of Vishnu. The aim of every Avatara is to save the world from some great danger, to destroy the wicked and protect the virtuous. The ten Avataras are: Matsya (The Fish), Kurma (The Tortoise), Varaha (The Boar), Narasimha (The Man-Lion), Vamana (The Dwarf), Parasurama (Rama with the axe, the destroyer of the Kshatriya race), Ramachandra (The hero of Ramayana—the son of Dasaratha), who destroyed Ravana, Sri Krishna, The teacher of the Gita, Buddha (The prince-ascetic, founder of Buddhism) and Kalki (The hero riding on a white horse, who is to come at the end of the Kali-Yuga).

The object of the Matsya Avatara was to save Vaivasvata Manu from destruction by a deluge. The object of Kurma Avatara was to enable the world to recover some precious things which were lost in the deluge. The Kurma gave its back for keeping the churning rod when the Gods and the Asuras churned the ocean of milk. The purpose of Varaha Avatara was to rescue, from the waters, the earth which had been dragged down by a demon named Hiranyaksha. The purpose of Narasimha Avatara, half-lion and half-man, was to free the world from the oppression of Hiranyakasipu, a demon, the father of Bhakta Prahlada. The object of Vamana Avatara was to restore the power of the gods which had been eclipsed by the penance and devotion of King Bali. The object of Parasurama Avatara was to deliver the country from the oppression of the Kshatriya rulers. Parasurama destroyed the Kshatriya race twenty-one times. The object of Rama was to destroy the wicked Ravana. The object of Sri Krishna Avatara was to destroy Kamsa and other demons, to deliver His wonderful message of the Gita in the Mahabharata war, and to become the centre of the Bhakti schools of India. The object of Buddha Avatara was to prohibit animal sacrifices and teach piety. The object of the Kalki Avatara is the destruction of the wicked and the re-establishment of virtue.

2.1.5 The Agamas

Another class of popular scriptures are the Agamas. The Agamas are theological treatises and practical manuals of divine worship. The Agamas include the Tantras, Mantras and Yantras. These are treatises explaining the external worship of God, in idols, temples, etc. All the Agamas treat of (i) Jnana or Knowledge, (ii) Yoga or Concentration, (iii) Kriya or Esoteric Ritual and (iv) Charya or Exoteric Worship. They also give elaborate details about ontology and cosmology, liberation, devotion, meditation, philosophy of

Mantras, mystic diagrams, charms and spells, temple-building, image-making, domestic observances, social rules, public festivals, etc.

The Agamas are divided into three sections: The Vaishnava, the Saiva and the Sakta. The three chief sects of Hinduism, viz., Vaishnavism, Saivism and Saktism, base their doctrines and dogmas on their respective Agamas. The Vaishnava Agamas or Pancharatra Agamas glorify God as Vishnu. The Saiva Agamas glorify God as Siva and have given rise to an important school of philosophy known as Saiva-Siddhanta, which prevails in South India, particularly in the districts of Tirunelveli and Madurai. The Sakta Agamas or Tantras glorify God as the Mother of the Universe, under one of the many names of Devi.

The Agamas do not derive their authority from the Vedas, but are not antagonistic to them. They are all Vedic in spirit and character. That is the reason why they are regarded as authoritative.

2.1.6 The Six Darsanas

These are the intellectual section of the Hindu writings, while the first four are intuitional, and the fifth inspirational and emotional. Darsanas are schools of philosophy based on the Vedas. The Agamas are theological. The Darsana literature is philosophical. The Darsanas are meant for the erudite scholars who are endowed with acute acumen, good understanding, power of reasoning and subtle intellect. The Itihasas, Puranas and Agamas are meant for the masses. The Darsanas appeal to the intellect, while the Itihasas, Puranas, etc., appeal to the heart.

Philosophy has six divisions—Shad-darsana—the six Darsanas or ways of seeing things, usually called the six systems or six different schools of thought. The six schools of philosophy are the six instruments of true teaching or the six demonstrations of Truth. Each school has developed, systematised and correlated the various parts of the Veda in its own way. Each system has its Sutrakara, i.e., the one great Rishi who systematised the doctrines of the school and put them in short aphorisms or Sutras.

The Sutras are terse and laconic. The Rishis have condensed their thoughts in the aphorisms. It is very difficult to understand them without the help of commentaries by great sages or Rishis. Hence, there arose many commentators or Bhashyakaras. There are glosses, notes and, later, commentaries on the original commentaries.

The Shad-Darsanas (the six schools of philosophy) or the Shat-Sastras are: the Nyaya, founded by Gautama Rishi, the Vaiseshika by Kanada Rishi, the Sankhya by Kapila Muni, the Yoga by Patanjali Maharshi, the Purva Mimansa by Jaimini, and the Uttara Mimansa or Vedanta by Badarayana or Vyasa. The Darsanas are divided into three pairs of aphoristic compositions which explain the philosophy of the Vedas in a rationalistic method of approach. They are: the Nyaya and the Vaiseshika, the Sankhya and the Yoga, and the Mimamsa and the Vedanta. Each set of Sutras has got its Bhashya, Vritti, Varttika, Vyakhyana or Tika and Tippani.

(i) Sutra

A Sutra or an aphorism is a short formula with the least possible number of letters, without any ambiguity or doubtful assertion, containing the very essence, embracing all meanings, without any stop or obstruction and absolutely faultless in nature.

The Sutrakara or the composer of the aphorisms is said to be as happy as one would be while getting the first male child, if he is but able to reduce one letter in his abstruse Sutra of far-fetched words and ideas. The best example of the greatest, the tersest and the most perfect of Sutra literature is the series of aphorisms called the Ashtadhyayi composed by Panini. Panini is the father of all Sutrakaras from whom all others seem to have borrowed the method of composition. The Sutras are meant to explain a big volume of knowledge in short assertions suitable to be kept in memory at all times. The six Vedangas and the six systems of Hindu philosophy form the twelve sets of Sutra literature of the world. In addition to these, there are later compositions like the Narada-Bhakti Sutras, the Sandilya-Bhakti Sutras, etc., which also wish to assume an equal form with the famous Sutras mentioned above.

(ii) Bhashya

A Bhashya is an elaborate exposition, a commentary on the Sutras, with word by word meaning of the aphoristic precepts, their running translation, together with the individual views of the commentator or the Bhashyakara. The best and the exemplary Bhashya in Sanskrit literature is the one written by Patanjali on the Vyakarana Sutras of Panini. This Bhashya is so very famous and important that it is called the MAHABHASHYA and its celebrated author is specially called the BHASHYAKARA. Patanjali is the father of Bhashyakaras. The next important Bhashya is the one on the Mimamsa Sutras written by Sabara-Swamin who learnt the art from Patanjali's commentary. The third important Bhashya was written by Sankara on the Brahma Sutras, in close following with the Sabara-Bhashya. The Bhashyas on the six sets of aphorisms dealing with Indian philosophy were written by Vatsyayana, Prasastapada, Vijnanabhikshu, Vyasa, Sabara and Sankara. On the Vedanta or Brahma Sutras, there are about sixteen Bhashyas, like those of Ramanuja, Madhva, Vallabha, Nimbarka, etc.

2.2 Five Stages of Love According to Ancient Hindu Philosophy

There are very interesting stories and origins of love in Hinduism (Hindu Dharma). One origin has it that there used to live a super-being known as 'Purusha', who had no desire, craving, fear, or any impulse to do anything as the created universe was perfect and complete.

Then Lord Brahma, the creator, took things upon his hands and split Purusha in two. Then, the Sky separated from the Earth, the darkness separated from light, the life separated from death, and finally, the male separated from the female. Each of the halves then went on a quench to satisfy itself by reuniting with its other half.
As either male or female on this earth, we are seeking our other half

too, and that search is known to be 'Love'. Today, we are completely indulged in the romantic and sexual elements: there are dating sites to find "partners", advertisers exploit this "love" to sell everything, and then there are movies that keep us on our toes with romantic involvement.

But the sages of ancient India say that the love we're chasing is not love; instead, it is the fleeting emotional high of "falling in love", which can collapse at any moment. The sage philosophers kept pondering on this topic way before Christ, and freshly developed the ideas during the revival of Bhakti Yoga during the 15th century.

They found that love transits at five different stages. These stages are:

2.2.1 Kama – Sensory Craving

The desire to merge initiates from physical attraction. The Kama means "craving for sense objects", which is usually translated as "sexual desire". It is to be noted that unlike Judeo-Christian myth where sexual desires are considered to be the "fall of man", Hindu dharma doesn't associate sex with shame, instead, a joyous aspect of human existence. This is where Kamasutra comes into play, which is not just about different positions of sex, but more about the philosophy of love and the questions of love. The sages agree that kama can be a goal of Hindu life, but it is not the sole factor that can lead to wholeness.

2.2.2 Shringara – Rapturous Intimacy

Only sex can fulfil physical desires, but there would be no emotional feeling if we indulge in sex without true intimacy and sharing. This is where the Indian sages focused on the emotional content and developed a rich context to understand the moods and emotions. This is where 'Shringara' was born, which is romance. The erotic attraction from just sensory cravings is stirred up when they share secrets with each other, make affectionate names of another, play games, exchange inventive gifts. This sort of imaginative play of love is symbolized by the relationship between Radha and Krishna, where they were involved in adventure, music, dance, poetry, and many other romantic gestures.

But the ancient sages understood that just finding our "soulmates" would not be able to solve all our problems. However, it does provide us with the foretaste of something good, something much greater.

2.2.3 Maitri – Generous Compassion

There is love in little things we can do. This could just be a simple smile to a stranger or food to hungry. Mahatma Gandhi says "The simplest acts of kindness are by far more powerful than a thousand heads bowing in prayer." Compassion just like the natural love we feel towards children and pets. The "Matru-Prema", which in Sanskrit means motherly love, and it is the kind of love that is the most giving and least selfish. Maitri is the motherly love, not just for your partner or children, but for all living beings.

Compassion for everyone might be hard for all. Thus, there are practices in Hindu and Buddhist dharma that can help you develop this ability. And when you are more compassionate with everyone, you become even more compassionate with your partner.

There is a beautiful shloka (in Sanskrit) wishing the welfare of everyone, which says:

Oṃ sarve bhavantu sukhinaḥ, sarve santu nirāmayāḥ. Sarve bhadrāṇi paśyantu, mā kaścidduḥ khabhāgbhaveta
Oṃ śāntiḥ śāntiḥ śāntiḥ ||

Meaning: *May all sentient beings be at peace, may no one suffer from illness, May all see what is auspicious, may no one suffer. Om peace, peace, peace.*

2.2.4 Bhakti – Impersonal Devotion

Compassion is just a start, and not a final rubber stamp. The ancient sages went beyond interpersonal love and envisioned a form of love that expanded to the whole of creation. This path to finding this love is known as "Bhakti Yoga", where you are not only cultivating the love for others but also to the love of God. The love of God doesn't need to be the God that we use in the usual self. It can be the highest form of kindness, truth, or justice. People like Dalai Lama are passionate and committed to these highest forms of truth, kindness, and justice. Real love is clearsighted–never blind–whereas infatuation masquerading as love is both blinding and blindness.

2.2.5 Atma Prema – Unconditional Self-Love

There is a cycle to everything. The love that started by directing towards others is then again directed towards the inside – the self. Atma Prema could be translated as self-love. Indian mystical poet Kabir says, "The river that flows in you also flows in me." This means that what we see in others, we see others in ourselves.

Once we achieve self-love, we recognize that we are all one, in that we recognize that our genetic heritage and upbringing have little value in the distinction of our self. The true self is all. Atma-Prema leads us to understand that we are part of the Purusha, and we are the children of the highest. Thus, when we love ourselves and others in the most profound manner, the love knows no boundaries and thus becomes unconditional.

Thus, the ancient philosophers of Hindu dharma proposed these five stages of a lover's journey as mutually exclusive and that we don't need to renounce physical love and romance to pursue higher love. When we develop ourselves in these five stages, we free ourselves from the attachment of physical romance only and thus be able to live love in the most unconditional way.

2.3 Love in Brihadaranyaka Upanishad (Self-Love)

There was a great sage called Yajnavalkya. His name occurs in the

Brihadaranyaka Upanishad. He was a master of spiritual wisdom. One day, when he had become aged, he told his wife Maitreyi, and another wife known as Katyayani, that he was retiring; and he said:

maitreyīti hovāca yājñavalkyaḥ, udyāsyanvā
are'hamasmātsthānādasmi,hanta te'nayā kātyāyanyāntaṃ
karavāṇīti || 2.4.1 ||

'Maitreyī, my dear,' said the sage Yājñavalkya, I am going to renounce this householder's life —I intend to take up the life of renunciation, which is the next higher life. Hence, I ask your permission. Further I wish to finish between you and my second wife, Kātyāyanī, that is, put an end to the relationship that existed between you through me, your common husband; by dividing my property between you I will separate you through wealth, and go.' The younger wife, Katyayani, was very happy. "Good riddance! Now the old man goes," she perhaps thought. But the other wife, Maitreyi, was very mature.

sa hovāca maitreyī, yannu ma iyaṃ bhagoḥ sarvā pṛthivī
vittenapūrṇā syātkathaṃ tenāmṛtā syāmiti; neti hovāca
yājñavalkyaḥ,
yathaivopakaraṇavatāṃ jīvitaṃ tathaiva te jīvitaṃ syāt,
amṛtatvasya tu nāśāsti vitteneti || 2.4.2 ||

Thereupon Maitreyī said, 'Sir, if indeed this whole earth full of wealth be mine, shall I be immortal through that?' 'No,' replied Yājñavalkya, 'your life will be just like that of people who have plenty of things, but there is no hope of immortality through wealth.'

Thus addressed, Maitreyī said, 'Sir, if indeed this whole earth girdled by the ocean and full of wealth be mine, shall I be immortal through that, That is, through rites such as the Agnihotra, which can be performed with the entire wealth of the earth? 'Shall I be immortal?' 'No,' replied Yājñavalkya. If the word 'how' indicates disbelief, Yājñavalkya's word 'No' is an approval. If it has an interrogative force, his reply means, 'You can never be immortal; as is the life of people of means filled with materials of enjoyment, so will your life be; but there is no hope, even in thought, of immortality through wealth, that is, rites performed with wealth.'

sa hovāca maitreyī, yenāhaṃ nāmṛtā syāṃ kimahaṃ tena kuryām?
yadeva bhagavānveda tadeva me brūhīti || *2.4.3* ||

Thus addressed, Maitreyī said in reply, 'If this is so, what shall I do with that wealth which will not make me immortal? Tell me, sir, of that alone which you know to be the only means of immortality.'

sa hovāca yājñavalkyaḥ, priyā batāre naḥ satī priyaṃ bhāṣase,
ehi, āssva, vyākhyāsyāmi te, vyācakṣāṇasya tu me nididhyāsasveti
|| *2.4.4* ||

When rites performed with wealth were rejected as a means to immortality, Yājñavalkya, seeing that Maitreyī concurred with his views, was pleased and said, 'O Maitreyī, you have been my beloved even before, and now you say what is just after my heart. Therefore, come and take your seat, I will explain to you what you desire—that knowledge of the Self which confers immortality. But as I explain it, meditate, or desire to reflect steadfastly, on the meaning of my words.' The particle 'bata' is suggestive of tenderness.

sa hovāca: na vā are patyuḥ kāmāya patiḥ priyo bhavati,
ātmanastu kāmāya patiḥ priyo bhavati |
na vā are jāyāyai kāmāya jāyā priyā bhavati,
ātmanastu kāmāya jāyā priyā bhavati |
na vā are pūtrāṇāṃ kāmāya putrāḥ priyā bhavanti,
ātmanastu kāmāya putrāḥ priyā bhavanti |
na vā are vittasya kāmāya vittaṃ priyaṃ bhavati,
ātmanastu kāmāya vittaṃ priyaṃ bhavati |
na vā are brahmaṇaḥ kāmāya brahma priyaṃ bhavati,
ātmanastu kāmāya brahma priyaṃ bhavati |
na vā are kṣatrasya kāmāya kṣatraṃ priyaṃ bhavati,
ātmanastu kāmāya kṣatraṃ priyaṃ bhavati |

na vā are lokānāṃ kāmāya lokāḥ priyā bhavanti,
ātmanastu kāmāya lokāḥ priyā bhavanti |
na vā are devānāṃ kāmāya devāḥ priyā bhavanti,
ātmanastu kāmāya devāḥ priyā bhavanti |
na vā are bhūtānāṃ kāmāya bhūtāni priyāṇi bhavanti,
ātmanastu kāmāya bhūtāni priyāṇi bhavanti |
na vā are sarvasya kāmāya sarvaṃ priyaṃ bhavati,
ātmanastu kāmāya sarvaṃ priyaṃ bhavati |
ātmā vā are draṣṭavyaḥ śrotavyo mantavyo nididhyāsitavyo maitreyi,
ātmano vā are darśanena śravaṇena matyā vijñānenedaṃ sarvaṃ viditam || 2.4.5 ||

He said: It is not for the sake of the husband, my dear, that he is loved, but for one's own sake that he is loved. It is not for the sake of the wife, my dear, that she is loved, but for one's own sake that she is loved. It is not for the sake of the sons, my dear, that they are loved, but for one's own sake that they are loved. It is not for the sake of wealth, my dear, that it is loved, but for one's own sake that it is loved. It is not for the sake of the Brāhmaṇa, my dear, that he is loved, but for one's own sake that he is loved. It is not for the sake of the Kṣatriya, my dear, that he is loved, but for one's own sake that he is loved. It is not for the sake of the worlds, my dear, that they are loved, but for one's own sake that they are loved. It is not for the sake of the gods, my dear, that they are loved, but for one's own sake that they are loved. It is not for the sake of the beings, my dear, that they are loved, but for one's own sake that they are loved. It is not for the sake of all, my dear, that all are loved, but for one's own sake that it is loved. The Self, my dear Maitreyī, should be realised—should be heard of, reflected on and meditated upon. By the realisation of the Self, my dear, through hearing, reflection and meditation, all this is known.

Hence it is a well-known fact that the Self alone is dear, and nothing else. Therefore, our love for other objects is secondary, since they contribute to the pleasure of the Self; and our love for the Self alone is primary. Therefore, 'the Self, my dear Maitreyī, should he realised, is worthy of realisation, or should be made the object of realisation. It should first be heard of from a teacher and from the scriptures, then reflected on through reasoning, and then steadfastly meditated upon.' Thus, only is It realised—when these means, viz. hearing, reflection and meditation, have been gone through. When these three are combined, then only true realisation of the unity of Brahman is accomplished, not otherwise—by hearing alone. The different castes such as the Brāhmaṇa or the Kṣatriya, the various orders of life, and so on, upon which rites depend, and which consist of actions, their factors and their results, are objects of notions superimposed on the Self by ignorance—based on false notions like that of a snake in a rope. In order to destroy these, he says, 'By the realisation of the Self, my dear, through hearing, reflection and meditation, all this is known.'

brahma taṃ parādādyo'nyatrātmano brahma veda,
kṣatraṃ taṃ parādādyo'nyatrātmanaḥ kṣatraṃ veda,
lokāstaṃ parāduryo'nyatrātmano lokānveda,
devāstaṃ parāduryo'nyatrātmano devānveda,
bhūtāni taṃ parāduryo'nyatrātmano bhūtāni veda,
sarvaṃ taṃ parādādyo'nyatrātmanaḥ sarvaṃ veda;
idaṃ brahma, idaṃ kṣatram, ime lokāḥ,
ime devāḥ, imāmi bhūtāni, idaṃ sarvaṃ yadayamātmā || 2.4.6 ||

The Brāhmaṇa ousts one who knows him as different from the Self. The Kṣatriya ousts one who knows him as different from the Self. The worlds oust one who knows them as different from the Self. The gods oust one who knows them as different from the Self. The beings oust one who knows them as different from the Self. All ousts one who knows it as different from the Self. This Brāhmaṇa, this Kṣatriya, these worlds, these gods, these beings, and this all are the Self.

2.4 Love in Bhagavad Gita

In the Bhagavad Gita (the Song of the Lord) Krishna comforts and advises his troubled disciple Arjuna by telling him about three paths. Each, he says, is a kind of yoga—a way to live in the world and at the same time maintain inner peace. They are the path of action(Karma Yoga), the path of devotion(Bhakti Yoga), and the path of knowledge (Jnana Yoga). Karma yoga, Lord Krishna says, is the ability to conscientiously evaluate one's motivation, to act with skill and determination, and yet not be attached to the outcome of the action. On the path of bhakti yoga, help is proffered and spirits are healed through love—through the soul's love for that which is eternal, and through the love of the eternal for each soul.

In Chapters 7–12 of the Gita Krishna teaches the path of devotion and love, bhakti yoga. This path is commonly associated with those who express themselves through music, poetry, dance, and other fine arts, and it is synonymous with a life of service, prayer, and meditation—a life devoted to God. But you do not need to be an artist or a member of a religious order to find joy on the path of devotion. Ultimately, this path is about uplifting human hearts. On the path of bhakti yoga, help is proffered and spirits are healed through love—through the soul's love for that which is eternal, and through the love of the eternal for each soul. The path of bhakti yoga unfolds spontaneously. For some, its appeal stems from an inherent attraction to God. For others, gratitude toward yoga matures into love and respect for a teacher, for a system of practice, or for the natural universe.

I am the same to all beings, and my love is ever the same; but those who worship me with devotion, they are in me and I am in them. For if even one who does evil were to worship me with all his soul, he must be considered righteous, because of his righteous will. He will soon become pure and reach everlasting peace. For be aware, Arjuna, that he who loves me shall not perish. (9:29–31)

When we are summoned by Krishna's voice, however, we are not expected to join a new religion or develop a sentimental dependence upon a teacher. And if some of us find ourselves drawn to Krishna's stories and teachings, we are not compelled in yoga to accept Krishna's tradition. The call of the self is to know the Self. It is a call issued by one's heart—a call that clears away fears and past faults. In yogic terms, Krishna's voice is the voice of love, truth, and self-acceptance, flowing through one's own soul.

Our biggest problem here is our habit of projecting energy outward. When we seek recognition as a holy person or demand love and attention from a teacher, our emotional needs have been projected onto the trappings of spiritual life. The outcome is invariably disappointing. But when we cultivate love, not for what the world sees as glorious, but for the flower of life blossoming in us—then our devotion will surely bear fruit. For, as Krishna tells us,

Of all knowledge, I am the knowledge of the Soul. Of the many paths of speech, I am the one that leads to Truth. (10:32)

Only by undistracted love can men see me, and know me, and enter into me.

He who does my work, who loves me, who sees me as the highest, free from attachment to all things, and with love for all creation, he in truth comes to me. (11:53–55)

When we love someone, we want to be near them—to give gifts, share experiences, and receive the other's love. Out of love, we offer support during periods of illness, and encouragement during challenging times. We do not hurt or harm those we love. Love unites us.

Giving, receiving, sharing, and uniting are love's way.

But why does love compel us to behave like this? What is it about love that is so transforming? There is no answer to these questions. It is simply love's nature. Giving, receiving, sharing, and uniting are love's way. They are the blossoms that bloom wherever love grows.

Krishna appeals to us to love. Still speaking in the first person, he asks that we behave as one who is in love. Unseen and unheard

except in the quietness of the soul, he calls:
Give me your mind and give me your heart, give me your offerings and your adoration; and thus, with your soul in harmony, and making me your goal supreme, you will in truth come to me. (9:34)

But how do we do this? What change in life announces that we have discovered Love and worship it in the midst of life's busy affairs?

Krishna asks us to give, but he is also the giver, the Lord of life. We feel his hidden presence in the splendour of nature, in the beauty of human life, and in acts of personal sacrifice. But we are so often consumed by our daily lives that we lose sight of the significance of these gifts. Rabindranath Tagore, the Nobel Prize-winning poet of India, reminds us of their importance:

Krishna asks us to give, but he is also the giver, the Lord of life.

Love spontaneously gives itself in endless gifts. But those gifts lose their fullest significance if through them we do not reach that love, which is the giver.

Bhakti is a path of goodwill. With love in our heart, it is possible to see beyond the faults and Judgements which often colour our relationships with others and with ourself. Try rescuing a relationship that is inherently good, but has gone sour, by returning to it with love in your heart.

According to Bhagavad Gita (3.41):

Tasmattvamindriyanyadau niyamya bharatarshabha.
Papamanam prajahi hyenaṁ jnanavijnananashanam. (3.41)

Meaning: Therefore, O Arjuna, best of the Bhāratas, in the very beginning curb this great symbol of sin [lust] by regulating the senses, and slay this destroyer of knowledge and self-realization.

The Lord advised Arjuna to regulate the senses from the very beginning so that he could curb the greatest sinful enemy, lust, which destroys the urge for self-realization, and specifically, knowledge of the self. Jñānam refers to knowledge of self as distinguished from non-self, or, in other words, knowledge that the spirit soul is not the body. Vijñānam refers to specific knowledge of the spirit soul and knowledge of one's constitutional position and his relationship to the Supreme Soul. It is explained thus in the Śrīmad-Bhāgavatam: jñānaṁ parama-guhyaṁ me yad-vijñāna-samanvitam / sarahasyaṁ tad-aṅgaṁ ca gṛhāna gaditaṁ mayā: "The knowledge of the self and the Supreme Self is very confidential and mysterious, being veiled by māyā, but such knowledge and specific realization can be understood if it is explained by the Lord Himself." Bhagavad-gītā gives us that knowledge, specifically knowledge of the self. The living entities are parts and parcels of the Lord, and therefore they are simply meant to serve the Lord. This consciousness is called Krishṇa consciousness. So, from the very beginning of life one has to learn this Krishṇa consciousness, and thereby one may become fully Krishṇa conscious and act accordingly.

Lust is only the perverted reflection of the love of God which is natural for every living entity. But if one is educated in Krishṇa consciousness from the very beginning, that natural love of God cannot deteriorate into lust. When love of God deteriorates into lust, it is very difficult to return to the normal condition. Nonetheless, Krishṇa consciousness is so powerful that even a late beginner can become a lover of God by following the regulative principles of devotional service. So, from any stage of life, or from the time of understanding its urgency, one can begin regulating the senses in Krishṇa consciousness, devotional service of the Lord, and turn the lust into love of Godhead-the highest perfectional stage of human life.

2.5 Some Interesting Love Stories in Mahabharata

1. Krishna and Rukmini

Krishna kidnaps Rukmini and rides away in his chariot. Though most of the stories tell the tale of how Krishna fell in love with a Gopi Radha, the ancient scriptures don't mention about Radha at all. Instead, it is mentioned that Krishna's favourite was Rukmini, among his seven other wives. The story is full of drama as Krishna fell in love with Rukmini and abducted her against her parent's will. Rukmini was also in love with Krishna, and they both married to live happily thereafter. Some consider Rukmini to be the incarnation of Goddess Laxmi.

2. Arjuna and Ulupi

Arjuna had four wives, and among them, Ulupi was the second. They met when Arjun was in exile. But it is interesting how in this case, Ulupi was the one who abducted Arjun and convinced him to get married. Ulupi was the Naga princess with a half-maiden and half-serpent body. Later, they even had a son named Iravan. Ulupi also granted Arjuna a boon that the water kingdom will obey him and that he will never be defeated underwater.

3. Ganga and Shantanu

Shantanu was the Kuru King of Hastinapur when he met a beautiful girl in white saree on the banks of Ganges. He instantly fell in love with her beauty, and thus, proposed her to get married. But Ganga put forth a condition that no matter what she does, he should not ask her any questions about her actions. Shantanu agreed. Later, Ganga drowned their sons, one by one. She drowned seven of their sons.

Since Shantanu had promised her not to ask her any questions about her actions, he stayed quiet, until Ganga was about to drown their eighth son when Shantanu couldn't bear it. Shantanu broke the promise, and so Ganga disappeared with her son, but she had promised that she would return the son one day when everything is in the right place. For 16 years, there was no news. Then one day (after 16 years), he was reunited with his eighth son Devrath, who we know as Bhishma Pitamah

4. Bhima and Hidimbi

When the Pandavas escaped the Lakshagraha, they reached a forest. All of them fell asleep, except Bhima. In that forest, there used to live a demon Hidimba, who was living with his demon sister Hidimbi. Hidimbi smelled Bhima and asked Hidimba to lure him so that they could eat him. Hidimbi went forth to lure him, only to fall in love in with Bhima at first glance. She confessed the truth to Bhima and expressed her will to marry him. But Bhima denied, and became furious; he instead killed her brother and was about to kill Hidimbi when Yudhisthira stopped him from committing this sin. Hidimbi begged Kunti to convince Bhima to get married. Bhima set a condition that he would leave Hidimbi after the birth of their first child if they get married. Hidimbi agreed and they got married. When their first son Ghatotkacha was born, Bhima left both of them.

5. Pandavas and Draupadi

Commonly referred to as Draupadi, Panchali was the wife of all five Pandavas. Arjuna won her hand in Swayamvara. What happened was Arjuna had won a competition and they came to their mother Kunti to tell her about it. Hearing this, Kunti told them to share the prize. To keep up with their mother's command, they shared Draupadi. She gave birth to each of the Pandava brothers. Some feel that Draupadi had a feeling for Arjuna, but Arjuna was in love with Subhadra. So, she found solace in Yudhisthira who lusted after her. But it was Bhima who genuinely loved Draupadi and tried to give out to all the demands of her wishes. Sahadev and Nakul only obliged to the commands of Yudhishthira.

6. Arjuna and Subhadra

Arjuna abducted Subhadra so that he could save her from marrying Duryodhana. Arjuna was completely in love with Subhadra when he first fell into the beauty of Subhadra. He even wanted to marry her. Knowing this, Subhadra's half-brother, Krishna sensed their mutual feelings and after the consent from Balarama, the two got married.

They later had a son together, who we know as Abhimanyu.

7. Gandhari and Dhritarashtra

Gandhari is considered to be an example for all women, the Pativrata. She is the epitome of virtue and the wife of Dhritarashtra, the blind king of Hastinapur. When they got married, she tied a piece of cloth on her eyes and pledged to live the rest of her life as a blind woman in order to share the same pain with her husband. They had 100 kids together.

8. Parashar Rishi and Satyavati

Parashar was a Maharishi and when Satyavati was ferrying her across the river Yamuna, he asked her to satisfy his lust. And so, he held her hand. As a Brahmin, the action doesn't suit his stature to desire a woman who smelled of fish, according to Satyavati. She asked him to be patient until they reached the shore and set forth three conditions so that she could fulfil his lust. First, she wanted the smell of fish to be replaced by a pleasant, lusting fragrance. He turned her into a Yojanagandha. Second, no one should be able to see what they were doing in the broad daylight. He created an artificial mist around them. Third, their virginity should remain intact after intercourse. The Maharishi agreed that she would get her virginity back when she gave birth to their child. With the blessings to have all the three wishes, Satyavati and Parashar made love. They gave birth to a son. He was Vyasa, the one who wrote Mahabharata.

9. Arjuna and Chitrangada

The princess of Manipur, Chitrangada met Arjuna on the banks of Kaveri river. Both of them fell in love in the place and Arjuna asked her hand from her father Chitravahana. He wanted their son to lead Manipur as his successor to the throne. Arjuna agreed. They had a son by the name Babruvahana. Arjuna left them to join his brothers at Indraprastha. Chitrangada and Babruvahana were left behind. Later, Babruvahana became the king of Manipur and even defeated his father in part of a war.

2.6 Eternal Love Story Of Kama And Rati

India was once known, among other things, as the land of the Kamasutra. We were that much 'forward' nation that not only we gave the world fascinating sex manuals but also put images of amorous couples on our temple walls. Sex was not a taboo subject to be avoided or spoken of in bad metaphors but something to be celebrated. The Kama, or sensual pleasure, was counted among the four purusharthas (goals of life), the other three being dharma (righteous duty), artha (wealth) and moksha (liberation). It was not just a right but a duty unto oneself, without which life would neither be wholesome nor complete. Love was sport and art. It was serious business and celebration. Love was divine because it was ruled by the gods. That is why Kamadeva is important. He is considered to be the Hindu God of love and lust, the India Cupid.

The word, Kama, used to denote pleasure, is also the name of the God who controls it. Known as Manmatha, Madana, Atanu, or Ananga, Kamadeva is one of Brahma's sons by many mythological accounts. He lords over and is the personification of love, lust and sensuality. Much like the western Eros or Cupid, he signifies the attraction between two people. Visually, he is represented as a handsome young man with a parrot as his vahana (vehicle), a sugarcane bow, with bees forming the bowstring and flower-tipped arrows. He is often accompanied by his wife, Rati, who is the Goddess of carnal desire, lust, passion and sexual pleasure. She, too, is described in mythological texts as a woman of great youth and beauty and is one of the many daughters of Daksha Prajapati.

Together, Kama and Rati have a son named 'Harsh'; or by some accounts, two sons – the other one being 'Yash'. The names of these offspring of Kama couple are worth noting here, for the metaphors are more than evident: sexual union and harmony result in joy and grace. Our seer-poets didn't miss a thing.

How Kama and Rati came to be together. It is related to the beauteous form of Lakshmi called Saundarya Lakshmi. It so happened that the goddess, Rati, was once rather plain-looking. Being unable to attract any suitors made Rati very doleful, but then she earned Lakshmi's benevolence. Lakshmi imparted the art of solah (sixteen) shringara to Rati, which made her the most beautiful woman in the three worlds. Inevitably, Kamadeva was bewitched by her and made her his chief consort. Incidentally, the word shringara includes the term shri, which is another name for the goddess Lakshmi. The Gods of love, then, had the blessings of the goddess of prosperity. Kamadeva was captivated by Rati's beauty.

But another god wasn't quite pleased with this couple. This famous story of Madana Bhasma is told about the time Lord Shiva was deep in meditation. Having lost his wife, Sati, Shiva had withdrawn from the world. But a world terrorized by the terrible demon, Tarakasura, needed a 'son of Shiva' for deliverance. For Shiva to have a son, he would have to get married, and for him to get married, he would first have to be drawn out of his meditative trance. So that Shiva could be united with Parvati – who was Sati reborn – the gods conspired. Kamadeva's services were enlisted and he was sent to create an untimely spring and shoot these arrows of lust at the recluse God. Kamadeva succeeded in his job alright, but at the cost of his life. Terribly angered at the intrusion, Shiva opened his third eye and burnt Kamadeva to ashes. Rati was inconsolable at having lost her lover and mate and sought redress.

When Shiva calmed down, he realized his folly and offered to undo it by bringing him back to life. However, Kamadeva would not have a body anymore and thus came to be known as the bodiless one (Ananga). Eventually, Shiva married Parvati and their son, Kartikeya, killed Tarakasura. The day was saved by love, so what if it was now formless.

2.7 Love of Meera for Lord Krishna

Meera (1498 - 1557) was a Rajput princess who lived in the north

Indian state of Rajasthan. When she was just four years of age on watching a marriage procession Meera , the child, asked her mother innocently, "Dear mother, who will be my bridegroom?" Meera's mother smiled, and half in jest pointed towards the image of Sri Krishna and said, "My dear Meera, Lord Krishna is going to be your bridegroom". She manifested a deep devotion to Krishna. Meera lost her mother soon.

As Meera grew up, she believed that Lord Krishna would come to marry her. Meera was beautiful, soft-spoken, mild-mannered, gifted, sweet, and she sang with a melodious voice. Very reluctantly she consented to marry Rana Sangha, the powerful King of Mewar. After her household duties were over, Meera would go to the temple of Lord Krishna, worship, sing and dance before Lord Krishna's Idol daily. Her mother-in-law and other ladies did not like her ways and forced her to worship Durga; but she maintained, "I have already given up my life to my beloved Lord Krishna".

Meera's sister-in-law Udabai conspired to defame the innocent Meera. She informed Rana Kumbha that Meera was secretly in love with someone. Kumbha ran with a sword in hand towards Meera but was calmed down .With his sister he went to the temple at night broke open the door, and found Meera alone in her ecstatic mood talking and singing to Krishna's idol. He shouted "Meera, show me your lover with whom you are talking now". Meera replied, "There sits He—my Lord She stood unruffled in the face of accusations of immoral character and said that she was married to Krishna. Her husband was heart-broken but he remained good and sympathized with her until his death.

Meera was sent a basket with a cobra inside and a message that the basket contained a garland of flowers. Meera opened the basket and found inside a lovely idol of Sri Krishna with a garland of flowers. She was sent her a cup of poison saying that it was nectar. Meera offered it to her Lord Krishna as Prasad. It was real nectar to her. The bed of nails that Rana sent transformed into a bed of roses when Meera reposed on it.

After so many attempts on her life, Meera proceeded to the river to drown herself. Chanting "Govinda, Giridhari, Gopala", She danced in ecstasy on her way to the river. A hand from behind grasped her and embraced her. She turned and saw her beloved Giridhari (Lord Krishna). She fainted on him. Lord Krishna smiled and gently whispered: "My dear Meera, your life with your mortal relatives is over now. You are absolutely free. Be cheerful. You are and have always been mine." She then shifted to Vrindaban thereafter.

2.8 Love between Radha and Krishna

Radha was a consort of the god Krishna. She is worshipped as the goddess of love, tenderness, compassion and devotion. She is described as the chief of gopis (milkmaids). During Krishna's youth, she appears as his lover and companion, though he was not married to her. In contrast, some traditions accord Radha the status of the primary consort and wife of Krishna.

Radha is considered as a metaphor for the human spirit (atma), her love and longing for Krishna is theologically viewed as symbolic of the human quest for spiritual growth and union with the divine (brahman). She has inspired numerous literary works, and her Rasa lila dance with Krishna has inspired many types of performance arts. Radha is an important goddess in the Vaishnavite traditions of Hinduism. Her traits, manifestations, descriptions, and roles vary by region. Radha is intrinsical with Krishna. In early During the Bhakti movement era in the sixteenth century, she became more well known as her extraordinary love for Krishna was highlighted.

Radha also appears in the late puranas namely the Padma Purana (as an avatar of Lakshmi), the Devi-Bhagavata Purana (as a form of Mahadevi) and the Brahma Vaivarta Purana (as Radha-Krishna supreme deity). The 15th and 16th century Krishnaite Bhakti poet-saints Vidyapati, Chandidas, Meera Bai, Surdas, Swami Haridas, as well as not special vaishnava Narsinh Mehta (1350–1450), who preceded all of them, wrote about the romance of Krishna and Radha too.

The birthplace of Radha is Raval which is near to Gokul but is often said to be Barsana. It is in Barsana that the Lathmar Holi is practiced depicting the episode of Krishna going to Barsana and then running away escaping the beating from the womenfolk of Barsana. Radha and Krishna share two kinds of relationships, Parakiya (Love without any social limitation) and Svakiya (married relationship). Radha asked Krishna why he can't marry her, the reply came "Marriage is a union of two souls. You and I are one soul, how can I marry myself?" The Brahmavaivarta Purana and the Garg Samhita mention that Krishna secretly married Radha in presence of Lord Brahma in the Bhandirvan forest, near Vrindavan. But to give importance to Parakiya relationship (love without any social foundation) over Svakiya's (married relationship), this marriage was never publicized and kept hidden.

In some devotional (bhakti) Krishnaite traditions of Vaishnavism that focus on Krishna, Radha represents "the feeling of love towards Krishna". For some of the adherents of these traditions, her importance approaches or even exceeds that of Krishna. Radha is worshipped along with Krishna in Bengal, Assam and Odisha by Vaishnava Hindus. Elsewhere, such as with Visnusvamins, she is a revered deity.

2.9 Love in Ramayana: Lord Rama and Sita

Rama and Sita are perceived to be 'ideal' couple of Indian mythology. Indeed, this is the way all Adarsh (ideal) Indian couples are expected to behave.

Notice how only the Ramayana is read out in homes and not the Mahabharata, for we want our women to behave like the sinless Sita, and not the perfervid Panchali.

Rama and Sita are looked upon as the perfect couple in mythology. The story of love between Rama and Sita is told and retold because as a woman Sita is looked at as the person who traded the hardships of living in a forest with her life in the palace, just to be with her husband. Her husband also did not leave her side for a moment, took care of her and protected her but destiny had other plans.

The Ramayana has long been treated as something of a moral codebook in Hindu society. This is especially true of Tulsidas' version of the epic – the Ramacharitamanas, which catapults Valmiki's yet human heroes into the realm of divine infallibility. Even if Tulsidas adheres to the main storyline, he colours it differently. Every action of Rama and Sita is treated as part of a godly plan, and the sweet imperfections of a man-woman relationship are forgotten.

Speak to even half a feminist, and you're likely to meet with some ready repugnance for Rama. Which self-respecting, freethinking woman, after all, would approve of a man who not only victim shames his wife but also abandons her during her pregnancy? But this view is as reductive as the traditional one, which upholds Rama as the maryada purushottam (role model of code of conduct). With some extra tinsel, mythology ultimately reflects human truths; and life, as we know it, is rarely so black and white. But why is the story of Rama and Sita important? We are coming to that.

Rama's character must be considered in its entirety, especially in the light of the roles he plays. As a hero, superlative he must be, whether as a son, brother, husband or king. In most cases, he takes a morally hard stand, but he is almost pliant as a husband. It just takes a little patient reading of the man to see that. It is advisable to revisit the episode of Sita's abduction to see this. Rama is an indulgent partner by any measure. Knowing fully well that the golden deer is an illusory rakshasa, Ram concedes to Sita's demands and agrees to fetch it for her. Could an uncaring spouse simply not refuse?

Rama's proof of love, unfortunately, becomes the morbid turning point of the tale and Sita is abducted by Ravana. We all know of this dramatic episode, but what follows is rarely discussed.

When Rama returns to find Sita gone, is perhaps a moment of epiphany for him. It has been known that love knows not its own depth until the hour of separation. Rama is disconsolate, shattered. In his haze of grief, he starts asking the animals and trees if they've seen Sita. He loses his will to live. Who, among the broken-hearted, will not understand this? It is only when Lakshman hammers some sense into his disconsolate elder brother that Rama comes around and becomes a man with a mission. This is a very important turning point of the love story Rama and Sita.

Another rather charming episode from the Ramayana helps us explore the romantic side of Rama-Sita's relationship. Sita narrates this to Hanumana when he first goes to Lanka to get news of her. One day, on the Chitrakuta hill, when the couple was resting, a hungry crow attacks Sita. He pecks at her breasts a couple of times, distressing her greatly. Seeing his beloved so, an agitated Rama plucks a blade of kusha grass, breathes magic into it, turns it into a brahmastra (the most powerful weapon) and unleashes it on the erring bird. Scared, the bird flies around the world, but the divine arrow doesn't stop chasing it. In the end, it surrenders to Rama and seeks his protection. But a brahmastra once unleashed cannot be taken back, so the compassionate hero (Rama) modifies the clause. He spares the crow's life and says that the weapon would strike him only in one eye.

Sita's acquiescence to everything Rama does is not mere wifely obedience either. She is feisty in her own way and if she chooses silence or suffering, it is for the cause of love.

Sita knows and values Rama's love too much to want to stay behind in Ayodhya or to give in to Ravana's threats and temptations. Sita too keeps her side of the marital pact as long as she lives. The love story of Ram and Sita has many layers we just need to be perceptive to understand better.

2.10 Love between Shabari and Lord Rama

Shabari was a woman from a tribal village. She was a seeker of knowledge and wanted to know the meaning of Dharma. After days of travel, she met Sage Matanga at the foot of Mount Rishyamukha. She accepted him as guru, serving him with devotion for many years. When Matanga was about to die, Shabari, now elderly, stated that after serving him throughout her life, she now sought to reach for herself the same "abode of peace" which Matanga had reached. The sage responded that, if she offered seva (service), Lord Rama would give her darshana. He told her to wait for Rama's arrival. Then, while sitting in lotus posture, the sage attained Mahasamadhi. Following her guru's advice, Shabari awaited Rama's arrival.

Every day, Shabari would go out of her ashram, with the help of a walking stick, and pluck berries for Lord Rama. She would pluck one, taste it and, if it was sweet, she would put it in her basket, discarding the bitter ones. She wanted to give the good berries to Rama. She didn't know that offerings must not be tasted. Thus, collecting a few berries, Shabari would return to the ashram and eagerly await Lord Rama's arrival.

According to the scriptural account, even though hundreds of other yogis were waiting to receive Rama in their ashrams, Rama went only to Shabari's ashram because of her sincere devotion. On seeing Rama, Shabari became ecstatic and said, "There were so many exalted yogis waiting for your darshan, but you came to this unworthy devotee (...) This clearly shows that you will neither see whether a devotee lives in a palace or humble hut, whether he is erudite or ignorant (...) neither see caste nor colour; you will only see the true bhakti (...) I do not have anything to offer other than my heart, but here are some berries. May it please you, my Lord." Shabari offered the fruits which she had meticulously collected. As Rama tasted them, Lakshmana raised the concern that Shabari had already tasted them and they were, therefore, unworthy of eating. To this, Rama responded that, of the many types of food he had tasted, "nothing could equal these berries, offered with such devotion. You taste them, then alone will you know. Whomsoever offers a fruit, leaf, flower or some water with love, I partake in it with great joy." Traditional writers use this narrative to indicate that in bhakti, faults are not seen by the deities.

Pleased with Shabari's devotion, Rama blesses her with his vision. Rama notices the donas, or bowls, of handmade leaves in which she had offered the fruits and is impressed by the hard work Shabari has gone through to make them and, hence, blesses the tree so that the leaves naturally grow in the shape of a bowl. Shabari also tells Rama to take help from Sugriva and where to find him. The Ramayana says that Shabari was a very bright and knowledgeable saint.

CHAPTER 3

Love in Buddhism

The monk who abides in the universal love and is deeply devoted to the Teaching of the Buddha, attains the peace of Nibbana, the bliss of the cessation of conditional things.

3.1 Buddhist Scriptures

Buddhist traditions have generally divided these texts with their own categories and divisions, such as that between buddhavacana "word of the Buddha," many of which are known as "sutras," and other texts, such as shastras (treatises) or Abhidharma.

The Buddhist texts are listed in the following:

3.1.1 Buddhavacana

The concept of buddhavacana (word of the Buddha) is important in understanding how Buddhists classify and see their texts. Buddhavacana texts have special status as sacred scriptures and are generally seen as in accord with the teachings of the Buddha, which is termed "the Dharma". The criteria for determining what should be considered buddhavacana were developed at an early stage, and that the early formulations do not suggest that Dharma is limited to what was spoken by the historical Buddha.

The Mahāsāṃghika and the Mūlasarvāstivāda considered both the Buddha's discourses, and of his disciples, to be buddhavacana. A number of different beings such as buddhas, disciples of the buddha, rishis, and devas were considered capable of transmitting buddhavacana. The content of such a discourse was then to be collated with the sūtras, compared with the Vinaya, and evaluated against the nature of the Dharma. These texts may then be certified as true buddhavacana by a buddha, a saṃgha, a small group of elders, or one knowledgeable elder.

In Theravāda Buddhism, the standard collection of buddhavacana is the Pāli Canon, also known as the Tipiṭaka ("three baskets"). Generally speaking, the Theravāda school rejects the Mahayana sutras as buddhavacana (word of the Buddha), and do not study or see these texts as reliable sources.

In East Asian Buddhism, what is considered buddhavacana is collected in the Chinese Buddhist canon. The most common edition of this is the Taishō Tripiṭaka, itself based on the Tripitaka Koreana. This collection, unlike the Pāli Tipiṭaka, contains Mahayana sutras, Śāstras (scholastic treatises) and Esoteric literature. Sometimes texts that are considered commentaries by some are regarded by others as buddhavacana.

In Indo-Tibetan Buddhism, what is considered buddhavacana is collected in the Kangyur ('The Translation of the Word'). The East Asian and Tibetan Buddhist canons always combined buddhavacana with other literature in their standard collected editions. tantras and other related tantric literature.

3.1.2 Early Buddhist Texts

The earliest Buddhist texts were passed down orally in Middle Indo-Aryan languages called Prakrits, including Gāndhārī language, the early Magadhan language and Pali through the use of repetition, communal recitation and mnemonic devices. These texts were later compiled into canons and written down in manuscripts. For example, the Pali canon was preserved in Sri Lanka where it was first written down in the first century BCE.

There are early texts from various Buddhist schools, the largest collections are from the Theravada and Sarvāstivāda schools, but there are also full texts and fragments from the Dharmaguptaka, Mahāsāṅghika, Mahīśāsaka, Mūlasarvāstivāda, and others. The most widely studied early Buddhist material are the first four Pali Nikayas, as well as the corresponding Chinese Āgamas. The modern study of early pre-sectarian Buddhism often relies on comparative scholarship using these various early Buddhist sources.

Various scholars of Buddhist studies such hold that early Buddhist texts contain material that could possibly be traced to the historical Buddha himself or at least to the early years of pre-sectarian Buddhism. In Mahayana Buddhism, these texts are sometimes referred to as "Hinayana" or "Śrāvakayāna". The Chinese Buddhist canon contains a complete collection of early sutras in Chinese translation, their content is very similar to the Pali, differing in detail but not in the core doctrinal content. The Tibetan canon contains some of these early texts as well, but not as complete collections. The earliest known Buddhist manuscripts containing early Buddhist texts are the Gandharan Buddhist Texts, dated to the 1st century BCE and constitute the Buddhist textual tradition of Gandharan Buddhism which was an important link between Indian and East Asian Buddhism. Parts of what is likely to be the canon of the Dharmaguptaka can be found among these Gandharan Buddhist Texts.

There are different genres of Early Buddhist texts, including prose "suttas" (discourses), disciplinary works (Vinaya), various forms of verse compositions (such as gāthā and udāna), mixed prose and verse works (geya), and also lists (matika) of monastic rules or doctrinal topics. A large portion of Early Buddhist literature is part of the "sutta" or "sutra" genre. The Sūtras (Pali Sutta) are mostly discourses attributed to the Buddha or one of his close disciples. They are considered to be buddhavacana by all schools. The Buddha's discourses were perhaps originally organized according to the style in which they were delivered. They were later organized into collections called Nikāyas ('volumes') or Āgamas ('scriptures'), which were further collected into the Sūtra Piṭaka ("Basket of Discourses") of the canons of the early schools.

Out of the early sutras that have survived are from Sthavira nikaya schools; no complete collection has survived from the other early branch of Buddhism, the Mahāsāṃghika. However, some individual texts have survived, such as the Śālistamba Sūtra (rice stalk sūtra). This sūtra contains many parallel passages to the Pali suttas. This text is in general agreement with the basic doctrines of the early sutras of the Sthavira schools such as dependent origination, the "middle way" between eternalism and annihilationism, the "five aggregates", the "three unwholesome roots", the four noble truths and the noble eightfold path. Another important source for Mahāsāṃghika sutras is the Mahāvastu ("Great Event"), which is a collection of various texts compiled into a biography of the Buddha. Within it can be found quotations and whole sutras, such as the Mahāsāṃghika version of the Dharmacakrapravartana.

The other major type of texts aside from the sutras are the Vinayas. Vinaya literature is primarily concerned with aspects of the monastic discipline and the rules and procedures that govern the Buddhist monastic community (sangha). However, Vinaya as a term is also contrasted with Dharma, where the pair (Dhamma-Vinaya) mean something like 'doctrine and discipline'. The Vinaya literature in fact contains a considerable range of texts. There are, of course, those that discuss the monastic rules, how they came about, how they developed, and how they were applied. But the vinaya also contains some doctrinal expositions, ritual and liturgical texts, biographical stories, and some elements of the "Jatakas", or birth stories. Various Vinaya collections survive in full, including those of the following schools: Theravāda (in Pali), Mula-Sarvāstivāda (in Tibetan translation) and the Mahāsānghika, Sarvāstivāda, Mahīshāsika, and Dharmaguptaka (in Chinese translations). In addition, portions survive of a number of Vinayas in various languages.

Aside from the Sutras and the Vinayas, some schools also had collections of "minor" or miscellaneous texts. The Theravāda Khuddaka Nikāya ('Minor Collection') is one example of such a collection, while there is evidence that the Dharmaguptaka school had a similar collection, known as the Kṣudraka Āgama. Fragments of the Dharmaguptaka minor collection have been found in Gandhari.

The Sarvāstivāda school also seems to have had a Kṣudraka collection of texts, but they did not see it as an "Āgama". These "minor" collections seem to have been a category for miscellaneous texts, and was perhaps never definitively established among many early schools.

Early Buddhist texts which appear in such "minor" collections include:

The Dharmapadas. These texts are collections of sayings and aphorisms, the most well-known of which is the Pali Dhammapada, but there are various versions in different languages, such as the Patna Dharmapada and the Gāndhārī Dharmapada.

The Pali Udana and the Sarvāstivāda Udānavarga. These are other collections of "inspired sayings."

The Pali Itivuttaka ("as it was said") and the Chinese translation of the by Xuanzang.

The Pali Sutta Nipata, including texts such as the Aṭṭhakavagga and Pārāyanavagga. There is also a parallel in the Chinese translation of the Arthavargīya.

Theragāthā and Therīgāthā, the two collections of verses related to the elder disciples of the Buddha. A Sanskrit Sthaviragāthā is also known to have existed.

3.1.3 Abhidharma Texts

Abhidharma texts contain "an abstract and highly technical systematization" of doctrinal material appearing in the Buddhist sutras. It is an attempt to best express the Buddhist view of "ultimate reality" (paramartha-satya) without using the conventional language and narrative stories found in the sutras. Modern scholars generally believe that the canonical Abhidharma texts emerged after the time of the Buddha, in around the 3rd century BCE. Therefore, the canonical Abhidharma works are generally claimed by scholars not to represent the words of the Buddha himself, but those of later Buddhists.

There are different types and historical layers of Abhidharma literature. The early canonical Abhidharma works (like the Abhidhamma Pitaka) are not philosophical treatises, but mainly summaries and expositions of early doctrinal lists with their accompanying explanations. These texts developed out of early Buddhist lists or matrices (mātṛkās) of key teachings, such as the 37 factors leading to Awakening. There is an "ancient core" of early pre-sectarian material in the earliest Abhidharma works, such as in the Theravada Vibhanga, the Dharmaskandha of the Sarvastivada, and the Śāriputrābhidharma of the Dharmaguptaka school.

Only two full canonical Abhidharma collections have survived, both containing seven texts, the Theravāda Abhidhamma and the Sarvastivada Abhidharma, which survives in Chinese translation. However, texts of other tradition have survived, such as the Śāriputrābhidharma of the Dharmaguptaka school, the Tattvasiddhi Śāstra (Chéngshílun) and various Abhidharma type works from the Pudgalavada school.

3.1.4 Other Texts

One of the largest categories of texts that were neither Sutra, Vinaya nor Abhidharma includes various collections of stories such as the Jātaka tales and the Avadānas (Pali: Apadāna). These are moral fables and legends dealing with the previous births of Gautama Buddha in both human and animal form. The different Buddhist schools had their own collections of these tales and often disagreed on which stories were canonical.

Another genre that developed over time in the various early schools were biographies of the Buddha. Buddha's biographies include the Mahāvastu of the Lokottaravadin school, the northern tradition's Lalitavistara Sūtra, the Theravada Nidānakathā and the

Dharmaguptaka Abhiniṣkramaṇa Sūtra. One of the most famous of biographies is the Buddhacarita, an epic poem in Classical Sanskrit by Aśvaghoṣa. Aśvaghoṣa also wrote other poems, as well as Sanskrit dramas. Another Sanskrit Buddhist poet was Mātṛceṭa, who composed various pious hymns in slokas. Other later hagiographical texts include the Buddhavaṃsa, the Cariyāpiṭaka and the Vimanavatthu (as well as its Chinese parallel, the Vimānāvadāna).

There are also some unique individual texts like the Milinda pañha (literally The Questions of Milinda) and its parallel in Chinese, the Nāgasena Bhikśu Sūtra. These texts depict a dialogue between the monk Nagasena, and the Indo-Greek King Menander (Pali: Milinda). It is a compendium of doctrine, and covers a range of subjects.

3.1.5 Theravāda Texts

The Theravāda tradition has an extensive commentarial literature, much of which is still untranslated. These are attributed to scholars working in Sri Lanka such as Buddhaghosa (5th century CE) and Dhammapala. There are also sub-commentaries (ṭīkā) or commentaries on the commentaries. Buddhaghosa was also the author of the Visuddhimagga, or Path of Purification, which is a manual of doctrine and practice according to the Mahavihara tradition of Sri Lanka. According to Nanamoli Bhikkhu, this text is regarded as "the principal non-canonical authority of the Theravada." A similar albeit shorter work is the Vimuttimagga. Another highly influential Pali Theravada work is the Abhidhammattha-sangaha (11th or 12th century), a short 50-page introductory summary to the Abhidhamma, which is widely used to teach Abhidhamma.

Buddhaghosa is known to have worked from Buddhist commentaries in the Sri Lankan Sinhala language, which are now lost. Sri Lankan literature in the vernacular contains many Buddhists works, including as classical Sinhala poems such as the Muvadevāvata (The Story of the Bodhisattva's Birth as King Mukhadeva, 12th century) and the Sasadāvata (The Story of the Bodhisattva's Birth as a Hare, 12th century) as well as prose works like the Dhampiyātuvā gätapadaya

(Commentary on the Blessed Doctrine), a commentary on words and phrases in the Pāli Dhammapada.

The Theravāda textual tradition spread into Burma and Thailand where Pali scholarship continued to flourish with such works as the Aggavamsa of Saddaniti and the Jinakalamali of Ratanapañña. Pali literature continued to be composed into the modern era, especially in Burma, and writers such as Mahasi Sayadaw translated some of their texts into Pali.

Burmese Buddhist literature developed unique poetic forms from the 1450s onwards, a major type of poetry is the pyui' which are long and embellished translations of Pali Buddhist works, mainly jatakas. A famous example of pyui' poetry is the Kui khan pyui' (the pyui' in nine sections, 1523). There is also a genre of Burmese commentaries or nissayas which were used to teach Pali. The nineteenth century saw a flowering of Burmese Buddhist literature in various genres including religious biography, Abhidharma, legal literature and meditation literature.

An influential text of Thai literature is the "Three Worlds According to King Ruang" (1345) by Phya Lithai, which is an extensive Cosmological and visionary survey of the Thai Buddhist universe.

3.1.6 Mahāyāna Texts

Around the beginning of the common era, a new genre of sutra literature began to be written with a focus on the Bodhisattva ideal, commonly known as Mahāyāna ("Great Vehicle") or Bodhisattvayāna ("Bodhisattva Vehicle"). The earliest of these sutras do not call themselves 'Mahāyāna,' but use the terms Vaipulya (extensive, expansive) sutras, or Gambhira (deep, profound) sutras.

Mahāyāna seems to have been emerged "primarily a textual movement, focused on the revelation, preaching, and dissemination of Mahāyāna sutras, that developed within, and never really departed from, traditional Buddhist social and institutional structures." Early dharmabhanakas (preachers, reciters of these sutras) were influential figures, and promoted these new texts throughout the Buddhist communities.

Many of these Mahāyāna sūtras were written in Sanskrit (in hybrid forms and in classical Sanskrit) and then later translated into the Tibetan and Chinese Buddhist canons (the Kangyur and the Taishō Tripiṭaka respectively) which then developed their own textual histories.

Mahāyāna sūtras are also generally regarded by the Mahāyāna tradition as being more profound than the śrāvaka texts as well as generating more spiritual merit and benefit. Thus, they are seen as superior and more virtuous to non-Mahāyāna sutras. The Mahāyāna sūtras are traditionally considered by Mahāyāna Buddhists to be the word of the Buddha. Mahāyāna Buddhists explained the emergence of these new texts by arguing that they had been transmitted in secret, via lineages of supernatural beings (such as the nagas) until people were ready to hear them, or by stating that they had been revealed directly through visions and meditative experiences to a select few.

The literary style of the Mahāyāna sūtras reveals how these texts were mainly composed as written works and how they also needed to legitimate themselves to other Buddhists. They used different literary and narrative ways to defend the legitimacy of these texts as Buddha word. Mahāyāna sūtras such as the Gaṇḍavyūha also often criticize early Buddhist figures, such as Sariputra for lacking knowledge and goodness, and thus, these elders or śrāvaka are seen as not intelligent enough to receive the Mahāyāna teachings, while more the advanced elite, the bodhisattvas, are depicted as those who can see the highest teachings.

Mahāyāna sūtras contain several elements besides the promotion of the bodhisattva ideal, including "expanded cosmologies and mythical histories, ideas of pure lands and great, 'celestial' Buddhas and bodhisattvas, descriptions of powerful new religious practices, new ideas on the nature of the Buddha, and a range of new philosophical perspectives." These texts present stories of revelation in which the Buddha teaches Mahāyāna sutras to certain bodhisattvas who vow to teach and spread these sutras. These texts also promoted new religious practices that were supposed to make Buddhahood easy to achieve, such as "hearing the names of certain Buddhas or bodhisattvas, maintaining Buddhist precepts, and listening to, memorizing, and copying sutras." Some Mahāyāna sūtras claim that these practices lead to rebirth in Pure lands such as Abhirati and Sukhavati, where becoming a Buddha is much easier to achieve.

Several Mahāyāna sūtras also depict important Buddhas or Bodhisattvas not found in earlier texts, such as the Buddhas Amitabha, Akshobhya and Vairocana, and the bodhisattvas Maitreya, Mañjusri, Ksitigarbha, and Avalokiteshvara. An important feature of Mahāyāna is the way that it understands the nature of Buddhahood. Mahāyāna texts see Buddhas (and to a lesser extent, certain bodhisattvas as well) as transcendental or supramundane (lokuttara) beings, who live for eons constantly helping others through their activity.

Some Mahāyāna sūtras are also thought to display a distinctly tantric character, like some of the shorter Perfection of Wisdom sutras and the Mahavairocana Sutra. At least some editions of the Kangyur include the Heart Sutra in the tantra division. Such overlap is not confined to "neighboring" yanas: at least nine "Sravakayana" texts can be found in the tantra divisions of some editions of the Kangyur. One of them, the Atanatiya Sutra, is also included in the Mikkyo (esoteric) division of the standard modern collected edition of Sino-Japanese Buddhist literature. Some Mahāyāna texts also contain dhāraṇī, which are chants that are believed to have magical and spiritual power.

Central to much of Mahāyāna philosophy are the works of the Indian scholar Nagarjuna. Especially important is his magnum opus, the Mūlamadhyamika-karikā, or Root Verses on the Middle Way, a seminal text on the Madhyamika philosophy. Various other authors of the Madhyamaka school followed him and wrote commentaries to his texts or their own treatises.

Another very influential work which traditionally attributed to NagarjunaInEastAsiaistheDàzhìdùlùn(Mahāprajñāpāramitopadeśa, The Great Discourse on Prajñāpāramitā). This is a massive Mahayana Buddhist treatise and commentary on the Prajñāpāramitā sutra in Twenty-five Thousand Lines, and it has been extremely important in the development of the major Chinese Buddhist traditions.

The Yogācārabhūmi-Śāstra (fourth century CE) is another very large treatise which focuses on yogic praxis and the doctrines of the Indian Yogacara school. Unlike the Dà zhìdù lùn, it was studied and transmitted in both the East Asian Buddhist and the Tibetan Buddhist traditions.

The 9th Century Indian Buddhist Shantideva produced two texts: the Bodhicaryāvatāra has been a strong influence in many schools of the Mahayana. It is notably a favorite text of the 14th Dalai Lama.

Dignāga is associated with a school of Buddhist logic that tried to establish which texts were valid sources of knowledge (see also Epistemology). He produced the Pramāna-samuccaya, and later Dharmakirti wrote the Pramāna-vārttikā, which was a commentary and reworking of the Dignaga text.

3.1.7 East Asian Works

The Awakening of Faith in the Mahayana (Dàshéng Qǐxìn Lùn) is an influential text in East Asian Buddhism, especially in the Hua-yen school of China, and its Japanese equivalent, Kegon. While it is traditionally attributed to Ashvaghosha, most scholars now hold it is a Chinese composition. The Dhyāna sutras (Chan-jing) are a group of early Buddhist meditation texts which contain meditation teachings from the Sarvastivada school along with some early proto-Mahayana meditations. They were mostly the work of Buddhist Yoga teachers from Kashmir and were translated into Chinese early on.

East Asian Buddhism began to develop its own unique doctrinal literature with the rise of the Tiantai School and its major representative, Zhiyi (538–597 CE) who wrote important commentaries on the Lotus sutra as well as the first major comprehensive work on meditation composed in China, the Mohe Zhiguan. Another important school of Chinese Buddhism is Huayan, which focused on developing their philosophical texts from the Avatamsaka. An important patriarch of this school is Fazang who wrote many commentaries and treatises.

The Tripitaka Koreana, which was crafted in two versions (the first one was destroyed by fire during the Mongol invasions of Korea), is a Korean collection of the Tripitaka carved onto 81,258 wooden printing blocks during the 13th century. Still intact in good condition after some 750 years, it has been described by the UNESCO committee as "one of the most important and most complete corpus of Buddhist doctrinal texts in the world".

Zen Buddhism developed a large literary tradition based on the teachings and sayings of Chinese Zen masters. One of the key texts in this genre is the Platform Sutra attributed to Zen patriarch Huineng, it gives an autobiographical account of his succession as Ch'an Patriarch, as well as teachings about Ch'an theory and practice. Other texts are Koan collections, which are compilations of the sayings of Chinese masters such as the Blue Cliff Record and The Gateless Gate. Another key genre is that of compilations of Zen master biographies, such as the Transmission of the Lamp. Buddhist poetry was also an important contribution to the literature of the tradition.

3.1.8 Buddhist Tantras

The late Seventh century saw the rise of another new class of Buddhist texts, the Tantras, which focused on ritual practices and yogic techniques such as the use of Mantras, Dharanis, Mandalas, Mudras and Fire offerings. Many early Buddhist Tantric texts, later termed "action Tantras" (kriyā tantra), are mostly collections of magical mantras or phrases for mostly worldly ends called mantrakalpas (mantra manuals) and they do not call themselves Tantras.

Later Tantric texts from the eighth century onward (termed variously Yogatantra, Mahayoga, and Yogini Tantras) advocated union with a deity (deity yoga), sacred sounds (mantras), techniques for manipulation of the subtle body and other secret methods with which to achieve swift Buddhahood. In East Asian Esoteric Buddhism and its Japanese offshoot, the Shingon school, the most influential tantras are those which focus on Vairocana Buddha, mainly, the Mahavairocana Tantra and the Vajrasekhara Sutra.

Buddhist Tantras are key texts in Vajrayana Buddhism, which is the dominant form of Buddhism in Tibet, Bhutan and Mongolia. They can be found in the Chinese canon, but even more so in the Tibetan Kangyur which contains translations of almost 500 tantras. In the Tibetan tradition, there are various categories of tantra.

3.1.9 Other products of the Vajrayana literature

Tibetan Buddhism has a unique and special class of texts called terma (Tibetan: gTer-ma). These are texts (or ritual objects, etc.) believed either composed or hidden by tantric masters and/or elementally secreted or encoded in the elements and retrieved, accessed or rediscovered by other tantric masters when appropriate. Termas are discovered by tertöns (Tibetan: gTer-stons), whose special function is to reveal these texts. Some termas are hidden in caves or similar places, but a few are said to be 'mind termas,' which are 'discovered' in the mind of the tertön. The Nyingma school (and Bön tradition) has a large terma literature. Many of the terma texts are said to have been written by Padmasambhava, who is particularly important to the Nyingmas. Probably the best known terma text is the so-called Tibetan book of the dead, the Bardo Thodol.

A sadhana is a tantric spiritual practice text used by practitioners, primarily to practice the mandala or a particular yidam, or meditation deity. The Sādhanamālā is a collection of sadhanas.

Vajrayana adepts, known as mahasiddha, often expounded their teachings in the form of songs of realization. Collections of these songs such as the Caryāgīti, or the Charyapada are still in existence. The Dohakosha is a collection of doha songs by the yogi Saraha from the 9th century. A collection known in English as The Hundred Thousand Songs of Milarepa was composed by Tibetan Buddhist yogi Milarepa and is especially popular amongst members of the Kagyu school.

3.2 What does Love mean in Buddhism?

What does love mean, exactly? We have applied to it our finest definitions; we have examined its psychology and outlined it in philosophical frameworks; we have even devised a mathematical formula for attaining it. And yet anyone who has ever taken this wholehearted leap of faith knows that love remains a mystery — perhaps the mystery of the human experience.

Learning to meet this mystery with the full realness of our being — to show up for it with absolute clarity of intention — is the dance of life. That's what legendary Vietnamese Zen Buddhist monk, teacher, and peace activist Thich Nhat Hanh (b. October 11, 1926) explores in How to Love.

At the heart of Nhat Hanh's teachings is the idea that "understanding is love's other name" — that to love another means to fully understand his or her suffering. ("Suffering" sounds rather dramatic, but in Buddhism it refers to any source of profound dissatisfaction — be it physical or psycho-emotional or spiritual.) Understanding, after all, is what everybody needs — but even if we grasp this on a theoretical level, we habitually get too caught in the smallness of our fixations to be able to offer such expansive understanding. He illustrates this mismatch of scales with an apt metaphor:

If you pour a handful of salt into a cup of water, the water becomes undrinkable. But if you pour the salt into a river, people can continue to draw the water to cook, wash, and drink. The river is immense, and it has the capacity to receive, embrace, and transform. When our hearts are small, our understanding and compassion are limited, and we suffer. We can't accept or tolerate others and their shortcomings, and we demand that they change. But when our hearts expand, these same things don't make us suffer anymore. We have a lot of understanding and compassion and can embrace others. We accept others as they are, and then they have a chance to transform.

The question then becomes how to grow our own hearts, which begins with a commitment to understand and bear witness to our own suffering. When we feed and support our own happiness, we are nourishing our ability to love. That's why to love means to learn the art of nourishing our happiness. Understanding someone's suffering is the best gift you can give another person. Understanding is love's other name. If you don't understand, you can't love.

And yet because love is a learned "dynamic interaction," we form our patterns of understanding and misunderstanding — early in life, by osmosis and imitation rather than conscious creation. Nhat Hanh writes: "If our parents didn't love and understand each other, how are we to know what love looks like? … The most precious inheritance that parents can give their children is their own happiness. Our parents may be able to leave us money, houses, and land, but they may not be happy people. If we have happy parents, we have received the richest inheritance of all."

Nhat Hanh points out the crucial difference between infatuation, which replaces any real understanding of the other with a fantasy of who he or she can be for us, and true love. Often, we get crushes on others not because we truly love and understand them, but to distract ourselves from our suffering. When we learn to love and understand ourselves and have true compassion for ourselves, then we can truly love and understand another person. Out of this incomplete understanding of ourselves spring our illusory infatuations, which Nhat Hanh captures with equal parts wisdom and wit:

The essence of loving kindness is being able to offer happiness. You can be the sunshine for another person. You can't offer happiness until you have it for yourself. So, build a home inside by accepting yourself and learning to love and heal yourself. Learn how to practice mindfulness in such a way that you can create moments of happiness and joy for your own nourishment. Then you have something to offer the other person. If you have enough understanding and love, then every moment — whether it's spent making breakfast, driving the car, watering the garden, or doing anything else in your day — can be a moment of joy.

This interrelatedness of self and other is manifested in the fourth element as well, equanimity, the Sanskrit word for which — upeksha — is also translated as "inclusiveness" and "nondiscrimination":

In a deep relationship, there's no longer a boundary between you and the other person. You are her and she is you. Your suffering is her suffering. Your understanding of your own suffering helps your loved one to suffer less. Suffering and happiness are no longer individual matters. What happens to your loved one happens to you. What happens to you happens to your loved one. In true love, there's no more separation or discrimination. His happiness is your happiness. Your suffering is his suffering. You can no longer say, "That's your problem."

To love without knowing how to love wounds the person we love. To know how to love someone, we have to understand them. To understand, we need to listen. When you love someone, you should have the capacity to bring relief and help him to suffer less. This is an art. If you don't understand the roots of his suffering, you can't help, just as a doctor can't help heal your illness if she doesn't know the cause. You need to understand the cause of your loved one's suffering in order to help bring relief. The more you understand, the more you love; the more you love, the more you understand. They are two sides of one reality. The mind of love and the mind of understanding are the same.

3.3 Love in Buddhism (Mettà)

The Pàli word Mettà (in Buddhism) is a multi-significant term meaning universal love, loving-kindness, friendliness, goodwill, benevolence, fellowship, amity, concord, inoffensiveness and non-violence. The Pàli commentators define Mettà as the strong wish for the welfare and happiness of others (parahitaparasukha-kàmanà). When Mettà infuses the mind, one refuses to be offensive and renounces bitterness, resentment and animosity of any kind. Instead, one develops a mind of friendliness, accommodation and benevolence seeking the well-being and happiness of others. True Mettà is devoid of self-interest. It evokes within a warm-hearted feeling of fellowship, sympathy and love, which grows boundless with practice and overcomes all social, religious, racial, political and economic barriers. Mettà is indeed a universal, unselfish and all-embracing love.

When Buddha decided to break from the worldly life, he made four great vows:

(i) To save all people;

(ii) To renounce all worldly desires;

(iii) To learn all the teachings; and

(iv) to attain perfect Enlightenment.

These vows were manifestations of the love and compassion that are fundamental to the nature of Buddhahood. He trained himself to avoid anger, and he wished that all people might love one another.

"Your suffering is my suffering and your happiness is my happiness," said Buddha, and, just as a mother always loves her child, He does not forget that spirit even for a single moment, for it is the nature of Buddhahood to be compassionate." Hatreds never cease by hatreds in this world. By love alone they cease. This is an ancient Law. (Dhammapada, 5)

There is a story of a physician and his children, While the physician was away from home, his children accidentally took some poison. When the physician returned, he noticed their sickness and prepared antidote. Some of the children who were not seriously poisoned accepted the medicine and were cured, but others were so seriously affected that they refused to take the medicine. The physician, prompted by his paternal love for his children, decided on an extreme method to press the cure upon them. He said to the children: "I must go off on a long journey. I am old and may pass away any day. If I am with you I can care for you, but if I should pass away, you will become worse. If you hear of my death, I implore you to take the antidote and be cured of this subtle poisoning." Then he went on the long journey. After some time, he sent a messenger to his children to inform them about his death. The children, receiving the message, were deeply affected by the thought of their father's death and by the realization that they would no longer have the benefit of his benevolent care. Recalling his parting request, in a feeling of sorrow and helplessness, they took the medicine and recovered.

Tathagat Buddha has given first sila in Panchshila, which is based on metta bhavana .

Panatipata veramani sikkhapadam samadhiyami, which means to abstain from killing any living creature signifying to generating metta bhavana in mind for all living being that is metta. Concept of nonviolence in Buddhism is based on Metta bhvana.

Mettà makes one a pure font of well-being and safety for others. "Just as a mother gives her own life to protect her only child", so Mettà only gives and never wants anything in return. To promote one's own interest is a primordial motivation of human nature. When this urge is transformed into a wish to promote the interest and happiness of others, then self-seeking is overcome. And the mind becomes universal by identifying its own interest with the interest of all. By making this change one also promotes one's own well-being in the best possible manner.

Mettà is the protective and immensely patient attitude of a mother who forbears all difficulties for the sake of her child and ever protects it despite its misbehavior. Mettà is also the attitude of a friend who wants to give the best to further one's wellbeing. If these qualities of Mettà are sufficiently cultivated through Mettà-bhàvanà, meditation on universal love, the result is acquisition of tremendous inner power which preserves, protects and heals both oneself and others.

Apart from its higher implications, today Mettà is a pragmatic necessity. In a world menaced by all kinds of destructiveness, Mettà in deed, word and thought is the only constructive means to bring harmony, peace and mutual understanding. Indeed, Mettà is the only means for bringing about interfaith amity among the followers of all the religions. It is also the basis for all benevolent activities intended to promote human well-being.

3.3.1 The Karaõãya Mettà Sutta

1. Karaõãya matthakusalena,
Yaÿ taÿ santaÿ padaÿ abhisamecca,
Sakko ujå ca såjå ca,
Suvaco cassa mudu anatimàni.

Whoso his welfare seeks to promote, With a grasped of the state of Perfect Peace, He should be competent, honest and upright, Gentle in speech, meek and not proud.

2. Santussako ca subharo ca,
Appakicco ca sallahukavutti,
Santindriyo ca nipako ca,
Appagabbho kulesu ananugiddho.

He should be contented and easy to support, Be not over-busy, but live a simple life, With restrained senses, be ever prudent, Not be brazened nor fawn on families.

3. Naca khuddaÿ samàcare ki¤ci,

Yena vi¤¤å pare upavadeyyuÿ,

Sukhino và khemino hontu,

Sabbe sattà bhavantu sukhitattà.

He should refrain from any action, That gives the wiser reason to reprove. May all beings be happy and secure, May all be well-disposed at heart!

4. Ye keci pàõabhåtatthi,

Tasà và thàvarà và anavasesà,

Dãghà và ye mahantà và

Majjhimà rassakànukathulà.

Whatever living beings there be, Without exception, weak or strong. Long or huge, middle-sized, Short, minute or bulky,

5. Diññhà và yeva adiññhà,

Ye ca dåre vasanti avidåre,

Bhåtà và sambhavesi và,

Sabbe sattà bhavantu sukhitattà.

Whether visible or invisible, And those living afar or near, The born and those seeking birth,

May all beings be happy!

6. Na paro paraÿ nikubbetha,

nàtimanetha katthacinaÿ kanci.

Byàrosanà pañighasannà,

Nànnamanassa dukkhamiccheyya.

Let none deceive or decry His fellow anywhere. Let none with resentment or hate Ever wish to harm others.

7. Màtà yathà niyaÿ puttaÿ

âyusà ekaputtamanurakkhe,

Evaÿpi sabbabhåtesu,

Mànasaÿ bhàvaye aparimànaÿ.

Just as a mother would shield, With her own life an only child, Even so let him develop a mind, Of boundless love for all beings.

8. Metta¤ca sabbalokasmiÿ,

Mànasaÿ bhàvaye aparimànaÿ,

Uddhaÿ adho ca tiriyanca,

Asambàdhaÿ averaÿ asapattaÿ.

Let him cultivate a mind of boundless love, Towards all, throughout the universe, In all its height, depth and breadth, Love that is unobstructed And free from hatred or enmity.

9. Tiññhaÿ caraÿ nisinno và,

Sayàno và yàvatassa vigatamiddho

Etaÿ satim adhiññheyya,

Brahmametaÿ vihàraÿ idhamàhu.

Whether he stands, walks, sits or lies down, As long as he is awake, Let him preserve this mindfulness of love, Deemed here a Divine State.

10.Diññhinca anupagamma sãlavà

Dassanena sampanno,

Kàmesu vineyya gedhaÿ

Na hi jàtu gabbhaseyyaÿ punaretã'ti.

Holding no wrong views, being virtuous, Endowed with the Vision of Nibbàna, Ultimate reality, Having overcome all sensual desires,

Never in a womb is he born again.

3.3.2 Three Aspects of Metta

The *Mettà Sutta* consists of three parts, each of which focuses on a distinct aspect of *Mettà*. The first part covers that aspect which requires a thorough and systematic application of loving-kindness in one's day-to-day conduct. The second part expresses loving-kindness as a distinct technique of meditation or culture of mind leading to *samàdhi* — higher consciousness induced by meditative absorption. And the third part underlines a total commitment to the philosophy of universal love and its personal, social and empirical extensions, that is, loving-kindness through all bodily, verbal and mental activities.

Mettà has been identified as that specific factor which 'ripens' the accumulated merit *(puntha)* acquired by the ten courses of meritorious deeds *(dasapunnakiriyavatthu),* such as, the practice of generosity, virtue, etc. Again, it is *Mettà* which brings to maturity the ten exalted spiritual qualities known as 'perfections' *(pàramã).* Thus, the practice of *Mettà* is like growing a great tree. From the time the seed is sown to the time the tree is laden with fruits, sending forth sweet odour far and wide and attracting myriads of creatures to enjoy the nutritious bounty. The sprouting of the seed and the growth of the plant are, as it were, brought about by the first part of the sutta. In the second part, the tree, now well developed and robust, is fully covered with fragrant and beautiful flowers. As a pattern of behaviour, the first aspect of Mettà makes one's life grow like generous and noble tree. Mettà, as meditation, is that spiritual efflorescence whereby one's entire life becomes a source of joy for all. The third part envisages in this imagery the fruition of that process of spiritual development by which one brings about an all-embracing application of universal love. This stage of the practice of Mettà affects the whole society and leads one to the height of transcendental realization.

3.3.3 Ten Perfections and Four Brahmaviharas in Buddhism

There are the ten "Perfections" (pāramī, or pāramitā), also known as the "Transcendental Virtues". These are ten qualities leading to Buddhahood. They are:

(i) Generosity (dāna);

(ii) Morality (sīla);

(iii) Renunciation (nekkhamma);

(iv) Wisdom (paññā);

(v) Energy (viriya);

(vi) Patience (khanti);

(vii) Truthfulness (sacca);

(viii) Determination (adhiṭṭhāna);

(ix) Loving-kindness (mettā); and

(x) Equanimity (upekkhā).

Likewise, there are the four "Divine Abodes" (**brahmavihāras**). They are also called appamaññā "limitless, boundless", because these thoughts are radiated towards all beings without limit or obstruction. The system of meditation on the Divine Abodes has come to occupy a central position in the field of mental training (bhāvanā) in Buddhism. Its exercises include the development of the following four higher sentiments:

(i) Loving-kindness (mettā);

(ii) Compassion (karuṇā);

(iii) Sympathetic, or altruistic, joy (muditā); and

(iv) Equanimity (upekkhā).

From an ethical point of view, these four principles emphasize the moral foundation of every form of religious life and are considered indispensable to spiritual development.

Generally, people love their egoistic comfort, which is a love of fame and praise. But fame and praise are like incense that consumes itself and soon disappears. If people chase after honours and public acclaim and leave the way of truth, they are in serious danger and will soon have cause for regret. A man who chases after fame and wealth and love affairs is like a child who licks honey from the blade of a knife. While he is tasting the sweetness of honey, he has to risk hurting his tongue. He is like a man who carries a torch against a strong wind; the flame will surely burn his hands and face.

3.4 Eight Buddhist Verses in Love and Compassion

In Tibetan Buddhism, compassion is the key and central training within their religion. Mahayana Buddhists believe that love and compassion can overcome all obstacles, awaken the mind to enlightenment and bring enormous benefit to yourself and others.

In compassion training, you have to actually give it a go to see for yourself how it works but essentially it's impossible for anger, hatred, jealousy and selfishness to exist in the company of genuine love and compassion. Love and compassion have the potential to bring about harmony and understanding between all the people of the world.

There is a guide to living a compassionate and enlightened life from an 11th Century Tibetan Buddhist monk, Langri Thangpa, called 8 Verses for Training the Heart Mind. It's from the Mahayana tradition, where they place a very high value in training in love and compassion; claiming it's absolutely necessary to achieve full enlightenment.

These 8 verses are:

1. By thinking of all sentient beings, As more precious than a wish-fulfilling jewel, For accomplishing the highest aim, I will always hold them dear.

2. Whenever I'm in the company of others, I will regard myself as the lowest among all, And from the depths of my heart Cherish others as supreme.

3. In my every action, I will watch my mind, And the moment destructive emotions arise, I will confront them strongly and avert them, Since they will hurt both me and others.

4. Whenever I see ill-natured beings, Or those overwhelmed by heavy misdeeds or suffering, I will cherish them as something rare, As though I'd found a priceless treasure. Whenever I see those overwhelmed by suffering, I will cherish them as something rare.

5. Whenever someone out of envy, Does me wrong by attacking or belittling me, I will take defeat upon myself, And give the victory to others.

6. Even when someone I have helped, Or in whom I have placed great hopes, Mistreats me very unjustly, I will view that person as a true spiritual teacher.

7. In brief, directly or indirectly, I will offer help and happiness to all others, And secretly take upon myself All their hurt and suffering.

8. I will learn to keep all these practices Untainted by thoughts of the eight worldly concerns. May I recognize all things as like illusions, And, without attachment, gain freedom from bondage.

Research has shown your own happiness is increased by practicing love and compassion. In fact, love and compassion are not just good for happiness, they also have a positive impact on health as well, reducing blood pressure and boosting the immune system. But it is not always easy. It is a radical departure from our usual selfish ways of behaviour; instead, the training embodies a compassionate way of being; cherishing others more than ourselves, with the goal of alleviating suffering from the entire world.

3.5 Buddhism and Romantic Relationships

In regards to romantic relationships, Buddhism has very liberal views. Buddhism encourages independence through non-attachment. Non-attachment is the idea that in order to be fulfilled and happy in life, a person cannot be attached to any one thing because this thing can cause suffering. In order to be happy and to follow the path of enlightenment, Buddhism teaches people to discard all things in life that can cause pain. This idea is not referring to worldly objects in the physical sense, but in a spiritual sense. To achieve non-attachment, one must detach from the idea of a perfect person and holding one's partner to an impossible standard. Instead, one must accept a partner for who they are unconditionally. In Buddhism, this is the key to a happy romantic relationship. Accepting a partner for who they are, for who they are throughout their life no matter what changes, and making the best of every situation is how one achieves personal fulfillment in a romantic relationship.

The idea of unconditional love is essentially what Buddhism teaches. Marriage is a social construct that has changed vastly throughout the course of history. People married for a variety of reasons including: status, wealth, power and love. Buddhist texts do not delve too deeply into the idea of marriage because Buddhism leaves the decision to marry up to each individual person. In Buddhism, marriage is not a religious obligation, a means for procreation, or a romantic notion of love. It is simply an option for each individual to make. If an individual believes marriage will bring them happiness and keep them on the path of enlightenment, then they are free to make that choice. Buddhism does not provide rules or traditions about marriage, instead, the philosophy offers advice to help a person live happily within a marriage. This advice is thought to help give people the best chance at a happy relationship. In Buddhist texts, The Buddha thought that the biggest hurdle of marriage is spousal weakness to other partners. He saw the weakness and trouble that other romantic interests can bring to a family and advised against it. Instead of a religious obligation, marriage is seen as an individual choice. Buddhism allows for each person to make the decision of whether or not they want to be married, how many children they want to have, and who they want to marry.

Buddhists do not prohibit divorce, but the idea of living the Buddhist lifestyle would suggest that one need not divorce. If a person is living by the ideals of Buddhism and accepting someone for who they are and following the path of enlightenment, it stands to reason that they would never need a divorce because they would be fulfilled with their marriage and their partner. It is also stated that separation is preferable to being miserable for a prolonged period of time. The philosophy prefers that a couple separate rather than live together and be counterproductive to personal fulfillment and enlightenment. Buddhism also states that to prevent divorce, older men should not have younger wives and older women should not have younger husbands. The claim was that the age difference would make them incompatible and cause problems leading to divorce. Overall, Buddhism says that any person is free to divorce, especially if it is hindering their path to personal fulfillment. However, it makes the important distinction that living a Buddhist lifestyle would mean creating a happy and strong relationship that would not end in divorce.

CHAPTER 4

Love in Sufism

Lovers don't finally meet somewhere.
They're in each other all along. — RUMI

4.1 History of Love in Sufism

Love has been an integral component of Sufism from the second century ah until today. Despite extensive discussions of love in Sufism, there has been no detailed examination of the precise manner in which the teachings on love from the early Sufi tradition (spanning the second to fifth Islamic centuries) influenced later developments. In the early period, the majority of teachings on love are contained in poems and brief statements that focus upon the human love for God, wherein there is always a duality between the human lover and the Divine Beloved. But in the early sixth/ twelfth century love comes to be discussed as the Divine Essence beyond all duality. This marks the beginning of what some scholars have called 'the path of love' or 'the school of love'. This 'school' is not a direct succession of Sufi initiates marked by a definitive spiritual genealogy like the Sufi orders, rather it is a trend within Sufi thought in which all aspects of creation and spiritual aspiration are presented in an imaginal language fired by love.

The first Sufi text in which a full metaphysics of love is expressed is the masterful *Sawanaih* of Shaykh Ahmad al-Ghazl; Ahmad devoted himself to the Sufi path, focusing all of his efforts upon the purification of the heart through spiritual realization. Written in Persian in the year 508, the *Sawanaih* presents all of reality as an unfolding of love (ishq) through the complex interrelations of loverness (ishq;) and belovedness (mashuq;), both of which are said to be derived from love and ultimately return to this eternal point of origin. All phases of the descent of creation and the spiritual ascent of the human being are thus seen as phases of love. Like Ahmad, previous Sufis, such as Shaqiq Balkhi and others, had envisaged the spiritual path as degrees of love. But in his *Sawanaih*, Ahmad makes a revolutionary move in Sufi thought by placing love at the centre of metaphysics. The poetry of such famous Sufi figures as Rabia may appear to indicate a centrality of love similar to that expressed by Ahmad , such authors emphasize a human love for God which is absolute, not a love which is the Absolute Itself—and this is the crux of the matter.

The aforementioned Rubia is often recognized as the first to speak of love as being due to God alone. She expressed this realization in short poems such as these oft cited verses. The sentiment that God alone is worthy of love is echoed throughout the literature of early Sufism. Personalities such as the famous Abu Bakr, who was known for his teachings on love, spoke of love (mahabba) as 'a fire in the heart, consuming all save the will of the Beloved', or as that which 'erases all that is other than God from the heart', and thus considered mystical love as an intense desire centering one's spiritual aspiration (himma) on God alone and cutting one off from all that is other than the Divine.

In contrast, Ahmad made ishq the centre of an intellectual discourse on the nature of reality and the stages of the Sufi path, discussing all aspects of creation and of spiritual wayfaring in terms of ishq. Whereas previous Sufis recognized love as a Divine attribute and, in turn, one of the highest human attributes, or like Nasr al-Sartaj , author of Kitab al-Luma6 (The Book of Illumination), one of the most important early Sufi handbooks, as a particular state or station on the path of spiritual wayfaring, Ahmad saw it as the Divine Essence Itself. Though previous accounts express the need for unconditional love for God alone and can be interpreted to present the path of spiritual wayfaring as degrees of love, they do not express the subtle metaphysics of love found in the *Sawanaih* and later writings of the Persian Sufi tradition.

4.2 Introduction to Sufi Philosophy

The term “Sufi” derives from the Arabic word “Soof” (meaning “wool”) and was applied to Muslim ascetics and mystics because they wore garments made out of wool. The ecstatic state of the mystic can sometimes produce extreme behaviour or statements that on occasion appear to border on the blasphemous. The cause of this is that the Sufis can sometimes feel so close to God that they lose a sense of their own self-identity and feel themselves to be completely absorbed into God. This in fact is the goal of the Sufi. Through following a series of devotional practices, which lead to higher levels of ecstatic state, Sufis aspire to realize a condition in which they are in direct communion with God. Ultimately the individual human personality passes away and the Sufi feels his soul absorbed into God- known in Tassawuf or Sufism as Fanaa - Annihilation of Self and Baqaa - Mystical Union with God.

Sufi philosophy includes the schools of thought unique to Sufism, a mystical branch within Islam, also termed as Tasawwuf or Faqr according to its adherents. Sufism and its philosophical traditions may be associated with both Sunni Islam and Shia Islam. It has been suggested that Sufi thought emerged from the Middle East in the eighth century, but adherents are now found around the world. According to Sufism, it is a part of the Islamic teaching that deals with the purification of inner self and is the way which removes all the veils between divine and man. It was around 1000 CE that early Sufi literature, in the form of manuals, treatises, discourses and poetry, became the source of Sufi thinking and meditations. Sufi philosophy, like all other major philosophical traditions, has several sub-branches including metaphysics and cosmology as well as several unique concepts.

The emergence of Sufi thought is commonly linked to the historical developments of the Middle East in the seventh and eighth centuries following the life of Prophet Muhammad, and its development took place throughout the centuries after that. Between the tenth and twelfth centuries, Sufism became a widely spread discipline. One influential early writer on Sufi philosophy was Al-Ghazali (1058–1111). He discussed the concept of the self and the causes of its misery and happiness. By the end of the thirteenth century, Sufism had become a well-defined science of spiritual awakening throughout the Islamic World, an "Islamic Golden Age". No important domain in the civilization of Islam remained unaffected by Sufism in this period. Several tariqahs (Sufi orders) were found. Also a class of notable Sufi philosophers, theologians and jurists such as Hankari, Ibn Arabi, Abu Saeed Mubarak Makhzoomi, led this age who trained and generated historical specimens of philosophers and geniuses now read worldwide such as Al-Ghazali, Avicenna, etc. An important mark made in the history of Sufi philosophy has been made by Abdul Qadir Jilani with his jurisprudence and philosophy of Sufism that made him define the Sufi orders. Jilani's adopted order was Qadiriyya and the offshoot he started later became known as Sarwari Qadiri. Several other orders were also founded in this era. Sufis were influential in spreading Islam particularly to the farthest outposts of the Muslim world in Africa, he Balkans and Caucasus, the Indian subcontinent, and East and Southeast Asia. Some scholars have argued that Sufis, Muslim mystics, played a decisive role in converting the Mongols in Iran to Islam in the thirteenth and fourteenth centuries, mainly because of the similarity between the extreme Sufis (the dervishes) and the Shamans of the traditional Mongol religion.

4.3 Sufi Metaphysics

Major ideas in Sufi metaphysics have surrounded the concept of ***Wahdat*** or "Unity with God". Two main Sufi philosophies prevail on this controversial topic. Wahdat-ul-Wujood (Unity of Being) essentially states that the only truth within the universe is God, and that all things exist within God only. Wahdat-ul-Shuhud (Apparentism, or Unity of Witness), on the other hand, holds that any experience of unity between God and the created world is only in the mind of the believer and that God and his creation are entirely separate. It is the state where there is no difference between God and human being who is trying to achieve a particular state, that is, 'No One Except God'. The concept of Sufi Metaphysics was first deeply discussed in written form by Ibn Arabi in one of his most prolific works titled, "Fusus-al-hikam", where he applies deep analysis on the issue of Oneness through the metaphor of mirror. In this metaphor, al-Arabi compares an object being reflected in countless mirrors to the relationship between God and his creatures. God's essence is seen in the existent human being, as God is the object and humans being the mirrors. Meaning two things, that since humans are mere reflections of God there can be no distinction or separation between the two and without God the creatures would be non-existent. When an individual understands that there is no separation between human and God they begin on the path of ultimate oneness. This metaphysics of Sufi philosophy is also narrated in the hadith: "Whoever recognized his self, undoubtedly recognized his Rabb (Allah)".

4.4 Lataif-e-sitta

Drawing from Qur'anic verses, virtually all Sufis distinguish Lataif-as-Sitta ("the six subtleties") as: Nafs, Qalb, Sirr, Ruh, Khafi, and Akhfa. These lataif (singular: latifa) designate various psycho spiritual "organs" or, sometimes, faculties of sensory and suprasensory perception. They are thought to be parts of the self in a similar manner to thc way glands and organs are part of the body.

4.5 Subtle Bodies

4.5.1 Ruh (spirit)

Some mystics named ruh as "batin" or "the esoteric self" or "qalb". The Sufi, mostly believes in a strong soul as it brings him close to Divine. Soul is strengthened by the spiritual training given by the perfect spiritual guide. This eventually leads to the nearness to Allah (God). Also, it is stated in hadith Qudsi that "Whoever recognizes his self, undoubtedly, recognized his Allah". Hence, death is not the end but, in fact, it is the beginning to the eternal life which is only endowed to the soul and not to the body.

4.5.2 Nasma

Nasma is the Sufi term for the subtle or Astral Body. It is not to be confused with the Ruh (spirit) which transcends both nasma and physical form.

4.5.3 Physical body (Jism)

Sufism demarcates the physical body from the Nasma. According to Sufi beliefs, physical body is a reflection of spiritual body or 'batin' or 'ruh', as also stated in one of the famous hadiths of Prophet Mohammad ,"Actions are but by intentions".

4.6 Spiritual States

4.6.1 Hāl

A hāl (pl. aḥwāl) is a state of consciousness that arises in the course of spiritual wayfaring (sulūk), either within or outside of the formal practice of remembrance (dhikr). Among these are states of bliss (wajd), bewilderment (hayrah), and various others. The transient nature of such states is contrasted with the more abiding quality of a maqām (station), i.e. a stage along the spiritual path. Both aḥwāl and maqāmat are considered gifts from God, not experiences generated by any technique in itself. While they are auspicious signs, the sālik is exhorted not to be diverted by their charms but to remain steadfast in seeking God alone through love and knowledge.

4.6.2 Manzil

A Manzil, which literally means destination, is a terminology in Sufism, is a plane of consciousness. There are seven Manzils along the path to God. The Manzils are also parts of the Qur'an which help in protecting on sorcery (the use of black message).

4.6.3 Maqaam

A maqaam is one's spiritual station or developmental level, as distinct from one's haal, or state of consciousness. This is seen as the outcome of one's effort to transform oneself, whereas the haal is a gift.

4.7 Concepts in Gnosis (knowledge of spiritual mysteries)

4.7.1 Baqaa

A person's baqaa, which literally means "permanency", is a term in Sufi philosophy which describes a particular state of life with God and is a manzil or abobe, that comes after the station of fanaa. The ideal perfection, called Baqa by Sufis, is termed 'Najat' in Islam, 'Nirvana' in Buddhism, 'Salvation' in Christianity, and 'Moksha' in Hinduism. This is the highest condition attainable, and all ancient prophets and sages experienced it, and taught it to the world. Baqaa is the original state of God. At this state everyone must arrive someday, consciously or unconsciously, before or after death. The beginning and end of all beings is the same, difference only existing during the journey.

4.7.2 Yaqeen

Yaqeen is generally translated as "certainty", and is considered the summit of the many maqaams (stations) by which the path of walaya (sometimes translated as Sainthood) is fully completed.

4.8 Other Concepts

4.8.1 Haqiqa

Haqiqa or Haqiqat is the Sufi term for the supreme Truth or absolute Reality.

4.8.2 Marifa

Marifa (or alternatively 'marifah') literally means knowledge or recognition. According to mysticism, the truth behind creation of man and essence of all prayers is the recognition of Allah. The term is used by Sufi Muslims to describe mystical intuitive knowledge, knowledge of spiritual truth as reached through ecstatic experiences rather than revealed or rationally acquired.

4.8.2 Ihsan

Ihsan is an Arabic term meaning "perfection" or "excellence." Ihsan is the goal or aim of Sufi practices and is achieved when a seeker surrenders and submits himself completely to the will of Allah.

The Sufi may go into khalwat, solitude from the world where the believer meditates on God, man, and creation.

4.9 Iconic Personalities for Love in Sufism

Submitting to the requirements of love and to its purpose, the sufi poet worships not only the beloved but also the grief and sorrow of love. He acknowledges the grief and sorrow of love while being envious. His whole and gracious devotion is directed, one might say, toward love's apotheosis. Love's supremacy in Persian lyrics is quite intense. It is illustrated in a half-lyrical, half-mystical fashion, not only as the Almighty overseeing all beings, but also as God's reason and tenacity. The Sufis viewed the following statement of the Prophet about God and creation as the source of their principles: "I was a hidden treasure; I loved to be known, so I created creation."

The Sufism is "Dil Allah", that is Sufism is God's Heart Garden. This Garden is His Heart. If one likes to see the beauty of this Garden and to be nourished from it, he must be a Sufi. To enter into this Garden one ought to try to gain the consent of God. For this, one must learn and apply His commandments and prohibitions. It is possible only through obeying the Islamic Sharia truly.

The humans ought to love first God and then His Messenger. To win the consent of God and His Messenger that he loves, must fulfill of their requests. In the case of loving Him, God addresses to His Messenger in the following verse as:

“Say, “If you love God, follow me and God will love you and forgive you your sins; God is most forgiving, and most merciful.” (Al-Imran, verse 31)

According to this verse, the head of love in Islam is to obey the Prophet Muhammad and to assume that he brought and to comply fully with the binding duties and sunna.

Almighty God created the universe out of Love. This love is spread to all the creations and all businesses. In a hadith is said that:

“There was Allah and was nothing but Allah”

That is, there are not worlds, heavens, angels, demons and people but Our Lord exists. In another sacred hadith Our Lord states that:

“I was a hidden treasure, I liked to be known and created all creatures for them to know me.”

According to this sacred hadith, Our Lord created all existences in the universe to know Him. What is then our duty according to this hadith? Our duty is to know God and to seek Him.

Almighty God created first the soul and light of Prophet Muhammad. Then He created all creatures from the Prophet’s light. Almighty God helped the people to know Him by removing up the veil of His Garden of Heart. Only after this it would be possible to see the secrets and beauty of His Heart Garden by the wisdoms. And they invited the people to know God by Love of ecstasy. This love of ecstasy is placed in the hearts of servants and so the hearts of servants could be fond of God. This can be achieved through the Sufi path.

Affection is to feel a tendency towards an object which gives pleasure to him. If this affection is strengthened, then it is called love. The degree of Love could be so high that everything may be sacrificed for the beloved.

According to Sufism, love is to tear the curtains of God's Heart Garden and to discover the secrets in it. The author of the book "Fütûhât-I Mekkiyye", Ibn Arabî (pubh) explains the signs of love of people who love God as follows:

"Revealed a split in the hearts of those who truly love God. Thus, they see the glory of God with their lights of hearts. They wander among the ranks of the angels and observe what works in reality. They worship Him fondly with their most forces without desiring the heaven and fearing the fire."

Below are mentioned some of the statements of Sufis about love in Sufism.

► Love is the turning towards beloved through the surrounding all parts of love.

► Love is an attribute of God.

► Divine love is that God loves us for us and for Himself.

► The pleasure of Wisdom saves us the life in which there is no human death.

► Supererogatory worships and keeping on them regularly save the servants the sovereignty of the God's attributes. And those obligatory provide his whole to become light.

► There is no more beautiful than the universe, because God loves the universe. God is the most beautiful, and God is loved because of the essence of His beauty. Therefore, all universe loves God. The beauty of God's creating spreads on all creations and the universe is the place of the reflection of His Pleasure and Beauty.

► God saw His Beauty in the universe and loved His Beauty.

► God liked the affirming His Unity in His creations. So, who unities Him, is beloved of God.

► God does not like the person who does not unity Him.

► Wise man knows that all seeing, all hearings and all talking are from God. So, God manifests this reality to His Lovers.

► If a servant is honest in his claim loving Lord, he has to have conduct through the names of God.

► If one wants to enter the presence of God, he must leave his mind and put the Sharia in front of him.

► Happy people are who stand in God's borders and does not go beyond of them.

► Wherever and whatever is the case, try to be friendly and lover. When affection is your property, you could be lover forever, whether you are in grave or in the Day of Judgement or in heaven. If you sow wheat, it is grown wheat and you get wheat in your granary and on your tandour.

► The evidence of affection is the statement: "I thank God for His granting us everything." The evidence of love is the statement: "I thank God in every case."

Following are three of the many iconic personalities of Love in Sufism:

4.9.1 Rumi

Jalāl ad-Dīn Mohammad, more popularly simply as Rumi (30 September 1207 – 17 December 1273), was a 13th-century Persian poet. Rumi's influence transcends national borders and ethnic divisions: Iranians, Tajiks, Turks, Greeks, Pashtuns, other Central Asian Muslims, and the Muslims of the Indian subcontinent have greatly appreciated his spiritual legacy for the past seven centuries.

His poems have been widely translated into many of the world's languages and transposed into various formats. Rumi's works are written mostly in Persian, but occasionally he also used Turkish, Arabic, and Greek in his verse. His Masnavi (Mathnawi), composed in Konya, is considered one of the greatest poems of the Persian language.

Rumi was born to native Persian-speaking parents, originally from the Balkh, which at the time was part of the Khwarezmian Empire, but is now in present-day Afghanistan. He was born either in Wakhsh, a village on the Vakhsh River in present-day Tajikistan, or in the city of Balkh, in present-day Afghanistan. Greater Balkh was at that time a major centre of Persian culture and Sufism had developed there for several centuries. The most important influences upon Rumi, besides his father, were the Persian poets. Rumi lived most of his life under the Persianate Seljuk Sultanate of Rum, where he produced his works and died in 1273 AD.

Like other mystic and Sufi poets of Persian literature, Rumi's poetry speaks of love which infuses the world. Rumi's teachings also express the tenets summarized in the Quranic verse which Shams-e Tabrizi cited as the essence of prophetic guidance: "Know that 'There is no god but He,' and ask forgiveness for your sin" (Q. 47:19). In the interpretation attributed to Shams, the first part of the verse commands the humanity to seek knowledge of tawhid (oneness of God), while the second instructs them to negate their own existence. In Rumi's terms, tawhid is lived most fully through love, with the connection being made explicit in his verse that describes love as "that flame which, when it blazes up, burns away everything except the Everlasting Beloved." Rumi's longing and desire to attain this ideal is evident in the following poem from his book the Masnavi:

I died to the mineral state and became a plant,
I died to the vegetal state and reached animality,
I died to the animal state and became a man,
Then what should I fear? I have never become less from dying.
At the next charge (forward) I will die to human nature,

So that I may lift up (my) head and wings (and soar) among the angels,
And I must (also) jump from the river of (the state of) the angel,
Everything perishes except His Face,
Once again I will become sacrificed from (the state of) the angel,
I will become that which cannot come into the imagination,
Then I will become non-existent; non-existence says to me (in tones) like an organ.

Following are a couple of more short poems of Rumi about his love for God:

(i) Masnawi I 3686-87

Love is the Water of Life
Everything other than love for the most beautiful God
though it be sugar- eating.
What is agony of the spirit?
To advance toward death without seizing
hold of the Water of Life.

(ii) Mathnawi VI, 1967-1974

Love is reckless; not reason.
Reason seeks a profit.
Love comes on strong,
consuming herself, unabashed.
Yet, in the midst of suffering,
Love proceeds like a milestone,
hard surfaced and straightforward.
Having died of self-interest,
she risks everything and asks for nothing.
Love gambles away every gift God bestows.
Without cause, God gave us Being.

(iii) Mathnawi III, 1417-1424

Love has nothing to do with
the five senses and the six directions:
its goal is only to experience
the attraction exerted by the Beloved.
Afterwards, perhaps, permission
will come from God:
the secrets that ought to be told with be told
with an eloquence nearer to the understanding
that these subtle confusing allusions.
The secret is partner with none
but the knower of the secret:
in the sceptic's ear
the secret is no secret at all.

4.9.2 Yunus Emre

Yunus Emre was a poet who was constant to Islamic Sufism. Accordingly, he expressed his opinion about the Divine Love in his poetry. The main point of his sight is that there is only one real being in Sufism. It is the one God, Allah. As all of the other Sufis he acts from this thought. He illuminates the concept of presence, death, love and the universe from this perspective. Yunus focuses on Allah, Divine Love, existence and abstinence, life, death and the love of other human beings. He was born on 1240 in Sarıköy, Anatolia and died in 1320.

The main study of Yunus includes his real poems, which is called **"Poetry of Yunus Emre"**. Although there are over one thousand poems attributed to Yunus, there are approximately 300 of his poems in his divan (a collection of poems). Some of his poems about the Divine Love are given below:

When in love, the soul burns,
Melts like wax as it churns.
Stone hearts are like winter,
Dark, harsh, with all warmth gone.
Yunus, leave such fears behind,

Drive all care out of your mind.
Love is what one must first find,
One's a mystic from then on.
Burning, burning, I drift and tread,
Love spattered my body with blood,
I'm not in my senses nor mad,
Come, see what love has done to me.
I'm Yunus, mystic of sorrow,
Suffering wounds from top to toe,
In the friend's hands I writhe in woe,
Come, see what love has done to me.
Yunus is my name, I'm out of my mind,
Love serves as my guide to the very end,
All alone, toward the majestic Friend,
I was kissing the ground – and I arrive
Re-union with that Beloved of his
Gives Yunus the lover his ecstasies
I have smashed the bottle against the stones,
What would I do with honor and prudence?
The lover's heart is the Creator's throne
God admires and accepts it as his own
The man who breaks a heart shall groan and moan
In both worlds, suffering sorrows and cares.
I have disclosed all my secrets today,
And found my soul by giving it away
Heart and soul adoring the Beloved,
In whose embrace I cherish my heyday
I found the Loved One, I need no one else
Let my store be plundered this very day
Earth is mine, sky is mine, heavens are mine
Under my tent, I put them in array
No wonder the name Yunus is disgraced
They read my poems and learn what I say.

4.9.3 Rabia of Basra

Rābiʿa al-ʿAdawiy was a Muslim saint and Sufi mystic. She is known in some parts of the world as, Hazrat Bibi Rabia Basri, Rabia Al Basri or simply Rabia Basri. Rābi'a is said to have been born between 714 and 718 CE (95 and 98 Hijri) in Basra, Iraq, of the Qays tribe. Much of her early life has been recounted by Farid ud-Din Attar, a later Sufi saint and poet.

She herself left no written works about her life. She was the fourth daughter of her family and therefore named Rābi'a, meaning "fourth". Rabia went into the desert to pray and became an ascetic, living a life of semi-seclusion. She is often cited as being the queen of saintly women, and was known for her complete devotion in the form of "pure unconditional love of God." As an exemplar among others devoted to God, she provided a model of mutual love between God and His creation; her example is one in which the loving devotee on earth becomes one with the Beloved.

One day, Rabia was seen running through the streets of Basra carrying a pot of fire in one hand and a bucket of water in the other. When asked what she was doing, she said, "I want to put out the fires of hell, and burn down the rewards of paradise. They block the way to Allah. I do not want to worship from fear of punishment or for the promise of reward, but simply for the love of Allah. She prayed:

"O Lord, if I worship You because of Fear of Hell,
then burn me in Hell;

If I worship You because I desire Paradise,
then exclude me from Paradise;

But if I worship You for Yourself alone,
then deny me not your Eternal Beauty".

4.10 Laylâ and Majnûn: An Eternal Love Story in Sufism

Laylâ and Majnûn is the best-known love story of the Middle

East, and for the Sufism it is an allegory of mystical love. Sufis are lovers of God, wayfarers travelling through the desert of the world, making the journey from separation back to union with God. For these mystics the relationship with God is that of lover and Beloved, and it is the longing for their Beloved that turns them away from the world, drawing them deeper and deeper into the mystery of the heart. These lovers of God have made Laylâ and Majnûn their own story, full of symbols and images of this great love affair of the soul, a love affair as mad, dangerous and destructive as that experienced by the young man Qays, whose love for Laylâ changes his name to Majnûn, the mad one.

Laylâ is the beloved, Majnûn the lover, and his story is that of the seeker consumed by longing, burnt by love. Their relationship is rich in Sufi symbolism—as when Majnûn, driven by the pain of separation, creeps to Laylâ's tent. All the radiance of this morning was Laylâ, yet a candle was burning in front of her, consuming itself with desire. She was the most beautiful garden and Majnûn was a torch of longing. She planted the rose bush; he watered it with his tears.

The candle held against the light of the sun is a Sufi image of the light of the lover before the radiance of God. Majnûn is the lover, consuming himself like a candle in the fire of his own longing, and his beloved holds in her hand the wine of love whose very scent intoxicates him. For the Sufi, wine is a symbol of a divine love that is both intoxicating and addictive. Just one sip of the wine of divine love and one will give away everything for another sip. This wine is the most dangerous substance in creation, which is why the Sufi says, "Keep away, keep away, from the lane of Love."

Qays (Majnûn) and Laylâ begin with the innocence of childhood sweethearts, but only too soon they are separated, and the pain of separation turns Qays into Majnûn. The pain of separation, that we are separate from God, the lover separate from the Beloved—is at the very foundation of mystical life.

Anyone who has entered the lane of love, who has been awakened to this love affair, has felt this pain within the heart. Nothing is more painful that the primal sorrow of separation, this cry of the soul. It is said that Sufism was "at first heartache, only later it became something to speak about." And the ninth-century Sufi, Râbi'a of Basra, who is attributed as introducing the theme of divine love into early Islamic mysticism, described how this heartfelt grief can only be healed by divine union:

All lovers know this pain that tears apart the very fabric of one's being, the longing that makes one bleed tears of love. And this longing is infinitely precious because it draws one directly back to God. To quote the ninth-century Sufi Bâyezîd Bistâmî:

If the eight Paradises were opened in my hut, and the rule of both worlds were given in my hands, I would not give for them that single sigh which rises at morning-time from the depth of my soul in remembering my longing for Him.

Majnûn had become the slave of love and a prisoner of longing. His longing, this divine sickness of the soul, had begun its work of breaking him free from the chains of normal existence, from the conditioned life of the ego:

O who can cure my sickness? An outcast I have become. Family and home where are they? No path leads back to them and none to my beloved. Broken are my name, my reputation, like a glass smashed on a rock; broken is the drum which once spread the good news, and my ears now hear only the drumbeat of separation.

This is the path of love that has chosen Majnûn, that has made him appear mad in the eyes of the world but become a figure of mystical love in the tradition of the Sufis.

As an ideal of lovers, Majnûn is seen by the Sufis as embodying many of the qualities of the lover. His very madness images how, in the words of 'Attâr, "When love comes, reason disappears. Reason cannot live with the folly of love."

A king has Majnûn summoned and presents him with a number of beautiful girls in the hope that when he sees them, he'll forget his insane love for Laylâ. Majnûn doesn't deign to look upon the girls, and says: "Love stands upright in my soul with a drawn sword in its hand and threatens to kill me if I cast a glance at anyone but Laylâ." Through the faculty of active or creative imagination we can have access to an intermediary, symbolic world that is a stepping-stone to the reality of the soul. The use of the imagination in this way makes perceptible the symbolic essence of a material form, as it exists in the world of Mystery. The inner, ideal Laylâ is no fantasy, but an inner reality that nourishes Majnûn.

Love itself, rather than any external object of love, is the desire of the lover. And through the image of Laylâ, Majnûn has begun to access a deeper, more overwhelming truth of love—that this love is not limited to a single form. The inner Laylâ consumes Majnûn's attention to such a degree that finally he seeks and finds her everywhere, until all that exists for him is Laylâ. As was the case with Majnûn of the Banû 'Amir: if he looked at the wild animals, he would say "Laylâ", if he looked at the people, he would say: "Laylâ", and if anyone asked him: "What's your name and how are you?" he would say "Laylâ." For the mystic this intense inner identification with the Beloved becomes a state in which the Beloved is seen everywhere in the inner and outer worlds, until finally one reaches the stage in which "Wheresoever you turn, there is the face of God."

The people of Majnûn's tribe came together and said to Laylâ's people: "This man will be destroyed out of love. What harm would it do if he were allowed to see Laylâ once?" They answered: "We've nothing against this, but Majnûn himself doesn't have the strength to endure seeing her." They brought Majnûn and lifted the curtain over the door of Laylâ's tent. One could still scarcely make out Laylâ's shadow, when Majnûn, true to his name (the madman), collapsed by the door. They said, "It's just as we told you. He doesn't have the strength to see her."

The inner image and the path itself lead us gradually along; love draws us slowly from separation back to union. More and more the feeling of love consumes us. So many tears we cry, so many nights we are kept awake with longing. So many days we feel, like Majnûn, helpless, desolate, abandoned by love. The joys, pleasures and attachments of the outer world fall away, and we walk the same desert that Majnûn trod, crying like him, "I have sold my life for love's sake."

Majnûn knows mainly the cruelty of love, the longing that drives him into the desert of desolation, that makes him lose his family, his father, even his own name. Interestingly the name Laylâ means the dark one, which in the culture of the Middle East suggests that she is not even beautiful, but could also allude to this dark side of love, the love that annihilates the lover.

Majnûn, consumed by love, ceases to exist. He becomes so absorbed by the object of his love that the lover and the beloved become one. In such a state there is no longer any separation: "If you knew what it means to be a lover, you would realize that one only has to scratch him and out falls the beloved." Rich with his love, Majnun cares for nothing else. In the wilderness he lives on roots, grass and fruit, and having died to himself is afraid of nothing. The wild beasts sense his unusual power, and, rather than attack him, befriend him. They forget their hunger and become tame and friendly. The fox, the wild ass, the lion, the wolf and the panther travel with him and are his companions, watching over him when he sleeps. Majnûn's love transforms the wildest animals, suggesting that within the lover the deepest, wildest instinctual forces are transformed through the power of love. These instinctual energies are not tamed by force or will power, as in the path of ascetic, but by love itself.

Majnûn describes the truth that is at the heart of the mystical journey: the love that destroys the ego self is the love that reveals the eternal presence of the Beloved within one's heart. The illusion of separation is burnt away and the reality of union remains. When the ego is gone the Beloved is present. From the very beginning of the journey the lover knows that it is the "I" that separates us from God, as the in words of the prince of lovers, al-Hallâj,

Laylâ and Majnûn is a story about a pair of star-crossed lovers, whose unfulfilled love has tragic consequences. Laylâ dies young of a broken heart, and Majnûn spends the last days of his life at Laylâ's tomb, weeping, mourning the loss of her, until finally he is buried at Laylâ's side. But the Sufis have infused this story of with the symbolism of the mystical journey back to God. Sufism is a love affair with God in which the glance of the Beloved awakens the longing of the heart, the primal pain of separation. Majnûn, whose heart is awakened by Laylâ, has become the mystical lover crying tears of separation from his beloved. Every wayfarer is like Majnûn, whose tears draw him into the desert, where love transforms him. Love burns away all sense of separation, finally revealing the truth that lover and Beloved are one. This oneness with the Beloved is traditionally the secret of the Sufis, these wayfarers of the heart's tears. They know the cry of the heart and experience the death of the ego that awakens the lover into the presence of the Beloved—the mystery of merging where all separation dissolves and there is only God.

CHAPTER 5

Love in Christianity

Love is the fullness and the completeness of the Christian character for the believer is "made perfect in love." - (1 John 4:18)

5.1 Introduction to Christianity

Christianity is an Abrahamic monotheistic religion based on the life and teachings of Jesus of Nazareth. It is the world's largest religion, with about 2.4 billion followers. Its adherents, known as Christians, make up a majority of the population in 157 countries and territories, and believe that Jesus is the Christ, whose coming as the Messiah was prophesied in the Hebrew Bible, called the Old Testament in Christianity, and chronicled in the New Testament.

Christianity remains culturally diverse in its Western and Eastern branches, as well as in its doctrines concerning justification and the nature of salvation, ecclesiology, ordination, and Christology. Their creeds generally hold in common Jesus as the Son of God—the Logos incarnated—who ministered, suffered, and died on a cross, but rose from the dead for the salvation of mankind; and referred to as the gospel, meaning the "good news". Describing Jesus' life and teachings are the four canonical gospels of Matthew, Mark, Luke and John, with the Old Testament as the gospel's respected background.

The four largest branches of Christianity are the Catholic Church, Protestantism, the Eastern Orthodox Church, and Oriental Orthodoxy. While Christians worldwide share basic convictions, there are also differences of interpretations and opinions of the Bible and sacred traditions on which Christianity is based.

5.1.1 Jesus

The central tenet of Christianity is the belief in Jesus as the Son of

God and the Messiah (Christ). Christians believe that Jesus, as the Messiah, was anointed by God as savior of humanity and hold that Jesus' coming was the fulfillment of messianic prophecies of the Old Testament.

According to the canonical gospels of Matthew and Luke, Jesus was conceived by the Holy Spirit and born from the Virgin Mary. Little of Jesus' childhood is recorded in the canonical gospels, although infancy gospels were popular in antiquity. In comparison, his adulthood, especially the week before his death, is well documented in the gospels contained within the New Testament, because that part of his life is believed to be most important. The biblical accounts of Jesus' ministry include: his baptism, miracles, preaching, teaching, and deeds.

5.1.2 Death and resurrection

Christians consider the resurrection of Jesus to be the cornerstone of their faith and the most important event in history. Among Christian beliefs, the death and resurrection of Jesus are two core events on which much of Christian doctrine and theology is based. According to the New Testament, Jesus was crucified, died a physical death, was buried within a tomb, and rose from the dead three days later. Jesus' death and resurrection are commemorated by Christians in all worship services, with special emphasis during Holy Week, which includes Good Friday and Easter Sunday.

5.1.3 Death and afterlife

Most Christians believe that human beings experience divine Judgement and are rewarded either with eternal life or eternal damnation. This includes the general Judgement at the resurrection of the dead as well as the belief (held by Catholics, Orthodox and most Protestants) in a Judgement particular to the individual soul upon physical death.

Some Christian groups, such as Seventh-day Adventists, hold to mortalism, the belief that the human soul is not naturally immortal, and is unconscious during the intermediate state between bodily death and resurrection. These Christians also hold to Annihilationism, the belief that subsequent to the final judgement, the wicked will cease to exist rather than suffer everlasting torment.

5.1.4 Christian worship and Church service

Depending on the specific denomination of Christianity, practices may include baptism, the Eucharist (Holy Communion or the Lord's Supper), prayer (including the Lord's Prayer), confession, confirmation, burial rites, marriage rites and the religious education of children. Most denominations have ordained clergy who lead regular communal worship services. And on the day called Sunday, all who live in cities or in the country gather together to one place, and the memoirs of the apostles or the writings of the prophets are read, as long as time permits; then, when the reader has ceased, the president verbally instructs, and exhorts to the imitation of these good things.

5.1.5 Sacrament

In Christian belief and practice, a sacrament is a rite, instituted by Christ, that confers grace, constituting a sacred mystery. The term is derived from the Latin word sacramentum, which was used to translate the Greek word for mystery. Views concerning both which rites are sacramental, and what it means for an act to be a sacrament, vary among Christian denominations and traditions.

5.1.6 Baptism

Baptism is the ritual act, with the use of water, by which a person is admitted to membership of the Church. Beliefs on baptism vary among denominations. Differences occur firstly on whether the act has any spiritual significance

5.1.7 Prayer in Christianity

"... 'Our Father in heaven, hallowed be your name. Your kingdom comes. Your will be done on earth as it is in heaven. Give us today our daily bread. Forgive us our debts, as we also forgive our debtors. Lead us not into temptation, but deliver us from evil.'"
— The Lord's Prayer, Matthew 6:9–13, EHV

In the Gospel of Saint Matthew, Jesus taught the Lord's Prayer, which has been seen as a model for Christian prayer.[131] The injunction for Christians to pray the Lord's prayer thrice daily was given in the Didache and came to be recited by Christians at 9 am, 12 pm, and 3 pm.

5.2 Scriptures in Christianity

The Bible is the sacred book in Christianity. Christianity, like other religions, has adherents whose beliefs and biblical interpretations vary. Christianity regards the biblical canon, the Old Testament and the New Testament, as the inspired word of God. The traditional view of inspiration is that God worked through human authors so that what they produced was what God wished to communicate.

Some believe that divine inspiration makes our present Bibles inerrant (incapable of being wrong). Others claim inerrancy for the Bible in its original manuscripts, although none of those are extant. Another closely related view is biblical infallibility or limited inerrancy, which affirms that the Bible is free of error as a guide to salvation, but may include errors on matters such as history, geography, or science.

The books of the Bible accepted by the Orthodox, Catholic, and Protestant churches vary somewhat, with Jews accepting only the Hebrew Bible as canonical; however, there is substantial overlap. These variations are a reflection of the range of traditions, and of the councils that have convened on the subject. Every version of the Old Testament always includes the books of the Tanakh, the canon of the Hebrew Bible. The Catholic and Orthodox canons, in addition to the Tanakh, also include the deuterocanonical books as part of the Old Testament. These books appear in the Septuagint, but are regarded by Protestants to be apocryphal. However, they are considered to be important historical documents which help to inform the understanding of words, grammar, and syntax used in the historical period of their conception. The New Testament, originally written in Koine Greek, contains 27 books which are agreed upon by all major churches.

5.3 Trinity

The Christian doctrine of the Trinity ("threefold") holds that God is one God, but three coeternal and consubstantial persons: the Father, the Son (Jesus Christ), and the Holy Spirit. The three persons are distinct, yet are one "substance, essence or nature" (homoousios). In this context, a "nature" is what one is, whereas a "person" is who one is.

The subset of Christianity that accepts this doctrine is collectively known as Trinitarianism, while the subset that does not is referred to as Nontrinitarianism (see also Arianism). Trinitarianism contrasts with positions such as Binitarianism (one deity in two persons) and Monarchianism (no plurality of persons within God), of which Modalistic Monarchianism (one deity revealed in three modes) and Unitarianism (one deity in one person) are subsets.

While the developed doctrine of the Trinity is not explicit in the books that constitute the New Testament, the New Testament possesses a "triadic" understanding of God and contains a number of Trinitarian formulas. The doctrine of the Trinity was first formulated among the early Christians and fathers of the Church as early Christians attempted to understand the relationship between Jesus and God in their scriptural documents and prior traditions.

5.4 God in the New Testament

5.4.1 Before the Council of Nicaea

While the developed doctrine of the Trinity is not explicit in the books that constitute the New Testament, it was first formulated as early Christians attempted to understand the relationship between Jesus and God in their scriptural documents and prior traditions.

An early Trinitarian formula appears towards the end of the first century, where Clement of Rome rhetorically asks in his epistle as to why corruption exists among some in the Christian community; "Do we not have one God, and one Christ, and one gracious Spirit that has been poured out upon us, and one calling in Christ?" (1 Clement 46:6). Around the turn of the first century, the Didache directs Christians to "baptize in the name of the Father and of the Son and of the Holy Spirit." Ignatius of Antioch provides early support for the Trinity around 110, exhorting obedience to "Christ, and to the Father, and to the Spirit".

The pseudonymous Ascension of Isaiah, written sometime between the end of the first century and the beginning of the third century, possesses a "proto-trinitarian" view, such as in its narrative of how the inhabitants of the sixth heaven sing praises to "the primal Father and his Beloved Christ, and the Holy Spirit". Justin Martyr (AD 100–c. 165) also writes, "in the name of God, the Father and Lord of the universe, and of our Savior Jesus Christ, and of the Holy Spirit".

The first of the early church fathers to be recorded using the word "Trinity" was Theophilus of Antioch writing in the late 2nd century. He defines the Trinity as God, His Word (Logos) and His Wisdom (Sophia) in the context of a discussion of the first three days of creation, following the early Christian practice of identifying the Holy Spirit as the Wisdom of God. The first defence of the doctrine of the Trinity was in the early 3rd century by the early church father Tertullian. He explicitly defined the Trinity as Father, Son, and Holy Spirit and defended his theology against "Praxeas", though he noted that the majority of the believers in his day found issue with his doctrine.

St. Justin and Clement of Alexandria used the Trinity in their doxologies and St. Basil likewise, in the evening lighting of lamps. Origen of Alexandria (AD 185-c. 253) has often been interpreted as Subordinationist, but some modern researchers have argued that Origen might have actually been anti-Subordinationist and that his own Trinitarian theology inspired the Trinitarian theology of the later Cappadocian Fathers.

Among the Non-Trinitarian beliefs, the Sabellianism taught that the Father, the Son, and the Holy Spirit are essentially one and the same, the difference being simply verbal, describing different aspects or roles of a single being.

5.4.2 First Council of Nicaea

The Glory of Saint Nicholas, by António Manuel da Fonseca. Nicholas of Myra, a participant in the First Council of Nicaea, achieves the beatific vision in the shape of the Holy Trinity. In the fourth century, Arianism, as traditionally understood, taught that the Father existed prior to the Son who was not, by nature, God but rather a changeable creature who was granted the dignity of becoming "Son of God". In 325, the First Council of Nicaea adopted the Nicene Creed which described Christ as "God of God, Light of Light, very God of very God, begotten, not made, being of one substance with the Father", and the "Holy Ghost" as the one by which "was incarnate... of the Virgin Mary". ("the Word was made flesh and dwelled among us"). About the Father and the Son, the creed used the term homoousios (of one substance) to define the relationship between the Father and the Son. After more than fifty years of debate, homoousios was recognized as the hallmark of orthodoxy, and was further developed into the formula of "three persons, one being".

The Confession of the First Council of Nicaea, the Nicene Creed, said little about the Holy Spirit. At the First Council of Nicea (325) all attention was focused on the relationship between the Father and the Son, without making any similar statement about the Holy Spirit:

"We believe in one God, the Father Almighty, Maker of all things

visible and invisible. And in one Lord Jesus Christ, the Son of God, begotten of the Father [the only-begotten; that is, of the essence of the Father, God of God,] Light of Light, very God of very God, begotten, not made, being of one substance with the Father; (...) And [we believe] in the Holy Ghost. (...)."
— Nicene Creed

5.5 Some Characteristics of True Love according to Bible

If you want to know and understand what true love really is, here are some signs, qualities or characteristics of a genuine love according to the verses in the Holy Bible.

1. Love is patient.

True love can tolerate pain or suffering without complaining or getting angry.

2. Love is kind.

True love has a gentle, caring and compassionate heart. It feels your sorrow; it feels your joy.

3. Love is not envious.

True love is content and thankful for its blessings and current possessions. It doesn't envy other people.

4. Love is humble.

True love is not proud and boastful. It is humble enough to admit its own mistakes and strive to correct them. It also forgives to get rid of hatred and enjoy the peacefulness.

5. Love is respectful.

True love respects and honours you as a person. It doesn't put you into shame or humiliation.

6. Love is selfless.

True love is always thoughtful and concerned about the welfare of its beloved. It's not selfish, inconsiderate, and greedy.

7. Love is calm.

True love always maintains the clarity of mind and softness of heart. Its heart is deep and its mind is not narrow.

8. Love is righteous.

True love always does the right thing. It disciplines itself to avoid wrongdoings.

9. Love is honest.

True love is truthful. It's happy living an honest life. It doesn't lie and hide in darkness.

10. Love protects.

True love always protects you and wants you to be safe.

11. Love is trusting.

True love trusts. It relies and depends on you. It recognizes your abilities, talents, skills and the good things in you.

12. Love is hopeful.

True love is optimistic. It includes you in its plans. It sees a bright future with you.

13. Love is persistent.

True love doesn't easily give up. It always protects, always trusts, always hopes, always perseveres.

14. Love banishes fear.

True love eliminates fear, anxieties and insecurities that torment one's heart, mind, and soul.

15. Love loves even those who don't love it.

True love does good things even to those who hate it. It will love you even though you are treating it as your enemy.

16. Love comes from God.

True love brings you closer to God.

17. Love makes great sacrifice.

True love does extraordinary things. It goes out of its comfort zone or sacrifices things important to it just to show its love.

18. Love loves through true actions.

True love is not based on words or hypocritical deeds, but it is based on truthful actions. It doesn't only believe or hope, but it does actions that will make the things it believes or hopes a reality.

19. Love loves itself.

True love takes care of itself, not hurt itself. It develops itself to be stronger, healthier and more capable to continue on loving.

20. Love binds a person's good virtues in perfect unity.

True love transforms you into a whole new and better person.

21. Love gives you the confidence to face even the end of time.

True love keeps you away from sins and cleanses your soul so that you may become confident even on the Day of Judgement.

5.6 Love in Christianity

God is love, He wants believers to know and enjoy that Divine attribute. In a thousand ways and with ten thousand voices God has been shouting to mankind, *"I love you!"* But for some strange reason man has not heard the gospel message distinctly. Even when God took upon Himself the form of a man and personally demonstrated authentic love, people misunderstood and they tried to kill Love. At first, hatred seemed to be successful, but even death cannot destroy Love (Song of Sol. 8:7) and so it was that Love walked out of the grave. What did Love have to say?

- Love said, *"Father, forgive them, they know not what they do."* (Luke 23:34)
- Love said, *"Come unto me and I will give you rest."* (Matt. 11:28)
- Love said, *"Behold I stand at the door and knock. If any man hears my voice, and opens the door, I will come in to him, and will sup with him, and he with me."*

(Rev. 3:20)

What does Bible say on Divine Love?

1 John 4:8 ESV /
Anyone who does not love does not know God, because God is love.

1 John 4:18 ESV /
There is no fear in love, but perfect love casts out fear. For fear has to do with punishment, and whoever fears has not been perfected in love.

1 Corinthians 13:4-7 ESV /
Love is patient and kind; love does not envy or boast; it is not arrogant or rude. It does not insist on its own way; it is not irritable or resentful; it does not rejoice at wrongdoing, but rejoices with the truth. Love bears all things, believes all things, hopes all things, endures all things.

John 3:16 ESV /
"For God so loved the world, that he gave his only Son, that whoever believes in him should not perish but have eternal life.

1 John 4:7 ESV /
Beloved, let us love one another, for love is from God, and whoever loves has been born of God and knows God.

Zephaniah 3:17 ESV /
The Lord your God is in your midst, a mighty one who will save; he will rejoice over you with gladness; he will quiet you by his love; he will exult over you with loud singing.

Galatians 3:28 ESV /
There is neither Jew nor Greek, there is neither slave nor free, there is no male and female, for you are all one in Christ Jesus.

1 John 3:16 ESV /
By this we know love, that he laid down his life for us, and we ought to lay down our lives for the brothers.

1 Peter 4:8 ESV /
Above all, keep loving one another earnestly, since love covers a multitude of sins.

Galatians 5:22 ESV /
But the fruit of the Spirit is love, joy, peace, patience, kindness, goodness, faithfulness,

John 15:13 ESV /

Greater love has no one than this, that someone lay down his life for his friends.

1 John 4:19 ESV /
We love because he first loved us.

1 John 3:18 ESV /
Little children, let us not love in word or talk but indeed and in truth.

Galatians 3:23-25 ESV /
Now before faith came, we were held captive under the law, imprisoned until the coming faith would be revealed. So then, the law was our guardian until Christ came, in order that we might be justified by faith. But now that faith has come, we are no longer under a guardian,

1 Corinthians 2:14 ESV /
The natural person does not accept the things of the Spirit of God, for they are folly to him, and he is not able to understand them because they are spiritually discerned.

Romans 5:8 ESV /
But God shows his love for us in that while we were still sinners, Christ died for us.

Ephesians 3:17-19 ESV /
So that Christ may dwell in your hearts through faith—that you, being rooted and grounded in love, may have strength to comprehend with all the saints what is the breadth and length and height and depth, and to know the love of Christ that surpasses knowledge, that you may be filled with all the fullness of God.

Romans 1:26-27 ESV /
For this reason, God gave them up to dishonorable passions. For their women exchanged natural relations for those that are contrary to nature; and the men likewise gave up natural relations with women and were consumed with passion for one another, men committing

shameless acts with men and receiving in themselves the due penalty for their error.

Genesis 3:15 ESV /
I will put enmity between you and the woman, and between your offspring and her offspring; he shall bruise your head, and you shall bruise his heel."

1 John 4:16 ESV /
So, we have come to know and to believe the love that God has for us. God is love, and whoever abides in love abides in God, and God abides in him.

Ephesians 5:25 ESV /
Husbands, love your wives, as Christ loved the church and gave himself up for her,

Ephesians 2:8-9 ESV /
For by grace, you have been saved through faith. And this is not your own doing; it is the gift of God, not a result of works, so that no one may boast.

John 21:15 ESV /
When they had finished breakfast, Jesus said to Simon Peter, "Simon, son of John, do you love me more than these?" He said to him, "Yes, Lord; you know that I love you." He said to him, "Feed my lambs."

John 20:2 ESV /
So, she ran and went to Simon Peter and the other disciple, the one whom Jesus loved, and said to them, "They have taken the Lord out of the tomb, and we do not know where they have laid him."

John 13:34 ESV /
A new commandment I give to you, that you love one another: just as I have loved you, you also are to love one another.

Luke 11:43 ESV /

Woe to you Pharisees! For you love the best seat in the synagogues and greetings in the marketplaces.

Matthew 23:6 ESV /
And they love the place of honor at feasts and the best seats in the synagogues

1 John 3:2 ESV /
Beloved, we are God's children now, and what we will be has not yet appeared; but we know that when he appears we shall be like him, because we shall see him as he is.

2 Timothy 4:10 ESV /
For Demas, in love with this present world, has deserted me and gone to Thessalonica. Crescents has gone to Galatia, Titus to Dalmatia.

Ephesians 5:2 ESV /
And walk in love, as Christ loved us and gave himself up for us, a fragrant offering and sacrifice to God.

Galatians 5:14 ESV /
For the whole law is fulfilled in one word: "You shall love your neighbor as yourself."

1 Corinthians 13:8 ESV /
Love never ends. As for prophecies, they will pass away; as for tongues, they will cease; as for knowledge, it will pass away.

Romans 8:29 ESV /
For those whom he foreknew he also predestined to be conformed to the image of his Son, in order that he might be the firstborn among many brothers.

Romans 5:5 ESV /
And hope does not put us to shame, because God's love has been poured into our hearts through the Holy Spirit who has been given to us.

John 16:27 ESV /
For the Father himself loves you, because you have loved me and have believed that I came from God.

John 13:31-35 ESV /
When he had gone out, Jesus said, "Now is the Son of Man glorified, and God is glorified in him. If God is glorified in him, God will also glorify him in himself, and glorify him at once. Little children, yet a little while I am with you. You will seek me, and just as I said to the Jews, so now I also say to you, 'Where I am going you cannot come.' A new commandment I give to you, that you love one another: just as I have loved you, you also are to love one another. By this all people will know that you are my disciples, if you have love for one another."

John 11:36 ESV /
So, the Jews said, "See how he loved him!"

John 5:20 ESV /
For the Father loves the Son and shows him all that he himself is doing. And greater works than these will he show him, so that you may marvel.

Isaiah 62:5 ESV /
For as a young man marries a young woman, so shall your sons marry you, and as the bridegroom rejoices over the bride, so shall your God rejoice over you.

5.7 The Tenderness of Love

One day, a woman was pushed roughly through a crowd and thrown down into the dirt before the feet of Jesus. There was a tremendous amount of noise. Men with strong voices bellowed forth the thunder and lightning of Mount. Sinai as they told Jesus, "Master this woman was taken to adultery, in the very act. Now Moses in the law commanded us, that such should be stoned: but what sayest thou?" (John 8:4,5). It is a good question. What does one say to someone who has been caught in a terrible transgression.

• Some people express moral outrage.

• Others shout words of condemnation.

• Most shake their heads in amazement.

"But Jesus stooped down, and with his finger wrote on the ground, as though he heard them not. So, when they continued asking him, he lifted up himself, and said unto them, He that is without sin among you, let him cast a stone at her. And again, he stooped down, and wrote on the ground. And they which heard it, being convicted by their own conscience, went out one by one, beginning at the eldest, even unto the last: and Jesus was left alone, and the woman standing in the midst" (John 8:6b-9).

How many Christians would be as gracious as Jesus with a woman caught in the very act of adultery? How many Christians weep over the world that will soon perish? Until we learn to weep again, until we learn the language of love, we have yet to know what Paul is talking about in 1 Corinthians 13:1 when he writes,

"Though I speak with the tongues of men and of angels
And have not charity, I am become as sounding brass, Or a tinkling cymbal."

The challenge to every Church and to every Christian is to learn a little bit about love.

While the souls of men are dying—
for a little bit of love;
As the children too are crying—
for a little bit of love;
Stand no longer idly by
You may help them if you try,
Go then saying,

'Here am I'—
with a little bit of love.

5.8 Men of Unusual Abilities

5.8.1 Moses

Throughout the course of human history God has singled out certain individuals to be the recipients of extra-ordinary gifts. Moses was such a person. While still an obscure herdsman on the backside of a desert God revealed Himself. Moses saw a bush burn and not be consumed. Then he heard God speak and his life was changed forever.

Like Moses, you and I must hear God speak personally if we want to live extraordinary lives. One reason why so much preaching falls upon dull and deaf ears is because men and women are not listening for the voice of God through humble but natural elements. But if the words of God ever break forth, life will be forever different. Moses was made to be a prophet, a priest, and a presenter of the Law of the Lord. Because of that great privilege granted to him, rivers parted, plagues fell upon people, and two million people were prepared to create a new nation.

5.8.2 David

David had great privileges bestowed upon him. Trading his sling for a harp and a pen, David was used by God to write some of the most inspiring Psalms in all the world.

5.8.3 Daniel

In a similar manner Daniel knew something of the extra-ordinary privileges of divine mercy. When the nation of Israel fell to the Babylonian army in 586 BC, Daniel and his friends were not butchered as many others. They were taken to the king's palace where great mercy and favour was bestowed upon him. Being a young man of high moral standards and spiritual insight, the godly ethics of the youth captured the imagination and attention of the Queen. Hear how the Queen of Babylon speaks to Belshazzar about the young people from a foreign land. "*There is a man in thy kingdom, in whom is the spirit of the holy gods; and in the days of thy father light and understanding and wisdom, like the wisdom of the gods, was found in him; whom the king Nebuchadnezzar thy father, the king, I say, thy father, made master of the magicians, astrologers, Chaldeans, and soothsayers; For as much as an excellent spirit, and knowledge, and understanding, interpreting of dreams, and shewing of hard sentences, and dissolving of doubts, were found in the same Daniel, whom the king named Belteshazzar: now let Daniel be called, and he will shew the interpretation*" (Dan. 5:11,12).

5.8.4 The Apostles.

Moving from the Old Testament era to the New Testament, it can be observed that the apostles were granted a measure of extra-ordinary gifts and for good reason, the Church is built upon the apostles and prophets, Jesus Christ Himself bring the chief corner-stone (Ephesians 2:20). So, it is a great privilege to receive the special privileges of divine favour. Moses and David, Daniel and the Twelve Apostles are honoured and exalted for the special place they have in the history of the Church. And yet, Paul writes that despite being the recipient of extra-ordinary gifts, if there is not love, such a person is nothing.

SECTION 3

(HEALING)

CHAPTER 6

Healing in Hinduism

Healing is a course of action of the restitution of health to an unbalanced, diseased or injured organism. Healing was correlated with themes of wholeness, narrative, and spirituality. Spiritual healing leads to the maintenance of health, emphasizing meditation, specific movements of the body so that the health of the individual is restored to its normal state.

In western culture, different forms of possession, mental illness, and spiritual disorders are often categorized as pathological and abnormal; these pathologies are usually treated with psychoanalysis, psychiatry and mass amounts of medication with less frequent attention paid to spiritual treatment. In the east, and more specifically, in the Hindu tradition, spiritual abnormalities and anomalies are treated most of the times using various religious practices and spiritual healing techniques that date back to the time of the Vedas.

Modern medicine, particularly in the west, restores the health of the individuals but not to heal. The role of the physicians has transferred from being the healer to the curer of the disease. Thus, religion has taken up a massive foothold in the field of providing healing to its followers. The Hindu religion as a whole consists of a large number of measures by which a person is healed from the physical suffering they are going through.

6.1 Healing traditions across different time periods in Hinduism

Encroachment of the population into the Indian sub-continent has been a factor since the pre-historic times. The medicinal values of the plants and many other associated factors have been playing a major role in the Hindu tradition of healing of the individuals since the pre-historic times.

6.1.1 Pre-historic period

Medical practices such as dentistry and trepanation were practiced since 7000 BCE in the Indian subcontinents. The importance of medicinal plants, trees and emphasis on health, hygiene as well as water sanitation was considered to be essential since the prehistoric time period. Archaeo-botanical excavations provide indication for the application in the Middle Gangetic region of medicinal plants ever since the 2nd millennium BCE is still used by Ayurvedic physicians and folk healers.

6.1.2 Vedic Period

In Rigveda, there is a reference of Indo-Aryans using the juice of 'Soma' Plant as a medicinal agent. In Vedic literature, there are also references of preparations like Swarasa, Kalka, Madya, Sura, Phanta, Lehya, Churna and so on. Special preparations for nasal installation of medicine are also known to man during Vedic periods. Apart from medicinal preparations, various dietic preparations were also mentioned in Vedic literature. In Kausika Sutra, a supplement to Vedic literature, there are descriptions of about 50 varieties of herbs. In Vishnu dharma dietic preparations were classified into: Bhojyam, Bhakshyam, Lehyam, Chooshyam and Peyam.

The fourth and last Veda of Hindu literature the Atharvaveda (AV) contains medical information in its various stages of evolution and contains the most primitive as well as some of the most highly developed stages of therapy. AV mentions a large number of diseases both major and minor. AV is also known as 'Bhaisajyaveda' because its hymns represent Ayurveda of Vedic period and the name Atharvan is almost synonymous with Bhesaja, that is, medicine. Aetiological factors, origin, method of treatment of diseases especially the "Yaksma (consumption)", are described in AV.

According to AV, Rudra is the best physician, he possesses healing remedies, he is the first divine physician; he can cause the diseases and performs the cure as well. Rohini is the drug prescribed for the healing of fracture, Silaci for the healing of wounds. Most of the Vedic healing verses occur in the Atharva Veda. Over 100 of its hymns are devoted to conditions like fever, leprosy, consumption, heart disease, headache, rheumatism, epilepsy etc. Natural forces like the sun and water and human contrivances were all used therapeutically in the Vedic era.

The Vedic hymns of the nomad Aryan tribes are the earliest literary foundation of knowledge about the healing practices in the sub-continent. These hymns give a close acquaintance into the diseases which were rampant during the period. These hymns provide information about the causes of the diseases too. The hymns in the Atharva Veda are composed after the Aryans, were well settled in the Indian sub-continent. It indicates that the native non-Aryan healing practices had controlled the Vedic Aryan healers.

6.1.3 Post-Vedic Period

Influence of the Sanskrit-speaking Vedic Aryan spread gradually eastward from the Punjab and Doab region towards the Middle Gangetic plains, which had its own socio-cultural and linguistic context. It was during this period that diverse cultures interacted with each other and awareness on health and well-being eventually increased among the people. Spiritual healing became one of the foremost and prime option among the individuals as they believed that they can get their near and dear ones treated well by the application of the healing strategies.

6.2 Healing---Body, Mind and Spirit

The healing traditions is one of the chief factors which gives rise to spiritual consciousness, relaxation of the mind, curer of the diseases; overall one can say that the healing traditions develop the proper functioning of the body, mind and the spirit together. Even in the medical sphere, understanding the body and the mind is one of the crucial factors while analysing the patients. Healing traditions related to one's diet and healthy digestion of the consumed food involved therapeutic treatment which invariably acts as the technique of the balance of behaviour and emotions. Use of the medicinal plants also acts as vital healing strategies by which the body can be cured of the pathology it is suffering from. These traditional plants are known to be the "natural antibiotics". Therefore, the healing traditions strengthen the immune system and the homeostatic mechanism of our body.

6.3 Types of Healing in the Hindu Tradition

There are different ways and forms by which a Hindu healer tries to heal a patient out of its pathology. These mainly include Ayurveda, reiki and other rituals related to healing.

6.3.1 Ayurveda

The formal scientific culture of healing is known as Ayurveda. Ayurveda is the traditional Hindu science of medicine that is carried out in one form or another by 80% of people of the Indian descent. It is one of the oldest healing sciences. The word "Ayurveda", in Sanskrit, means the "Science of Life". It originated around 5000 years ago and is referred to as by many people as the "Mother of all Healing". Ayurveda puts a great amount of emphasis on the deterrence and encouragement for the healthy maintenance of one's life by maintaining a balanced life-style with proper diet.

There are three basic types of energy identified in Ayurveda. These are vata, pitta and kapha6. There is the requirement of energy to create movements of the body fluids and nutrients so that the total body can function properly. Body, mind and consciousness works together in a flow under the umbrella of Ayurveda. Vata includes the energy associated with movements. Thus, it is composed of Space and Air. It governs breathing, blinking of the eyes, pulse of the heart etc. Pitta implies the body's metabolic system. Therefore, it's composed of Fire and Water. It governs the nutrition, body temperature, digestion. Pitta leads to the production of intelligence and understanding. Anger, jealousy and hatred can crop up if the pitta is out of one's control. Kapha includes the energy that forms the body's structure, that is, bones, muscles. It supplies water for all the body parts. If the Kapha is in balance then it can produce live, calmness but if it is out of control then responses like greed, attachment, envy results from it. Ayurveda doesn't put its spotlight on the diseases rather on the balances of the energies within the body. It provides description of how to treat the diseases through medicinal herbs.

The Ayurveda is the oldest of traditional healing guides that Hinduism has to offer us. "Diet, herbs, water, minerals, and other treatments are [typically] used for cures" in this system of healing. Traditionally, yoga (which has presently become popularized in the west, as mere physical postures, called 'asanas') was therapeutically used as a part of Ayurvedic practices to delve into the actualization of the true self (atman) and the nature of reality (Brahman). Spiritually speaking, the Ayurveda and the practice of yoga ultimately seek to liberate the soul (jiva) from the cycles of rebirth (samsara) and the tremendous constraining moral principle that is karma.

6.3.2 Yoga

Yoga is considered to be a part of healing, spirituality and meditation. It is a philosophy of the ancient and is considered as a practice of well-being of the individuals. By doing Yoga, one can control the mind. The mind is the ultimate source from where concentration emanates. Therefore, the ability to focus and discipline the mind is the work of the yoga. Yoga may not cure an individual from any kind of diseases but it can give strength to the individual and heal his mind to bear with the consequences. There are different types of yoga, such as:

(i) **Hatha Yoga**--- Hatha had its origination in India in the 15th century. It is slow-paced, gentle, and focused on breathing and meditation. It relieves stress and improves breathing along with physical exercise.

(ii) Raj Yoga---It is an inclusive of all yogas. It emphasises on meditation and self-realization as well as the evolution of the consciousness.

(iii) Tantra Yoga---It aims at expanding consciousness. It promotes a one-pointedness and centeredness that helps us to free the consciousness from any kind of limitations.

Apart from these above forms or types of yoga there are other types of yoga too, which emanates the mind from all kinds of limitations that create a constraint in the mind of the individuals. Yoga emphasises relationship as a healing modality.

6.3.3 Concept of Healing in the Bhagavad Gita:

The words of Lord Krishna to Arjun in the Bhagavad Gita provide a solemnity to the minds of the readers. The strong words as uttered by Lord Krishna provide healing of the mind to the individuals. It calls for abandonment of worldly ties for the sake of self-realization. People in their time of deluge refer to the words of the Gita, which thereby provides them with a strong mind and makes them able to face the odds in life. As lord Krishna said:

aha kratur aha yaja
svadhāham aham au adham
mantro 'ham aham evājyam
aham agnir aha hutam

The above words of Lord Krishna refer that—"But it is I who am the ritual, I the sacrifice, the offering to the ancestors, the healing herb, the transcendental chant. I am the butter and the fire and the offering."
Therefore, Lord Krishna is believed to be the Yajna, Shraddha, aushadham (has the potency for healing as the healing herb), mantra, ajam or ghee, ahavaniyas (fire)--- all these concepts laid down in the Gita act as a source of healing to all its readers in their crisis period.

6.3.4 Healing in the Hindu Mythology

Healing narratives from the Hindu mythologies such as Ramayana and Mahabharata are striking examples to point out that the healing traditions emanates from these narratives too. In the Ramayana, the pregnant Sita is abandoned by brother-in-law Laxman, on order of Ram, by which she had brought up her twin sons with only nature acting as the aid. Another example from the narratives of Ramayana can be pointed out whereby Hanuman brings medicinal herbs from the "Gandhomadon Parbat" in order to heal dying Laxman.

The strong words blurted out by Lord Krishna during the Kurukshetra to Arjuna acts as a source of healing to those who feel mentally deprived and faces lack of concentration due to the odds in life. It helps the individuals to guide him and give a direction to his with the sturdy words of Lord Krishna. Therefore, the concept of healing is imbibed within.

6.4 Spiritual Healing

To understand spirituality and spiritual healing in Hinduism one must first understand the ultimate goal in Hindu philosophy, which is to free oneself from the cyclical nature of existence. This liberation is termed 'moksha', which is essentially the same ultimate goal in the practice of yoga, termed kaivalya. Techniques such as mantras and meditations used in yoga, which have been adopted from the Ayurveda, attempt to spiritually link the self and consciousness to the natural world that surrounds it. This broad look at the spiritual focus of Hindu philosophies to maintain the well-being of the self is linked to the spiritual healing that accompanies anomalies in one's spirit, such as spiritual possession.

Essentially, the goal of spiritual healing in Hindu philosophy seeks to protect the soul from demonic spiritual powers; the influence of this negative spiritual energy can be, and should be, warded off. Negative spiritual possession can be counteracted by the use of Soma, which is an intoxicating, mind-altering, hallucinogenic drink that is perceived as divine and therefore connects the spirit of the ingesting person to higher understanding and consciousness. Negative influences on the mind and spirit in general have been understood as celestially caused; the inauspiciousness that is associated with the universe at certain times is counteracted by the wearing of specific gemstones that repel negative spirits from interacting with the body. Vedic or other Hindu textual verses are held, they are usually made of copper, brass or iron, similar to the ta'wiz in the Islamic tradition. Interestingly, the sacred healing ash (vibhuti) is oftentimes placed inside the amulet for the same spiritual protection purposes.

Contemporary, exorcisms, gemstones, intoxicating substances and yoga still play important spiritual healing roles not only in India but in the west as well. Mindfulness, spiritual awareness and yoga are implicated in contemporary western conceptions of spiritual well-being. The present psychological healing that Hindu rituals have on positive thinking and spirituality worldwide shows that spiritual healing should not be underestimated as a powerful tool in curing mental illness. The most vital aspect to understanding our own consciousness is to understand how the spirit can be healed and refurbished with guidance from the spiritual healing practices of the Hindu tradition.

All the spiritual practices in the Hinduism have got an explanation rather a justification on why the practices exist among the followers. The Hindus wears a mark on their forehead in the form of tilak or pottu as the entire body emanates energy in the form of electromagnetic waves – the forehead and especially between the eyebrows. The tilak and pottu cools the forehead, guards the person and prevents energy loss. Sometimes the total forehead is covered with chandan or bhasma (which is also known as the holy ash) as a mark of fast healing from any disease. Bhasma is also applied in different parts of the body. Many a time it is also consumed by the ascetics. Bhasma means, "That by which our sins are destroyed and the Lord is remembered". The appliance of bhasma connotes annihilation of the evil and commemoration of the divine. Bhasma is also called vibhuti (which implies "glory"). It gives glory to one who applies it and "raksha" (which means a source of protection) from ill health and evil, by purifying the wearer. Individuals are perceived to heal faster by the application of any holy material. Many a time the holy flower from the flower bed of the God or Goddesses is kept in touch with the ill patients as they are thought to heal faster.

The first great Hindu physician known, Charaka, practiced about 1000 BC. Susruta, in the 5th century AD, noted the relationship of malaria to mosquitoes and of plague to rats, knew of more than 700 medicinal plants, and described more than 100 surgical instruments. He treated fractures, removed tumors and kidney stones, and delivered babies by Caesarian section. The tulsi is considered to have huge medicinal value and its perveived by the followers of Ayurveda so that they can be healed from cough and cold. The leaves of the neem tree are considered to have important medicinal value and are provided to the person suffering generally from chicken pox. The medical providers can be classified into two heads--- a) Baidhya-Kabiraj and b) Jadi-butiwala. Baidhya and kabiraj are ayurvedic physicians who use elixirs, metal preparations and herbs to treat infirmity while the jadi-buti walas use only herbs to treat illness. Therefore, Ayurveda is one of the most essential elements which are given prime importance under the Hindu healing traditions.

Everything in creation is, at its most refined level, sound or vibration. Every tree, every flower, every part of your body has its own unique vibration. Even the qualities you express in your life such as happiness, joy, abundance, and love are vibrations. Mantras are sounds or vibrations that create a desired effect, such as healing, transformation, or self-awareness, to a specific area of your body and/or life.

When you are healthy, happy, and vibrant, these vibrations are harmonizing with each other like a magnificent cosmic symphony. However, if the vibration of any area becomes distorted, the harmony breaks down, leading to a lack of wholeness and some discomfort in your life. Many forms of healing are based on knowing the correct sound or vibration and reintroducing it into that area, whereby you can restore the balance, harmony, and comfort once again.

Nature itself is full of sounds—birds singing, the wind blowing through the trees, waves breaking on the beach, innocent children laughing, and so many more. Unfortunately, for much of our time nowadays, we separate ourselves from nature. When you spend time in nature, listening to these sounds, your physiology becomes harmonized with the rhythms and flow of nature.

All traditions of the world have used sound for healing, whether the beating of a drum, a bell, a gong, or a sacred chant. The ancient Vedic Tradition of India has taken this a step further, exploring and refining the use of sound over thousands of years to formulate it into the Vedic Science of Mantras.

Mantras are specific sounds or vibrations whose effects are known. When either chanted aloud or repeated silently, they can create a desired effect in any area of your physiology or life—for healing, transformation, and inner awakening.

6.4.1 Mantras for Healing

Reintroducing the correct sound helps to restore the harmony in that area. Healing mantras are normally repeated with the attention in the area of discomfort—or, you could say, directing the vibration to where it is needed.

There are some powerful healing mantras, some of the simpler ones are:

For the sinuses: *Mmmmm*

For the ears: *Nnnnnnn*

For the eyes: *Eeemmm*

For the throat: *Gaa Gha*

For the jaw: *Yaa Yu Yai*

The following vowels sounds can also be used for healing:

Aaa

Eeeee

Eye

Ooooo

Uuuuuu

These are non-local, meaning you can chant one of them and direct its vibration wherever you choose.

6.4.2 Anuswaram (Nasal Sound), MMMM and Production of Nitric Oxide in the Body

The anuswaram (nasal sound) MMMM (equivalent to the sound of a honey bee) humming boosts the production of Nitric oxide in the body. This was known to Indians and documented more than 7000 years ago. Nadaswaram (Shehnai) is an ancient musical instrument which produces similar nasal sound. Many mantras which end with Anuswaram, produce Nitric oxide, which is a molecule that our body produces to help its 50 trillion cells communicate with each other by transmitting signals throughout the entire body. Nitric Oxide (NO) is an important regulator and mediator of numerous processes in the nervous, immune, and cardiovascular systems. These include vascular smooth muscle relaxation, resulting in arterial vasodilation and increasing blood flow. People with diabetes usually have lower levels of Nitric oxide than those without diabetes. Stems and Flowers cut from their original plants can survive for longer time if supplied with Nitric Oxide. Opiate drug Morphine , the addictive pain killer, works by an increase in Nitric Oxide release. Nitroglycerin and Amyl Nitrite tablets serve as vasodilators because they are converted to

Nitric Oxide in the body, to ease angina pain (heart pain). Sufficient amounts of Nitric Oxide in blood controls Blood Pressure. When the human body reaches the age of 27 years, the secretion of nitric oxide is at its peak. As one gets older, the production of nitric oxide in the human body declines gradually.

CHAPTER 7

Healing in Buddhism

7.1 Healing in Buddhism

In the wake of the "mindfulness revolution" in the past two decades, it is now common for many people around the globe to think of meditation primarily as a tool for cultivating mental health and well-being. Yet even as this perspective has become mainstream, more committed practitioners of Buddhism have articulated the critique that an exclusive interest in health outcomes is misguided, vastly inferior to an "authentic" practice of meditation focused on liberation. A broader perspective, one that looks at the history and the wider context of contemporary Buddhist practice worldwide, may help to examine—and question—some of the assumptions behind both sides of this debate.

Perhaps most surprisingly for some, there can be no doubt that this-worldly health-seeking practices have been closely associated with Buddhism since its very inception. Practical tools for mental and physical healing—including but not limited to meditation—were adapted and elaborated across virtually all of Asia for most of Buddhism's history, and indeed have often played a major role in the popularization of the religion in its new host cultures. Approaching this topic from a historical and global perspective, however, also brings to light ruptures with the past that have affected and reshaped modern Buddhist notions of health and healing.

Buddhism's connection with health goes as far back as the Pali canon, the primary collection of early scriptures that was first written down in Sri Lanka beginning in the 1st century B.C.E. and is assumed to represent an earlier oral tradition from India. While medical knowledge was by no means the primary concern of these texts, it was mentioned tangentially in a great number of medical metaphors, similes, and analogies, such as the frequent comparison of the Buddha to a physician and his teachings to medicine. A number of parables and narratives involve doctors, surgery, medicines, and other health matters, such as the famous "parable of the poisoned arrow," in which the Buddha discourages questioning that would distract a person from dealing with the existential problem at hand. Meditation texts such as the influential Satipatthana Sutta describe the physical components of the body—the organs, fluids, and elements (earth, water, fire, wind, and so on)—in ways that are strikingly similar to lists appearing in Indian Ayurvedic medical treatises from around the same period. Additionally, the Pali Vinaya, or monastic code, lists numerous contemporary medicines and procedures, and specifies whether the Buddha approved or disapproved of each one in turn. Finally, several stories in the sutta literature tell of the healing powers of reflecting or contemplating certain aspects of the dharma, such as the seven factors of awakening. These stories seem not to refer to structured meditation practice, but rather to claim that even simply being reminded of the dharma has a healing effect on the body.

Less tangential, and more relevant to health care per se, are narratives in which the Buddha is personally involved in healing activities. In one iconic story in the Vinaya, the Buddha comes across a monk with dysentery who has been abandoned by his fellow monastics. After caring for the monk with Ananda's help, the Buddha admonishes the sangha. "Whoever would tend to me," he says, "should tend to the sick." Other sections of the monastic code discourage monks and nuns from engaging in healing or other "worldly arts" for personal profit, and the Buddha's words in this story are meant to advocate that monastics care for one another, not for the laity. However, Buddhists the world over have interpreted the story of the monk with dysentery—which appears in many versions in multiple languages—as an imperative to become involved in healing, nursing, and palliative care as an embodiment of the Buddhist values of compassion and merit-making.

With the linking up of the Silk Road and maritime trade routes across Asia, Buddhism began a period of expansion from the 1st century B.C.E. to the 8th century C.E. Aspects of Indian medicine that are reflected in early Pali and Sanskrit texts—stories, metaphors, models of the body, specific therapies—were embedded in Buddhist tradition and came along for the ride. Just as some might refer to Buddhism today as one of the first "world religions" in the sense that it expanded beyond its original cultural and linguistic context, one might similarly think of Buddhist healing as one of the first "world medicines."

7.2 Bhaiṣajyaguru (Medicine Buddha: The Earliest Healer in Buddhism)

Bhaiṣajyaguru is the Buddha-healing and medicine in Mahāyāna Buddhism. Commonly referred to as the "Medicine Buddha", he is described as a doctor who cures suffering using the medicine of his teachings.

Bhaiṣajyaguru's original name and title was rāja (King), but Xuanzang translated it as Tathāgata (Buddha). Subsequent translations and commentaries followed Xuanzang in describing him as a Buddha. The image of Bhaiṣajyaguru is usually expressed with a canonical Buddha-like form holding a gallipot and, in some versions, possessing blue skin. Though also considered to be a guardian of the East, in most cases Akshobhya is given that role. As an exceptional case, the honzon of Mount Kōya's Kongōbu Temple was changed from Akshobhya to Bhaiṣajyaguru.

Bhaiṣajyaguru is described in the eponymous Bhaiṣajyaguru-guru-vaiḍūrya-prabhā-rāja Sūtra, commonly called the Medicine Buddha Sutra, as a bodhisattva who made twelve great vows. On achieving Buddhahood, he became the Buddha of the eastern pure land of Vaiḍūryanirbhāsa "Pure Lapis Lazuli". There, he is attended to by two bodhisattvas symbolizing the light of the sun and the light of the moon respectively.

7.2.1 The Twelve Vows of Medicine Buddha

The Twelve Vows of the Medicine Buddha upon attaining Enlightenment, according to the Medicine Buddha Sutra are:

1. I vow that my body shall shine as beams of brilliant light on this infinite and boundless world, showering on all beings, getting rid of their ignorance and worries with my teachings. May all beings be like me, with a perfect status and character, upright mind and soul, and finally attaining enlightenment like the Buddha.

2. I vow that my body be like crystal, pure and flawless, radiating rays of splendid light to every corner, brightening up and enlightening all beings with wisdom. With the blessings of compassion, may all beings strengthen their spiritual power and physical energy, so that they could fulfil their dreams on the right track.

3. I vow that I shall grant by means of boundless wisdom, all beings with the inexhaustible things that they require, and relieving them from all pains and guilt resulting from materialistic desires. Although clothing, food, accommodation and transport are essentials, it should be utilized wisely as well. Besides self-consumption, the remaining should be generously shared with the community so that all could live harmoniously together.

4. I vow to lead those who have gone astray back to the path of righteousness. Let them be corrected and returned to the Buddha way for enlightenment.

5. I vow that I shall enable all sentient beings to observe precepts for spiritual purity and moral conduct. Should there be any relapse or violation, they shall be guided by repentance. Provided they sincerely regret their wrong-doings, and vow for a change with constant prayers and strong faith in the Buddha, they could receive the rays of forgiveness, recover their lost moral and purity.

6. I vow that all beings who are physically disabled or sick in all aspects be blessed with good health, both physically and mentally.

All who pay homage to Buddha faithfully will be blessed.

7. I vow to relieve all pain and poverty of the very sick and poor. The sick be cured, the helpless be helped, the poor be assisted.

8. I vow to help women who are undergoing sufferings and tortures and seeking for transformation into men. By hearing my name, paying homage and praying, their wishes would be granted and ultimately attain Buddhahood.

9. I vow to free all beings from evil thought and its control. I shall lead them onto the path of light through inculcating them with righteousness and honour so that they will walk the Buddha way.

10. I vow to save prisoners who have genuinely repented and victims of natural disasters. My supreme powers will bless those who are sincere and be freed from sufferings.

11. I vow to save those who suffer from starvation and those who committed a crime to obtain food. If they hear my name and faithfully cherish it, I shall lead them to the advantages of Dharma and favour them with the best food that they may eventually lead a tranquil and happy life.

12. I vow to save those who suffer from poverty, tormented by mosquitoes and wasps day and night. If they come across my name, cherish it with sincerity and practice dharma to strengthen their merits, they will be able to achieve their wishes.

7.2.2 Dharani and Mantra

In the Bhaiṣajyaguru-guru-vaiḍūrya-prabhā-rāja Sūtra, the Medicine Buddha is described as having entered into a state of samadhi called "Eliminating All the Suffering and Afflictions of Sentient Beings." From this samadhi state he spoke the Medicine Buddha Dharani.

namo bhagavate bhaiṣajyaguru vaiḍūryaprabharājāya tathāgatāya arahate samyaksambuddhāya tadyathā: oṃ bhaiṣajye bhaiṣajye mahābhaiṣajya-samudgate svāhā

The last line of the dharani is used as Bhaiṣajyaguru's short form mantra. There are several other mantras for the Medicine Buddha as well that are used in different schools of Vajrayana Buddhism.

7.3 Role in Japanese Buddhism in Healing

Starting in the 7th century in Japan, Yakushi was prayed to in the place of Ashuku (Akshobhya). Some of Yakushi's role has been taken over by Jizō (Ksitigarbha), but Yakushi is still invoked in the traditional memorial services for the dead.

Older temples, those mostly found in the Tendai and Shingon sects, especially those around Kyoto, Nara and the Kinki region often have Yakushi as the center of devotion, unlike later Buddhist sects which focus on Amitabha Buddha or Kannon Bodhisattva almost exclusively. Often, when Yakushi is the center of devotion in a Buddhist temple, he is flanked by the Twelve Heavenly Generals, who were twelve yaksha generals who had been converted through hearing the Bhaiṣajyaguruvaiḍūryaprabhārāja Sūtra.

Wherever this sutra circulates or wherever there are sentient beings who hold fast to the name of the Medicine Buddha [Yakushi Buddha] and respectfully make offerings to him, whether in villages, towns, kingdoms or in the wilderness, we [the Twelve Generals] will all protect them. We will release them from all suffering and calamities and see to it that all their wishes are fulfilled.

7.4 Role of Tibetan Buddhism in Healing

The practice of Medicine Buddha, the Supreme Healer (or Sangye Menla in Tibetan) is not only a powerful method for healing and increasing healing powers both for oneself and others, also for overcoming the inner sickness of attachment, hatred, and ignorance, thus to meditate on the Medicine Buddha can help decrease physical and mental illness and suffering.

The Medicine Buddha mantra is held to be extremely powerful for healing of physical illnesses-healing and purification of negative karma. One form of practice based on the Medicine Buddha is done when one is stricken by disease. The patient is to recite the long Medicine Buddha mantra 108 times over a glass of water. The water is now believed to be blessed by the power of the mantra and the blessing of the Medicine Buddha himself, and the patient is to drink the water. This practice is then repeated each day until the illness is cured.

7.5 Buddhist Perspective on Health and Healing

7.5.1 Understanding Health in Buddhism

The meaning of health relates to the ways of supervising health including the ways to explore the causes of illness, the ways to be concerned for patients, or the ways to encourage health. Health is the state of wholly free from all anguish that is nibbana. Lord Buddha said in the Māgaṇḍiya Sutta that: "This is that health, this is that nibbāna" (M.I 511 in Horner, 1989: 190) or "Health is the highest gain, nibbāna the highest bliss; And of ways, the Eightfold leads to deathlessness, to security10." (M.I 510 in ibid.: 189). Illness is the outcome of karma (law of cause and effect), therefore an unavoidable outcome of actions either in this life or in one's previous life. Health is holistic in nature (that is, it connects between mind and body); therefore, mental cures are important. Few Buddhists are of belief that a spiritually alert person will not become sick. If illness occurs in human body, then people are of belief that a cure can be found by thinking positively or using medicinal herbs. Few presume that if they expose their body to harsh natural conditions, they are less likely to fall sick because their immune system will be braced up.

7.5.2 Understanding Healing

'He who tends to the sick tends to me' – The Buddha.

Healing is a trail of activities for the restitution of physical form from a troubled, diseased or damaged organism. Healing is many a time compared with the thought of in-depth, vivid and spirituality. Spiritual healing shows the path to the shield of health, highlights on meditation, specific movements of the body so that the health of the person is rescheduled to its normal state. The Buddha expected his followers to look after the sick. A caregiver should also be sympathetic, kind and should not be nauseated by saliva, phlegm, urine, stools or sores of the patient. He recommended the contemplation of the Seven Limbs of Enlightenment which are 1. mindfulness; 2. investigation of things (dharmas); 3. striving; 4. joy; 5. serenity; 6. meditative trance (samadhi); and 7. equanimity. Therefore, meditation on these factors was a process of overcoming inner poisons of envy, anger and illusion. Liberation is the outcome of healing according to Buddha. The Buddha said "Beings of the future may hear the names of the two Bodhisattvas", that is, the King of Healing (Bhaisajya-raja) and Supreme Healer (Bhaisajya-samudgate) by achieving the five prerequisites—

1. One should shower loving kindness on the others.
2. One should abstain from following unwholesome deeds in life.
3. One should have peace and calmness in life.
4. One should listen to the texts of Mahayana and Theravada.
5. One should believe and have faith on the eternity of Buddha and one must always abide
by the truth.

7.5.3 Buddhist Healing Practices

Gautama Buddha discovered that enlightenment could come only when there was a healthy mind in a healthy body. Spiritual development can only come when one avoids hedonism (the pursuit of pleasure), devotion to pleasure or asceticism, mortification of the body. Healing in Buddhism involves surrendering oneself and liberating his mind so that they can work for the good of the people.

Welfare of others is the key to one's own healthiness. Karma is the architect of all happiness and misery. Buddhism affirms that for long-lasting healing to take place, it is essential to heal not only the existing disease with proper medications and other methods of treatment, but also the root of the disease, which initiates from the mind. This brings in the concept of "ultimate healing". This promotes the notion of ridding all the negative thoughts away from the mind of the individuals, as a healthy mind is the secret to one's healthy body. One must not be selfish in nature; it is only then that he/she can heal faster in life. Kind words and acts are helpful in bringing in expectations and console to a vulnerable patient. Metta and Karuna are inspirational sentiments (brahamavihara). Narration of the enlightenment aspects (Bojjhanga) is functional in healing physical disorders. The ten perceptions put forward by Buddha on healing are based on the 1. impermanence, 2. egolessness, 3. pollution of the body, 4. evil consequences (of bodily survival), 5. abolition (of sensual pleasures), 6. aloofness, 7. cessation, 8. disillusionment with the entire world, 9. impermanence of all things, and 10. mindfulness of breathing. It is thus by these ways that Buddha has proclaimed the different spiritual healing practices to his followers.

7.5.4 Healing and Psychotherapy

Well-known and celebrated psychologists like William James, Carl Jung, and Eric Fromm viewed that much of the importance in Buddhist philosophy is in its constructive impact on mental health. Contemporary health practitioners have gathered facts which maintain the fact that Buddhism possesses the secret to the healing of the mind of the individuals. Mental health can be looked after properly by following the principles laid down in Buddhism. Psychotherapy is defined as a treatment of emotional, behavioural, character disorders based chiefly upon "verbal or nonverbal communication". Buddhism is a course of mind schooling. Buddhist psychotherapy is founded on the Buddhist model of the cause of mental suffering (that is, the noble fourfold truths) and the conceptions of attachment, eternalness and adhering to the fact of self as the forces of mental suffering. It deals with self-knowledge,

Judgement, outlook and measures to reduce the psychological suffering. The Buddhist philosophy talks about the human mind and its pathological and non-pathological sections. In Abhidhamma (which is the higher teaching of the Buddha) analyses the human mental progression. In Abhidhamma man is portrayed as a psycho-physical being consisting of both mind and matter. The Buddhist Jathaka story book deals with the DSM (Diagnostic and Statistical Manual of Mental Disorders) which is based on mental illnesses. Buddhist psychotherapy is based on the Buddhist replica of the cause of mental affliction. It has a constructive impact on mental health and it can be used to take care of a wide variety of mental illnesses of human beings.

7.5.5 Meditation and Healing

Meditation is a coordinated mind-body performance and deliberate effort that helps in converting the mind. In Buddhism meditation is observed as one of the processes of the Eight-Fold Path. The theory of mindfulness is based on Vipassana meditation technique. Mindfulness is explained as a practice of knowledge to put concentration on moment-by-moment understanding with an approach of inquisitiveness, openness, and acceptance. Vipassana meditation calls to mind a state of increased perceptual lucidity and decreased programmed reaction. Metta Meditation or Loving-kindness Meditation is largely used by many admirers. It increases the feelings of kindness and empathy for self and others. Anapanasati meditation or 'mindfulness of breathing' is a meditation developed by the Buddha in the Maha-Satipatthana Sutta which is the Great Discourse on the Foundations of Mindfulness. Mindful breathing increases oxygen intake and has stress reducing impact. These processes in turn make the human beings to heal faster and lead a healthy lifestyle.

7.5.6 Prayer and Healing in Buddhism

"Just as the soft rains fill the streams,
Pour into the rivers, and join together in the oceans,
So may the power of every moment of your goodness

Flow forth to awaken and heal all beings–
Those here now, those gone before, those yet to come."
----Lord Buddha

Prayer, or chanting in Buddhism, is generally in Pali and is proposed to pay reverence to the Triple Gems--the Buddha (the Enlightened One), the Dhamma (the Teaching), the Sangha (the Order)--and to remind the individuals of the noble qualities of Buddha and his instructions. It tries to secure blessings and safeguard of oneself. One of the widely known prayers for its healing effect is bojjhanga paritta. Paritta implies "protection" and bojjhanga refers to the seven factors of enlightenment (bodhinana). It is chanted to ward off illness and to promote healing among individuals. It is a tradition among the Theravada community to chant prayers for the welfare of the sick. Spinning the written form of the mantra around in a Mani wheel (prayer wheel) is also believed to give the individuals healing in all aspects of one's life. 16 It is believed that the truth of the Dhamma and the Buddha's boundless compassion embodied in the verses chanted have great power to promote healing.

7.5.7 The Concept of Giving and Healing

Dana or giving is another way of healing of the individuals. It involves the giving of material gifts (amisadana) to individual monks or to the poor and the down-trodden; the giving of spiritual gifts (dhammadana) to those who are in need of it. It also involves the sharing of time, power, wisdom, and experience for the benefit as well as welfare of others. People who practice dana is seen by the practitioners to heal faster. Voluntary offerings and doing good for the people, enhances one's soul and spirit and brings in positive impact in the minds of the individuals which thereby helps the individuals to heal from their ailments. Even if dana alone cannot restore to health the deadly disease, it can heal the mind by eroding away all the negative thoughts. As the mind can manipulate the body, physical health recovers when the mind is sound. This happens when dana is given in true compassion, consideration and devoid of any self-interest. Therefore, such altruistic feelings in one lead one to reach nibbana which is the ultimate goal of Buddhism.

7.5.8 Healing in Tripitaka

Tripitaka is a Pali word meaning three baskets. It contains the three baskets of teachings: a Sūtra Piṭaka, a Vinaya Piṭaka and an Abhidharma Piṭaka. To cure any kind of diseases of both the body as well as the mind, the Buddha devoted his complete life to passing down the information of the Tripitaka. He emphasized in the holy book that one must start the treatment of any disease in the human beings by studying the minds of the individuals. If the mind can be healed of its wound then a person can have a quick recuperation in his health condition.

7.6 More on Healing in Buddhism

Buddhism is an optimistic system and proposes a cure or healing. Whatever has a cause can be remedied by removing the cause. The way to remove the cause is known as the Noble Eightfold Path It includes: 1. Right View, 2. Right Intentions, 3. Right Speech, 4. Right Action, 5. Right Livelihood, 6. Right Effort, 7. Right Mindfulness, and 8. Right Concentration.

The system is a total spiritual discipline involving the body and mind. It aims not only at improving life, but also to liberate one from the bondage to finite existence and repeated reincarnations in the stream of births and deaths. The goal is ultimately Nirvana.

Though Buddhism aims at a final solution to the problems of existence, it also provides a pattern for living holistically in this world. Initially, it was for monks but its principles have relevance for ordinary life. The system of eight aspects of Buddhist spirituality begins with Right Views, which contributes to mental health. By having a proper and realistic understanding of the self as a dynamic, evolving process, we may become more adaptable and flexible confronting life situations. Accepting the impermanence of life and things, we may become more tranquil. There is a famous story about a mother, Kisa Gotami. Her baby had died and she was distraught. She pleaded with the Buddha to restore her child. The Buddha agreed, on the condition that she bring a mustard seed from a home where there had never been a death. She searched but could not find such a home. She gained insight and returned to the Buddha, now understanding that her child suffered death as all others do. She then accepted the death of her child.

The five aspects of Right Intentions, Right Speech, Right Action, Right Livelihood, Right Effort, take up the inner and outer dimensions of our life activities. Buddhism focuses on the activities of the mind, body and speech, which are involved in all our activities. These should be integrated and in harmony with our understanding of reality. It involves ethical, spiritual and physical dimensions of living.

Right Mindfulness, and Right Concentration are perhaps the best-known features because we hear so much about meditation in Buddhism and other traditions. Mindfulness is maintaining a focus of attention, an awareness of what is going on without focusing on a particular objects. It is a detached observation of what is happening within us and around us in the present moment.

Right Concentration describes the unification of all mental functions on an object of meditation. It involves deep attentiveness and tranquillity. Essentially meditation enables a detachment from the distracting flow of stimuli that assault the mind and permits an inner unification of the psyche to develop. As Jon Kabat-Zinn has written on mindfulness and meditation, it is like climbing out of a raging current in a stream and watching the stream from the bank. This unification can become the basis for more creative activity or involvement. We call it centring or working from the inner quietude of our minds. In meditation our egoism and its stake in things is set aside, allowing other perceptions and alternatives to emerge. When people get angry and wish to retaliate for a hurt, we say count to 10. That is, give space for the mind to truly assess the situation and find a more proper response. Meditation is a more developed spiritual approach to our problems.

Buddhism contributes to mental and physical health through encouraging the development of a unified and centred personal approach to our life affairs. It assists the well-being of the body through the body-mind synthesis in which the physical elements and the psychological and spiritual dimensions are all part of a continuum and a dynamic interrelation. In the west, we are prone to distinguish flesh and body, matter and spirit, body and soul, etc. However, Buddhism sees things as a process in which all features of existence are interdependent and ultimately one. According to Jon Kabat-Zinn:

"Since the mind plays such an important part in people's experience of their bodies and what's possible in their lives, it seemed that a hospital would be a perfect place to train people in meditative awareness. They could optimize their inner resources for healing and take responsibility for their health."

According to Kabat-Zinn, meditation-mindfulness can help in reducing stress, pain and depression. By letting go of stress, one may even enhance the body's self-healing powers. Studies have shown that anger and hostility affect our health. According to one study, they influence heart disease.

The role of Buddhism in creating healthy life-conditions does not involve miracle cures, but employs methods for dealing with the emotional elements that accompany pain and even intensify it. The Dalai Lama indicates that happiness is not merely a feeling, but is the result of right thinking. Our problems begin with negative thinking. However, negative thought is not intrinsic to our minds and the mind can be trained to develop positive attitudes of love, compassion, patience and generosity. This approach has taken form in what is known as cognitive therapy, which seeks the source of negative and self-defeating ideas. Right thinking is not just a matter of correct information and belief. Right thinking in Buddhism means a transformation in one's understanding of the nature of existence.

Enlightenment is transformation of one's total being.

There are forms of therapy based in Buddhism. From the Pure Land tradition, there is the method of Naikan therapy which is a system of introspection to make one aware of our interdependence with others and to arouse the sense of gratitude for their contribution to our lives. This positive force can offset personal problems that induce negativity.

There is also Morita therapy based in Zen Buddhism and is reality therapy, that is living in harmony with reality as it is. According to Morita therapy, "the gap between the world as it is and the world as we think it ought to be, can fill with pain. When we do not look at the way we think we ought to look and when we cannot accomplish our goals as rapidly and effortlessly as we think we ought to be able to accomplish them, we worry that either there is something wrong with us or we are victims of injustice. Rather than futilely railing against nature or trying to force it into complying with our ideals, we can learn to live in harmony with it. To live in harmony with nature, we accept as parts of ourselves our talents, imperfections, painful feelings and real desires."

Buddhism has all the elements of folk religions common around the world. There are Buddhas and bodhisattvas who offer healing and prayers requesting their blessing. There are shrines and services where people seek alleviation and healing from their illnesses. Among the most common figures are: Yakushi Buddha, the Buddha of healing; Kuan-yin, the Bodhisattva of compassion (a central figure in healing); and Jizo Bodhisattva who cares for children and the dead and also heals. The Heart Sutra, a profound philosophy, is often recited in times of disaster and personal problems. There are practitioners who are considered to have special powers for healing and are consulted for many problems. There are practitioners in this community, some well-known and others not.

Buddhism is a complex of spiritual principles, practices and practitioners all designed to enhance the life of people corresponding to the level of their understanding and devotion. The heart of Buddhism is the Buddha's compassion, which takes many forms and applications.

7.7 Healing in Early Buddhism (Last days of the Buddha's Life)

When studying the practice of healing in early Buddhism, a central source of information can be found in Vinaya narratives. In the Pāli Vinaya, the cures effected by the royal physician Jīvaka stand out as testimonies of an impressive medical ability, going even as far as the successful performance of cranial surgery. Understandably such material has been somewhat at the forefront of studies of healing as reflected in early Buddhist texts. However, Jīvaka reportedly learnt his art in Takkasilā, so his abilities should be understood as reflecting general ancient medical knowledge and skills. In other words, aside from the fact that he was a Buddhist lay follower and offered free medical service to Buddhist monastics, there is nothing particularly Buddhist about his cures.

The Buddha's overcoming of a disease

The first case is of a prolonged narrative of the events that preceded the Buddha's demise, found in the Mahāparinibbāna-sutta and its parallels. The passage in question describes how the Buddha overcame what appears to have been a rather serious case of illness. In what follows in the Dīrghaāgama record of this event, followed by studying the means used by the Buddha to recover, is the translated portion has its placing within the overall narrative after the Buddha had met the famous courtesan Ambapālī and accepted the gift of her grove.

At that time in that region there was a famine and the grain was expensive; it was difficult to get food by begging. The Buddha said to Ānanda: 'Tell all the monks who are now within this region to gather in the assembly hall.' He replied: 'Yes, indeed.' Having received the instruction, he informed those far and near that they should all gather in the assembly hall. Then, when the great community of those within this region had gathered, Ānanda said to the Buddha: 'The great community has gathered, may the Noble One know the time has come [for instructing them].' At that time the Blessed One rose from his seat and approached the assembly hall. He sat on a prepared seat and said to the monks: 'There is a famine in this region and it is difficult to get food by begging. You should each divide into groups and go to Vesālī or the Vajjī country to spend the rains retreat, according to where you have friends, so that hopefully you will not experience want. I will spend the rains retreat here alone with Ānanda. Why is that? Lest there be deprivations.' Then the monks received the instruction and carried it out. The Buddha and Ānanda remained alone.

Afterwards, during that summer's rainy season, a disease arose in the Buddha's body and his whole body was completely in pain. The Buddha thought to himself: 'Now a disease has arisen in me and the whole body is in much pain. None of my disciples is with me. It would not be appropriate for me to take up [entry into final] Nirvāṇa now. I shall energetically with my own strength keep on living.' Then the Blessed One came out of his hut and sat in a cool spot. Having seen him, Ānanda quickly approached him and said: 'Now seeing the Venerable One's face it seems [to me] that the disease has diminished.' Ānanda further said: 'When the Blessed One was ill, my mind was in fear and tied up with worry. I was lost and confused, no longer recognizing the directions. Yet I slightly recovered myself as your breath had not stopped, thinking quietly [to myself]: "The Tathāgata has not yet attained Parinirvāṇa, the Eye of the World has not yet ceased, the great Dharma has not yet suffered a loss. Why has there up to now not been a [final] instruction to the community of disciples?" The Buddha said to Ānanda: 'What does the community of monks expect from me? If someone were to say of himself: "I manage the community of monks, I control the community of monks"; such a person should give a [final] instruction to the community. The Tathāgata does not say: "I manage the community of monks I control the community of monks." Why should he give a [final] instruction to the community? Ānanda the Dharma I have taught is already complete, within and without. I never kept to myself, what I have seen and realized. Indeed, I am already old, having been eighty years for some time. My body is just like an old cart which by being expediently patched up and adjusted reaches the place to which it is going. By expedient strength I can maintain it alive a little [longer], through my own strength. and energy, putting up with these painful feelings. When I do not give attention to any signs and enter sign-less concentration, then my body is at ease and there are no afflictions.

Therefore, Ānanda, you should be a light to yourself, a light in the Dharma, without another light; you should be a refuge to yourself, a refuge in the Dharma, without another refuge. How can you be a light to yourself, a light in the Dharma, without another light, a refuge to yourself, a refuge in the Dharma, without another refuge? Ānanda, a monk contemplates the body internally, diligently without laxity, with undistracted mindfulness, removing desire and discontent for the world. He contemplates the body externally … contemplates the body internally and externally, diligently without laxity, with undistracted mindfulness, removing desire and discontent for the world. He contemplates feeling … mental states … dharmas …also in this way. Ānanda, this is reckoned being a light to yourself, a light in the Dharma, without another light, being a refuge to yourself, a refuge in the Dharma, without another refuge.' The Buddha said to Ānanda: 'After my Parinirvāṇa, those who are able to cultivate this teaching are truly my disciples and foremost in the training.'

In the above-translated extract the Buddha falls ill while being alone with Ānanda, and this then causes mental affliction to Ānanda. In response to being told of this mental affliction, the Buddha gives him a teaching on self-reliance through mindfulness practice. The way the Buddha overcame his own physical disease, however, was through making an effort. In addition, sign-less concentration receives a highlight as being particularly helpful for bringing about a sense of physical ease.

The Buddha's actual overcoming of his disease in the Theravāda version in the Dīgha-nikāya is similar. The passage reads as follows: 'Then the Blessed One dwelled, having overcome this illness with energy, determined on the life force. Then the illness of the Blessed One abated.' Later on, the Theravāda version also refers to the sign-less concentration as what helped the Buddha to dwell without pain. In the Sarvāstivāda/Mūlasarvāstivāda version preserved in Sanskrit fragments, sign-lessness already features in the Buddha's overcoming of his actual disease, together with energy.

CHAPTER 8

Healing in Sufism

"Mankind! there has come to you a guidance from your Lord and a healing for your hearts, and for those who believe a guidance and a mercy." [Quran, 4, 57]

Healing is a natural gift inherent in every human being which can be used to heal oneself as well as others. The Islamic Terminology for healing is Shifaʿ. Muslims have a staunch belief that each word of the divine book "Quran" carries Shifaʿ, however in the holy tradition; the Prophet Muhammad (SAW) mentioned the healing properties of specific verses and section (Surah) of the Quran for different remedies. The major characteristics of Sufi practitioner is the utilization of the healing properties of blessed verses of the Quran.

Just as the most prominent characteristic or attribute of Allah is His compassion for humanity, so, too, do the Sufis strive to spread and bestow this among the people. Of all the service to humanity, that which is considered superior is the healing of the sick and suffering. Certainly, the great proportion of Sufi shaykhs have been known for their ability to effect results in the realm of healing various ailments. Of course, it is Allah Who does the actual healing, the shaykh being only the agent for the will of Allah, exalted is He!

The philosophy of Sufism is best summed up in the words of the final kliutbah (sermon) of Hazrat Khwaja Muinuddin Chishti (r.a.), which he delivered to his followers just one month before his demise. The great saint said:

Love all and hate none.
Mere talk of peace will avail you naught.
Mere talk of God and religion will not take you far.
Bring out all of the latent powers of your being

and reveal the full magnificence
of your immortal self.
Be surcharged with peace and joy,
And scatter them wherever you are
and wherever you go.
Be a blazing fire of truth,
Be a beauteous blossom of love
And be a soothing balm of peace. With your spiritual light,
dispel the darkness of ignorance;
dissolve the clouds of discord and war
and spread goodwill, peace, and harmony among the people.
Never seek any help, charity, or favours
from anybody except God.
Never go to the courts of kings,
but never refuse to bless and help the needy and the poor,
the widow, and the orphan, if they come to your door.
This is your mission, to serve the people ...

8.1 Early Healing in Sufism

The first healer, Aba, began his career at twenty and took an apprenticeship with older religious healers. He claimed that after a long period of fasting he heard voices telling him to stop his fast and receive the gift of healing powers as a reward. His healing methods consisted of placing a copper key between each patient's fingers and examining the patient by touching the forehead, tracing the pulse and manipulating the diseased part of the body. Occasionally, pieces of paper, inscribed with quotations from the Quran were placed on the affected area. Evil spirits were exorcised by bathing the patient, at which ceremony the patient was required to provide white cloth, chickens and other items.

The second healer began his career when he was 6 years old. Then his advice would be administered after a spirit consultation: this facility was obtained by being 'taken away' by the spirits for 3 days. He did not enter trance to communicate with the spirits. However, after marrying, at 17, his methods changed, and he could only cure when possessed by the spirits. Trance was achieved after calling up the spirits and their advice to the conveyed to the patient. Treatment is made up of herbs.

The last healer was a female, and belonged to an affluent middle class. She began healing after a 3-month illness, when she started speaking to her husband in a strange voice and announcing herself to be Cik Maris (ibid .). The spirit agreed to leave her body , and during this trance the healer spoke in a strange language. He identified illnesses by placing a broken needle on a plate and a magnet or a dagger on the affected part. After diagnosis the healer again consulted the spirits and conveyed conditionally, and she then told her husband that she had healing powers given to her, the persistence of which required sacrifice to be made regularly. Curing for her involved trance and possession by the spirit Cik Maris. The patient and the spirit commune and advice and herbs were usually suggested after a fee was paid. In difficult cases Cik Maris might issue an amulet. After the healer had recovered from her trance she claimed to remember nothing.

8.2 Spiritual Healing Practices in Sufism

Spiritual healing is defined as the awakening of the self, awakening those qualities of the human soul which have positive impact in their lives such as love and compassion, patience, tolerance, forgiveness, contentment, a sense of responsibility, a sense of peace and harmony that brings happiness to both self and others around him. Spiritual healing opens one's heart to divine love and leads to inner awakening. From the Sufi point of view, "spiritual healing" is an endeavour to "clear the cloak" or " images" that captured on the hearts of people, causing to encounter detachment from The Divine, themselves, and each other. Sufi healing practices are based on the Quran, hadith and Sunnah (the recorded acts and the sacred saying of the Prophet Muhammad (PBUH)) and also the examples from the life of the Prophet and his companions. The role of Sufi Spiritual Healing is not only to cure the suffering humanity but to teach them the ways to awaken the God gifted hidden treasure.

Some are gifted with healing ability that people recognize them as natural healers while others are given the ability of healing in transmission (as disciples in sufi order) and others through their inner calling take upon this or perform healing out of compassion. Some healers are unaware of their healing ability yet they help others to heal, thus they are saved from their ego-based claim since behind all healing is as-Shafi (the One Healer).

The significant aspect of Sufi healing is the transmission of energy from a qualified guide in the path himself is connected through chain of transmission through his earlier masters, all the way to the Prophet (PBUH) and eventually to Allah. The Sufi healer never claims self-seeking of himself or herself being the healer, but always stress upon being a medium / instrument of Allah Who is the Sole Healer. Sufi healers act as a mediator or harbinger who draw the energy from divine power, One Invisible, Unseen All Intelligent Source and transmit to the sufferer. The most popular method to draw the divine energy is through meditation. Meditation is being practiced by all religions saint according to their belief system. Islamic Sufi tradition is rich in the practice of Spiritual Healing, it is a belief of the Muslim that illness comes from Allah and Allah alone is the one who can heal it.

The Chishtiyyah Order of Sufis, one of the four largest in Islam, has carried on this tradition of serving the downtrodden of humanity-the sick and ailing-for the past eight hundred years, ever since the founding of the order. A large herbal-medicine clinic is attached to the dargah premises at Ajmer, and all persons coming there (upward of sixty thousand per day) are provided whatever treatment they need, free of charge or obligation. Masha' Allah!

If Allah touch thee with affliction,
none can remove it but He. (Qur'an 6:17)

The above verse has been written to provide specific means to attain a true health of the body, mind, and soul. For these suggestions to be put into practice successfully requires only the state of being known as tawwakul Allah (trust in Almighty Allah).

8.2.1 Types of Healing Methods

Some of the known healing methods can be categorized in four types:

(i) Modern (counselling therapy)

(ii) Traditional (reiki, acupressure, acupuncture, Ayurveda, herb remedies, homeopathy etc.)

(iii) Spiritual (yoga, tai chi, shiatsu, magnetism, hypnosis, breathing exercise, etc.), and

(iv) Divine Spiritual Power (meditation, zikr etc).

8.2.2 Healing, as mentioned in Quran

The Islamic Terminology for healing is Shifaʿ. Muslims have a staunch belief that each word of the divine book "Quran" carries Shifaʿ, however in the holy tradition; the Prophet Muhammad (SAW) mentioned the healing properties of specific verses and section (Surah) of the Quran for different remedies. The major characteristics of Sufi practitioner is the utilization of the healing properties of blessed verses of the Quran. Ruqya can be defined as a spiritual healing prayer in which verses from the Quran or the supplication taught by the Prophet Muhammad (PBUH) are practiced; hence Ruqya is a Sunnah of our beloved Prophet Muhammad (PBUH). The term Ruqya applied for the healing through recitation of the specific verses of the Quran or to make supplication by reciting specific words that are mentioned in the saying of the Prophet Muhammad (SAW).

Based on the Prophetic tradition the following are called "Ayat Al-Shifa" or s "There issues from within the bodies of the bee a drink of varying colours wherein is healing for mankind verses of healing, used in Sufi Spiritual Healing:

1. "And God shall heal the inner heart of the believers." [3, 14]

2. "Mankind! there has come to you a guidance from your Lord and a healing for your hearts, and for those who believe a guidance and a mercy." [4, 57]

3. "There issues from within the bodies of the bee a drink of varying colours wherein is healing for mankind." [5, 69]

4. "And We sent down in the Quran such things that have healing and mercy for the believers." [6, 82]

5. "And when I am ill, it is God who cures me." [7,80]

6. "And declare that the Quran is a guidance and healing for the believers." [8, 44]

Sufi Spiritual healing usually integrates energy work, as well as herbal and natural remedies belonging to ancient knowledge and other healing techniques principally used by Prophet Muhammad (PBUH) himself. Sufi orders consider service to humanity the utmost duty and among this service they give the most importance to healing of the sick. Their method is called the Sufi Healing.

8.3 Healing Methods and Techniques practiced by the Sufis

In Arabic, nafs is the word for the body and its appetites. Nafs means all of the demands of the body-for food, for warmth, for fame and fortune (all of these include emotional needs or drives). All physical diseases can be marked out by one or more of these physical dimensions.

The word nafs has many meanings: breath, animal life, soul, self, a person, essence, and more. In Sufism, the progression of the soul is described by considering the evolution of the nafs, which manifests in human behaviour as one's entire character, personality, and behaviour. The nafsi-nm-mara is the commanding soul, which creates inordinate appetites. This is the condition of the nafs referred to when one occupies the station of egotism (maqam-an-nafs). The behaviours recommended in the Qur'an (shariat) are meant to control and subdue these inordinate appetites, leading the nafs to a more refined status. The soul that has been entirely purified is called nafsi kull, meaning "universal soul," which unites with Allah in the final stage of Sufism. However, even at the latest stages of Sufi practice, one cannot assume oneself to be immune to the blemishes of the soul.

There are three categories for health practices:

(i) Those related to the body;

(ii) For the mind or emotions; and

(iii) Those related to soul.

The paramount and ideal amongst these are the one related to the Soul. The practices involved for the soul are highly divine in nature and have blessings from God.

8.3.1 Medicine

There are numerous sorts of materials used to influence positive change in Sufi healing practices. Medicine contains spiritual quality, for example, words from the Holy Quran, or can be as merely physical as chicken soup. Numerous remedies are a mix of "profound" and "material" cures. Since Sufis see all power structures to be both divine and material, these types are utilized here for the advancement.

8.3.2 Spiritual Medicine

1) Suras and Verses from the Quran

Allah ordained in the Quran that His Book of Wisdom is healing and mercy for those who believe. The Words of Allah in the Quran show a divine energy having spiritual powers that affects and heal the minds, heart and bodies as well as the some specific Surahs and Verses are prescribed for different ailments.

2) Allah's Most Beautiful Names/Attributes

Allah portrays Himself regarding qualities, called Allah's Most Beautiful Names. There are ninety-nine Names of Allah specified in the Holy Quran. It is mentioned in Hadith (sayings of the Prophet Muhammad (SAW) that each name/attribute has a significant quality as well as a particular energy connected with it and can be utilized to influence a longing result.

8.3.3 Material Medicine

1) Diet and Physical Exercise

The purpose of the Sufi healing is to seek the simplest and most persistent form of therapy. The key factors to maintain the health are nourishing food and healthy drinks as well as the appropriate amounts of physical exercises. For this purpose, the medicinal herbs are often prescribed.

2) Environment

The need of clean and pleasant environment is the requirement of the human being in which he flourishes. Adding to that purity and calmness provide an atmosphere negative energy and negative forces cannot hit upon a comfortable corner to rest or settle.

8.4 Sufism and Healing in the Middle East

Sufism is a devotional branch of Islam. Sufi sheikhs understand it as the spiritual side and interpretation of Islam. Over time Sufism developed into various orders that follow different leaders or masters ("sheikhs" in Arabic), all of which trace their origin back to the Prophet Mohammed. Today, Sufism has many followers throughout the Middle East, in the West, and globally. The orders that are perhaps best known to Western observers are the "Whirling Dervishes;' a term derived from the old Persian word Darwish, for a supplicant "one who goes door-to-door." "Dervish" applies equally to the sheikh and his followers, in the sense that the term connotes a "Sufi." The Whirling Dervishes belong to the Mawlawi Order, a term derived from "Mawlana," which means "our master" and refers to Jalal ad-Din Rumi (1207-1273), founder of the order. Members of the Mawlawi Order are geographically found from North Africa, the Arabian Peninsula, Turkey, Afghanistan, and into Southeast Asia.

The orthodox practices of Islam at various times in history were not accepted as outward practice by some of the Sufis. In the same way, some Sufi orders are also notable for their practice of deliberately caused bodily damage (DCBD) as a devotional practice, something not condoned by orthodox Islam. Under such circumstances, remarkable healing has been observed. The Tariqa Kasnazaniyah school (or "order") of Sufi mysticism in Baghdad, Iraq, is one of the largest Sufi school, in the Middle. Followers (dervishes) of this Sufi school have demonstrated instantaneous healing of DCBD. For example, dervishes have inserted a variety of sharp instruments (for example, spikes, skewers) into the body, hammered daggers into the skull bone and clavicle, and chewed and swallowed glass and sharp razor blades without harm to the body and with complete control over pain, bleeding, and infection, as well as rapid wound healing within 4 to 10 seconds. The Tariqa Kasnazaniyah School has described extraordinary phenomena of instantaneous healing of wounds from DCBD. The School's name, Tariqa Kasnazaniyah, can be attributed to three of its senior scholars: Imam Ali bin Abi Talib; Sheikh Abd al-Qadir al-Gaylani; and Sheikh Abd alKarim Shah al-Kasnazan.

During the period of isolation, Sheikh Abd al Karim experienced the sublime joy and love of drawing nearer to Allah. Following his period of isolation, dedication, and worshiping Allah, Allah's messenger, the Prophet Muhammad, gave him spiritual secrets related to power over nature. DCBD and other forms of healing are manifestations of these spiritual secrets. They include the extraordinary ability to tolerate without harm strong electrical shocks, immunity against snakes and scorpions, rapid healing from being stabbed or shot, protection against being burned, and healing of clinical conditions such as cancers, heart disease, infertility, depression, and psychosis.

The interaction of the three realms (or the activation of the physical and mental realms by the soul realm) is carried out by means of the spirit. Many people use the words "spirit" and "soul" to mean the same thing, yet they are distinctly different and separate. The spirit is what activates the physical level existence, including thought processes. The word for this spirit activator is nafs. It is activated at the point of the breath. The point of the lips where in-breath and out-breath unite is the link between life and death.

We can live without mental activity and without physical movement. But without breath, life ceases in a very short time. There are people who live without mental existence. Although an electroencephalograph shows that their brain waves are not functioning, they may be kept "alive" by mechanical means. They are called "brain dead," yet they are still regarded as living; we do not bury them. This means that there is something superior to this mental existence and physical existence. Such persons still have something left of life in them, and that something is the breath.

The Sufis consider that the breath of life exists and continues by virtue of the idhn, or permission of God, the One Who has created us all. What we call the Creator-God, Allah, Yahweh, or whatever-does not matter. In His ultimately reality, God is one. He gives His permission for human life to exist in the first place, and as long as that permission remains, we may draw breath in and out. Regardless of which system of healing we may wish to apply, or how skilled the practitioner, even if all the healers of the world came together, they could not counteract the idhn. When the permission is withdrawn, there is no more breath; life ceases.

CHAPTER 9

Healing in Christianity

The Bible says God promises us healing and long life. - TIME 10:10

Christians often look at the healing ministry of Christ from a biological and physiological perspective. Hence when they face physical ailments, they hope to witness the power of healing in their lives, they want God to intervene and restore their physical health.

In today's world, we distinguish between three different levels of healing:

(i) **Physically**, healing means the restoration of physical or mental functions;

(ii) Psychosocially, it means the restoration of harmonious social relationships, self-awareness and self-determination; and

(iii) Metaphysically and/or religiously, the focus is on processes which create and give meaning, even if restrictions on physical function remain – for instance, coming to terms by coping with serious illness or accidents ("coping with disease").

There is a growing hunger among people for a holistic form of healing that encompasses body, mind and spirit, social relationships and spirituality.

When afflicted with serious sickness, Roman Catholics often receive the Sacrament of Anointing of the Sick. The Rite includes both a proclamation of Scripture and certain liturgical actions, most notably the anointing with oil. Together, these create the opportunity for sick people to experience holistic healing from Jesus Christ. Together, these create the opportunity for sick people to experience holistic healing from Jesus Christ. This encounter can transform their own religious narrative into one more in keeping with Jesus' healing ministry, and can help them cope positively with their sickness.

9.1 Faith Healing in Christianity

Faith healing is the practice of prayer and gestures (such as laying on of hands) that are believed by some to elicit divine intervention in spiritual and physical healing, especially the Christian practice. Believers assert that the healing of disease and disability can be brought about by religious faith through prayer or other rituals that, according to adherents, can stimulate a divine presence and power. Religious belief in divine intervention does not depend on empirical evidence of an evidence-based outcome achieved via faith healing.

Claims that "a myriad of techniques" such as prayer, divine intervention, or the ministrations of an individual healer can cure illness have been popular throughout history. There have been claims that faith can cure blindness, deafness, cancer, HIV/AIDS, developmental disorders, anemia, arthritis, corns, defective speech, multiple sclerosis, skin rashes, total body paralysis, and various injuries. Recoveries have been attributed to many techniques commonly classified as faith healing. It can involve prayer, a visit to a religious shrine, or simply a strong belief in a supreme being.

Many people interpret the Bible, especially the New Testament, as teaching belief in, and the practice of, faith healing. According to a survey, nearly 72 percent of Americans said they believe that praying to God can cure someone, even if science says the person has an incurable disease. Unlike faith healing, advocates of spiritual healing make no attempt to seek divine intervention, instead believing in divine energy. Faith healing can be classified as a spiritual, supernatural, or paranormal topic, and, in some cases, belief in faith healing can be classified as magical thinking.

Regarded mainly as a Christian belief that God heals people through the power of the Holy Spirit, faith healing often involves the laying on of hands. It is also called supernatural healing, divine healing, and miracle healing, among other things. Healing in the Bible is often associated with the ministry of specific individuals including Elijah, Jesus and Paul.

Christian physician Reginald B. Cherry views faith healing as a pathway of healing in which God uses both the natural and the supernatural to heal. Being healed has been described as a privilege of accepting Christ's redemption on the cross. Matthew 8:17, after describing Jesus exorcising at sunset and healing all of the sick who were brought to him, quotes these miracles as a fulfillment of the prophecy in Isaiah 53:5: "He took up our infirmities and carried our diseases". When you are healed rests entirely on what the sovereign purposes of the Healer are. Proponents of faith healing say it may come later, and it may not come in this life. "The truth is that your healing may manifest in eternity, not in time".

9.1.1 New Testament

Parts of the four gospels in the New Testament say that Jesus cured physical ailments well outside the capacity of first-century medicine. Jesus' healing acts are considered miraculous and spectacular due to the results being impossible or statistically improbable. One example is the case of "a woman who had a discharge of blood for twelve years, and who had suffered much under many physicians, and had spent all that she had, and was not better but rather grew worse". [Mark 5:26–27] After healing her, Jesus tells her "Daughter, your faith has made you well. Go in peace! Be cured from your illness". [Mark 5:34] At least two other times Jesus credited the sufferer's faith as the means of being healed: Mark 10:52 and Luke 19:10.

Jesus endorsed the use of the medical assistance of the time (medicines of oil and wine) when he told the parable of the Good Samaritan (Luke 10:25–37), who "bound up [an injured man's] wounds, pouring on oil and wine" (verse 34) as a physician would. Jesus then told the doubting teacher of the law (who had elicited this parable by his self-justifying question, "And who is my neighbor?"

in verse 29) to "go, and do likewise" in loving others with whom he would never ordinarily associate (verse 37).[20]

The healing in the gospels is referred to as a "sign"[John 6:2] to prove Jesus' divinity and to foster belief in him as the Christ.[John 4:48] However, when asked for other types of miracles, Jesus refused some[Matthew 12:38–42] but granted others[Luke 9:38–43] in consideration of the motive of the request. Some theologians' understanding is that Jesus healed all who were present every single time. Sometimes he determines whether they had faith that he would heal them. Four of the seven miraculous signs performed in the Fourth Gospel that indicated he was sent from God were acts of healing or resurrection. He heals the Capernaum official's son, heals a paralytic by the pool in Bethsaida, healing a man born blind, and resurrecting Lazarus of Bethany.

Jesus told his followers to heal the sick and stated that signs such as healing are evidence of faith. Jesus also told his followers to "cure sick people, raise up dead persons, make lepers clean, expel demons. You received free, give free".[Matthew 10:8][Mark 16:17–18]

Jesus sternly ordered many who received healing from him: "Do not tell anyone!" Jesus did not approve of anyone asking for a sign just for the spectacle of it, describing such as coming from a "wicked and adulterous generation".[Matthew 12:38–39]

The apostle Paul believed healing is one of the special gifts of the Holy Spirit, [1 Corinthians 12:9] [26] and that the possibility exists that certain persons may possess this gift to an extraordinarily high degree.

In the New Testament Epistle of James,[5:14] the faithful are told that to be healed, those who are sick should call upon the elders of the church to pray over [them] and anoint [them] with oil in the name of the Lord.

The New Testament says that during Jesus' ministry and after his

Resurrection, the apostles healed the sick and cast out demons, made lame men walk, raised the dead and performed other miracles. Apostles were holy men who had direct access to God and could channel his power to help and heal people. For example, Saint Peter healed a crippled man. [Luke 3:1-10]

Jesus used miracles to convince people that he was inaugurating the Messianic Age, as in Mt 12.28. Scholars have described Jesus' miracles as establishing the kingdom during his lifetime.

9.1.2 Case of the Tillmans

Steve and Marion Tillman live in rural Alabama. Marion is a retired schoolteacher, and Steve has recently retired from the local manufacturing plant. Steve is six feet and three inches in height, and is overweight. A strong man, he has worked hard all his life in the factory. His major source of exercise is taking care of their large piece of property. For his diet, he enjoys Marion's rich southern cooking, and has been on high blood pressure medication for several years. He does not drink, though he does use chewing tobacco. The Tillmans have three grown children, several grandchildren, and two great-grandchildren. They have attended the same small rural Roman Catholic Church for many years and have participated in various service opportunities. They are excited to have reached retirement, and look forward to traveling and spending more time with their family and friends.

On a particularly hot day, Steve lies down on the couch to take a nap after working in the yard. Surprised at the unusually longer length of Steve's nap, Marion is unable to wake him up. She calls 911 and, within several minutes, the paramedics take Steve to the hospital. After evaluation, the tests reveal that Steve had a significant left hemisphere ischemic cerebrovascular accident, more commonly known as a stroke. Although Steve will live, the doctors are unable to determine to what extent the stroke will affect him.

When Steve awakens, he is unable to speak and cannot move his right side. Tests confirm that Steve has expressive aphasia, right hemiplegia, and some difficulty swallowing. The expressive aphasia means that Steve can understand what people are saying, but he has lost the ability to form words and sentences. The hemiplegia means that Steve has lost the use of his right extremities, with the arm more affected than his leg. This is unfortunate because Steve is right-handed. Due to the effects of the stroke, Steve is very weak and sleeps a lot.

Marion is grateful that Steve is alive, but she is very shaken up. Her children and grandchildren have come to help her and check on Steve. The hospital chaplain pays them a visit. The members of the parish pray for Steve and also lend their support to Marion by preparing meals and visiting her. Steve and Marion plead with God often and fervently that Steve will make a full recovery. Their religious faith and network of family and friends will remain an important means of support throughout the various stages of the recovery process.

After a week in the hospital, the doctors recommend that Steve spend a month in an intensive rehabilitation centre about two hours from their home. The Tillmans agree and make arrangements to go there. After spending a month in the rehabilitation centre, Steve has made some progress. He can roll by himself in both directions in the bed, but he needs Marion's help to sit up on the side of the bed and to put on his clothes. He is able to swallow, but can only make certain sounds. Aided by fellow church members the Tillmans' children have built a ramp to give Steve wheelchair access to their house. Although satisfied with his progress, Steve and Marion wish that it was both faster and more pronounced. Also, they begin to long for the days when everything would return to normal.

The doctors recommend that Steve continue speech, occupational, and physical therapy on an outpatient basis. This will require Marion to assist Steve in and out of both his wheelchair and the car, which she is able to do by herself, though it requires much effort. She will also have to drive him the thirty minutes into town for his thrice-weekly appointments, and then must wait the two hours for them to take place. The reality that Steve's recovery may take longer than the Tillmans expected sinks into their consciousness, and they both begin to think that Steve may not make a full recovery.

With this in mind, they set up a meeting with their pastor. When the pastor asks them how they are doing, Marion begins to cry, and Steve lets out a sigh. The pastor asks what is wrong. Through her tears, Marion explains that she does not know why God is doing this to them. She continues by expressing how she and Steve have lived a good life. They have gone to church regularly and prayed faithfully. They have also helped other people. More importantly, they have not done anything wrong. She is confused and does not know why God is punishing them in this way. What is worse is that she also feels that God has abandoned them when they have needed God the most. She begins to sob, and Steve begins to cry as well. To understand how the Tillmans have arrived at this state, one needs to have an understanding of religion, religious coping, and religious narrative. When Steve has the stroke, they cannot understand why God would let this happen because they were doing their part; that is, they were keeping up their end of the "bargain."

The Tillmans believe that in exchange for their years of faithful service to Jesus that Jesus will cure Steve. After reading these passages, they begin to beg Jesus for a cure. When Steve does not get well, they could seek out their pastor to receive the ritual actions of the Anointing of the Sick. On the way, they might both agree to give all glory and praise to God if Steve is cured. They would also commit to reforming their ways in exchange for a cure, but they cannot recall a wrong that deserved the stroke.

Since the Tillman's religious narrative is not helping them cope in a positive way with Steve's stroke, they have become frozen in it and cannot see a way out. In order for Marion and Steve to move forward, they must first let go of their religious narrative that sees his sickness as punishment for sin. Next, they need to be reminded of to appreciate other aspects of their religious faith in order to create more plot material. This will allow them to rewrite their religious narrative that can give new meaning to Steve's sickness and include healing from God.

Sickness refers to the patient's complete experience of being ill. Sickness includes the physical effects as well as the psychological, spiritual, and social effects. In this way, sickness encompasses the whole person. Because of the care that Steve received, he survived and continues living with his sickness, the condition deriving from the stroke. This means that the Tillmans have to deal not only with the stroke's physical symptoms but also with the full range of emotions, questions of faith, and changes in relationships that the experience of sickness presents.

9.2 Jesus Christ Himself as the First Healer

Jesus comes into the world to bring "life … to the full" (cf. John 10:10 NIV). This "life to the full" corresponds to the sense of shalom, and applies not only to physical wholeness and not only to individuals but always encompasses the world as a whole, and centres around life in unbroken relationships.

Jesus comes alongside human beings and cares particularly for those whose dignity was not respected in his day. He notices and takes seriously the physical life of each individual, something that was as significant in those days as it is today: for over the centuries Christians have often found it hard to see the human body as God's creation and hence as something to be highly valued. On the other hand, though, we must not miss the fact that Jesus' healing ministry has a far greater aim than simply curing the physical or mental symptoms of certain individuals.

In healing the men, Jesus removes the blindness and deafness that prevents them from really hearing what he has to say and clearly seeing who he is. For sick people, such healing can often be a slow and gradual process. Like the blind man, sick people may need to progress from "no sight" to "partial sight" to "full sight." With eyes to see and ears to hear, sick people find that it is easier to follow Jesus. This helps them let go of certain expectations and beliefs about the way that Jesus should or should not act.

By following Jesus, sick people are led to healing, but this is often down a different path than the one they would have chosen for themselves. Sick people frequently want to race down the path of a cure in order to return to how things were before their sickness. Instead, Jesus might want to take sick people down the path to healing, which begins with acceptance of their condition, moves to understanding it, and culminates in a change of attitude. This progression allows sick people to exchange their old desire, wanting things to be like they used to be, for a new one.

Goodness is an attribute of the Person of God as is revealed in creation. When God created the heavens and earth, disease, sickness and weakness did not exist. The Bible says that everything that God made was very good (Genesis 1:31) (revelation of the person & character of God. He is good). Man was created in the image and likeness of God (Genesis 1:26) and was free from sickness and disease. God's intention was that man should live a pure healthy life on earth forever. We are told that Jesus Christ "went about doing good and healing ... " in his earthly ministry. (Acts 10:38) Jesus was the exact representation of the invisible God while on earth. (Hebrews 1:3) "If you have seen me, you have seen the Father." (John 14:9). The eternal goodness and purpose of God was seen in Christ as He fulfilled the will of the Father in every act of healing (John 6:17-20) (Jesus said that its God working in him). Scripture reveals that sickness is an enemy of man that destroys the creation of God and is inconsistent with the nature of God.

After crossing the Red Sea and journeying in the wilderness for three days they found water that was bitter and could not drink it. God showed Moses a tree (symbolized cross) and told Him to cut it down and cast it in and the water would be healed. Afterward, God initiated His covenant of healing using the title of Jehovah Rapha, meaning "the Lord our Healer". God's promise to Israel also foreshadowed the work of Christ on Calvary where healing would be provided for Jew and Gentile alike. The tree Moses cut down and threw into the water symbolized the cross where Jesus bore our sickness and carried our diseases (Isaiah 53:4-6). Cursed is everyone that hangeth on a tree (Galatians 3:13). When Moses was telling the people of God's plan for them once inside the promised land, he reiterated the promise of healing. It was God's will that they should be free from all the sickness they had known in Egypt (Deuteronomy 7:15). Egypt is a type of the world under the dominion of Satan (Pharaoh), and sickness is their reward for service under the cruel taskmaster. However, God has promised total protection from all the diseases on earth for them who live obediently and put their trust in God (Psalm 91:10).

God has made provision for our healing through the substitutionary work of Christ on Calvary. Just as "surely" as He has borne our sin, He has also borne our sickness' (Isaiah 53:4-6). Christ not only bore our sins to the cross, but He bore the penalty as well. "Who His own self bore our sins in His body on the tree, that we being dead to sin, should live unto righteousness; by whose stripes ye were healed" (1 Peter 2:24). The word "stripes-molops" means a blow or mark. When Jesus was lashed with the cat-o-nine tails by the burly Roman soldier, His flesh was torn as the price for our healing. Notice the verb Peter uses is past tense, "were" healed, indicating a finished work.

When the priest laid his hands on the scapegoat and sent him into the wilderness (Leviticus 16:10), it typified Christ who would also carry away our sins as far as the east is from the west. Regarding our sickness. Matthew says "Himself TOOK our infirmities and carried our diseases," Matthew 8:17. God has provided righteousness for our sinfulness, and healing for our sickness, we can now declare on the authority of His Word that "We are righteous and We are healed."

When the believers of today "do the works of Jesus" John 14:12-14 there will be no doubt about God's will to heal because we will be "proving" the will of God Romans 12:2 as Jesus did when He was on earth. Therefore, the greatest cure for unbelief and failure to receive healing is for the Spirit-empowered church of Jesus Christ to preach, teach and perform the will of God as Jesus commanded in the great commission of Mark 16:17-20 and Luke 9:1,2,6.

The modern approach to miracles would describe them as breaking the natural laws of nature that God made. They are extraordinary. Some people try various ways to explain them away as some sort of fiction, a fable. But the believers experience a miracle everything the Mass is celebrated when bread and wine become the Body and Blood of Christ. The Biblical Approach would view them as "mighty deeds, wonders, and signs, which God worked" (Acts 2:22). The God who created the earth had renewed the earth through His healing actions, wonders, miracles. The God who liberated the Israelites from the Egyptians in the Exodus now frees His people through wondrous signs, miracles. They are one of the ways that God interacts with His people. The Synoptic Gospels (Matthew, Mark and Luke) used the Greek word "dynamics" "act of power" to describe Jesus' miracles. For wonders Jesus did, John used two Greek words "erga" translated as "works" and "sēmeion" as "signs". "A large crowd followed him, because they saw the signs, he was performing on the sick." (John 6:2). For all the Gospels, the healing works done by Jesus flowed from God's primal.

9.3 Healing in Mark 2:1-12

How sick people may read Jesus' healing of the paralyzed man in Mark 2:1-12. How they can use this passage to confirm or construct a religious narrative that sickness is punishment for sin. How this understanding leads them to believe that if they ask Jesus to forgive them that he will cure them. Although this passage highlights Jesus' ability to forgive sin, it also invites sick people to a different understanding of the connection between sin and sickness on the one hand, and forgiveness and healing on the other.

During the time of Jesus, there were several faith and magic healers, but no one who claimed to forgive sins. The forgiveness of sin was a power reserved for God. By pronouncing forgiveness of the man's sin, Jesus manifests that he has this divine prerogative. By using this ability, Jesus reveals that he is intimately related to God. The scribes do not believe this; therefore, they accuse him of blaspheming.

Jesus realizes they are thinking this. In response, he takes the opportunity of the man's healing to demonstrate who he is and his divine right. He heals the man to offer proof that he has in fact forgiven the man's sins. That Jesus has the power and the authority to forgive sins is the key message of this passage. It is not to reveal a causal connection between sin and sickness, and forgiveness and curing.

9.4 Some Healing Verses from Bible

The Bible says God promises us healing and long life. - TIME 10:10

The earth-walk of Jesus and his Ministry of Healing. - TIME 18:56

Healing is one of the greater works. - TIME 47:16

There is healing in the name of Jesus. - TIME 50:25

The Bible says you can receive healing by your faith. - TIME 102:04

Let's give God glory as we receive your healing right now from Jesus. - TIME 110:27 - 110:56

The Bible says God promises us healing and long life. - Ephesians 5:30

Let's take a look at the earth walk of Jesus and His Ministry of Healing. Jesus Heals All Sickness and Disease. -Matthew 4:23-24

And Jesus went about all the cities and villages, teaching in their synagogues, and preaching the gospel of the kingdom, and healing every sickness and every disease among the people.

How God anointed Jesus of Nazareth with the Holy Ghost and with power: who went about doing good, and healing all that were oppressed of the devil; for God was with him. - Hebrews 13:8

The Bible says healing is one of the greater works. The Healing Prayer of Faith, James 5:14-16

The Bible says there is healing in the name of Jesus.- Malachi 4:2

But unto you that fear my name shall the Sun of righteousness arise with healing in his wings; and ye shall go forth, and grow up as calves of the stall.

The Bible says you can receive healing by your faith. - Matthew 18:19

SECTION 4

(HAPPINESS)

CHAPTER 10

Happiness in Hinduism

Peace arises from cultivating friendship with those who are happy, compassion towards those who are in distress, joy towards those who are virtuous, and sameness towards those who are not virtuous. - Yogasutras 1.33

Who wants to be happy? Everyone! Pursuit of happiness is the goal of all religions and almost all spiritual writings describe the ways how to achieve it.

Brihadaaranyaka Upanishad (1.4.14), an ancient Hindu scripture, says:

Sarve Bhavantu Sukhinah, Sarve Santu Niraamayah,
Sarve Bhadraani Pashyantu, Maa Kaschid Dukha Mapnuyat.

Meaning: May all be happy; May all be without disease; May all look for well-being of others; May none have misery of any sort. - Brihadaaranyaka Upanishad 1.4.14

According to Sri Aurobindo, happiness is the natural state of humanity, as he mentions in his book 'The Life Divine', he informs about it as delight of existence. Srimad Bhagavad Gita interprets happiness as derived via good thoughts and good deeds that depend on the state and on the control of the mind. Through evenness of temper and mind, the state of supreme bliss is reached in all aspects of one's life. According to the Vishishtadvaita Vedanta school, which was proposed by Ramanujacharya, true happiness can only be through divine grace, which can be achieved by surrender of one's ego to the Divine. According to Ramana Maharshi, happiness is within us and can be known only through discovering our true self. The happiness can be attained by inner enquiry, using the thought "Who am I?

10.1 Concept of Happiness

10.1.1 What is Happiness?

Happiness is the meaning and the purpose of life, the whole aim and end of human existence.

Everyone in this world desires happiness, although few know exactly what is meant by this word. How do you define happiness? According to a large number of spiritual philosophers, happiness is our birth-right. It is ours for the experiencing. Nevertheless, if we don't really know what true happiness is, or how to cultivate its sweet fragrance inside ourselves, then our efforts to find true happiness in outer circumstances alone are likely to be in vain.

Happiness is a state of inner fulfilment, not the gratification of inexhaustible desires for outward things. Genuine happiness may be influenced by the circumstances, but it is not dependent on it. It actually gives us the inner resources to deal better with those circumstances. Happiness is to understand that we are one with others, and this not only leads to obtaining happiness, but also brings peace and harmony into the lives of others. The more we care for the happiness of others, the greater our own sense of happiness becomes. According to the ancient Hindu scriptures, happiness is a fundamental state of existence that aligns the sacred self with the timeless, infinite dimension of the cosmos.

Doing what you like is freedom. Liking what you do is happiness.
- Frank Tyger

Men and women are rushing hither and thither in the blind search for happiness, and cannot find it; nor ever will until they recognize that happiness is already within them and round about them, filling the universe, and that they, in their selfish searching, are shutting themselves out from it. - James Allen

According to Augustine, "Eternity is the now that does not pass away." A happiness anchored in the now is eternal. The Self lives in the now; the 'I' lives in time. Shifting your centre of awareness from the 'I' to the 'Self' means anchoring your consciousness in the now. At first we can do this only for brief moments. But we can learn to take the temporal happiness of the 'I' lightly and enjoy more and more the "now-happiness" of the Self, the condition that accounts for genuine happiness.

10.1.2 What is Pleasure?

Pleasure is satisfying the need of five senses: A good meal, a good smell, a good sex, a good scene, looking a beautiful face, listening to good music etc. The pleasure is dependent of external objects. If there is no such object, the pleasure will go away. The experience of pleasure is subjective and different individuals experience different kinds and amounts of pleasure in the same situation. Pleasure is short-lived, at times leading to pain, guilt or depression as its after-effects. Pleasure is temporary, and generally is centred on the self, which can make us selfish and sometimes is in conflict with the well-being of others.

10.1.3 What is the Difference between Happiness and Pleasure?

Happiness is often equated with a maximization of pleasure, and some imagine that true happiness would consist of an interrupted succession of pleasurable experience. There is no reason to deprive ourselves of the enjoyment of a magnificent landscape, of swimming in the sea or of the scent of a rose, but we must understand that the experience of pleasure is dependent upon circumstance, on a specific location or moment in time. It is unstable by nature, and the sensation it evokes can soon become neutral or even unpleasant. In other words, pleasure is externally motivated and fleeting, while happiness is internally generated and constant. Happiness is not necessarily dependent on any external or internal pleasurable stimuli.

10.1.4 What is the Difference between Happiness and Success?

"Success is getting what you want; happiness is: wanting what you get."- Ingrid Bergman. Success is meeting the deadlines. Happiness is working toward your goals. Success is focusing on accumulating wealth. Happiness is focusing on improving your life. Success is promotion above your peers. Happiness is being respected by your peers. "When I look back on all these worries, I remember the story of the old man who said on his deathbed that he had had a lot of trouble in his life, most of which had never happened." -Winston Churchill. Success is finding a life partner. Happiness is keeping your partner for life. Success is keeping the knowledge you glean to yourself. Happiness is sharing your expertise freely.

One of my Facebook friends recently wrote on her post, "Success is father, and happiness is mother. Father wants his children to be successful but mother always wishes her children to be happy."

10.1.5 What is the Difference between Happiness and Satisfaction?

'Happiness' is defined as both a state of mind and an emotion. Man can choose to be happy. It is relevant to note that even people who are poor can be happy despite the fact that not all their needs are met, even the most basic ones. 'Satisfaction,' on the other hand, is the state wherein your desires are met. You will find it in the possession and enjoyment of things that you desire. In effect, it, too, is a state of mind wherein you find contentment knowing that your demands and desires are made possible.

Meeting the desires of your heart and the demands of your needs will not necessarily make you happy despite the fact that you will never want for anything when you are satisfied. Everything actually depends on your beliefs. If you see poverty as a blessing rather than a curse and be content with what you have, then your chances of being happy are greater than the person who sees material things as a necessity in life.

10.1.6 What is the Difference between Joy and Bliss?

When you have joy, that joy is in the central being, in the heart itself. When you are really joyful, that joy usually remains inside the heart with utmost confidence. Inner joy means real inner security. But if you are happy, it can be on a much lower plane of consciousness — on the physical plane, the vital plane, or the mental plane. Joy is superior to happiness. Bliss is much higher, much superior to joy. It is infinitely superior to both joy and happiness.

When we are immersed in doing an activity that we truly love, we transform ourselves into a refreshing and tranquil state. When that activity, which we love to engross in, results into the enhancement of human potential and/or welfare of others, we achieve happiness. Happiness is synchronizing with the flow of nature while doing such activity with effortless acceptance and with zero resistance and no expectations.

10.2 In Pursuit of Happiness

A man always wants more, not less, happiness than he has already. He errs, however, when he thinks he can increase his happiness by adding to his possessions rather than expanding his awareness. Any effort to increase his happiness without at the same time expanding his sensitivity to the world around him, and his sense of identity with it, will be self-defeating. Whenever a person acts selfishly, he deadens the capacity to perceive his essential unity with all life. He becomes, as a result, petty and mean. The expansion of happiness necessarily entails the expansion of awareness, not the expansion of property. For happiness is not a thing, and cannot be found in mere things. It is a quality of consciousness: something that one is aware with, rather than of.

Reason therefore suggests, and inner experience confirms that happiness is an intrinsic quality of human nature. We enjoy things only to the extent that we satisfy the thought in our own minds that things are enjoyable. In fact, it is never things themselves that we enjoy at all, but only a deeper reality within our own being. The clearest proof that things are not enjoyable in themselves may be seen in the fact that different people can have such very different ideas as to what gives them happiness. The theory of non-dualism is emphatic in its conviction that man is endowed with an innate quality of being (sat), consciousness (chit) and unalloyed happiness (ananda): he has only to look within to realise experientially that the jiva is an embodiment of the macrosmic existence.

The desire to attain happiness is actually symptomatic of the desire for self-discovery, for self-fulfilment. By the same token, the desire to avoid suffering is essentially a desire to eschew 'non-happiness' as foreign to our nature. We suffer only when something withholds from us that degree of happiness which we feel rightfully ours.

10.3 Concept of Happiness in Hinduism

According to Hinduism, happiness in human life arises mainly from one's own actions, past life karma, actions of gods and others, and the grace of God. In Hindu scriptures we find references to mainly three types of happiness as stated below.

(i) Physical (bhautika) happiness, or sukham, which arises from comforts of life, sensual enjoyment, and bodily pleasures.

(ii) Mental (manasika) happiness, or anandam, which arises from sense of fulfilment and freedom from worries, afflictions, and anxieties.

(iii) Spiritual (adhyatmika) happiness, or atmanandam, which arises from freedom from the cycle of births and deaths, and union with Self.

According to Hinduism, an embodied being's ultimate purpose is enjoyment of supreme bliss as a free soul (mukta) in the highest heaven. This aspect will be described in a subsequent chapter in this book. Enjoyment is also the basis of happiness upon earth. However, in mortal life happiness should not be pursued for happiness sake alone, because mere pursuit of happiness in a bound state (baddha) leads to attachment (Yogasutras 2.7), and bondage. It should be pursued as part of a way of life in which liberation or union with the Self should be the highest goal. Human beings can temporarily secure happiness upon earth by doing their duties, or permanently in the highest heaven by achieving liberation.

An intermediary approach is to prolong happiness by doing good karmas and going to the ancestral heaven where souls can stay for longer periods than upon earth. However, such happiness would not last forever, because when their good karma is exhausted souls have to return to the earth and take another birth to continue their existence. The best strategy therefore is to secure happiness here, and liberation hereafter. In the following discussion we will examine how Hinduism expects each practitioner to achieve this rather difficult goal. The impediments to peace and happiness are egoism (aham), ignorance (avidya), impurities (malas), delusion (maya), past actions (karma), desires (kama) and attachments (pasas).

10.3.1 A Structured Approach to Happiness in the Moral World

To secure happiness here in mortal life, Hinduism prescribes a holistic method, which takes into consideration both the material and spiritual needs of human beings. It recognizes four chief aims of human life, called purusharthas, by pursuing which human beings can experience physical, mental, and spiritual happiness. They are also called the four chief purposes (purusharthas) of existence, because they are also chosen by God (Purusha) himself for his own enjoyment. Broadly speaking, these four purusharthas are (i) morality, (ii) prosperity, (iii) enjoyment, and (iv) spirituality. Specifically, in a religious sense, they refer to religious and moral duty (dharma), wealth (artha), conjugal bliss (kama) and liberation (moksha).

Let us examine how they contribute to our happiness. By pursuing dharma, you enjoy name and fame, social status, and respect in society. By pursuing wealth, you enjoy the comforts of life, status in society, and the satisfaction of fulfilling your obligations to family and society. By pursuing kama (sex) you enjoy conjugal bliss, companionship with your spouse, family life, and the happiness of having children, relations, and continuation of family lineage. Finally, pursuing liberation, you can secure the ultimate happiness of being absolutely and eternally free from all obligations. For a human being, these four aims are the best means to secure happiness upon earth and lay a firm foundation for future happiness in the world of Brahman, the highest Self.

Hindu scriptures further suggest that a person has better chances of securing happiness and enjoying life if he pursues these four aims according to the four phases of human life, called ashramas, during which he has to fulfil the duties and obligations that are specific to each of them. The four phases of human life are, brahmacharya, grihastha, vanaprastha, and sanyasa. In Brahmacharya, which corresponds to childhood and young age, a person has to study the Vedas and learn about his duties and responsibilities (dharma), apart from the knowledge of the Self and the Supreme Self. In Grihastha, which corresponds to the adult life, he has to perform his obligatory duties (dharma) and earn wealth (artha) to ensure the welfare, order and regularity of his family and society. In Vanaprastha, which corresponds to the old age, he has to retire into seclusion and contemplate upon his experiential wisdom (dharma) and the ultimate purpose of human life (liberation). In Sanyasa, which corresponds to the last phase of human life, he has to renounce everything, including his knowledge of the scriptures (dharma), and work for his liberation (moksha). In each of these stages it is possible to experience peace and happiness by following the injunctions specified in the scriptures. If he follows them strictly, at the end of the journey he is bound to become liberated and enter the world of bliss.

10.3.2 Eternal Happiness through Complete Freedom

True enjoyment and happiness in life are not possible, unless it is secured on a lasting basis. Like Buddhism, Hinduism also clearly and emphatically recognizes the suffering that is inherent to earthly life and traces its root cause to desire only. Beings are unhappy because they are bound to impermanent things and cannot easily escape from their attraction and aversion to them. Because they are driven by their desire for impermanent things, and pairs of opposites, their happiness upon earth remains temporary and elusive. No one is free from suffering because of impermanence, which manifests in our lives as loss, union, aging, sickness, decay, death, and destruction.

Duality is another important cause. We experience unhappiness, because of union and separation, or attraction and aversion to the objects and conditions that we like or dislike. We are happy when we are with those that we like, or unhappy when we are with those that we dislike. One may experience temporary happiness when we pursue sense objects. However, it is a trap, since the pursuit of objects results in attachment. From attachment arise karma, delusion, and bondage, which aggravate our suffering and make our chances of enjoying life increasingly difficult.

Thus, chasing happiness upon earth by worldly means is like chasing a mirage. To escape from this predicament, one should subordinate earthly happiness to spiritual happiness and, earthly goals to spiritual goals, and aim for permanent happiness, which can be secured only when a being is completely free from all attachments, and the limitations of mortal life. True happiness of the divine kind arises not from having things or fulfilling our desires, but by restraining our minds and bodies, and becoming free from our dependence upon them. When we are free from all attachments, from the impurity of maya and desires, we return to our soul's essential nature, which is permanent bliss. Reaching this state is called liberation, which one can achieve even when one is alive upon earth.

10.4 What does Bhagavad Gita say about Happiness?

We may be keen on performing certain actions and indulging in certain activities because those, we think, will make us happy. But, are we aware of the true meaning of happiness? Sri Krishna enlightens us about this elusive concept through his conversation with Arjun in Bhagavad Gita.

10.4.1 What is Happiness?

In Chapter II, Verse 70 of the Bhagavad Gita, Sri Krishna says,

"aapurya-manam achala-prathistham
samudram apah pravishanti yadvat
tadvat-kama yam pravishanti sarve
sa shantim-apnoti na kama-kaami"

"As the waters (of different rivers) enters the Great Ocean, which though full on all sides remains undisturbed, likewise a person who is not disturbed by the incessant flow of desires, can alone achieve peace, and not the man who runs after these desires & strives to satisfy such desires."

10.4.2 Three Types of Happiness

Sri Krishna says to Arjun,

"sukhaṁ tu idaniṁ tri-vidhaṁ shrinu me bharatarshabha
abhyasad ramate yatra duhkhantam cha nigachchhati"

"And now hear from me, O Arjun, of the three kinds of happiness in which the embodied soul rejoices, and can even reach the end of all suffering."

- Bhagavad Gita, Chapter 18, Verse 36

(i) Satvik or Pure happiness: It is the happiness that arises from the elevation of the soul. However, attaining this is not easy. One pursuing satvik or pure happiness has to practice a lot of discipline. That is why, it feels like poison in the beginning but nectar in the end.

"yat tad agre viham iva pariname mitopamam
tat sukham sattvikam proktam atma-buddhi-prasada-jam"

"That which seems like poison at first, but tastes like nectar in the end, is said to be happiness in the mode of goodness. It is generated by the pure intellect that is situated in self-knowledge."

- Bhagavad Gita, Chapter 18, Verse 37

(ii) Rajasic or result-oriented happiness: This is the materialistic pleasure that is derived when the senses come in contact with external objects that create a feeling of gratification. However, this kind of happiness is temporary.

"vishayendriya-sanyogad yat tad agre mritopamam
pariname visham iva tat sukham rajasam smritam"

"Happiness is said to be in the mode of passion when it is derived from the contact of the senses with their objects. Such happiness is like nectar at first but poison at the end."

- Bhagavad Gita, Chapter 18, Verse 38

(iii) Tamasic or slothful happiness: This is the lowest form of happiness and is derived from sleeping or being lazy. The soul is never nurtured through these practices yet since there is a tiny sense of pleasure associated with it, people wrongfully consider it to be a state of happiness.

"yad agre chanubandhe cha sukham mohanam atmanah
nidralasya-pramadottha tat tamasam udahritam"

"That happiness which covers the nature of the self from beginning to end, and which is derived from sleep, indolence, and negligence, is said to be in the mode of ignorance."

- Bhagavad Gita, Chapter 18, Verse 39.

10.5 28 Bhagavad Gita Quotes on Happiness

1. *A gift is pure when it is given from the heart to the right*

person, at the right time, at the right place and when we expect nothing in return.

2. *The happiness which comes from long practice, which leads to the end of suffering, which at first is like poison, but at last like nectar – this kind of happiness arises from the serenity of one's own mind.*

3. *The impermanent appearance of happiness and distress and their disappearance in due course are like the appearance and disappearance of winter and summer seasons. They arise from the sense of perception, and one must learn to tolerate them without being disturbed.*

4. *Happiness derived from a combination of the senses and the sense objects is always a cause of distress and should be avoided by all means.*

5. *Man is made by his beliefs. As he believes so he is.*

6. *There is neither this world nor the world beyond nor happiness for the one who doubts.*

7. *You grieve for those who should not be grieved for, Yet you speak wise words. Neither for the dead nor those alive do the wise grieve for.*

8. *All happiness in the material world has a beginning and an end, but happiness in Krishna is unlimited, and there is no end.*

9. *Pleasures conceived in the world of the senses have a beginning and an end and give birth to misery, Arjuna. The wise do not look for happiness in them. But those who overcome the impulses of lust and anger which arise in the body are made whole and live-in joy. They find their joy, their rest, and their light completely within themselves. United with the Lord, they attain nirvana in Brahman.*

10. *Those who realize the self are always satisfied. Having found the source of joy and fulfilment they no longer seek happiness from the external world. Happiness can only be found within self.*

11. *He who has no attachments can love others, For his love is pure and divine. And it is from those small acts of love you truly can be happy.*

12. *There is neither in this world or the world beyond that happiness exists for someone who doubts.*

13. *Free from all thoughts of 'I' and 'mine', man finds absolute peace.*

14. *Meet this transient world with neither grasping nor fear, Trust the unfolding of life and you will attain true serenity.*

15. *You came here empty handed and so will you leave. What is yours today belonged to someone else yesterday. And Tomorrow someone else will call it his.*

16. *The person who is not disturbed by happiness and distress and is steady in both is certainly eligible for liberation.*

17. *Happiness is of the soul. The soul can never be cut to pieces. Nor burned by fire, nor moistened by water or withered by wind.*

18. *Make it easy for yourself. Get Organized, Live the moment. Your day-to-day activities should not steal your happiness.*

19. *Little by Little. Through patience and repeated effort, The mind will become stilled in self.*

20. *One has to learn tolerance in the face of dualities, Such as happiness or distress, Or cold and warmth and by tolerating such dualities, become free from anxieties regarding gain and loss.*

21. *There is neither Self-knowledge nor Self-perception to those whose senses are not under control; Without self-perception, there is no peace and without peace, there can be no happiness.*

22. *Delusion arises from anger; The mind is bewildered by delusion; Reasoning is destroyed when the mind is bewildered; One falls down when reasoning is destroyed.*

23. *We are like fish out of water; Just as fish cannot be happy unless he is in water; We cannot be happy apart from the spiritual world.*

24. *The real sense of happiness is not cursing your destiny, Not wanting every second to change your scene, to change another mind, But to change your own mind to change the world.*

25. *The Key to happiness is the Reduction of desires.*

26. *When you move amidst the world of sense; free from the attachments and aversions alike, there comes the peace in which the sorrow ends, and you live in the wisdom of the self.*

27. *One who is peaceful amidst good or evil, Whose aim and happiness are within, He is released from material bondage.*

28. *It is better to live your own destiny imperfectly but happily than to live an imitation of somebody's life with perfection and sorrow.*

10.6 Some more Sanskrit Shlokas (with English Translation) On Happiness

Lokah Samastah Sukhino Bhavantu

Meaning: Let the entire world be happy.

Om Sarve Bhavantu Sukhinah
Sarve Santu Niraamayaah |
Sarve Bhadraanni Pashyantu
Maa Kashhid-Duhkha-Bhaag-Bhavet |
Om Shaantih Shaantih Shaantih ||

Meaning: Om, May All be Happy,
May All be Free from Illness.
May All See what is Auspicious,
May no one Suffer.
Om Peace, Peace, Peace.

svastiprajābhyaḥ paripālayantāṃ nyāyena mārgeṇa mahīṃ mahīśāḥ ।
gobrāhmaṇebhyaḥ śubhamastu nityaṃ lokāḥ samastāḥ sukhino bhavantu ॥

Meaning: May the well-being of all people be protected by the powerful and mighty leaders be with law and justice. May the success be with all divinity and scholars, May all the worlds become happy.

Chitte prasanne bhuvana chitte vishanne bhuvanam .
Atoabhilasho yadi te sukhe syat chittaprasade prathamam yatasva.

Meaning: If the mind is happy, the entire world (seems) happy. If the mind is despondent, the entire world (seems) despondent. Hence, if you desire happiness, strive towards the happiness of the mind first.

10.7 Happiness in Upanishads

The Upanishads advance a unique and powerful notion that the qualitative distinction between pleasure and happiness resides within a temporal context. To elaborate, the pleasure is short-lived: meaning that it is temporally local; on the other hand, happiness is long lasting: meaning that it is temporally nonlocal.

Isa-Vasya-Upanishad gives knowledge of the All-pervading Deity. The dominant thought running through it is that we cannot enjoy life or realize true happiness unless we consciously "cover" all with the Omnipresent Lord. If we are not fully conscious of that which sustains our life, how can we live wisely and perform our duties? Whatever we see, movable or immovable, good or bad, it is all "That." We must not divide our conception of the universe; for in dividing it, we have only fragmentary knowledge and we thus limit ourselves.

Katha Upanishad beautifully distinguishes between the 'happiness' and the 'pleasure' in the following two shlokas:

anyacchreyo 'nyadutaiva preya-
ste ubhe nānārthe puruṣa~ sinītaḥ |
tayoḥ śreya ādadānasya sadhu
bhavati hīyate'rthādya u preyo vṛṇīte (1.2.1)

śreyaśca preyaśca manuṣyametaḥ
tau samparītya vivinakti dhīraḥ |
śreyo hi dhīro›bhi preyaso vṛṇīte
preyo mando yogakṣemādvṛṇīte (1.2.2)

Meaning: There is the path of happiness, and there is the path of pleasure. Both attract the soul. Who follows the first (means the happiness) comes to good; who follows the path of pleasure fails to reach the end goal. The two paths lie in front of man. Discriminating between them the wise one chooses the path of happiness; the simple-minded choose the path of pleasure." (Katha Upanishad I.2, 1-2).

In this context, some shlokas from the **Chandogya Upanishad** are quoted here below:

yadā vai sukhaṃ labhate'tha karoti nāsukhaṃ labdhvā karoti
sukhameva labdhvā karoti sukhaṃ tveva
vijijñāsitavyamiti sukhaṃ bhagavo vijijñāsa iti (7.22.1)

Meaning: 'A person works when he gets happiness. He does not care to work if he does not get happiness. By getting happiness one does one's duty. But one must try to understand the true nature of this happincss.' Nārada replied, 'Sir, I want to know well the true nature of happiness'.

yo vai bhūmā tatsukhaṃ nālpe sukhamasti bhūmaiva sukhaṃ
bhūmā tveva vijijñāsitavya iti bhūmānaṃ bhagavo vijijñāsa iti
|| 7.23.1 ||

Meaning: 'That which is infinite is the source of happiness. There is no happiness in the finite. Happiness is only in the infinite. But one must try to understand what the infinite is.' Nārada replied, 'Sir, I want to clearly understand the infinite'.

yatra nānyatpaśyati nānyacchṛṇoti nānyadvijānāti sa bhūmātha
yatrānyatpaśyatyanyacchṛṇotyanyadvijānāti tadalpaṃ yo vai
bhūmā tadamṛtamatha yadalpaṃ tanmartyṃ sa bhagavaḥ
kasminpratiṣṭhita iti sve mahimni yadi vā na mahimnīti
(7.24.1)

Meaning: 'Bhūmā [the infinitc] is that in which one sees nothing else, hears nothing else, and knows [i.e., finds] nothing else. But alpa [the finite] is that in which one sees something else, hears something else, and knows something else. That which is infinite is immortal, and that which is finite is mortal.' Nārada asked, 'Sir, what does bhūmā rest on?' Sanatkumāra replied, 'It rests on its own power—or not even on that power [i.e., it depends on nothing else]'.

sa evādhastātsa upariṣṭātsa paścātsa purastātsa dakṣiṇataḥ
sa uttarataḥ sa evedaṃ sarvamityathāto 'haṃkārādeśa
evāhamevādhastādahamupariṣṭādahaṃ paścādahaṃ
purastādahaṃ dakṣiṇato 'hamuttarato 'hamevedaṃ sarvamiti ||
7.25.1 ||

Meaning: That bhūmā is below; it is above; it is behind; it is in front; it is to the right; it is to the left. All this is bhūmā. Now, as regards one's own identity: I am below; I am above; I am behind; I am in front; I am to the right; I am to the left. I am all this.

One of the verses in Isha Upanishad says:

"Well may he be content to live a hundred years who acts without attachment who works his work with earnestness, but without desire, not yearning for its fruits–he, and he alone."

It is generally felt that this verse–and other passages from scriptures and books on spiritual life–indicates that one hundred years is the normal lifespan for a human being. On the other hand, the figure of one hundred years may also symbolize the complete lifespan of a person, however brief or long, the idea here being that not one moment of our life need be a burden nor should we ever wish to shorten our life by a single breath–that life should be lived in fulfillment with peace and happiness all the way through. That this is possible has been shown well by the saints and Masters of all religions and ages. We need only know how to do it; and these words give the way.

Katha Upanishad (2-II-12):

Eternal happiness belongs to the intelligent – not to others – who realize in their hearts Him who is one, the controller and the in-dwelling Self of all beings, and who makes the one form manifold.

Mandukya Karika of Gaudapada. III. ADVAITA PRAKARANA:

III-5. Just as when the ether confined within a particular jar contains dust and smoke, that is not the case with all jars, in the same way, all the individual souls are not associated with happiness etc.

III-45. In that state one should not enjoy the happiness, but should, by means of discrimination, become unattached. When the mind that has become still tends towards wandering, it should be unified (with the self) with efforts.

IV. ALATASANTI PRAKARANA

IV-2. I bow down to that Yoga which is devoid of touch with anything (that implics relationship), which conduces to the happiness of all beings and is beneficial, and which is free from dispute and contradiction and is taught by the scriptures.

Taittiriya Upanishad 1:4:2

Thou art the source of all happiness and of all prosperity. Do thou come to me as the goddess of prosperity and shower thy blessings upon me. May the seekers after truth gather round me, may they come from everywhere, that I may teach them thy word."

Chandogya Upanishad

VII-xxii-1: 'When one obtains happiness', then alone does one act. Without obtaining happiness one does not act. Only on obtaining happiness does one act. But one must desire to understand happiness'. 'Revered sir, I desire to understand happiness'.

Yoga Tattva Upanishad

11. Know that to be Jiva which is associated with happiness and misery and hence is the term Jiva applied to Paramatman which is pure.

Rama Uttara Tapaniya Upanishad

Om! He who is Ramachandra is verily the God. He is the 'non-dual soul of great happiness'. I salute him again and again in earth, bhuvar loka and Suvar loka. 3.1

This is followed by the repetition of the mantra 47 times with modification of the words with in quotes viz. "non-dual soul of great happiness."

CHAPTER 11

Happiness in Buddhism

If you want others to be happy, practice compassion.
If you want to be happy, practice compassion.- Dalai Lama

11.1 Happiness in Buddhism

People need happiness and peaceful societies; therefore, development approach needs to be holistic, covering humans, social, environmental, and economic development. Human development need to also focus on inner-self, mind and wisdom, which can drive human and national development into the right direction. Sustainable Development Goals (SDGs) should not neglect inner happiness from mind and wisdom based. The care for living with nature is likely to be driven from spiritual or inner happiness obtained by wisdom of knowing the interdependence of all kinds of livings and nature, as well as happiness from less use of resources or independent of materials.

Happiness in Buddhism or called in Pali language as "sukha" has its own meaning which is more precise than the term "Happiness" used in Western happiness studies. Sukha is the opposite situation of dukkha or suffering; thus, to have "sukha" means to reduce "dukkha" (including physical pain and mental status that people do not want to experience). In Buddhism, there are different levels of "sukha" or happiness for human development that each individuals can be trained to achieve higher and neater happiness; therefore, happiness is not viewed as a static, but it is a dynamic process in human development. The development of happiness or sukha from a basic to higher levels can be seen as a process of reducing dukkha or suffering until it is completely gone at the highest level of sukha, which is nibbānasukha. This is the whole process of practicing dhamma. Buddhist Sustainable Development (BSD) provides a new pathway for sustainability, with right views for living and true happiness, moderation in consumption and life style, understanding the interdependence of all beings and nature, leading towards caring for nature for humanity's well-being.

To attain happiness progressively in Buddhism is the process of reducing suffering from the root cause by true understanding of natural interdependence with right views, clear and purified mind. To be happy, one has to understand how to deal correctly with suffering. The Four Noble Truths describe nature, cause, and how to eliminate suffering. Therefore, human beings need to know about dissatisfaction or suffering, its causes, and how to follow the right path for cessation. When we have no dukkha or suffering, we have sukha or happiness. In practicing process, the more we can reduce dukkha, the higher sukha we can achieve.

11.2 Classifications or Levels of Happiness in Buddhism

In Buddhism, there are different kinds of classifications or levels of "sukha". No matter how many levels it is classified, its range starts from the lowest level – kāmasukha – which is happiness from acquisition or meeting sensual pleasures, to the highest level – nirodha samāpattisukha – with total extinction of suffering. Kāmasukha is a kind of happiness, but it can also cause and increase dukkha or suffering. Therefore, it is not considered as real happiness. Different ranks or levels of happiness also reflect degrees of real happiness.

However, this lowest rank of happiness at physical or material level is required for basic needs to relieve person's physical sufferings. After the basic needs are fulfilled, that person should develop further to gain higher level of happiness. Excessive material accumulation driven by greed may not lead to the increase of happiness and never keep happiness sustainable. Instead, it may increase problems, resulting in suffering and reducing happiness. This type of happiness depends on external pleasures to serve one's needs and may cause conflicts with others who also need them. People can get stress and tensions for that object dependent and their happiness can be faded down with higher desire and pressure. Thus, this type of happiness needs to be watched out or monitored by one's own mind and managed with wisdom that understands the natural truth of changes and true happiness.

Buddhism encourages human beings to have happiness with less dependent from materials outside oneself. Happiness can be obtained from non-acquisition which is mind- and wisdom- based. This is the higher level of happiness or inner happiness which can be generated inside human beings and independent to external factors. This level of happiness is considered as a neater type of happiness that human beings should be trained for and it should be the goal for complete human development. The advancement in developing oneself to gain happiness at higher level is the progress from practicing Dhamma, which can be achieved by continued practicing rightly. When people reach the true happiness with full wisdom, they are free from any attachment and will not move back to enjoy the lower level of happiness. In other words, true happiness means realizing Dhamma, and reaching true happiness means reaching Dhamma. Buddhism teaches how to achieve a good and happy life by reaching the essence of Dhamma. Human beings have to understand what is a good life and genuine happiness. However, there are many steps to reach true happiness and many detailed classifications of happiness in various Dhamma books.

11.2.1 Three levels, from the lowest to the highest ones

(i) Sensual Pleasures:

As described before, happiness from sensual pleasures is the lowest level of Buddhist happiness, obtained from 5 senses: eye, ear, nose, tongue, and body; such as nice forms, pleasant noises, good smell, sweet taste, and comfortable touches. These are the pleasures one enjoys these things at physical level. This sensual pleasures or kāmasukha is not real happiness because it may involve dissatisfaction and suffering (dhukha). Happiness at this level can be further divided into two categories: undeveloped and developed ones.

(a) First, the undeveloped one from untrained mind, driven by kilesa (defilements) which is a troublesome desire: This type of desire is driven with the ignorance of the three signs of truth (impermanent, suffering, and non-existing) and can push people into trouble with dissatisfaction and unlimited wants. This type of desire may be called as "taṇhā" (craving and attachment). When the desire is not met, it can cause frustration due to attachment from being anticipated.

(b) It is acceptable that people can be happy with sensual pleasures, if they have wisdom and practices for living appropriately in the society. People can have materials and wealth, but they know how to develop their lives as well as others' towards higher goals. In other words, material accumulations can be used to improve human development to benefit the society as a whole. Also, human sensual desires should limit and people must know what level is appropriate for themselves and well behave towards others. In the process of acquisition, of material wealth, one should not burden oneself as well as the others.

If people in the society have sīla (morality), dāna (generiousity, sharing), and paññā (wisdom), the society can gain positively from material development. Therefore, Buddhism does not reject materials or physical development, if it is supervised by Dhamma.

(ii) Mind-Based Happiness

This is the happiness that can be generated as mind-based, not from getting more materials or dependence with external factors. Happiness can be developed inside one's own mind. Therefore, this level of happiness is higher than the level of physical well-being which has to depend on other things outside oneself.

As indicated in Buddha Dhmama, development on the mind-level will allow the individual to have a mind that contains virtues like loving-kindness (mettā), compassion (karuṇa), faith (saddhā), gratitude (kataññūkataveditā) and so on. It is a mind with efficiency, strength, stability, diligence and patience, a mind that has mindfulness (sati) and knows its responsibilities, and so, it is in good health because it is peaceful, relaxed, clear, fresh, joyful, and happy.

With loving-kindness (mettā) and compassion (karuṇā) in mind, we want other people to be happy. Therefore, we are happy to give, share, or help others, instead of taking advantage from them. People can be generous (dāna) towards others rather than selfishness, and that can generate happiness to the givers. Instead of being happy from acquisitions, individuals can be happy from giving away and less acquisition. In that case, individual happiness from mind.

(iii) Happiness at the Level of Liberation

Happiness at this level is characterized by wisdom or insight (paññā), with full understanding of natural changes from the three signs of truth: the impermanance, the state of suffering, and the non-existing (or selflessness). Realizing that it is not worth to attach with, human beings then have purified minds and free from any attachment. Therefore, they are completely free from suffering as they have insight to understand all the natural laws, that is, changes as well as causes and effects. This is the highest level of happiness and the individual who has progress to reach this level is completely awakened or enlightened with natural freshness and joyfulness. Nothing can cause suffering to that person whose wisdom is able to solve all problems wisely with the mind of emptiness and unattached. They will neutrally understand everything under the natural truth without suffering. Although the person can have happiness at sensual pleasures (level 1) and mind-based (level 2), there would be no danger as that are supervised by wisdom and can positively be utilized for the benefits of others and the society.

This level is the ultimate goal of dhamma practice or happiness development to be called as lokuttara (beyond the world) level or paramattha (the highest level). Those who can achieve this level are noble individuals or called "Ariya". That individual who has achieved the highest happiness do not want anything for oneself anymore; therefore, that one can fully work for others for the benefit of the society. Whatever the individual does is driven from "chanda" to do good things with selflessness, as well as pure and perfect compassion. Consequently, the society has received benefit fully from this type of highly developed person.

11.3 Treating Mind through the Eightfold Path of Buddhism

For Buddha, the path to happiness starts from an understanding of the root causes of suffering. Those who consider Buddha a pessimist because of his concern with suffering have missed the point. In fact, he is a skilful doctor — he may break the bad news of our suffering, but he also prescribes a proactive course of treatment. In this metaphor, the medicine is the Buddha's teachings of wisdom and compassion known as Dharma, and the nurses that encourage us and show us how to take the medicine are the Buddhist community or Sangha. The illness however, can only be cured if the patient follows the doctor's advice and follows the course of treatment: the Eightfold Path, the core of which involves control of the mind.

In Buddhism, this treatment is not a simple medicine to be swallowed, but a daily practice of mindful thought and action that we ourselves can test scientifically through our own experience. Meditation is, of course, the most well-known tool of this practice, but contrary to popular belief, it is not about detaching from the world. Rather it is a tool to train the mind not to dwell in the past or the future, but to live in the here and now, the realm in which we can experience peace most readily.

All that we are is the result of what we have thought. It is founded on our thoughts. It is made up of our thoughts. If one speaks or acts with an evil thought, pain follows one, as the wheel follows the foot of the ox that draws the wagon.

All that we are is the result of what we have thought. It is founded on our thoughts. It is made up of our thoughts. If one speaks or acts with a pure thought, happiness follows one, like a shadow that never leaves.
- (Dhammapada 1-2 / Müller & Maguire, 2002.)

The first and second verses (abovc) of the Dhammapada, the earliest known collection of Buddha's sayings, talk about suffering and happiness. So, it's not surprising to discover that Buddhism has a lot to offer on the topic of happiness. Buddha's contemporaries described him as "ever-smiling" and portrayals of Buddha almost always depict him with a smile on his face (Laughing Buddha). But rather than the smile of a self-satisfied, materially-rich or celebrated man, Buddha's smile comes from a deep equanimity from within.

The Problem & The Solution: The Four Noble Truths & The Eightfold Path to Happiness

These Four Noble Truths, monks, are actual, unerring, not otherwise. Therefore, they are called noble truths. (Samyutta Nikaya 56.27)

The Eightfold Path

1. Right View/ understanding (wisdom), 2. Right Intention/ thought (wisdom), 3. Right Speech (Ethical conduct), 4. Right Action (Ethical conduct), 5. Right Livelihood (Ethical conduct), 6. Right Effort (Mental cultivation), 7. Right Mindfulness (Mental cultivation), and 8. Right Concentration (Mental cultivation).

The Eightfold Path is a practical and systematic way out of ignorance, eliminating dukkha from our minds and our lifestyle through mindful thoughts and actions. It is presented as a whole system, but the three paths associated with the area of mental cultivation are particularly relevant to the happiness that we can find in equanimity, or peace of mind.

Right Effort:

The Buddha once described the mind as a wild horse. In the Eightfold Path, he recommends practicing "right effort" by first avoiding and then clearing our minds of negative, unwholesome thoughts. Once that is achieved, one perfects a wholesome, tranquil state of mind through the practice of positive thinking. This ongoing effort promotes a state of mind that is conducive to the practice of mindfulness and concentration (meditation).

Mindfulness:

Mindfulness is one of the most influential teachings of Buddhism and has filtered into popular culture as well as modern psychotherapy. The Buddha felt that it was imperative to cultivate right mindfulness for all aspects of life in order to see things as they really are, or in other words, to "stop and smell the roses."

Right Concentration and Meditation:

A monk who with tranquil mind has chosen to live in a bare cell knows an unearthly delight in gaining a clearer and clearer perception of the true law.
(Dhammapada 373 / Müller & Maguire, 2002.)

Right Concentration is a mental discipline that aims to transform your mind. As the core practice of "meditation," right concentration is a foundational activity within Buddhist thought and practice.

11.4 Equanimity: Peace of Mind & Happiness

If by leaving a small pleasure one sees a great pleasure, let a wise person leave the small pleasure and look to the great. - (Dhammapada 290 / Müller & Maguire, 2002.)

Buddhism pursues happiness by using knowledge and practice to achieve mental equanimity. In Buddhism, equanimity, or peace of mind, is achieved by detaching oneself from the cycle of craving that produces dukkha. So, by achieving a mental state where you can detach from all the passions, needs and wants of life, you free yourself and achieve a state of transcendent bliss and well-being.

As described in the first verse of the Dhammapada, for Buddha, mental dysfunction begins in the mind. The Buddha encouraged his followers to pursue "tranquillity" and "insight" as the mental qualities that would lead to Nirvana, the Ultimate Reality. As mentioned earlier, the Eightfold Path as a whole is said to help one achieve these qualities. In particular, the areas of mental cultivation, which include right effort, right mindfulness and right concentration, are the mental skills and tools used for achieving happiness.

11.5 Research on Happiness

The concept of happiness as an achievable goal, something we can deliberately cultivate through practice and effort, is fundamental to the Buddhist view of happiness. In fact, the idea of training the mind has been the cornerstone of Buddhist practice for millennia. The impact is even being seen on the governmental level in nations around the world, with the country of Bhutan, for instance, replacing GDP with GNH (Gross National Happiness) as its most important measure of success as a nation. Policymakers in many nations are now even exploring the idea of shaping public policy based on happiness research. As one government official in Scotland exuberantly asserted, "If we can embrace this new science of positive psychology, we have the opportunity to create a new Enlightenment."

11.5.1 Benefits of Happiness

One of the factors fueling the Happiness Revolution has been the startling research in the past decade revealing the many benefits of happiness, benefits extending far beyond merely "feeling good." In fact, cultivating greater happiness can be seen as "one-stop shopping" for those seeking greater success in every major life domain. Scientific studies have shown that happy people are more likely to attract a mate, enjoy stronger and more satisfying marriages, and are better parents. Happy people are also healthier, with better immune function and less cardiovascular disease. There is even evidence that happy individuals live up to ten years longer than their less happy peers! In addition, happiness leads to better mental health, greater resilience, and an increased capacity to deal with adversity and trauma.

There are some who believe that happy people tend to be shallow and a bit stupid, a notion shared by the French novelist Gustave Flaubert, who once wrote: "To be stupid, selfish, and have good health are three requirements for happiness, though if stupidity is lacking, all is lost." Recent research, however, has proven this idea to be nothing but a myth, finding that happiness leads to greater creativity and improved mental functioning. The benefits of happiness extend to the workplace, as well, with happy individuals performing better and enjoying greater personal success on every level, including higher income. In fact, studies show that higher income is more directly related to one's level of happiness than to one's level of education. Extensive research has also shown that organizations with happy employees are more successful, consistently demonstrating greater profitability; this isn't surprising considering that happy workers are more productive, more loyal to the company, take fewer sick days, show up to work more consistently, have fewer conflicts with coworkers, quit their jobs less frequently, and generate greater customer satisfaction.

So there is no question that happiness brings tremendous personal rewards. But it is also critical to point out that cultivating greater happiness benefits not only oneself, but also one's family, community, and society. The beneficial effects of happiness extend to the broadest level of society; another study, for instance, found that increasing the average level of happiness among the population of a nation will result in an increase in freedom and democracy in that country! Other lines of evidence have found that happiness and positive emotions act as an antidote to prejudice, causing changes in the brain that prevent the instinctual bias against those we perceive as different, ultimately breaking down the barriers between us and them. With this in mind, it's important to recognize that the science of human happiness is still in its infancy. While we have learned a great deal, there is a lot that we still don't know.

Buddhism might have much to contribute to our understanding of happiness and how to achieve it, and some remarkable recent developments certainly suggest that this is the case. A fascinating line of evidence is based on some cutting-edge research conducted by Dr. Richard Davidson, a highly regarded neuroscientist at the University of Wisconsin in Madison. Using the latest technology, Dr. Davidson and colleagues identified a specific area in the left prefrontal cortex of the brain that is associated with states of happiness. He then measured the average level of activity in this "happiness" region among a large group of ordinary Americans. Later, he invited some Tibetan Buddhist monks into his lab and performed the same studies. He was astonished to find that their levels of activity in the happiness area of the brain were the highest he had ever seen, and by a huge margin—so far above the others that they were essentially off the chart! Of course, this may not be proof of anything, but nevertheless such extreme findings are highly suggestive of the potential value of Buddhist practices in the quest to find effective methods of increasing individual happiness.

11.6 Kindness and Compassion are the Pre-requisites for Happiness

There is an inextricable link between one's personal happiness and kindness, compassion, and caring for others. And this is a two-way street: increased happiness leads to greater compassion, and increased compassion leads to greater happiness.

In other words, studies have found not only that happier people tend to be more caring and more willing to reach out and help others, but that by deliberately cultivating greater kindness and compassion, a person will experience increased happiness. It is easy to see how such principles could have a profound impact on any society if people adopted them on a widespread scale. However, since it is unlikely that most people will "convert" to Buddhism as their primary spiritual path, they need to be presented in a secular context, which generally means investigating them from a scientific perspective.

11.7 Right to Happiness

The very purpose of our life is to seek happiness. That is clear. Whether one believes in religion or not, whether one believes in this religion or that religion, we all are seeking something better in life. The concept of achieving true happiness has, in the West, always seemed ill-defined, elusive, ungraspable. Even the word "happy" is derived from the Icelandic word happ, meaning luck or chance. Most of us, it seems, share this view of the mysterious nature of happiness. In those moments of joy that life brings, happiness feels like something that comes out of the blue. When we speak of this inner discipline, it can of course involve many things, many methods. But generally speaking, one begins by identifying those factors which lead to happiness and those factors which lead to suffering. Having done this, one then sets about gradually eliminating those factors which lead to suffering and cultivating those which lead to happiness. That is the way.

The basic premise that the purpose of our life is to seek happiness. It is a vision of happiness as a real objective, one that we can take positive steps toward achieving. And as we begin to identify the factors that lead to a happier life, we will learn how the search for happiness offers benefits not only for the individual but for the individual's family and for society at large as well.

11.8 Sources of Happiness

Talking at a superficial lever, a pay raise, a new car, or recognition from our peers may lift our mood for a while, but we soon return to our customary level of happiness. In the same way, an argument with a friend, a car in the repair shop, or a minor injury may put us in a foul mood, but within a matter of days our spirits rebound. This tendency isn't limited to trivial, everyday events but persists even under more extreme conditions of triumph or disaster. Researchers surveying Illinois state lottery winners and British pool winners, for instance, found that the initial high eventually wore off and the winners returned to their usual range of moment-to-moment happiness. And other studies have demonstrated that even those who are struck by catastrophic events such as cancer, blindness, or paralysis typically recover their normal or near-normal level of day-to-day happiness after an appropriate adjustment period.

So, if we tend to return to our characteristic baseline level of happiness no matter what our external conditions are, what determines this baseline? And, more important, can it be modified, set at a higher level? Some researchers have recently argued that an individual's characteristic level of happiness or well-being is genetically determined, at least to some degree. Studies such as one that found that identical twins (sharing the same genetic constitution) tend to have very similar levels of well-being—regardless of whether they were raised together or apart have led these investigators to postulate a biological set point for happiness, wired into the brain at birth.

But even if genetic makeup plays a role in happiness—and the verdict is still out on how large that role is—there is general agreement among psychologists that no matter what level of happiness we are endowed with by nature, there are steps we can take to work with the "mind factor," to enhance our feelings of happiness. This is because our moment-to-moment happiness is largely determined by our outlook. In fact, whether we are feeling happy or unhappy at any given moment often has very little to do with our absolute conditions but, rather it is a function of how we perceive our situation, how satisfied we are with what we have.

11.9 Some Buddha Quotes on Happiness

Buddha was not as chubby as many depictions of him make it seem – he was portrayed this way because, in the east, it was symbolic of happiness. Buddha practiced moderation, fasted regularly, and spent a lot of his time traveling by foot hundreds of miles, spreading his philosophy of enlightenment.

Following are some of the Buddha Quotes on Happiness:

- *If you are quiet enough, you will hear the flow of the universe. You will feel its rhythm. Go with this flow. Happiness lies ahead.*

Meditation is key.

- *Thousands of candles can be lit from a single candle, and the life of the candle will not be shortened. Happiness never decreases by being shared.*

- *There is no path to happiness. Happiness is the path.*

- *It is ridiculous to think that somebody else can make you happy or unhappy.*

- *Happiness does not depend on what you have or who you are. It solely relies on what you think.*

- *A disciplined mind brings happiness.*

- *Happiness is not having a lot. Happiness is giving a lot.*

- *Happiness never decreases by being shared.*

- *If you knew what about the power of giving you would not let a single meal pass without sharing it in some way.*

- *You only lose what you cling to.*

- *The past is already gone; the future is not yet here. There's only one moment for you to live.*

- *Your work is to discover your work and then with all your heart to give yourself to it.*

- *Teach this triple truth to all: A generous heart, kind speech, and a life of service and compassion are the things which renew humanity.*

- *Every human being is the author of his own health and*

happiness.

- *One should strive to understand what underlies sufferings and diseases – and aim for health and well-being while gaining in the path.*

CHAPTER 12

Happiness in Sufism

12.1 Concept of Happiness in Islam (Sufism)

From Islamic perspective, happiness is expressed by the term *sa'ādah*. The term contrary to *sa'ādah* is *shaqāwah*, which generally conveys the meaning of great misfortune and misery. The term *sa'ādah* is related to two dimensions of existence: the hereafter *(ukhrawiyah)* and the present world *(dunyawiyah)*. The term *sa'ādah* has a close relation to both the hereafter and the present world. In the case of the hereafter, *sa'ādah* indicates a meaning of an ultimate form of happiness, which is everlasting contentment and bliss, the highest vision of God, promised to those, who in the worldly life, have submitted themselves sincerely to serve God by obeying His commands, and avoiding His prohibitions. In other words, they observe the tenets of Islamic teachings.

The present world, on the other hand, is related to three things: (1) to the self *(nafsiyyah),* such as conduct pertaining to knowledge and good character, (2) to the body *(badaniyyah)*, such as good health and security, and (3) to things external to the self and the body *(khārijiyyah)*, such as wealth and other attributes. Based on the explanation above, it is clear that happiness affects not only our secular and regular life; in fact, it cannot be separated from the spiritual aspects of our existence as interpreted and guided by religion.

There are four group of means *(wasā'il) to happiness,* which man can utilise to achieve happiness in his life. Each of these four means has four forms of virtuousness. Thus, in actual fact, the total number of means amounts to sixteen. Nevertheless, not all of these means are equally relevant to happiness. In other words, they have their own functions, some are useful and some are necessary to attain happiness. The four groups of means are (1) the 'goods' of the *soul (al-fadā'il an-nafsiyya)*, (2) the bodily 'goods' *(al-fadā'il al-*

jismiyya), (3) the external 'goods' *(al-fadā'il al-khārijiyya),* and (4) the 'goods' of divine grace *(al-fadā'il at-tawfiqiyya).*

Al-Ghazzali was a practical mystic. His aim was to make men better by leading them from a merely notional acquiescence in the stereotyped creed of Islam to a real knowledge of God. The Ihya was written in Arabic and Ghazzali himself wrote an abridgment of it in Persian for popular use which he entitled Kimiya'e Saadat ("The Alchemy of Happiness"). The real self-knowledge consists in knowing the following things: What art thou in thyself, and from whence hast thou come? Whither art thou going, and for what purpose hast thou come to tarry here awhile, and in what does thy real happiness and misery consist? Some of thy attributes are those of animals, some of devils, and some of angels, and thou hast to find out to which of these attributes are accidental and which essential. Till thou knowest this, thou canst not find out where thy real happiness lies.

Anyone who will look into the matter will see that happiness is necessarily linked with the knowledge of God. Love is the seed of happiness, and love to God is fostered and developed by worship. All Muslims profess to believe that the Vision of God is the summit of human felicity, because it is so stated in the Law; but with many, this is a mere lip-profession which arouses no emotion in their hearts. This is quite natural, for how can a man long for a thing of which he has no knowledge? We must realise why the Vision of God is the greatest happiness to which a man can attain. For perfect happiness mere knowledge is not enough, unaccompanied by love, and the love of God cannot take possession of a man's heart till it be purified from love of the world, which purification can only be affected by abstinence and austerity. In brief, our future happiness will be in strict proportion to the degree in which we have loved God here.

12.2 How to Achieve Infinite Happiness according to Sufism?

Man is composed of three bodies. This creature that we call "man" is the most beloved creature of Allah. Allah wills this creature that He has created to be happy, to live in happiness. For this reason, He has created him differently from His other creatures, because we see that he has been created out of three different bodies. Another creature composed of three bodies has not been created in the universe and its being created is out of the question."Tasavvuf" (Sufism) is to act with the whole of the Noble Qur'an. It is to act not only with the verses concerning our physical body but also with the verses laying tasks on our soul and spirit, too. "Tasavvuf" (Sufism) is to live that which our Master the Prophet and his Companions (sahabe) had lived. The life that all the prophets and their dependents had lived was also "Tasavvuf" (Sufism). Tasavvuf (Sufism) is to surrender to Allâh our trusts (the spirit, the physical body, the soul and the free will) that He has confided to us. It is to reach "irshad", which is to be Islâm.

The first content of the word of Islâm is to believe in One Allah, its second content is the surrender (teslim, submission), its third content is peace and quietness (tranquility, serenity). Whoever has attained to the honour of becoming Islâm has reached the infinite happiness in three respects.

(i) As all the good qualities of the spirit are transferred to the soul in the inner world, man has reached peace and tranquility, because there is not any more state of conflict between the spirit and the soul.

(ii) Man has reached peace and tranquility in his relations with the outer world, that is, with other people, because there are not any more vices so that there may be conflicts with them.

(iii) The best relations have been established with Allahû Tealâ. Each order of our Exalted Lord has been fulfilled and each prohibition avoided. Henceforth, the virtues that the soul has possessed (that is, the good qualities of the spirit) feel a strong desire to execute the divine orders and never commit the prohibitions, because all the vices demanding to commit them have vanished. It has been thus seen that Islâm is a phase to be reached in order that an infinite happiness, a supreme delight, (hazzu'l 'azîm) should come into being.

For this reason, Allâh orders man to reach Irshad [2/Al-Baqarah – 186, 42/Ash-Shûra – 47]. Because only the person who has reached irshad has attained to Islâm, consequently to an infinite happiness. He has attained to the last rank of being a "perfect man" (Insân-ı Kâmil). He has been a perfect man from the point of view of happiness.

As this creature we name "man" is the most superior and beloved creature of Allahû Tealâ, He wishes him to live in Happiness, in Bliss. For this reason, He has created him differently from the creatures He had been creating up to that day, because we see that the man is composed of different bodies. Another creature created with the three different bodies has never been created in the Universe. His creation is out of the question, too. In the 26th verse of Hicr Sura, Allahû Tealâ makes known that our physical body was created out of soil. Allahû Tealâ wills this creature He loves the most to be happy. For this reason, The Torah, the Book of Psalms, the Gospel and the Glorious Qur'an have been sent down as an Invitation of Happiness to the humankind. That is to say, throughout the human history, Allah always wills the human beings to be happy.

You are a human being who cannot be happy in the sight of Allahû Tealâ. You are a person who cannot apply the prescription of happiness He has granted to you and therefore who will never be able to reach HAPPINESS as long as you will not apply that prescription. But when the person fulfils the Commands of Allah, he purifies his soul. If he surrenders his spirit to Allah, fulfill the subsequent surrenders, if he keeps trying in this direction, Allahû Tealâ will absolutely direct him from unhappiness to happiness. In such a system, man will gradually experience (taste) happiness. Allah is Able to do all things. But if men provoke wrong things through their wrong behaviours, he will never be able to reach Happiness neither in this worldly life nor in the Afterlife. If we scrutinize the Commands given by Allah carefully, we will see that the aim of Allah by saying: "purify your souls" is our happiness.

We name “Zikir” the iteration of the Name of Allah by beings (mankind and jinn) possessing the free will (faculty of choice). Zikir is a volitional event. This is an act made by the consent of the person and the unique means to make our worldly works into a worship. It is only zikir that can satify the (soul’s) heart. It is not possible for man to reach the happiness and the satisfaction without zikir.

The striving too is one of the means of remembering Allah. It is an occasion of zikir. That is to say, the goal is to repeat constantly Allah’s Name. But just as we should repeat the name of Allah in our hearts, we should also do zikir during our apparent actions. Now, the striving also is only one of the means to remember Allah. Striving against one’s soul in the Way of Allah has two meanings: Outwardly, to fight against the enemies of Islâm corporally. Inwardly, to struggle against one’s soul by means of zikir. Happiness will come after this fight, this struggle.

The fact that reaching Happiness is only possible by doing too much zikir has been expressed in the sacred verse below:

O you who are âmenû! When the call is made for prayer on Friday, then hasten to Allah’s zikir and leave off trading; that is better for you if you did but know! Then when the prayer is ended, then disperse in the land (earth) and seek of Allah’s Blessings (Virtue) and repeat Allah’s name too much, that you may reach the Salvation (Felâh: the Worldly Happiness and the Bliss of Paradise).

- 62/Al-Jumu’ah – 9, 10

Truly, man reaches “irshad” in person at the end of this invitation. For this reason, Allah calls all the human beings to “irshad”. For He wills man He loves the most to live happily in this world and in the next world. In case the person has not got rid of the tyranny of his soul through irshad, he cannot experience happiness neither in the life of this world nor in the Afterlife.

Allah sets forth a parable: There is a slave in whom are (several) partners disputing with one another, and there is another slave wholly owned by one man (master). Are the two alike in comparisoned?

(All) praise is due to Allah. Nay! Most of them do not know.

- 39/Az-Zumar – 29

Of a certainty, the slave who will conform to a single master, obey the orders of a single master will be in a better condition. Now, we shall attain the happiness when we abandon one of the masters from whom we take orders in opposite directions and act by order of a single Master. Insha Allah (if Allah wills it), to be able to attain this happiness is possible through reaching the third servanthood.

The fact that everything has been created for man and has been subjected to him demonstrates clearly that Allah loves mankind the most. Now on account of this boundless love that Allah has for man, He wills us to be happy. We can say briefly that Allah wishes solely mankind to be happy. But men are unhappy, are in stress. He has been seeking happiness everywhere in vain except the place where he should search for it. The Torah, the Psalms, Gospel and the Noble Qur'ân that Allah had sent down respectively for His human servants is an Invitation to Happiness and more owe a prescription of Happiness. Allah names the state of happiness as "hazzu'l 'azîm" (the boundless delight, the greatest gratification, the boundless happiness).

12.3 Pir-O-Murshid Inayat Khan, as a Symbol of Joy and Pain

Pir Vilayat Inayat Khan details the life, work, thinking and feelings of his Sufi Master, Pir-O-Murshid Inayat Khan. Murshid, according to Khan, "in his last years carried the signature of suffering written on his face, while one would have thought that a liberated master would radiate only joy". The author further explains that while one becomes increasingly sensitive with spiritual development, one is not carried exclusively to the land of joy, while ignoring the cries of pain and despair in the world. Instead, one becomes increasingly aware of all that is, was and will be, "in the Murshid one found joy and pain simultaneously, the way of the broken heart both agonizing and jubilant, never indifferent or low key".

The Sufi Master's words, "there is an incipient suffering ingrained in the very nature of life - life's inseparable companion". Suffering is found in birth and in death. Suffering is pervasive – even in a joy too intense, or unrcquited love, a loss of hope, guilt in not having given enough, or regret in having given too much.. Pir Vilayat Inayat Khan lost his sister in the Concentration Camps at Dauchau, and therefore, is deeply aware of and sensitive to global suffering, genocide, sadism, and humiliation. He has compassion for all the victims of cruelty, savagery, and natural disasters in this world. The collective Sufi consciousness is said to be aware that "everywhere and everyday there is endless bitter suffering. No matter how we may wish to protect people from it we cannot, because there must be room for the play of the forces set off by cosmic laws in motion. The only answer is to know how to harness the force that is suffering".

According to Pir Vilayat Inayat Khan we each have a certain threshold for physical pain in the human mind, with a "cut out mechanism" which is set very high for some people. Naturally, as one attempts to escape physical pain, the urgency of the pain keeps pulling one back to it and efforts to dissociate fail. The Murshid states, "The more one can bear, the more one is given to bear.

Pir Vilayat Inayat Kahn states "the more courageously you face physical suffering, the higher the threshold of suffering you can endure, and then at a moral level the more hardship one can endure". For the Sufis, accepting the situation and our suffering as part of the agony of the universe on a cosmic scale is the only way suffering can be sublimated . For us personally, the physical pain is simply pain.

According to the Murshid, it is not detachment that is the solution to our suffering; suffering is overcome by merging with all existence. As for joy, one is never so happy as when one has no reason to be because circumstances can never be so good as to suffice in making one happy. "Happiness cannot be bought or sold, nor can it be given. Happiness is in one's own being, one's own self, that Self that is the most precious thing in life." When one finds oneself face to face with the reality of suffering, and holds the belief that there is some intentional planning behind human affairs and destiny, we feel like storming the Universal force we perceive to be responsible. If one believes one is a victim, one feels the agony. All one can ask then is why, over and over. The Murshid points out that by blaming the cosmic planner, we become preoccupied with avoiding any suffering or bad karma that might bring more suffering upon us. We act as if happiness alone were our birth-right. It indicates that suffering is not part of left-over karma from a past life or even from this one, but is simply part of our training for life. Finding in everything its purpose, Murshid sees in pain "the lever devised by nature to make a person sincere and quickens one with life".

12.4 Essentials of Happiness in Major Sources in Sufism

The religion of Islam is accepting and being faithful to the teachings of God which He revealed to His last prophet, Muhammad. These teachings are prescribed in the Qur'an and the Sunnah (sayings and doings of the Prophet). Additional sources include analogical reasoning and the consensus of the community. In terms of belief, the Muslim should believe in One God; all of his messengers and previous books and revelations; the angels; the Last Day of Judgement; and finally, that what a human being faces in his life is God's will.

A first conclusion with regard to happiness in this system is that God is the origin of all good. He is the supplier and the Saviour. His continuous presence comforts one's life. The Qur'an describes this state by saying, "And when My servants question thee concerning Me, then surely I am nigh. I answer the prayer of the suppliant when he crieth unto Me. So let them hear My call and let them trust in Me, in order that they may be led aright" (Qur'an, 2:186). God metaphorically presents Himself in the Qur'an as the light of all existence, and it is that light that guides humans to true happiness. He says, "Allah is the Light of the heavens and the earth. The similitude of His light is as a niche wherein is a lamp. The lamp is in a glass. The glass is as it were a shining star. (This lamp is) kindled from a blessed tree, an olive neither of the East nor of the West, whose oil would almost glow forth (of itself) though no fire touched it. Light upon light. Allah guideth unto His light whom He will. And Allah setteth forth for man- kind similitudes, for Allah is Knower of all things" (Qur'an, 24:35). The Qur'an promises not only Heaven after life for those who act according to the words of God but also good life on earth: "Whosoever doeth right, whether male or female, and is a believer, him verily we shall quicken with good life, and We shall pay them a recompense in proportion to the best of what they used to do" (Qur'an, 16:97). He warns those who turn away from his remembrance unhappiness in life and after death: "But he who turneth away from remembrance of Me, his will be a narrow life, and I shall bring him blind to the assembly on the Day of Resurrection" (Qur'an, 20:124). Man occupies the position of God's viceroy on earth. In the Islamic narrative of the Creation of Adam, the Qur'an recounts, "And when thy Lord said unto the angels: Lo! I am about to place a viceroy in the earth, they said: Wilt thou place therein one who will do harm therein and will shed blood, while we, we hymn Thy praise and sanctify Thee? He said: Surely I know that which ye know not" (Qur'an 2:30). His life is then purposeful. But when it comes to his relation with the Creator, this must be of total submission. Submission to God has no prejudice to human beings but is rather presented as an act of recognition and gratefulness to all His gifts.

He challenges human's intelligence by saying, "He it is Who hath created for you, ears and eyes and hearts. Small thanks give ye! And He it is Who hath sown you broadcast in the earth, and unto Him ye will be gathered. And He it is Who giveth life and causeth death, and His is the difference of night and day. Have ye then no sense?" (Qur'an, 23:78–80). So, human beings, though holding the high rank of God's viceroy on earth, "And indeed, We have honoured the Children of Adam" (Qur'an, 17:70), cannot live a peaceful and a happy life without believing in the sustaining power. Moreover, the responsibility of humans is in line with this high rank among all creatures. He is responsible of all his sayings and doings and will be questioned on everything in the Last Day of Judgement: “Lo! We create man from a drop of thickened fluid to test him; So, We make him hearing, knowing” (Qur’an, 76:2).

12.5 The Falsafa (Philosophy) of Happiness in Sufism

Theoretical quests which are intimately linked to the Qur’an and the Hadith have accompanied the birth of Islam. They were further refined and extended as a result of Islam’s meeting with other cultures. For instance, the movement of Falsafa (philosophy) continued and recreated Greek philosophical thought. Happiness and social and political conducts were among the central themes of discussion. However, the shared frame of reference was the conception of “humans as ethical beings searching for happiness through the improvement of their natures and modes of conduct”. Happiness is conceived as transcendence beyond the physical or the sensual to achieve the long-lasting eternal happiness which is with the mercy of God and His heavens. So, earthly life is just a path toward the eternal home. Yet, the dichotomy between the two types of happiness is not easy to resolve as it may appear.

Big discrepancies could be noticed among Muslim scholars in approaching this issue. For instance, Al Farabi or Alpharabius (870–950) entitled one of his treaties “The attainment of happiness.” It discussed lengthily how individuals and nations could reach happiness. Deeply inspired by Aristotle, he proposed four kinds of happiness: theoretical virtues (knowledge naturally embedded in humans and those acquired through meditation, investigation and inference, instruction and study), deliberated virtues, moral virtues, and practical arts. Ibn Miskawayh (about 932–1030) displayed a main interest in ethics and how to reach ultimate happiness. He was deeply influenced by Aristotle and Neo-Platonism and held that happiness was the common aim for all human beings. Nevertheless, true happiness could not be found outside the boundaries of the divine word. Thus, the triumph is to succeed life tests and reach God’s blessings. Ibn Misquawayh agrees with Aristotle, clearly in opposition to Pythagoras, Hippocrates, and Plato, in that man’s happiness is in the perfection of both his spirit and body. Both Ibn Misquawayh and Aristotle maintain that the attainment of happiness is also possible in this world. Such things as health of body, moderation of temper and senses, wealth, good reputation, success in affaires, correctness of beliefs, moral virtues, and merited behaviour are a part of happiness, but the ultimate happiness is obtained through the accomplishment of all of the perfections related to spirit and body. Ibn Bajja or Avempace (about 1085–1139) is one of the main representatives of the falsafa in the Muslim West. In the Regimen of the Solitary, he maintained that the philosopher should isolate himself intellectually from the corrupted community, in order to attain the ultimate happiness of theoretical life. In The Conjunction of Intellect with Man, he argues that this ultimate happiness consists in the highest perfection of the human intellect.

12.6 Some Quotes / Verses on Happiness in Sufism

- *"Don't Worry Be Happy" — Meher Baba*

- *"Happiness comes from helping others, by being with others, and by sharing, even if it's only a smile."*
  — Zain Hashmi, A Blessed Olive Tree: A Spiritual Journey in Twenty Short Stories

- *"Whatever happens in your life, no matter how troubling things might seem, do not enter the neighborhood of despair. Even when all doors remain closed, God will open up a new path only for you. Be thankful! It is easy to be thankful when all is well. A Sufi is thankful not only for what he has been given but also for all that has been denied."*
  — Elif Shafak

- *The good deed and the evil deed cannot be equal. Repel (the evil) with one which is better; then verily he, between whom and you there was enmity, (will become) as though he was a close friend. But none is made to reach it (the above quality) except those who are patient – and none is made to reach it except the owner of the great portion (of happiness in the Hereafter that is, Paradise and of the happiness in this world).*

- *Fussilat – 34, 35*

- *The owners of Belief who wish to reach Allah! Be possessed of "Takvâ" towards Allah, And seek the Means to make you reach Him, and strive hard in His Way, so that you may reach Felâh (the Salvation the Bliss of Paradise and the worldly happiness).*

- *5/Al-Mâ'idah – 35*

- *Those who believed and emigrated and strove hard and fought in the Way of Allah with their property and their lives are far higher in degree in the Presence of Allah. It is those who have attained to Happiness.*

- *9/At-Taubah – 20*

-

- *And none are made to obtain (reach) it but those who are patient, and none are made to receive (reach) it but those who are the owners of great delight (happiness, portion).*

- *41/Fussilat – 35*

-

- *Let there arise from you a community who invite to goodness and enjoin what is right (el ma'rûf, what is ordered by Islâm) and forbid evil (el munker, what is forbidden by Islâm). Such are they who have reached the Salvation (Felâh = the happiness of the worldly life and the Bliss of Paradise).*

- *3/Âl-'Imrân – 104*

- *And he has indeed reached the Salvation (the worldly happiness and the bliss of Paradise) who purifies him.*

- *91/Ash-Shams – 9*

CHAPTER 13

Happiness in Christianity

"Happiness is the meaning and the purpose of life, the whole aim and end of human existence." ~ Aristotle

13.1 Happiness, Well-Being, and Flourishing in Christianity

When asked what people want for themselves and their children, happiness often tops the list. Human happiness is the core business of Positive Psychology. This field has been defined as the study of the conditions and processes that contribute to the flourishing or optimal functioning of peoples, groups, and institutions.

The concept of human happiness has been debated throughout the centuries. Flourishing, thriving, wellbeing, happiness, health, and optimal functioning are often used interchangeably, and one is often used to define the other. For instance, the World Health Organization defined health as "a complete state of physical, mental, and social wellbeing, not simply the absence of disease and disability". Numerous Positive Psychology scholars have proposed wellbeing theories, which intersect and diverge according to their own worldviews. Wellbeing and happiness are often viewed as meta constructs that subsume multiple other affective, cognitive, social, physical, and spiritual dimensions. Philosophically (returning to ancient Greek philosophers such as Aristotle and Socrates), theoretically and, happiness aligns along two primary dimensions: hedonic and eudaimonic .

13.2 Hedonic and Eudaimonic Happiness

Hedonic happiness is achieved through experiences of pleasure and enjoyment, while eudaimonic happiness is achieved through experiences of meaning and purpose. Both kinds of happiness are achieved and contribute to overall well-being in different ways.

13.2.1 Hedonic Happiness

Lay persons commonly associate happiness with hedonic wellbeing, which primarily refers to high levels of positive emotion (e.g., pleasure, excitement, contentment), low levels of negative emotion (e.g., sadness, anxiety, anger), and a general sense of satisfaction with life. Essentially hedonic wellbeing focuses on how wellbeing feels.

Positive emotion has been linked with numerous socially-valued outcomes, including better physical health, longer life, good social relationships, career advancement and success, lower levels of divorce, less mental illness, and greater creativity. The negative emotions narrow one's attention to the problem at hand, whereas positive emotions broaden one's psychological, social, and cognitive capacities. Evidence suggests that it is beneficial to have a greater proportion of positive emotions compared to negative emotions during the course of one's day. Positive emotions help people to connect with others and build resources, which can provide a buffer in times of stress. Positive and negative emotions can spread to others, potentially passed along through social networks.

Various interventions and exercises that can cultivate good feelings have been developed, which successfully temporarily relieve mental distress and improve self-reported wellbeing. Yet feelings are fleeting. Emotions change continuously throughout the day. We have a generally stable level of happiness, and despite good or bad experiences, we typically return to our baseline. While an entire industry of self-help books, entertainment, drugs, high-thrill activities, and the like have sprung up over the recent decades to help people 'feel good', the pursuit of pleasure often leaves a person feeling unfulfilled. Studies suggest that is possible to shift that level over time through one's activities, but it takes time and continued effort . Even while the idea of being happy sounds good, perhaps "all is vanity and a chasing after the wind".

13.2.2 Eudaimonic Happiness

Increasingly, Positive Psychology theory, research, and application has shifted its focus to eudaimonic wellbeing. Defined as "the good life", eudaimonia focuses on what makes life worth living. For example, self-determination theory suggests that humans have three core needs that drive behaviour: relationships, autonomy, and competence; happiness occurs when these needs are met. Psychological wellbeing is defined across six dimensions: positive social relationships, environmental mastery, autonomy, purpose in life, self-acceptance, and personal growth. These phenomenological indicators capture core aspects of what it means to be human. Studies over the past 25 years suggest that psychological wellbeing reduces the risk for disease and early mortality.

An aspect of eudaimonic wellbeing that has received a growing amount of attention in recent years is the meaning in life. The meaning involves two dimensions: comprehension, or an understanding of one's life (who one is, how one fits into the world, and a sense of direction), and purpose (feeling valuable, worthwhile, and that what one does matters). Studies have linked meaning and purpose to various subjective well-being measures, active engagement in life, better physical health, and lower mortality risk. The meaningful life is not necessarily happy from a hedonic perspective, but appears to lead to a variety of valued positive outcomes.

13.3 Christian Theology (Religious Belief) and Happiness

Christian theology has always been part of the happiness discourse. Realizing that temporary happiness is not sustainable and very fragile, theologians have indeed been very cautious to enter into the terminology and even the discussion of happiness. Because of the reality of death, happiness was thought to be unattainable in this life, and theologians generally resorted to eschatological terms to express their understanding of happiness as "eternal life". In ancient Aristotelian philosophy, happiness and morality were two sides of the same coin. Severing that bond in modernity, has placed theologians in a precarious position, where it became untenable to promote happiness on a Christian basis, for fear of it being identified too closely with hedonic happiness (the boosting of momentary and sensual experiences), detached from God and the moral good. But the theology can simultaneously hold both a moral and transcendent view on happiness, and recognize material pleasure and enjoyment, in a model of mutual affirmation.

A privatized, hedonic view of happiness can thus be overcome by the realization that social happiness is inevitably linked to individual happiness, and that goodness, creating more enduring societal happiness, need to be understood as an integral constituent part of happiness. In fact, it is generally recognized today that even sadness and despair can enrich one's life. A well-designed theological response will avoid both the extremes of other-worldliness on the one side and of mere materialism on the other. Claiming the connection between the spiritual and the material and grounding it in the theology of the incarnation and of the sacraments (as material means of grace) may show a way out of the impasse. The way in which the Old and the New Testament speak of or allude to happiness is indeed consistent with an integral connection of the spiritual and the material.

The Greek terms makarios and eudaimonia are used to denote "happiness". Makarios, in Homer, is used for describe the gods' state of happiness beyond care. From the time of Aristotle, the term has become weaker, denoting any happiness, also for humans. Aristotle still uses makarios to describe the gods' happiness, and uses eudaimonia to describe the happiness of humans. Seen in its Stoic context, eudaimonia is linked to the moral purpose (proairesis) of humankind, which means to live according to nature (kata phusin). It is further related to virtue (arete) and governed by reason (logos). So, for the Stoics eudaimonia is the ultimate goal in life, and it is primarily "to act virtuously so that one's life is in accordance with universal nature." Only secondarily it is "possibly a state of exhilaration" (chara, euphrosune) as a subsequent manifestation of virtuous activity.

The New Testament does not use eudaimonia to indicate happiness. Makarios and chairo are mostly used; with less frequent use of a few other terms as well. To the early Christians, understandably, happiness was a gift from the hand of God. According to the reports in Acts, they saw themselves as a community of joy and happiness. The coming of Jesus inaugurated a new era, that is, an era of happiness. The bridegroom has arrived; the fasting is over. The blind sees, the lame walks, the dead lives, and there is good news for the poor. There was a definite present aspect to this new view on happiness, but this happiness also included a future, where this happiness would be full and enduring. Especially in the gospel of Luke, this joyful theology is seen right from the birth narrative to the Easter accounts. With Paul this theology includes joy in suffering. Happiness is "happiness in Christ", which means sharing in his suffering and his glory. Happiness in spite of suffering and happiness in suffering is possible because of the future hope of sharing in Christ's triumph. In the Johannine writings special emphasis is laid on happiness as something that is fulfilled in the present." In Revelation happiness is on the new earth and in the new heaven when all unhappiness is removed forever. Vorster (1999:119) summarizes: Happiness is to be found in Christ. He is the inaugurator of happiness. In sorrow or pain, poverty or sadness, he is the reason why Christians can be happy. In Christ, God gives happiness. Happiness is both present and eschatological. In this sense, happiness appears to be a state of mind.

The "macarism" was known in both the Greek and Semitic worlds. It always refers to the "life-enhancing behaviour" of the believer, e.g., coming to Zion, fearing God, studying the Torah, caring for the poor, etc. The function (appearing almost exclusively in the Psalms and Wisdom literature) is to give moral instruction, indicating that persons following these instructions will be happy. Happiness corresponds with Israel's view on well-being, which mostly concerns the present: life, security, posterity, military success, prosperity, etc. In the inter-testamentary period, beatitude formulas start .

Because happiness is a gift from God and is found in the believers' relationship with God, it seems that happiness, according to early

Christianity is an inner state of the mind, a condition. Early Christians were also happy because of their conduct. Deeds have consequences, and proper conduct leads to happiness. Except for those who saw life in an apocalyptic perspective, both early Christians and Stoics had an optimistic view of life. They both accepted life as it was and tried to live happily. To be happy is to become wise in the eyes of both Stoics and early Christians.

The New Testament also speaks of suffering. Although it is not seen in a positive light, it is not seen to destroy the road to the highest good (or the Kingdom) of the faithful, as it contrasts that road, gives it profile, emphasises the urgency of being on that road, and trains the faithful in their determination to persevere towards the goal of the highest good. The New Testament does, however, promote the concept of life, understood both in its physical and eternal sense. Not losing your "soul" or "life" by winning the (material) world and following your selfish ways, is important. Christ promises life in abundance. This life is also described in very mundane terms to be calm (1 Tim 2:2), peaceful (Jm 3:17, 1 Tim 2:2 and 1 Tess 4:11) and unselfish (1 Cor 10:33).

Linking the life-promoting God to the concept of "blessing", Westermann (1968:44) shows that the Christian church stood in the long tradition which distinguished them from other religions of the time in that blessing would not only denote the showering with gifts because the worshippers of the particular God have performed the right rituals to appease the divine. Blessing was seen and experienced as God's power that enabled and sustained life and flourishing. It also protected from danger and despair. The Christians understood this notion of blessing to be proprietary connected to the salvation of God in Christ. Salvation in the Jewish tradition was not primarily seen then as salvation "from", but salvation to the empowering of the people of God in their existence in God's land. It is the Creator God who also blesses, and His blessing is continuation of his life-creating love. Westermann also shows the close relationship between blessing and wisdom. Where profane wisdom was about controlling your life in order to succeed, the reciprocal relationship between wisdom and blessing in Israel meant that wisdom was received as part of the blessing of God.

13.4 How to be happy in an unhappy world?

Frequently one is asked, "Is there any such thing as 'a happy life' in a world of 'Unhappiness, sin, suffering and sorrow'? If so, what is the recipe for it?" Surely anyone would be willing to pay a big price for such a recipe. But, there are as many recipes for happiness as there are recommended cures for a cold, However, in thinking of happiness as a permanent possession only One has an infallible recipe for it, Here is a recipe on to you because it never fails. Here it is:--

"Whoso trusteth in the lord, happy is he." Proberbs 16:20. " O, taste and see that the lord is good: happy is the man that trusteth in Him. n Psalm 34:8. "Happy is the man that walketh not in the counsel of the ungodly, nor standeth in the way of sinners, or sitteth in the seat of the scornful. But his delight is in the law of the lord. 11 Psalm l:l-2a, ''Happy is that people whose God is the Lord," Psalm 144:15.

In the light of these glorious truths, and the fact that there are two classes of people-the happy and the unhappy-lct us consider three things.

13.4.1 The Pursuit of Happiness

Everybody has a desire to be happy. Happiness is one thing for which all mankind is striving. Whether young or old, rich or poor, educated or. uneducated, saved or unsaved, all are pursuing happiness. Study the faces of people as they pass by on the street. What do those faces reveal that the people are thinking about and striving for? Is it money? Is it knowledge? Is it power? No, it is something behind all of these. It is happiness. Each one is trying to achieve happiness.

Some are concentrating all their energies in the pursuit of happiness, while others seem less hopeful, and more faint-hearted in their efforts. Bat, if the efforts that are being made to achieve happiness were only put forth in the right direction, many of the cups of happiness would be filled to overflowing. Much of the effort to secure happiness is made in the wrong way, so happiness is never achieved although it is desired and expected.

13.4.2 Preventiveness of Happiness

While all are pursuing happiness, it must be frankly admitted that the multitudes are not happy. Very few people are satisfied with what they have, but think if they had what some other people have they would be supremely happy. They fail to realize that a covetous soul can never be happy, even if it owned the whole world. Happiness does not consist in what you have, but in what you are. There are so many things that prevent people from being happy, but let us a few of them.

(i) An impossible or unattainable ambition.
(ii) A sell-interest which is so strong that it will not admit a social interest.
(iii) An unsatisfied craving, whether it be physical, social or mental.
(iv) tormenting conscience.
(v) An irritating or uncongenial environment.
(vi) Uncontrolled fear and anxiety.
(vii) Misdirected energies.
(viii) A spirit of covetousness.
(ix) An unsaved soul.

One can never experience happiness until his sins are forgiven and his soul is saved. “There is no peace, saith the Lord, unto the wicked.” Isaiah 48:22. ‘While an unsaved person is never happy, the Word of God says, “Happy is he whose transgression is forgiven, whose sin is covered. Happy is the man unto whom the lord imputeth not iniquity, and in whose spirit there is no guile.” Psalm 32:1-2.

(x) A disobedient life:

Saved people only are really happy. But one may ask, ''How do you account for the fact that many Christians are not happy?" That is an easy question to answer. They are living outside the circle of God's will for their lives. Any Christian who lives inside the circle of God's will for his life will be happy. God is the fountain of life and the source of all joy. Happiness is not something that we attain through increased possessions or through the achievement of some ambition; it is an attitude of life, a spirit within our own souls. If we do not have it on a small income, neither will we have it when our income grows larger. If it is not found where we are today, it will not be found in some place we may go tomorrow or next year. It is a flower that we my grow in the secret places of our own natures, and nowhere else in all the universe.

13.4.3 The Possessors of Happiness

Since all of us are in quest of' happiness, and the lord wants us to be happy, let us consider the best way to come into possession of happiness. One thing is certain, happiness cannot be found merely by running after it, because the source of happiness is within instead of without. Happiness depends on what lies. between the sole of your foot and the crown of your head. "Give us everything we want, the money we want, the recognition we want, the pleasures we want, and we shall be happy. Listen ! Money and happiness are not synonymous. Neither can you buy happiness. Real and abiding happiness is dependent not upon what we have in our hands, but upon what we have in our hearts.

Happiness is not to be found in unbelief. Happiness is not to be found in pleasure. Happiness is not to be found in money. Happiness is not to be found in position and fame. Happiness is not to be found in military glory. Alexander the Great conquered the known world in his day. Having done so, he wept in his tent, because, he said, "There are no more worlds to conquer."

where, then, is happiness to be found? In Christ alone. He said, "I will see you again, and your heart shall rejoice, and your joy no man take that from you." John 16:22.

In the light of the life and teachings of Jesus Christ, if you ever become the possessor of genuine happiness, it will come to you through the following channels.

(i) Salvation from sin;
(ii) Surrender to Christ;
(iii) Service for Christ; and
(iv) Share happiness with others.

"Lord Jesus I long to be perfectly whole; .

I want Thee forever to dwell in my soul;

Break down every idol, cast out every foe;

Oh wash me and I shall be whiter than snow.

13.5 Purpose for a Happy Life in Christianity

Positive Psychology (PP) theories focus on elements of the flourishing life, but lack a coherent purpose or outcome. Christianity adds the importance of telos – the realization of one's ultimate purpose, function, or design. The abundant theories of flourishing and happiness in the PP literature are predominantly self-driven, and interventions and activities aim to improve one's own happiness. The implied telos of PP is thus one of individual fulfillment and enjoyment. Yet the Bible suggests that such pursuits are meaningless (Ecclesiastes). In contrast, Christianity calls for a higher purpose that is defined by God. The source and meaning of happiness lie in God, rather than in the success or failure of one's own effort.

The Bible provides a specific purpose for humanity: humans were created in the image of God (the imago Dei) for the purpose of glorifying Him (1 Peter 4:11). Creation exists because God created it and humankind can only glimpse part of the full reality of God's purposes this side of heaven. Flourishing, or living the good life (i.e., a feeling of happiness and thriving), occurs when one lives in obedience to the design that God intended. This obedience is not simply a legalistic obedience confined by specific laws, but rather is a voluntary obedience to God's intentions for one's life, grounded in a close relationship with Him. As one's love for God grows, obedience to His commends becomes a natural response, and a sense of peace and happiness follow. It is a process of becoming who God uniquely intends one to be and becoming more Christ-like in one's attitudes, thoughts, and behaviour. Notably, Christ provides the ultimate example of human flourishing, demonstrating complete obedience to His design within the order of creation.

The Bible contains multiple words that in English all translate as "love". Storge refers to an empathetic bond or affection-based love, which is both need- and gift-related. It was responsible for 90% of human happiness. Philia is the love between friends, similar to that shown by Jonathan to David in the Old Testament (1 Samuel 18:1-4). Eros describes the emotional or sexual "being in love" feeling. Agape is God's unconditional love, which is extended to humankind regardless of circumstances or our response (John 3:16). These four types of love are only possible because of God's love for humankind.

13.6 Some Bible Verses About Joy and Happiness

God wants us to be happy and joyful. But what does that look like? How do we find happiness? The only way to find happiness is through Him. He created us! God knows us better than we know ourselves. Some of His ways may seem counterintuitive at first, but the verses that follow demonstrate where true contentment and joy is found—in Him!

The Bible contains many verses to provide wisdom and bring comfort in difficult times. There are also many verses about happiness to help guide you to a happy life.

You may have noticed that the Bible often uses the word joy instead of happiness. Finding happiness in the Bible isn't easy. And that's because the Bible isn't interested in making people happy. Instead, the Bible focuses on joy. These two words are often used interchangeably, but they aren't the same. The difference between joy and happiness is this: Joy is more consistent and is cultivated internally. It comes when you make peace with who you are, why you are and how you are, whereas happiness tends to be externally triggered and is based on other people, things, places, thoughts, and events.

In the modern world, joy is something we experience that is deeper and more meaningful. Happiness is something we feel because of our situation or circumstances. We are happy because something made us happy, but we are joyful because of something within us. The world tells us that we can only be happy if our situation is right. Many people that have everything they could ever want are not happy. And, on the other hand, many people have little in life but have a true joy that comes from deep within. When you study Bible verses about happiness, you will find how to experience true happiness.

Following are some of the verses in Bible about Joy and Happiness:

1 **Romans 15:13** Now may the God of hope fill you with all joy and peace in believing, that you may abound in hope by the power of the Holy Spirit.

2 **Hebrews 12:1-2** Therefore we also, since we are surrounded by so great a cloud of witnesses, let us lay aside every weight, and the sin which so easily ensnares us, and let us run with endurance the race that is set before us, looking unto Jesus, the author and finisher of our faith, who for the joy that was set before Him endured the cross, despising the shame, and has sat down at the right hand of

the throne of God.

3 **James 1:2-3** My brethren, count it all joy when you fall into various trials, knowing that the testing of your faith produces patience.

4 **Isaiah 9:3** You have multiplied the nation and increased its joy; they rejoice before You according to the joy of harvest, as men rejoice when they divide the spoil.

5 **Proverbs 10:28** The hope of the righteous will be gladness, but the expectation of the wicked will perish.

6 **Ecclesiastes 9:7** Go, eat your bread with joy, and drink your wine with a merry heart; for God has already accepted your works.

7 **Psalm 30:5** For His anger is but for a moment, His favour is for life; weeping may endure for a night, but joy comes in the morning.

8 **John 16:24** Until now you have asked nothing in My name. Ask, and you will receive, that your joy may be full.

9 **Psalm 34:8** Oh, taste and see that the Lord is good; blessed is the man who trusts in Him!

10. **Proverbs 16:20** He who heeds the word wisely will find good, and whoever trusts in the LORD, happy is he.

11 **Ecclesiastes 2:24** Nothing is better for a man than that he should eat and drink, and that his soul should enjoy good in his labour. This also, I saw, was from the hand of God.

12 **Psalm 144:15** Happy are the people whose God is the LORD!

13 **Psalm 16:11** You will show me the path of life; in Your

presence is fullness of joy; at Your right hand are pleasures forevermore.

14 **Proverbs 29:18** Where there is no revelation, the people cast off restraint; but happy is he who keeps the law.

15 **Romans 5:1-2** Therefore, having been justified by faith, we have peace with God through our Lord Jesus Christ, through whom also we have access by faith into this grace in which we stand, and rejoice in hope of the glory of God.

16 **Philippians 4:4** Rejoice in the Lord always. Again, I will say, rejoice!

17 **Matthew 5:9** Blessed are the peacemakers, for they shall be called sons of God.

18 **Matthew 5:4** Blessed are those who mourn, for they shall be comforted.

19 **Matthew 25:21** His lord said to him, "Well done, good and faithful servant; you were faithful over a few things, I will make you ruler over many things. Enter into the joy of your lord."

20 **Ecclesiastes 2:26** For God gives wisdom and knowledge and joy to a man who is good in His sight; but to the sinner He gives the work of gathering and collecting, that he may give to him who is good before God. This also is vanity and grasping for the wind.

21 **Psalm 37:4** Delight yourself also in the Lord, and He shall give you the desires of your heart.

22 **Psalms 126:5** Those who sow in tears shall reap in joy.

13.7 Happy are those who are Unhappy

The title of this message is a paradox, but so are all of the beatitudes.

Matthew 5:4 Blessed are those who mourn, For they shall be comforted.
"Blessed are those who mourn"

While this sounds more paradoxical or contradictory than others, actually it captures the spirit of all. It tells how to be happy when unhappy. It tells how to have deep joy when unhappy and things are bad enough to make you cry.

If we can only be happy when things around us make us happy, we don't have much. Our happiness is too easily taken away. The world says you can only be happy: if you have, if you get, if you join, and if you become.

Jesus says you can be happy without: having what they have, getting what they are selling, joining their group, and without becoming what they want you to be.

So that we may see Jesus' second prescription for how to have deep abiding happiness,

13.7.1 Who are Mourners?

Types of mourning – 15 words in the Bible mean to mourn.

1. Mourning over death – Abraham mourned when wife died
2. Mourning of discouragement – 2 Tim. 1:3-4
3. Mourning of disappointment – Jer. 9:1
4. Mourning of concern – Acts 20:31
5. Mourning of love – Mark 9:23
6. Mourning of devotion – Luke 7 (woman washes feet w/tears).

All of these in proper proportion are right and proper and some who have read this beatitude have concluded that it is just a statement of fact, "You feel better when you cry." Yes; sometimes; God designed the ability to cry to allow us to get feelings and emotions "washed out." But all of us who have mourned the loss of a loved one or mourned in discouragement or disappointment, or any other reason know that that kind of mourning does not necessarily result in marikos, the deep, pervading happiness that abides even when things are not going well!

13.7.2 The mourning Jesus describes in Matthew 5 is different – Penthos, Pentheo. Not used to describe outward display of grief though that sometimes accompanies it. But penthos itself describes the deep, inward, sorrow of the heart. Jesus is talking about spiritual mourning. Jesus is talking about mourning over what God mourns over. Jesus is talking about first and foremost mourning over our own sin. Jesus is describing a Godly sorrow over our sin that goes to the quick of the soul.

Such was the sin of David with Bathsheba and the murder of Uriah. Ps. 51:3-7 3

For I acknowledge my transgressions,
And my sin is always before me.
Against You, You only, have I sinned,
And done this evil in Your sight— ...
Behold, You desire truth in the inward parts, ...
Purge me with hyssop, and I shall be clean;
Wash me, and I shall be whiter than snow.

David fasted and prayed on ground before the Lord for seven days. Paul described this kind of sorrow in his letter to the Corinthians.14-09-07

For godly sorrow produces repentance leading to salvation, not to be regretted; but the sorrow of the world produces death. The kind of mourning Jesus is talking about is the Godly kind of sorrow for sin that turns life around. Mourning and repentance go hand in hand.

13.7.3 Mourning over sin is a necessary characteristic of those in the kingdom.

1. You must mourn over sin to get in. "Unless you repent you shall all likewise perish." Jesus said, "Repent for the kingdom of heaven is at hand." It follows close on the heels of poverty of spirit. The poor in spirit sees his spiritual bankruptcy and own unworthiness. He sees his sin as God sees it and grieves and sorrows and mourns over his sin. No man comes into the kingdom with the attitude of "My sin is not so bad." "My sins aren't so terrible." If Jesus had to die for our sin, if it took the blood of the Son of God to wash our robes clean, then our sin is indeed ghastly.

2. But like poverty of spirit, mourning over personal sin is to be a continual attitude. 1 Jn. 1:5-10 5. This is the message which we have heard from Him and declare to you, that God is light and in Him is no darkness at all. If we say that we have fellowship with Him, and walk in darkness, we lie and do not practice the truth. But if we walk in the light as He is in the light, we have fellowship with one another, and the blood of Jesus Christ His Son cleanses us from all sin. If we say that we have no sin, we deceive ourselves, and the truth is not in us. If we confess our sins, He is faithful and just to forgive us our sins and to cleanse us from all unrighteousness. If we say that we have not sinned, we make Him a liar, and His word is not in us.

John testifies of five marks of kingdom citizenship.
a. Walk in light
b. Fellowship with Him
c. Fellowship with other believers
d. Confession of sins – If we continually confess
e. Forgiveness of sins – He continually forgives and cleanses.

This passage is often called the "Christians bar of soap."
Repentance and faith cleansed us in the blood. Continual repentance and confession keeps our lives cleansed.

3. There is a need for mourning in the church today. The Bible is not against happiness – "A merry heart does good like a medicine." Jesus is not against happiness – "Happy are" Too frequently we

trade “marikos” – “abiding joy” for light-hearted frivolity.

James 4:8-10 8 Draw near to God and He will draw near to you. Cleanse your hands, you sinners; and purify your hearts, you double-minded. Lament and mourn and weep! Let your laughter be turned to mourning and your joy to gloom. Humble yourselves in the sight of the Lord, and He will lift you up. Jesus is saying that if we want lives full of real joy and true happiness, we need to pour out some of the trivial joviality and take some time to picture our sin and failures and shortcomings and compare them to the glory and perfection and sacrifice of God so we can mourn a little bit for “Blessed are those who mourn.”
Blessed are those who mourn, for they shall be comforted.

SECTION 5

(BLISS)

CHAPTER 14

Bliss in Hinduism

A particle of Its bliss supplies the bliss of the whole universe.
Everything becomes enlightened in Its light.
All else appears worthless after a sight of that essence.
I am indeed of this Supreme Eternal Self, - *Vijnananka*

Bliss refers to a state of ecstatic happiness, a perfect and exalted state of joy and love. It also refers to a state of contentment oblivious to any problems or suffering.

The term "bliss" is associated with the words "blithe" and "bless." Blithe refers to happiness —the person in this state is joyful and gay. Bless refers to religious consecration—especially with blood, as in the French verb "blesser," meaning to wound; it means to hallow or sanctify. The state of a person who is blessed is beatitude—the loving joy that arises from salvation.

Bliss may be associated with time and space. Times of bliss are usually in the future—the Rapture, the Millennium, the Messianic Age —though they may also be in the past as in the Golden Age of mankind described by Hesiod and Ovid; the Hindu Krita Yuga; and the Garden of Eden. Bliss may also refer to the places in which such states are experienced, such as the heavens of mystical Christianity and Kabbalistic Judaism, the Garden of Allah, the Jodo Shinsu Pure Land, Vaishnavism's eternal Vrindavana, and the Shaivite Kailash.

In the secular world, the word "bliss" may be used broadly to denote any form of happiness. It is used primarily in romantic love, in which the love object is idealized as a perfect being, and the lover is in a blissful state of intense love. Romantic love prevails in the courtly love tradition of Europe, but love poems reflecting this kind of love can also be found in ancient Egypt and India, and in Chinese poems of separation and loss. Additionally, bliss may describe new love, especially the love of a new mother for her infant.

14.1 Ānanda (Bliss) and Paramananda (Supreme Bliss) in Hinduism

Ānanda literally means bliss or happiness. In the Hindu Vedas, Upanishads and Bhagavad gita, ānanda signifies eternal bliss which accompanies the ending of the rebirth cycle. Those who renounce the fruits of their actions and submit themselves completely to the divine will, arrive at the final termination of the cyclical life process (saṃsāra) to enjoy eternal bliss (ānanda) in perfect union with the godhead. The tradition of seeking union with God through loving commitment is referred to as bhakti, or devotion.

Bliss is the favourable experience experienced by the embodied soul undertaking spiritual practice (jivatma), the God realised soul (Shivatma) or the soul in the state of union with The Supreme God (Shivadasha), when the functions of the five senses, mind and intellect have ceased.

Yasmin sthito na dukhena gurunapi avichalyate.

When the mind does not get disturbed even by intense sorrow and remains Blissful is itself the Bliss of Self-realisation (Atmanand).

Sukham atyantikam yat tat buddhigrahyam atindriyam.

Yam labdhva chaparam labham manyate nadhikam tatah.

After acquisition of that happiness which does not arise from the organs and which the pure intellect can realise to some extent, one does not desire to obtain any other type of happiness. This itself is known as the Bliss of Self-realisation (Atmanand).

Paramananda is a compound Sanskrit word composed of two words, Parama and Ānanda. Parma is usually taken to mean the Highest, the utmost or the most excellent, but actually means - "beyond". And Ānanda, which means, happiness and bliss and most often used to refer to joy though it does not exactly mean these because the original meaning implies permanence rather than just a momentary surge of delight or happiness; it also suggests a deep-seated spiritual emotion that is solidly entrenched. The Upanishadic Seers have used the word, Ānanda, to denote Brahman, the limitless, formless, infinite, indestructible, sole eternal Supreme Being or Sole Reality, to mean, Brahmanmayah, that is. full of Brahman.

A human being experiences joy or sorrow by means of his senses, mind and intellect. Looking at the beautiful sunrise or sunset, hearing harmonious music, the twitter of birds or the sound of the ocean waves, or empathising with the depth and range of emotions captured in literary masterpieces are examples of joys that give satisfaction. This aesthetic joy raises one above the mundane plane and exhilarates the mind and heart. But aesthetic satisfaction is at best only a poor substitute to the bliss of Brahmananda which the Upanishads state is far beyond any of the other joys that are accessible to man through his senses. Neither is this joy short-lived as these worldly joys.

The Upanishads also state that this ananda is the right of every jivatma and the ultimate goal as well, pointed out Velukkudi Sri Krishnan in a discourse. But how is this bliss of Brahman attainable to the jivatma?

The famous quote 'Raso Vai Saha' in the Taittiriya Upanishad captures the truth that Brahman is the essence of everlasting existence and bliss. He is the source of all creation and all objects of creation exist because of this bliss. Brahman is the support of all that is extraordinary and endless, of all the joys of this world and also of the joys that are beyond human grasp. He who knows and understands Brahman is known as 'Sat.' Not knowing Brahman is 'Asat.' The bliss of delight or 'Ananda' is possible only with association with Brahman. The conscious atma longs to experience the infinite bliss when he understands that the same Brahman is present everywhere and also in the deep recess within himself. So, he does 'Brahmopasana' to attain this infinite bliss.

A person experiences delight which follows from the contact of the senses with their objects of enjoyments, and there is also enjoyment derived through practice of adoration, meditation, etc.; whereby end of sorrow is reached. But even this is not the state of supreme or true happiness. Both, the Physical good and the Spiritual good, result in bliss; whereas the former by itself is an aspect of bliss, the latter constitutes the acme of bliss.

Jivanmukti

Joy, Happiness or Bliss, which is one of the four moral ends towards which human beings always direct all their efforts, is derived via decidedly good thoughts and good deeds that depend on the state and on the control of the mind, which means, depending on the evenness of one's own temper or in other words, through the practice of equanimity in the performance of every act without becoming instrumental in making those actions bear fruit ; the state of supreme bliss is reached through evenness of the mind with reference to all aspects of one's life. Vakya Vritti Sl.53. explains that Kaivalya is the final destination of evolution reaching which destination one gains the state of Absolute Oneness with the Divine, and by knowing one's own true essence enjoys endless immeasurable bliss called Padamapada.

To know that the Self already stands realised is not at all difficult for one becomes aware of Self-realisation at once with the dawn of the knowledge of the highest. But knowing this much and that too without experiencing the spiritual progress and the ecstasy in knowing it, is like not knowing the Self, it is like not knowing what purity actually means. In that state of realisation all finite ideas cease, the man of realisation simply exists as the Self who is the Eternal Bliss, and as the eternal subject distinct from all other objects. Hence, there is the experience of Paramananda to be gained as being distinct from Ānanda.

Even Absolute Truth (Sat), Absolute Consciousness (Chit) and Bliss (Anand) is not the real nature of Brahman as it is a spiritual emotion which has some attitude. Brahman means that devoid of an attitude (nivrutti), that is Serenity. In the nirvikalpa superconscious state (samadhi) one experiences Serenity. To simplify it, Brahman is a state of Bliss and Parabrahman that of Serenity. A quote from the Upanishads says '*Shantam upasitam*', which means that in the state of union with The Supreme God one experiences Serenity whereas in the state of the God realised soul (Shivatmadasha), one experiences Bliss.

'A vast multitude of Bliss is stored within one,

Waves of Bliss arise in the river of Bliss,

Blissful is the nature of Bliss.'

This is a quote by Tukaram Maharaj. Bliss is the basic nature, the very core of the embodied soul and the universe. Hence the embodied soul has an inherent tendency to return to its basic nature, that is to experience Bliss and on attaining it, tries to sustain it.

14.2 Means for achieving Bliss

The term "bliss" is more often used in relation to religious love. The Sanskrit term prem-ananda literally means the "bliss of love," which is based on selfless love (prema) rather than selfish and sensual love (kama). Historically, blissful love has been ascribed to Mahayana bodhisattvas, Catholic saints, and Sufi Pirs. However, the term is also used to describe the experience associated with two other religious states—divine wisdom and mystical union.

States of bliss are described in the greatest detail in three types of Hinduism: Vedanta, Tantra, and Bhakti. In the form of Vedanta known as Advaita or nondual Vedanta, the state of bliss arises from union with Brahman —the ground of being or Ultimate Reality. When the individual self or jivatman merges with the ultimate Self or paramatman, the individual merges with the universal as the drop of water flows into the sea. The resulting state of freedom and liberation is described as satchidananda—the state of perfect truth, pure consciousness, and ultimate bliss. Satchidananda is the highest attainment of the human spirit.

In the Tantric traditions, bliss is the result of union, which occurs on multiple levels. According to the philosopher Abhinavagupta, there are seven levels of bliss (ananda): innate bliss, transformative bliss, supreme bliss, bliss of Brahman, great bliss, consciousness bliss, and bliss of the world. Among the Bengali Tantric Bauls and Sahijiyas, God is found in bliss of love, and life is the carnival of love on the playground of the earth. Love causes the tantrika to be dazzled by the rays of divine beauty, which are like lightning in the clouds. In the West, Tantra is often associated with sexual bliss; in the Hindu tantric traditions, sexuality is only one dimension of a union that is complex and unites worlds and universes.

The states of bliss associated with love appear most strongly in the devotional or Bhakti traditions of Hinduism, in which the devotee loves the god or goddess intensely. In the Vaishnava tradition (which worships the god Vishnu), there are five traditional relational moods or bhavas of love: god as master and devotee as slave; god as friend and devotee as friend; god as child and devotee as parent; god as beloved and devotee as lover; and when both are realized as ultimately identical, sharing their identities. In the Shakta tradition of goddess worship, the bhavas are similar, except that the goddess may take on the role of the mother and the devotee that of the child.

In the Gaudiya Vaishnava school of Bengali Bhakti, the ideal state for the devotee is a blissful state of love that echoes the passion of Radha—the god Krishna' s beloved and perfect devotee, his Hladini Shakti, or power of bliss. In her most intense state of love, which is called Mahabhava, she experiences all states of passionate love simultaneously, including sorrow at the absence of the god and joy at his presence. By sharing in Radha's love, which is ever-new, the devotee gains an eternal future in Krishna's paradise of Vrindavana. One way that the devotee may do this is to take on a female soul, even if the devotee is physically male. Whereas the Gaudiya ideal is eternal romantic love, the Bengali Shakta ideal is eternal mother-child love, and the Shakta devotee looks forward to a joyful eternal life in the arms of a blissful mother.

Bliss is already within oneself. One should not expect someone else to give it to one. 'If one realises the eternal value of life then one will be able to obtain Bliss from impermanent things. However, without understanding the permanent, no matter how hard one tries to obtain happiness or Serenity from the impermanent, it proves futile. 'There is no permanent happiness in objects which are changing or have a limitation. That which is infinite and eternal is the true site of origin of happiness. It bestows everlasting Bliss and releases one from the bondage of unhappiness forever.'

The ways of realising the absolute value of life are as follows.

(i) Observing Righteousness (Dharma)

Sukharthah sarvabhutanam matah sarvah pravattayah.
Sukham na vina dharmat tasmat dharamparo bhavet.
-Vagbhaakrit ashtangahriday, 2.99

The tendency of all living beings is to attain happiness (in this context the word happiness is used synonymously with Bliss), but they cannot expect to get it without following the ethics of Righteousness. Hence they should be observed. The righteous individual whether knowledgeable or ignorant, will definitely experience happiness.

(ii) Spiritual practice

Only when the impressions of desires and instincts, likes and dislikes, temperamental characteristics, etc. are wiped off from the subconscious mind, that is only when nescience is destroyed, can one experience the Bliss lying dormant within oneself. This method of destroying impressions and nescience is called spiritual practice.

Repetition (chanting) of The Lord's Name, attending spiritual meetings or remaining in Satsang (holy company) of seekers or saints, service of the Absolute Truth (satseva), sacrifice and spiritual love (priti) for all are the main aspects of spiritual practice. Spiritual practice wipes off the impressions in the subconscious mind. Apart from this, the accumulated account of destiny decreases and the ability to withstand suffering due to destiny increases. Besides, by doing spiritual practice the satvik (sattva predominant) nature is enhanced. As a result, decisions made are more appropriate and errors in willful actions are avoided.

(iii) Company of Saints

A. The Bliss that an ordinary man experiences in the company of a woman, is constantly experienced by the one who is liberated from the cycle of birth and death; hence he does not harbor any sexual desire. – Saint Eknath Maharaj

'The less desires a person has the more enjoyable is his company. In spite of the desires being present in a subtle form in children they are very lovable. Then why should one consider it impossible for one whose desires have totally been destroyed by The Lord's grace to impart Bliss to others when in His company?' Saints emit frequencies of Bliss. Every seeker experiences them once he is able to perceive the subtle dimension beyond the five senses, mind and intellect.

B. In the company of an evildoer an individual begins to consider unhappiness, for instance stealing, drinking alcohol, etc. as happiness. In the company of a saint however, happiness appears like unhappiness. Actually, this is detachment (vairagya). Saints destroy the very desire for happiness. Similarly in the company of a saint, due to the acquisition of strength to endure unhappiness even that appears like happiness. Hence no unhappiness is felt, only Bliss is experienced in Their company.

C. Just as cancer cells are destroyed with certain radiations, so also dissolution of the mind and intellect occurs after exposure to frequencies of Bliss from a saint when in His company for a long time. In other words, the subtle and causal bodies and nescience are destroyed, and the individual experiences inner Bliss.

(iv) Sacrifice of happiness

One can acquire Bliss only by sacrificing happiness. Sacrificing all pleasures rather than indulging in them is of greater significance.

(v) Avoiding loss of energy

That pure energy which is utilized in wishing for happiness, is itself Blissful in nature. Once this is realized, desires will not be generated at all.

(vi) Becoming loving

Our culture teaches that an individual's happiness and unhappiness depend on his actions (karma). All can never get the same amount of happiness. Although happiness and unhappiness are dependent on action, love is independent of it. Hence, one can express empathy towards one who is suffering. This augments the individual psychological strength and he is able to tolerate the suffering. This itself is the special feature of our religion. Due to such a loving tendency, man's attitude becomes satvik (sattva predominant) and he learns to make greater sacrifices. Thus, his requirements go on reducing and gradually he is able to attain Self-realization.

(vii) Destroying Ego

'Righteousness (Dharma) proclaims that once one blends with the God's principle (Brahman), one experiences eternal happiness. If this is true, then from an individual's viewpoint attaining the Final Liberation (Moksha), that is blending of the soul with the God principle itself is the supreme goal. One should not only leave this body but should also destroy the awareness of 'I'ness. Righteousness states that even thereafter, one will experience happiness. If the one experiencing the happiness himself does not exist then he will acquire happiness, such is this strange concept (reality).' [When 'I'ness ends only the God principle exists and as Its nature is Absolute Truth (Sat), Absolute Consciousness (Chit) and Bliss (Anand), one gets the spiritual experience of Bliss. At that time there is non-duality between the one experiencing it and the experience itself.]

14.3 Happiness to Absolute Bliss

Happiness from any activity cannot last for a long time. There is always a search for eternal bliss.

Western psychologists have based the happiness index on various needs and activities. Maslow theory of human needs viz. physiological, safety, social, self-esteem and self-actualization, stress on these motivational factors for happiness. Seligman's acronym PERMA summarizes five factors correlated with happiness, that is, pleasure derived from material things, engagement in activity of interest, relationships, meaningful & purposeful activities and accomplishments & goal achievements. Whole of the western psychology revolves around meeting the needs of self.

Modern Medical Science has found correlation between happiness and release of a few hormones such as Dopamine, GABA, Serotonin and Endorphins. The levels of secretion of these hormones are dependent on the lifestyles adopted and various factors such as positive thoughts, regular exercise, yoga, meditation, gratitude, achievements, challenge of achievable goals etc.

14.3.1 Duration of Happiness

(i) Short Term: Sumptuous feast, good outing, gambling, watching favourite movie or TV show, wearing branded clothes, driving sports cars, etc. have brief durations of happiness. The principle of diminishing returns applies to the happiness from these material things.

(ii) Medium Term: The longer duration of happiness is a function of four dimensions viz. challenge, skill, love and focus on the activity. If one feels challenge in the activity, he works hard to achieve it. The given task should be achievable as per skills of the person with great efforts. Third is, one should have complete love to achieve the activity. Lastly, hundred percent focus need to be applied like Cobra snake which prepares to attack on the object with three attributes: With hood, he avoids all other distractions. Pay attention to the object, with full detachment of anything. Without caring the fruits of his action.

(iii) Long Term: Through following complete eight limbs of Patanjali Yoga and when Samadhi is attained, all desires, ignorance, afflictions, sufferings, impressions etc. retire and absolute bliss rise.

14.3.2 Wisdom of Bliss in Hinduism

Ancient rishis thousands of years ago deeply probed and experiment the happiness more from angle of permanency & longevity and to find eternal bliss. They observed that everything (person, place, age, moment, ego, love, sorrow etc.) goes, is transient; only our consciousness & supreme consciousness (Jivatma & Paramatma) are permanent.

They identified causes of pains and devised a comprehensive path for eternal bliss as under: One realizes that the universe is full of pains right from birth till death, pains of birth, pains in studies, pains after marriage, unsatisfied desires, pains in jobs/profession/business, pains of old age, pains of fear of death etc. which are intermittent with momentary pleasures.

To search eternal bliss, Hinduism has given four purpose of life Dharma, Artha, Kama and Moksha. Moksha brings eternal & permanent bliss. Our consciousness ultimately is destined to merge into universal consciousness (almighty) but when liberated from ignorance. When no duality is there, conflicts, differences, hatred, negative feelings go and positive feelings and pleasures comes in.

By self-surrender to almighty, all karma (actions) becomes absolute happiness and life becomes celebrations. It has following four stages:

Work and worship – doing the karma with sattvic attributes and worshipping and loving the personal god.

Work as worship – Doing the karma as worshipping the God.

Work is worship – Feel karma itself is God.

Non-duality – Oneness, that is, realizing self and everybody is Brahman (almighty).

Eight limbs of Patanjali Yoga Sutra are systematic way to achieve happiness not only in day-to-day life, but also ultimate bliss. These limbs are the steps to improve external behaviour, internal control, improve health, decision making & focus by observance of righteous actions. Rishi Patanjali prescribed eight limbs of the self-discipline of Yoga. Happiness, awareness and peace emerge with practice of each rule under the limbs. The eight limbs are as under:

(i) Yama (Self-restraints from violence, falsehood, theft, incontinence and collecting beyond needs),

(ii) Niyama (observances of rules- purity, contentment, austerity, self-study and self-surrender to almighty),

(iii) Asana (posture),

(iv) Pranayama (regulation of breath),

(v) Pratyahara (abstraction, withdrawing from outside distraction),

(vi Dharna (concentration),

(vii) Dhyana (meditation),

(viii) Samadhi (trance). When Samadhi is attained, all desires, ignorance, afflictions, sufferings, impressions etc. retire and absolute bliss rise.

Brahman is Satchidananda, that is, truth, existence/consciousness & bliss. The realization of Brahman is absolute bliss and happiness. Ignorance is removed after manifestation of true knowledge, duality of living beings disappears, karma becomes selfless service and love becomes devotion & bhakti. When no duality is there, conflicts, differences, hatred, negative feelings go and positive feelings and pleasures comes in.

14.4 Bliss in Upanishads

Kena Upanishad, IV-9

Yo va etamevam vedapahatya papmanamanante.
Loke jyeye pratitishthati pratitishthati.

He who knows this thus, with his sins destroyed, becomes firmly seated in the infinite, blissful and supreme Brahman. He becomes firmly seated (in Brahman).

Katha Upanishad 2-II-14

Tadetaditi manyanteanirdeshyam paramam.
Katham nu tadvijaniyam kimu bhati vibhati va.

How shall I know that indescribable and supreme Bliss which they think of as 'This'? Is It self-luminous or does It shine distinctly, (making Itself perceptible to the intellect), or does It not?

Mundaka Upanishad (II-ii-7):

Yah sarvagya sarvvidyayeisha mahima bhuvi.
Duvye brahmapure hyesha vyomnayatma pratishthah
Manomayah pranasarineta pratishit hridays.
Tada vijnanam paripashyanti dheera
Anandarupamritam yad vibhatih.

That Self which is omniscient in general and all-knowing in detail and which has such glory in this world – that Self, which is of this kind – is seated in the space within the luminous city of Brahman. It is conditioned by the mind, It is the carrier of the vital forces and the body, It is seated in food by placing the intellect (in the cavity of the heart). Through their knowledge, the discriminating people realize that Self as existing in Its fullness everywhere – the Self that shines surpassingly as blissfulness and immortality.

Mandukya Upanishad

Yatra supto na kanchana kamam kamayate na kanchana svapnam pashyati tat sushuptam.
Sushuptasthana Ekibhutah prajnanaghana evanandamayau hyanandabhuk chetomukhah prajnastritiyah padah. (5)

Where the sleeper desires not a thing of enjoyment and sees not any dream, that state is deep sleep. (The Self) seated in the state of deep sleep and called Prajna, in whom everything is unified, who is dense with consciousness, who is full of bliss, who is certainly the enjoyer of bliss, and who is the door to the knowledge (of the preceding two states), is the third quarter.

Mandukya Karika of Gaudapapa

I. AGAMA PRAKARANA (I-3)

Vishvo hi sthulabhunganityam teijasah praviviktabhuk.
Anandabhul tatha prajnastridha bhogam nibodhata.

Visva is ever the enjoyer of the gross, taijasa of the subtle, and, similarly, Prajna of bliss. Know (therefore) the enjoyment in three ways.

Brihadaranyaka Upanishad (II-i-19):

Atha yada susupto bhavati yada na kashyachana veda hita nama nadyo
Dvasaptih sahasrani hridayapuritatambhi prithante.

Tabhih pratavashripya puritati fields.
Jaise kumaro ya maharaja mahabrahmano va.
Tighanimanandasya gatva shyeityeimeveisha etachchete.

Again, when it becomes fast asleep – when it does not know anything – it comes back along the seventy-two thousand nerves called Hita, which extend from the heart to the pericardium (the whole body), and remains in the body. As a baby, or an emperor, or a noble Brahmana lives, having attained the acme of bliss, so does it remain.

Kaivalya Upanishad (14)

Punashcha janmantarakarmayogatsa eiva jivah svapiti prabuddhah.
Puratraye kridati yashcha jivastatastu jatam sakalam vichitram.
Aadharamanandamakhandabodham yasminnllayam yati puratrayam cha.

Again, through his connection with deeds done in previous births, that very Jiva returns to the dream-state, or the waking state. The being who sports in the three cities (viz., the states of wakefulness, dream and profound sleep) – from Him has sprung up all diversity. He is the substratum, the bliss, the indivisible Consciousness, in whom the three cities dissolve themselves.

Svetasvatara Upanishad (II-2):

Yuktena manasa vayam Devasya savituh save,
Suvargeyaya shaktya.

With our minds controlled so as to manifest the self-luminous Immanent Soul, we shall vigorously endeavour for the attainment of supreme bliss.

14.5 Bliss in Bhagavad Gita

Chapter 5, Verse 21

bāhya-sparśheṣhvasaktātmā vindatyātmani yat sukham
sa brahma-yoga-yuktātmā sukham akṣhayam aśhnute

Those who are not attached to external sense pleasures realize divine bliss in the self. Being united with God through Yoga, they experience unending happiness.

Chapter 5, Verse 22

ye hi sansparśha-jā bhogā duḥkha-yonaya eva te
ādyantavantaḥ kaunteya na teṣhu ramate budhaḥ

The pleasures that arise from contact with the sense objects, though appearing as enjoyable to worldly-minded people, are verily a source of misery. O son of Kunti, such pleasures have a beginning and an end, and so the wise do not delight in them.

Chapter 5, Verse 23

śhaknotīhaiva yaḥ soḍhuṁ prāk śharīra-vimokṣhaṇāt
kāma-krodhodbhavaṁ vegaṁ sa yuktaḥ sa sukhī naraḥ

Those persons are yogis, who before giving up the body are able to check the forces of desire and anger; and they alone are happy.

Chapter 5, Verse 24

yo 'ntaḥ-sukho 'ntar-ārāmas tathāntar-jyotir eva yaḥ
sa yogī brahma-nirvāṇaṁ brahma-bhūto 'dhigachchhati

Those who are happy within themselves, enjoying the delight of God within, and are illumined by the inner light, such yogis are united with the Lord and are liberated from material existence.

Chapter 6, Verse 21

sukham ātyantikaṁ yat tad buddhi-grāhyam atīndriyam
vetti yatra na chaivāyaṁ sthitaśh chalati tattvataḥ

In that joyous state of Yoga, called samādhi, one experiences supreme boundless divine bliss, and thus situated, one never deviates from the Eternal Truth.

Chapter 6, Verse 22

yaṁ labdhvā chāparaṁ lābhaṁ manyate nādhikaṁ tataḥ
yasmin sthito na duḥkhena guruṇāpi vichālyate

Having gained that state, one does not consider any attainment to be greater. Being thus established, one is not shaken even in the midst of the greatest calamity.

Chapter 6, Verse 23

taṁ vidyād duḥkha-sanyoga-viyogaṁ yogasañjñitam
sa niśhchayena yoktavyo yogo 'nirviṇṇa-chetasā

That state of severance from union with misery is known as Yoga. This Yoga should be resolutely practiced with determination free from pessimism.

Chapter 6, Verse 24-25

saṅkalpa-prabhavān kāmāns tyaktvā sarvān aśheṣhataḥ
manasaivendriya-grāmaṁ viniyamya samantataḥ
śhanaiḥ śhanair uparamed buddhyā dhṛiti-gṛihītayā
ātma-sansthaṁ manaḥ kṛitvā na kiñchid api chintayet

Completely renouncing all desires arising from thoughts of the world, one should restrain the senses from all sides with the mind. Slowly and steadily, with conviction in the intellect, the mind will become fixed in God alone, and will think of nothing else.

Chapter 6, Verse 26

yato yato niśhcharati manaśh chañchalam asthiram
tatas tato niyamyaitad ātmanyeva vaśhaṁ nayet

Whenever and wherever the restless and unsteady mind wanders, one should bring it back and continually focus it on God.

Chapter 6, Verse 27

praśhānta-manasaṁ hyenaṁ yoginaṁ sukham uttamam
upaiti śhānta-rajasaṁ brahma-bhūtam akalmaṣham

Great transcendental happiness comes to the yogi whose mind is calm, whose passions are subdued, who is without sin, and who sees everything in connection with God.

Chapter 6, Verse 28

yuñjann evaṁ sadātmānaṁ yogī vigata-kalmaṣhaḥ
sukhena brahma-sansparśham atyantaṁ sukham aśhnute

The self-controlled yogi, thus uniting the self with God, becomes free from material contamination, and being in constant touch with the Supreme, achieves the highest state of perfect happiness.

Chapter 6, Verse 29

sarva-bhūta-stham ātmānaṁ sarva-bhūtāni chātmani
īkṣhate yoga-yuktātmā sarvatra sama-darśhanaḥ

The true yogis, uniting their consciousness with God, see with equal eye, all living beings in God and God in all living beings.

CHAPTER 15

Bliss in Buddhism

"The Buddha of Infinite Light and Boundless Life is ever living and ever radiating His Truth. In His Pure Land there is no suffering and no darkness, and every hour is passed in joy; therefore, it is called the Land of Bliss." (AMIDA BUDDHA'S LAND OF PURITY)

15.1 Bliss in Buddhism

With the stilling of thought and examination, he enters and abides in the second jhana [which is characterized by] rapture and pleasure born of concentration, and accompanied by inner composure and singleness of mind, without thought and examination. (The Pali Sutras, as quoted in Shankman, 2008, p.43)

As everyday thoughts subside, a state of philosophical examination follows, perhaps over the nature of thought itself. Eventually, this examination stills and gives way to the feeling of bliss, as described in the quote above. This blissful state not only fills the mind but reportedly extends throughout the body as well.

Buddhism provides strong advice against the pursuit of worldly pleasures to attain the "good life." In contrast, many forms of meditation give rise to an immense and abiding joy. Most of these practices involve "stilling the mind," whereby all content-laden thought (e.g., fantasies, daydreams, plans) ceases, and the mind enters a state of openness, formlessness, clarity, and bliss. In Buddhism, the Theravada tradition emphasizes individual knowledge and liberation, while the Mahayana tradition stresses love and compassion. The ideal Mahayana figure is the bodhisattva, the person on the edge of liberation who steps back to help a suffering world. The love of the bodhisattva is both blissful and sorrowful, for he or she recognizes the tragedy of the world, but also the joy of its salvation. There are many schools of Mahayana, and one that speaks of bliss is the Jodo Shinshu or Pure Land form of Buddhism.

According to this tradition, Amida Buddha created a Land of Bliss or Pure Land in which all beings may attain perfect enlightenment. Amida did this because of his great and compassionate love for all beings. In Vajrayana Buddhism, bliss is found through experience of the Clear Light of the Void, as well as within the earthly world, the world of bliss (Sambhogakaya), and the world of liberation. The bliss world is the place of union of opposites—the set of meditative states through which the practitioner passes on his or her way to liberation.

15.2 The Land of Ultimate Bliss

Who would not like to end all suffering and enjoy every bliss? Shakyamuni Buddha spoke of the Amitabha Sutra to let all beings know of the power of Amitabha Buddha's great vows to lead all who recite his name with faith to rebirth in his Buddhaland, the Land of Ultimate Bliss, where they may cultivate and quickly realize Buddhahood. Sukhavati, or, as translated from the Chinese, Ultimate Bliss, is the name of this land. The large Sukhavati-vyuha explains the causal connections resulting in the Pure Land of Ultimate Bliss. It deals with Amitabha's vows of former lives and their realization in Sukhavati. In this Sutra, Shakyamuni Buddha, the teacher of the Saha world, speaks of the adornments of the Land of Ultimate Bliss and of its teacher, Amitabha Buddha. By the power of his vows, Amitabha Buddha leads all beings to rebirth in his country where they realize Buddhahood. This power attracts living beings to the Land of Ultimate Bliss, just as a magnet attracts iron filings.

The principles of this Sutra are Faith, Vows, and Practice-Holding the Buddha's name; these are the three prerequisites of the Pure Land Dharma-door. One who goes on a journey takes along some food and a little money. One who wishes to go to the Land of Ultimate Bliss needs faith, vows, and the practice of holding the Buddha's name.

15.2.1 Faith

Faith is the first prerequisite, for without it one will not make the vow to be born with Amitabha in the Pure Land of Ultimate Bliss, and thus will not realize the objective of this Sutra. You must have faith in Yourself, The Land of Ultimate Bliss, Cause and Effect, and Noumena and Phenomena.

What does it mean to believe in oneself? It is to believe that you certainly have the qualifications necessary to be born in the Land of Ultimate Bliss. You should not take yourself lightly and say, "I have committed so many offenses, I can't be born there." If you have heavy offense karma, you now have a good opportunity to take it with you to the Land of Ultimate Bliss. Regardless of the offenses you have committed in the past, if you change your mind and reform your conduct, you may be born there, offenses and all.

Taking your karma to the Pure Land refers to past karma, however, not to future karma. Once you have understood the Dharma, offenses should cease. If you continue to offend, you will absolutely not be reborn in the Land of Ultimate Bliss. You may recite the Buddha's name and bow to the Buddha, but you will only be making investments in future Buddhahood. You will not, in this life, be born in the Land of Ultimate Bliss because you clearly understood and yet deliberately violated the rules of the Dharma.

Before taking refuge with the Triple Jewel, doing things which are not in accord with the Dharma may be excusable, but to continue such behavior after taking refuge increases the gravity of one's offenses. Knowing your error, you must truly change your faults and say, "I most certainly can be reborn in the Land of Ultimate Bliss."

Secondly, you must have faith in the Western Land of Ultimate Bliss which is hundreds of thousands of millions of Buddhalands from here. Before he realized Buddhahood, Amitabha Buddha, as the Bhikshu Dharma Treasury, vowed to create a land where living beings who recited his name could be born. There's no need to do anything else; it's easy, simple, and convenient. It doesn't cost a thing, and yet this Dharma-door is the highest and most supreme, for if you just recite, "Namo Amitabha Buddha," you will be born in the Land of Ultimate Bliss.

15.2.2 Vows

Having discussed faith, we will now discuss vows. What is a vow? What you wish, the tendency of your thoughts, is a vow. In Buddhism there are four great vows:

I vow to save the limitless living beings.
I vow to cut off the inexhaustible afflictions.
I vow to study the immeasurable Dharma-doors.
I vow to realize the supreme Buddha Way.

All Buddhas and Bodhisattvas of the past, present, and future practiced the Bodhisattva conduct and attained Buddhahood by relying on these four great vows.

You may make the four great vows according to the Four Holy Truths.

According to the truth of suffering,
I vow to save the limitless living beings.
According to the truth of origination,
I vow to cut off the inexhaustible afflictions.
According to the truth of the Way,
I vow to study the immeasurable Dharma-doors.
According to the truth of extinction,
I vow to realize the supreme Buddha Way.

The four great vows come from an awareness of the suffering of living beings. For purposes of clarification, suffering is divided into groups of the three, eight, and limitless sufferings.

The three sufferings are:

1) Suffering within suffering. This is the poverty and misery of

all living beings.

2) The suffering of decay. Living beings may enjoy wealth and honor, but it eventually goes bad.

3) The suffering of process. Even without the sufferings of poverty and decay, the bitterness of the life-process from birth, to the prime of life, to old age and then to death is still suffering. The shift and change of each passing thought is called the suffering of process.

The eight sufferings are:

1) The suffering of birth.
2) The suffering of old age.
3) The suffering of sickness.
4) The suffering of death.

It was because Shakyamuni Buddha met with these four sufferings that he decided to leave the home-life and cultivate the Way.

5) The suffering of separation from what you love.
6) The suffering of being joined with what you hate.

If people are not apart from loved ones, they are involved with enemies. If you don't like someone, you'll find someone just like him wherever you go.

7) The suffering of not realizing aspirations.

You worry about getting something and once you have it you worry about losing it. This suffering is nothing compared to the next:

8) The suffering of the raging blaze of the five skandhas: form, feelings, perceptions, impulses, and consciousness. The five skandhas are like a raging fire. They are a constant shadow which we cannot escape.

According to the truth of suffering, I vow to save the limitless living beings:

15.2.3 Limitless Sufferings

Why are there limitless sufferings besides the eight?

In the past lives we planted the seeds of suffering as if they were old friends with which we were loath to part. Having established causes and conditions for suffering in the past, in the present we reap a bitter fruit.

From causes made in lives gone by
comes your present life;
Results you'll get in lives to come
arise from this life's deeds.
Plant good causes, reap good results;
Plant bad causes, reap bad results.

You fear the results. "Oh, I'm suffering too bitterly," you say, but you suffer because previously you planted the causes of suffering.

Living beings fear the results, not the causes from which they come, but Bodhisattvas fear the causes, not the results. Bodhisattvas are extremely careful not to plant the causes of suffering and so they do not reap the harvest of suffering. They endure their present suffering gladly. So Bodhisattvas, too, must sometimes suffer, but they do so willingly, knowing that

Enduring suffering ends suffering;
Enjoying blessings destroys blessings.

Living beings, on the other hand, are not afraid to plant the causes of suffering. "Good causes, bad causes, it doesn't matter," they say, "I'll do it anyway. It's not important." But when the results come, "Oh! I can't stand it," they moan. "How could this happen to me? Such bitterness!"

If you fear suffering you should not plant the causes of suffering, for if you do, you will certainly reap its bitter fruit. Born in the Land of Ultimate Bliss, one endures no suffering but enjoys every bliss. None of the three sufferings, eight sufferings, or the limitless sufferings are found there at all. The people are pure and free of greed, hatred, and stupidity. Without the three poisons there are no evil paths of rebirth because the evil paths are but manifestations of the poisons.

The Buddha saves living beings, but in reality there is not a single living being that he saves. He resolves to lead everyone to understand the Buddha dharma in order to leave suffering, attain bliss, and wake up. But when you take beings across, do not become attached to the mark of taking beings across.

If you recite the Buddha's name,
reciting without cease, The mouth recite "Amita"
and makes things of a piece.
Scattered thoughts do not arise,
samadhi you attain.
For rebirth in the Pure Land,
your hope is not in vain.
If all day you detest
the suffering Saha's pain,
Make rebirth in Ultimate Bliss
your mind's essential aim.
Cut off the red dust
thoughts within your mind.
Put down impure reflections,
and pure thoughts you will find.

15.3 Bliss and Emptiness in Buddhism

The twin aspects of tantra are: bliss and emptiness. Not emptiness alone or bliss alone, but both combined in a single entwined experience. Why is this? The fundamental experience of Buddha's enlightenment lies at the very heart of tantra. This is because that experience contained essentially two elements. The first was a sustained vision of the world as a dynamic state of flux, of continuous and unrelenting creation and destruction. That is the basis of emptiness. That nothing is permanent and thus everything is permeated by an underlying condition of impermanence and instability. That condition means that nothing exists of its own accord but only in codependence upon all other things. Thus, reality is contingent, a product, rather than a cause of itself.

This instability applies not only vividly, to the outer physical world, but also to the internal world of thoughts and feelings. Thus, the outer world is crumbling and collapsing before our gaze, and so too is the psychology of man. The vision of ourselves is almost as unstable and impermanent as that of the outer world. This could create a terrifying vision of identity-lessness and collapse of ego and self, which would be interpreted as very frightening. When viewed in that way it is disturbing to think that our thoughts and feelings from day to day are immensely fickle and transitory. Yet, we cling to the idea of permanence, a permanence within ourselves and a permanence without. There is no such permanence and it is deeply hurtful to us to know this. We resist the idea at every turn and will not confront the idea of our personal extinction. Thus, the problem Buddha revealed was not so much impermanence, but our deep clinging to the notion of permanence.

On its own and viewed in isolation, that emptiness would in most people signify a form of terror and nihilism. That is almost the view of the Zen school, which stresses emptiness above all else. The other component of the enlightenment experience is bliss. The Buddha experienced a continuous state of bliss, which was both physical and mental, and also non-fading, that is, indestructible. This combination of bliss and emptiness was fundamentally the experience of the enlightenment event. This event persisted for the rest of his life until his parinirvana (death). Everything is changeable, everything appears and disappears; there is no blissful peace until one passes beyond the agony of life and death.

There are many types of bliss, all of which have one thing in common: they are transient or impermanent. These include the blisses of looking at beautiful objects, hearing beautiful sounds, sensational pleasant fragrances and tastes, touches, et, including the blisses of foods, of physical sensation, of orgasm, etc. Yet they are all transitory, that is, they fade. But the bliss which Buddha experienced upon Enlightenment was non-fading. You could say that as a result of Enlightenment, he was plagued by continuous, intense and non-fading bliss.

The first 'turning of the wheel of dharma' established all the Hinayana teachings, the 8-fold path and the ethical basis of Buddhism, plus a small indication of the nature of impermanence. The second turning of the wheel of dharma the Prajnaparamita Sutras or perfection of wisdom sutras, from Vulture Peak, forms the basis of all the Mahayana teachings and presents a far more profound and complete view of impermanence and emptiness. This formed the basis for Nagarjuna's profound scriptures and the Zen school. The third turning of the wheel was as Vajradhara from which stem all the tantras of the secret mantra vehicle.

Bliss and emptiness are cultivated in tantra quite deliberately. That forms the basis of tantra and everything in it can be referred to one or the other as its basis. There are two other important ways in which bliss and emptiness are central to the enlightenment experience and thus to the tantric path. Because the view of combined emptiness and bliss is the vision of a Buddha, so constructing that from nothing as a path is bound to lead one closer and closer to the view itself and thus to enlightenment. In this sense the tantric path is seen very much as a dress-rehearsal for Buddhahood itself: by combining emptiness and bliss we cultivate a direct route to enlightenment. A second reason is that the view of emptiness and bliss translates into a view of the world as precious mandala and all beings as our precious mothers. Bliss is also a steady form of consciousness as well as being very strong. Thus, it can be used to deepen calm-abiding meditation and that can then be used to gain a steadier and deeper insight into impermanence and emptiness. It is said in the tantras that Buddha-hood is achieved when wisdom and method, or the profound and the manifest come together. That is the same as saying emptiness and bliss entwined.

In tantra the contemplation of the empty form of a deity can be described very accurately as a composite of bliss and emptiness and thus approximates very closely indeed to the nature of a Buddha. It serves several useful purposes -- like it generates bliss; it is by nature impermanent and empty; it generates great merit; it benefits all beings; it is a pure form; it is uncontaminated by ordinariness; it is free from desire, hatred and ignorance and thus of all defilements; it is essentially a part of a pure realm. It is also an example of the way that mind-stream is regarded virtually as a permanent entity residing beyond the impermanence of samsara. Anything which is vividly constructed in the mind produces deep karmic seeds and is passed forward and retained life upon life. Thus, generating a deity establishes very deep, very powerful and very beneficial seeds in the mind-steam.

The path of trantra relies to a very large extent upon cultivating bliss within one's ordinary waking life, on a moment-by-moment basis. This is an aspect of self-generation or deity yoga. It also relies upon a very profound and sustained cultivation of the view of emptiness of all phenomena. One can start by merely self-observation at what is pleasurable and which leads to bliss. Adjustment and control of this can then be achieved quite quickly.

Cultivation of the emptiness of external and internal phenomena, generates bliss anyway, but also leads to the collapse or crumbling of our domination by the senses and therefore, to a greater belief in the power of self-generated imagery as an alternative reality which is perfectly valid in its own right. It greatly increases disbelief in the power of external reality and thus correspondingly reduces its grip over us. Thus, pursuit of bliss based upon emptiness and emptiness based upon bliss and meditation on both leads most certainly to a self-generated 'Buddha- base'. Upon this base is also constructed the main practice of all tantric yoga: deity yoga, that is, generation of oneself as a deity (= a Buddha) and the outer world as mandala, buildings as mandala palaces, and all other beings as deities, speech as mantra, writings as dharma, etc. Sustained cultivation of this precious view negates/suspends the ordinary vision of the world and offers continuous protection from contamination by ordinary reality. Protection from contamination with the impure non- bliss of samsara. Thus, the path of tantra leads directly to the 'secret lair' of the experience of enlightenment itself, like a secret inner staircase which leads directly to a Buddha's view. Tantric practice thus leads straight into the cultivation of a Buddha's mind -- a selfless mind of bliss and emptiness.

Bliss without emptiness would be little more than indulgent sensuality; emptiness without bliss would come very close to terrifying nihilism. Buddhism needs both, arguably, because though emptiness is the correct view, it is hard without compassion and pleasure/joy to construct any kind of appealing path with it. Some softer dimension is also needed. Both together form a perfect combination but also accurately reflect the nature of the mind of enlightenment of a Buddha. The bliss which is cultivated in tantric practice is a pure form of bliss that relies upon a pure form rather than upon the impure forms of the senses.

15.4 Bliss through Mindful Meditation in Buddhism

Mindful meditation the way of letting go. In meditation you let go of the complex world outside in order to reach a powerful peace within. In all types of mysticism and in many spiritual traditions, meditation is the path to a pure and empowered mind. The experience of this pure mind, released from the world, is incredibly blissful. One of the many simple but profound statements of the Buddha is that "a meditator who makes letting go the main object easily achieves samādhi," that is, attentive stillness, the goal of meditation. Such a meditator gains these states of inner bliss almost automatically. The Buddha was saying that the major technique for attaining deep meditation and reaching these powerful states is the ability to abandon, to let go, to renounce.
To overcome the hindrance, do some metta (loving-kindness}

meditation. Give yourself a break. Say to yourself, "The door to my heart is open to all of me. I allow myself happiness. I allow myself peace. I have goodwill toward myself, enough goodwill to let myself become peaceful and to bliss out on this meditation." If you find it hard to extend loving-kindness toward yourself, ask why. There may be a deep-seated guilt complex inside, and you still expect punishment. You haven't given yourself unconditional forgiveness. Before you end the mettā meditation, pause for a minute or two and reflect on how you feel inside. Notice the effect that this meditation has had on you. Mettā meditation can produce heavenly bliss.

15.5 Gautama Buddha Quotes About Bliss

- *To master the pride of defiant self hood, that in truth is the highest bliss.*

- *Whenever and wherever, one encounters the arising and passing away of the mental-physical structure, one enjoys bliss and delight, which lead on to the deathless stage experienced by the wise.*

- *There is pleasure And there is bliss. Forgo the first to possess the second. If you are happy At the expense of another man's happiness, You are forever bound.*

- *When we feel happy and peaceful, our happiness and peace radiate around us, and others can enjoy it as well. This is called 'the enjoyment of others of our body of bliss'.*

- *Buddha Quotes on Happiness - "Blind is the world; here only a few possess insight. Only a few, like birds escaping from the net, go to realms of bliss." – The Buddha | Buddha quotes on love | Buddha quotes on karma | Buddha quotes on.*

- *Blind is the world; here only a few possess insight. Only a few, like birds escaping from the net, go to realms of bliss.*

- *Full of joy, full of faith in the Teaching of the Buddha, the monk attains the Peaceful State, the bliss of cessation of conditioned things.*

- *Happiness will never come to those who fail to appreciate what they already have. Should a person do good, let him do it again and again. Let him find pleasure therein, for blissful is the accumulation of good. Entangled by the bonds of hate, one who seeks happiness by inflicting pain on others is never delivered from hatred.*

- *Peace is the highest bliss. Shame on him who strikes a holy man, and more shame to him who gives way to anger.*

- *Should a person do good, let him do it again and again. Let him find pleasure therein, for blissful is the accumulation of good.*

- *Do not dwell in the past, do not dream of the future, concentrate the mind on the present moment.*

CHAPTER 16

Bliss in Sufism

What a relief to be empty! Then God can live your life. -Rumi

16.1 Bliss in Sufism

In the chaos that prevails around us, there is a growing feeling of desolation and misery. The pace of modern times has upset the rhythm of life and the music is slowly ebbing out. Living in a harsh world we have developed cynicism and hatred. Our inner life is marked by wrestling of competing forces. Love and jealousy, pleasure and pain, hope and fear life and death, ideal and reality, dream and truth are in a state of eternal conflict. Unifying values, around freedom and fairness, speech and civility are being shredded by rising communal and linguistic furies and passions. We face enemies intent on dividing us more. The most authentic hope comes from mystics whose philosophy combines the virtuous message of formal religion with the transcendental values of love and harmony.

Sufism (Tasawwuf) is the name given to mysticism in Islam. The term Sufism embraces the philosophy and practices which aim at direct communion between God and man, and those who practice Sufism are called Sufis. In Islam, bliss is found in the mystical Sufi traditions. It comes through appreciation of God's beauty and mercy. Beauty and love are like body and soul, and awareness of them can transform the human soul into light and allow its ascent to the one who is Truth and Unity. God is love, lover, and beloved. The blissful conditions are earthly love ('ishq), in which one sacrifices all for God; the state of fana, in which the person experiences divine love-madness; and the state of baqa, the state of stable perfection before God, which balances the madness. This love is shown in the story of Laila and Majnun, in which Majnun so loved Laila that the world was transformed into her image, and he lived in blissful madness surrounded by her presence. Her image eventually became that of

Allah, and Majnûn's love of a human woman was transformed into love of God.

The most authentic hope for a spiritual catharsis comes from Sufis whose philosophy combines the virtuous message of formal religion with the transcendental values of love and harmony. Sufism enables an individual to purge his mind of all toxic emotions and helps restore balance and harmony. As the acclaimed modern Sufi Inayat Khan says: "The secret of life is balance and the absence of balance is life's destruction."

Sufism consists of a variety of mystical paths that are designed to ascertain the nature of humanity and of God and to facilitate the experience of the presence of divine love and wisdom in the world. The personal spiritual life of Sufi masters is characterized by an untiring, seemingly mystical search for union with divinity and all of creation.

According to Sufi teachings, the path to experiencing the divine presence starts within. It is said that one who realizes oneself realizes the Lord. God is present, but individuals cannot see Him because curtains of ignorance veil their eyes and the sensual impressions encase their hearts. A common individual is ego-centred. It is only when he has polished the heart and purified the self-will the curtains lift, the dust of materialism will fall, and the eyes will attain the vision required to see God. Sufism connects us to the deeper layers of the authentic self and helps us in exploring it.

Sufism enables an individual to purge his mind of toxic emotions and restore to it, its incandescent luminosity. The great writer, Inayat Khan would emphasize that patience is the power of endurance. As resurrection follows crucifixion, happiness follows suffering. Spiritual paths and teachings give us access to the tools to do this inner work. For example, the practice of meditation can help to still the mind so that we are no longer distracted by its continual chatter. Psychological inner work can free us from the traumas, anger, anxiety and other feelings that may veil our light. Gradually we come to know more of our true nature, learn to live in the light of our real self. It is said that the goal of every spiritual path is to live a guided life, guided by that within us which is eternal. Rumi summed up his whole life in two lines:

"And the result is not more than these three words:
I burnt, and burnt, and burnt"

We all have a divine spark in us and we can experience glimpses of the divine when we forget our limitations in the beauty of nature, or art, or in deep love. Pursuing such experiences, and letting them grow deeper, he says, can lead us into the cosmic realm and enable us to celebrate celestial love. As the well-known Persian poet, Saadi says: "Every soul is born with a certain purpose and the light of that purpose is kindled in his soul."

Sufism has become a kind of new-age amalgam of spiritual practices, but its roots reach back to the earliest days of Islam. As the early Muslim conquerors took their faith to different lands, Sufism began to borrow from different traditions, including Greek and Hindu philosophy and Christian theology. Hence, many of the early Sufis believed that all faiths were equal, and that to privilege one religion was to deny the existence of the divine elsewhere.

The Sufi ideal is to combine the inner and outer life to be active in the world, for example, as an economist or a politician, and at the same time to be inspired by attuning to the divine ideal.

Sheikh Muzaffar says, "Keep your hands busy with your duties in this world, and your heart busy with God." Our faith has to be practised daily in our everyday lives. As Sahi, an eminent Sufi mystic exhorts: "A man should be in the marketplace while still working with true reality."

The purity of the Sufi is due to his constant remembrance of God. The more he remembers God, the more he comes to know Him; and the more he comes to know Him, the more he comes to love Him. This is why the act of polishing the mirror of the heart is the key to entering into a love-relationship with God. The Sufi's heart, in other words, is like white snow because of its purity, which it has attained through the remembrance of God. It is only a clarified heart that can help us perceive the true beauty and harmony of the universe.

In one important tale, the greatest of all Sufi masters, Rumi seeks to illustrate this idea in a more concrete way. He tells the story of a naked man who jumps into a pool of water in order to escape from being stung by a swarm of bees that have been chasing him and will not relent in their efforts to attack him. But since he cannot remain submerged for very long, he resurfaces for air only to find the bees waiting for him so they can resume their assault. The story sheds light on an important point, namely that the bees represent our remembrance for things in this world, while the water represents the act of remembering God. Rumi explains that the heart that is pure not only heads towards the Ocean, but it also becomes a part of it.

Nobel Laureate Doris Lessing has followed the Sufi path for a significant part of her life. She explains its attraction, "Sufi truth is at the core of every religion, its heart, and religions are only the outward vestments of an inner reality." She writes further: "They will find the word mysticism has lost its bizarre associations and that the way of the Sufi reveals itself as a sophisticated view of life, embodied in people who through the centuries have always been in advance of their time."

16.2 Understanding Bliss in Islamic Sufism

Sufism teaches how to purify one's self, improve one's morals, and build up one's inner and outer life in order to attain perpetual bliss. Its subject matter is the purification of the soul and its end or aim is the attainment of eternal felicity and blessedness. Following are the five Principal Teachings of Sufism:

1. Absolute Being (God) is also Absolute Beauty.

2. Since beauty tends towards manifestation, Absolute Being developed the phenomenal world.

3. Man should practice virtues like poverty, austerity, humility, fortitude and discipline. He should devote himself to the ways of inwardness like withdrawal, silence, solitariness, and self-examination. He should also keep in mind a constant awareness of God with faith, awe and desire. These virtues, inwardness and awareness will bring a sense of direct communication with God.

4. It would be better if such slogans are raised which work as remainders of the mystic belief and aim and as aids to concentration on the quest for unification.

5. Man should follow these directions with sufficient perseverance as they will advance through the standard mystic stages of concentration, apprehension of everything, sudden and unpredictable illumination, **blissful** ecstasy, sense of union with the deity, sense of nothingness and sense of the nothingness beyond nothingness.

The Sufis strive for and attest to having the experience of seeing God, Whom they call their Beloved One, face to face. There are instances of Sufis falling senseless when possessed by the ecstasy of extreme love. The Sufis say that the Prophet and some of his companions were totally absorbed in their prayers every time they prayed and that this complete absorption in prayer is the foundation of Tasawwuf.

According to the Sufis this higher level of excellence in worship, which might lead to ecstasy, may be achieved through dhikr. Dhikr literally means remembering God. The Qur'an says "Remember God always so that you may prosper." (62:10) At yet another place, it says: "Believers, be ever mindful of God: praise Him morning and evening." (33:41-42). The Sufis gave dhikr a formal, well-defined shape by attaching greater importance to its popular rather than the

Qur'anic meaning. They invented a number of ways for calling out the name of God—silently, loudly, and even accompanied by music or the beating of drums—as a means of achieving their goal.

According to an excerpt from Shaykh Ahmad's letters, published under the title Maktubat-e-Mujaddid:

"The mysticism of the Sufis and their relations and inspirations are to be accepted only if they conform to the shariah; otherwise, they are to be rejected... An abundance of miracles is not a sign of spiritual superiority... The real miracle of the saintly men is the purification of the souls of their disciples. The soul being immaterial, they have to turn their attention away from materialism. The distinction between a true and a false devotee is that the former adheres strictly to the shariah, while the latter adheres to his own whims and fancies... Submission to the Prophet's tradition is the real bliss."

16.3 The Age of Bliss in Sufism

From a worldly and egoistic perspective, the Age of Bliss was in no way a period of material happiness and comfort. On the contrary, it marked times of harsh living, a period filled with demanding struggles. But then again, they were also the times that stood witness to the invaluable blessings that were the life of the Noble Messenger blessings and peace- and the emergence of Islam. It was an era also in which the principles that ensured the happiness of humankind both in this world and in the Hereafter were founded. It was an age that watched on as a previously cruel, oppressive and tyrant mob of human were elevated through the truth, justice and good morals. It was an age that saw the greatest ever revolution in the history of mankind, where the dark desires of the ego were replaced by the glorious light of spirituality and in which spirits were set free from the captivity of the flesh. In short, it was an age when people began to take flight from evil towards eternal happiness.

Islam also prohibited wasting. So, in stark contrast to the feast of the times of Ignorance, not even a single meat of a sheep slaughtered in the Age of Bliss would go to waste. Again, from feelings of generosity and selflessness, it was not uncommon for meat to pass around seven different families only to return to the same place from where it had been handed out in the first place.

From the society of Ignorance, which could not raise a single man of importance for centuries on end, there all of a sudden hailed numerous exemplary figures endowed with the highest moral qualities, thanks to the spiritual training and teaching of the Blessed Prophet -upon him blessings and peace-. And they carried the inspiration they received from the Quran and Sunnah to the four corners of the world, as flames of wisdom and knowledge. They showed no sign of weariness or fatigue. Hearts had become the receptacles of the love of Allah, glory unto Him, and they began perceiving the created with eye of the Creator, so to speak. Taking eternity under its wings, the Light that had descended onto the desert preached the Truth and justice to humankind entire.

The Muslims of the Asr-u Saadah, reared under the training of the Prophet of Allah -upon him blessings and peace-, the quintessential example for entire humanity, became members of a society of knowledge, wisdom, compassion and elegance who not only knew the Blessed Prophet -upon him blessings and peace- externally but also internally, with their hearts. That period was an age of deep contemplation, a time to gain an intimate knowledge of the Almighty and His Messenger.

The Companions placed tawhid in the center of their thoughts and ideals. They were successful in destroy-ing worldly interests, selfish ambitions and the gods of desire that trickle into and wreak havoc in hearts. Life and wealth were demoted to being means rather than ends. Compassion grew deeper. Serving the Truth became a way of life. An enormous effort and sacrifice had the magnificent Islamic character put on display. Such that after traveling a month's distance just to confirm a hadith he already knew; a Companion would turn back after seeing that the man he had been seeking all along was tricking his horse with an empty fodder bag; an act of deception unbecoming of one to be trusted with the honourable task of confirming a hadith of the Prophet of Allah -upon him blessings and peace-.

Abu'l-Aliya, one of the great imams of the Tabiun generation, further explains this Islamic sensitivity in the following:
"Upon going next to someone with the intention of acquiring a hadith, we would observe the way he offered his ritual prayer. If we saw that he offered it nicely, we would think 'he must complete his other tasks in the same way' and then proceed to sit by his side and lend ear to him. Seeing him offer his ritual prayer in a sloppy manner, however, we would think 'this must be the case with all of his acts' and leave without giving him the time of the day."

The Muslims of the Age of Bliss were careful to be with wudu at all times and refresh it with each approaching salat. The Blessed Prophet -upon him blessings and peace- one day called Bilal Habashi -Allah be well-pleased with him- next to him and asked:

"Which deed was it you did that made you enter Paradise before me? Whenever I enter Paradise in my reams, I hear your shoes tapping in front of me. Last night I once again entered Paradise and heard the tap-ping of your shoes in front of me once again…"

"I make sure to offer two rakat of salat every time I hear the adhan, Messenger of Allah! When I break my wudu, I quickly refresh it and think that I owe Allah another two rakat," explained Bilal -Allah be well-pleased with him-. "Owing to those two, then", the Messenger of Allah -upon him blessings and peace. Abu Ghutayf al-Huzali explains:

"I listened to Abdullah ibn Omar in the Masjid as he spoke to us seated on the floor. When it was the time for zuhr salat, he got up from his spot, took wudu and offered salat. Once the time for asr salat came, he again got up from his spot, took another wudu despite retaining his previous wudu and offered salat. When it was time for maghrib salat, he again refreshed his wudu and offered the salat.

Afterwards, he returned to his spot.

'May Allah render you among the righteous', I said to him. 'Is it obligatory (fard) or voluntary (sun-nah) to refresh the wudu for each salat?'

During the Age of Bliss, the month of Ramadan was lived with enthusiasm and excitement and Muslims used to ensure their children also breathed this air of spirituality as much as they could. Omar -Allah be well-pleased with him- in fact once reproached a drunken man he came upon during Ramadan, say-ing, "Woe to you...Even our children are fasting right now!"

The age of Bliss is undoubtedly the most exceptional period in the history of mankind, typified by virtue, selflessness and moral excellence. It was that period in which the Blessed Prophet -upon him blessings and peace-, the reason for the existence of entire creation, graced the earth. It was a period moulded and inspired by his behaviour and spirituality. That age was, again, a time of getting to know the Almighty and His Messenger, with love and ecstasy, in an environment of deep contemplation.

16.4 Sakīna and Itminān and Riḍā in Sufism

(i) **Sakīna** literally means calmness, silence and steadiness such that a person experiences tranquillity. In the context of Islamic spirituality, it also means the heart has come to a state of bliss as a result of its connection with the presence of God or in the presence of angelic spirits, so it is not shaken by worldly fear, grief or anxiety, and finds peace, integrity and harmony between their inner world and the outer world. Someone with Sakīna, therefore, is able to deal with the challenges and difficulties that come with life without being shaken. There is an understanding of life and events in way that does not shudder the individual, but instead leaves them feeling content with whatever is being experienced.

Sakīna is affiliated with the unseen realm rather than drawing its strength from the world the physical eye can see. For example, a substance that resembled vapour or mist is believed to have surrounded Usayd ibn Khudayr, one of the companions of Prophet Muhammad, while he was reading the Qur'ān, which gave him a feeling of exhilaration. This feeling of exhilaration is attributed to Sakīna. Thus, it is like a positive energy that surrounds a person, giving them a feeling of peace. But this positive energy is dependent on the state of the person as well as their actions.

Sakīna is mentioned in the Qur'ān as a means of reaffirming one's faith: "It is He who sent down tranquillity (Sakīna) into the hearts of the believers that they would increase in faith along with their [present] faith ..." Maḥallī and Suyūṭī describe Sakīna as a spirit of peace sent down by God as a Divine reassurance to those who believe. In this respect, Sakīna is the result of faith, which is only possible through an intimate connection with God. The feeling of inner peace is generated or granted with having a strong conviction in God and the resultant strong faith. Ibn'Abbās explains how Sakīna further reaffirms and strengthens the faith of the believer, adding certainty, belief and knowledge to the faith one already has.

(ii) **Itminān** (peacefulness), on the other hand, is defined as the full satisfaction and contentment; so, one is in a state of complete rest in their inner world. It is a spiritual state surpassing Sakīna; if Sakīna is understood to be the "beginning of being freed from theoretical knowledge and awakened to the truth, Itminān is considered to be the final point or station." In other words, Sakīna leads to Itminān. Sakīna is a temporary state gifted by God in times of distress or when one experiences spiritual exhilaration, whereas Itminān is a constant state.

The Qur'ān mentions Itminān as one of the levels of the nafs (ego) that one aspires to achieve, known as al-nafs al-muṭma'innah (the nafs at peace). When one has reached this level of the nafs, it means one has attained peace and tranquillity. The Qur'ān mentions this level of the nafs as: "O you soul at rest (content). Return to your Lord, well-pleased (with Him), and well-pleasing to Him. Enter, then, among My servants (fully content with servanthood to Me)! And enter my Paradise!" God is talking to the nafs at peace directly as he talked to Moses. This is considered a great honour for the nafs and therefore a significant outcome of the purification process it has been through. It is also an indication of the closeness to God that one has achieved, deserving to be spoken to directly by God. The level of peace will increase as the level of knowledge of God (ma'rifa) contained within the nafs increases. Therefore, a clear association is made between knowledge of God and the purity of the nafs. At the level where the nafs is at peace, it means it is at a level of knowing God in this world. That is, true knowledge of God has been attained when one's nafs is at the level of muṭmaʾinnah. Such a nafs has calmness and certainty.

(iii) Rida: There is a link between Itminān and Riḍā in Qur'anic chapter 89 verses 27 to 30. When al-nafs al-muṭmaʾinnah is reached, the nafs is at the station of resignation (Riḍā). This state of Riḍā provides a sense of contentment, acceptance and peace for a person at this level of the nafs. At the same time, resignation and acceptance (Riḍā) lead to greater tranquillity (Itminān) of the heart. This is a critical aspect of how inner peace is nurtured by various states of the inner self.

When all three of these states are considered together, a collective understanding of inner peace emerges. It is an understanding of inner peace that evolves around the belief in the one God as highlighted by the Qur'anic verse "Verily in the remembrance of God do hearts find rest." After all, believing in the oneness of God (tawhid) is at the core of the Islamic faith, described as the "the cornerstone of Islam." It is the first tenet of the Islamic faith upon which all other beliefs of Islam are assembled. It is the belief there is no other deity but God, with a whole theology defining its understanding.

Furthermore, at the core of tawhid is the belief in a God "who has created everything in the best way." Many tafsīr scholars have commented on this verse. Ṭabarī explains this verse to mean, not only did God create everything perfectly, but everything is also perfectly calculated with a measure that demonstrates complete knowledge. In relation to this Qur'anic verse, Ṭabarī focuses on the notion that everything is created beautifully, with his focus being the perfection in design, symmetry and measure – the physical beauty of creation. Ibn Kathir has a similar focus. He explains that God is informing humankind of how He has created everything well and formed everything in a goodly fashion. He quotes Zayd bin Aslam's104 (d. 754) comments regarding this verse, who said: "'Who made everything He has created good" means "He created everything well and in a goodly fashion.'" Everything is created with wisdom and for a purpose: Whatever God created, He surely made it beautiful." The wisdom in creation can be understood in various ways. It can either suggest that creation has been created wisely and therefore everything serves multiple roles, which means it has been created with a good purpose. Or it can suggest that everything has been created with wisdom and therefore there must be good in all of creation.

16.5 The Will of Allah

"O you, who believe! Fear Allah as He should be feared, and die not except as Muslims." [Surah Ale-Imran (3), Ayah 102.]

"O Mankind! Be dutiful to your Lord, Who created you front a single person (Adam), and from him (Adam) He created his wife (Eve), and from them both He created many men and women. And fear Allah through Whom you demand your mutual (rights), and (do not cut the relations of) the wombs (Kinship). Surely, Allah is Ever an All-Watcher over you." [Surah An-Nisa (4), Ayah 1.]

"O you who believe! Keep your duty to Allah and fear Him, and always speak the truth. He will direct you to do righteous deeds arid will forgive you your sins. And whosoever obeys Allah and His Messenger, has indeed achieved a great achievement." [Surah Al-Ahzaab (33), Ayah 70-71.]

"But the greatest **bliss** is the good Pleasure of Allah: that is the supreme success." [Surah At-Taubah (9), Ayah 72.]

"And they have taken other gods besides Allah, that they might be helped. They are not able to help them, but they will be brought forward against those who worshipped them fat the time of Reckoning." [Surah Ya-Sin (36), Ayat 74-75.]

"And they have taken [other] gods besides Allah, that they may be [a source of] power for them. Not at all! They will reject their worship, and become their opponents." [Surah Maryam (19), Ayat 81-82.]

These 'gods' will disown them on the Day of Judgement and surrender them to their fate. It is strange that people reject the worship of Allah which brings them honour and glory in this life and eternal **bliss** in the Hereafter. It is really strange that they turn their backs on this, only to fall in the `mire' of shirk and the worship of false gods. They exalt these false gods, loving them, and approaching them with total humility and submission. These `gods', which do not benefit them in any way in this life, nor do they provide for them or help them, while it is they who protect these false gods. Furthermore, on the Day of Judgement these false `gods' will not intercede for them but will instead become their opponents: "And set not with Allah another god [for worship] lest you sit down disgraced [and] forsaken." [Surah Al-Israa' (17), Ayah 22.]

"What has he found who has lost God?
And what has he lost who has found God?"
— Ibn 'Ata' Allah Al-Iskandari

"The happiness of the drop is to die in the river."
— Imam Al-Ghazali

"Listen, O drop, give yourself up without regret,
and in exchange gain the Ocean.
Listen, O drop, bestow upon yourself this honour,
and in the arms of the Sea be secure.
Who indeed should be so fortunate?
An Ocean wooing a drop!
In God's name, in God's name, sell and buy at once!

Give a drop, and take this Sea full of pearls."
— Mawlana Jalal-al-Din Rumi

"You must empty out the dirty water before you fill the pitcher with clean."
— Idries Shah

CHAPTER 17

Bliss in Christianity

"Fear of the Lord is the beginning of wisdom." - *Hebrew Bible*

17.1 Bliss in Christianity

Bliss is an experience of wholeness, completeness, spiritual consummation. Its cognitive counterpart is the recognition that underlying and overarching the great diversity of the universe is an ultimate Unity with which one is, even in one's individuality, indissolubly connected. Bliss includes love, compassion, and inner peace. In Christianity, bliss may involve such visionary experiences as being caught up in the third heaven, hearing words in paradise, undergoing transformation in Christ, and becoming a new creature. There is the bliss of exaltation and glory, being risen with Christ and sharing his divine love. In Eastern Orthodoxy, the process of deification or theosis allows the person to share in the light and love and energies of the Trinity, participate in God's glory, and gain perfection through love and the fire of grace. In Catholic mysticism, the saints speak of the marriage of the human soul and the Word, the bliss that occurs through conformity of the soul in the union of divine love, and the role of soul as bride to God. Among Protestant charismatics, there is bliss in the gifts of the Holy Spirit. The goal is perfect love, with God's love communicated through the soul.

How are we to understand the reality of suffering from a spiritual perspective? I am asking something more fundamental: How can there be suffering in a reality that is fundamentally blissful? If the spiritual essence of God is bliss, as many religions teach, and everything else is somehow derived from God's blissful essence, then where does suffering come from? If bliss is ultimate, then suffering must arise from bliss. Suffering must be, in some sense, a mode of bliss.

But how are we to understand this? What is bliss such that, under certain conditions, it can manifest as suffering? What is suffering such that, under certain conditions, it can resolve itself as bliss? These are not idle questions. They are questions that lie at the heart of spiritual life, These are not idle questions. They are questions that lie at the heart of spiritual life, for spiritual life involves the endeavor to progress from states we experience as negative, states of suffering (dukkha in Buddhism), to a participation in, and enjoyment of, the bliss of God (nirvana; moksha; eternal life).

The ultimate goal of spiritual life is full participation in the bliss of God. This goal finds one of its fullest representations in the figure of Christ, the 'God-Man.' Christ is a revelation of the free, individual, human being who experiences (at the most profound level) unity/community with God. It is important to note that such unity does not obliterate freedom or individuality. Christ remains a free, self-determining, individual. But Christ's self-determination is informed by a perfected apprehension of the Whole to which he belongs. Thus, Christ's life is rooted in the bliss of God. Such bliss, of course, is not to be thought of as narcissistic self-satisfaction. : How can a divine reality of bliss give rise to a creation rife with suffering – how, unless divine bliss has already within it the potential to manifest as suffering under certain conditions? To approach this bliss, to participate in it, to express it, to celebrate it in its infinitely many forms, is the aim of spiritual of life.

17.2 Transmutation of Suffering into Bliss

How can a divine reality of bliss give rise to a creation rife with suffering – how, unless divine bliss has already within it the potential to manifest as suffering under certain conditions? Let us begin, then, by suggesting that bliss be thought of as analogous to white light. White light, separated from itself, breaks up into all the colours of the rainbow. Red is a fragment of white light, blue a fragment of white light, etc. All the diverse colors inhere within white light but appear as distinct when the light is divided from itself. When the fragments of light are joined together again, they combine as white.

Let us posit that something similar is true of the nature of divine bliss. All the affective modes, including the negative ones, are latent within bliss, fragments of it, so to speak – somewhat as the diverse colors of the spectrum are fragments of white. When separated, these fragments manifest as modes of relative dissatisfaction and suffering, when joined together they complement each other and satisfy one another. This satisfaction is bliss.

But reality is not a simple whole. It is a whole divided into elements each distinct from one another and distinct from the whole. These elements, when they achieve consciousness as separate elements (as in human beings), become aware of their isolation from the whole. A human being comes to see herself as an 'I' separated from the rest of reality, the 'not-I.' This awareness of separateness has its own affective modes, which may be understood as teleological fragments of bliss. They are 'teleological' in that they are modes of yearning for (re-)union with the whole. This yearning, when frustrated and unsatisfied, is suffering. Suffering is the frustrated desire for wholeness. Thus, we approach the bliss of ultimate reality, of sat-chit-ananda, as we come more and more to experience ourselves as conscious participants in the unity, the wholeness, of being. We experience suffering (deficient modes of bliss) as we experience ourselves as isolated from this unity. With this in mind, we might sketch out a progression, or regression, from the fullness of bliss to its most deficient modes; a ladder, so to speak, of spiritual devolution and evolution, deprivation and attainment. Spiritual life may be thought of as the endeavor to climb this spiritual ladder.

Bliss is love insofar as it is an experience of community with all things. To love God with all one's heart, soul, and might is not to love God to the exclusion of all else, but to love all else as included within God. Thus, Jesus tells us that the commandment to love God is "of a kind" (homoousios) with the command to love one's neighbor as oneself. Bliss is compassion insofar as it entails an empathic participation with all who suffer states of disunity and fragmentation. In Christianity, this empathic participation of God in human suffering is figured in the Cross of Christ.

Bliss is peace. Such divine peace finds expression in the Jewish notion of the Sabbath. The Sabbath is the seventh day (seven being a symbol of wholeness) when God rests from all God's work. God's 'work' is the work of bringing the diversity of the creation into accord with the unity of the Creator. This work is ongoing. It does not come to an end at some point in time, but achieves its end, its telos, at a point beyond time. This point beyond time is the Sabbath. The Sabbath is not a moment in time, but a mode of spiritual awareness; an awareness of divine bliss overarching time itself, unifying the disparate moments of time into wholeness. From the perspective of the Sabbath, one sees the ultimate wholeness and fulfillment of the creation even in its diversity and relative unfulfillment. Bliss is 'pure actuality,' to use an Aristotelian phrase. It does not seek to actualize anything beyond itself. It is satisfied in itself. As dynamic, however, it seeks something within itself. The dynamic life of bliss is joy.

17.3 Eschatological (Relating to Judgement) Views in Christianity

Let theism in general be the belief that a supremely powerful, supremely wise, and supremely good (loving, just, merciful) personal being exists as the Creator of the universe. Christian theism is, of course, more specific than that, and Christian theists typically make the following two-fold assumption: first, that the highest possible good for created persons (true blessedness, if you will) requires that they enter into a proper relationship (or even a kind of union) with their Creator, and second, that a complete severance from the divine nature, without even an implicit experience of God would be a terrifying evil. Although most Christians would probably agree with this, some may want additional clarity on the nature of the union and the separation in question here. But in any case, whereas heaven is in general thought of as a realm in which people experience the bliss of perfect fellowship and harmony with God and with each other, hell is in general thought of as a realm in which people experience the greatest possible estrangement from God, the greatest possible sense of alienation, and perhaps also an intense hatred of everyone including themselves.

All human sinners are equal objects of God's redemptive love in the sense that God wills or aims to win over each one of them over time and thereby to prepare each one of them for the bliss of union with the divine nature. God's redemptive love will triumph in the end and successfully win over each and every object of that love, thereby preparing each one of them for the bliss of union with the divine nature. Some human sinners will never be reconciled to God and will therefore remain separated from the divine nature forever.

So, one way to organize our thinking here is against the backdrop of the following inconsistent set of three propositions:

1. All human sinners are *equal* objects of God's redemptive love in the sense that God wills or aims to win over each one of them over time and thereby to prepare each one of them for the bliss of union with the divine nature.

2. God's redemptive love will triumph in the end and successfully win over each and every object of that love, thereby preparing each one of them for the bliss of union with the divine nature.

3. Some human sinners will never be reconciled to God and will therefore remain separated from the divine nature forever.

An issue concerning heaven that sometimes arises is whether everlasting bliss is even a possible state of affairs.

17.4 What does Bible say about Bliss?

John 3:16

For God so loved the world, that he gave his only Son, that whoever believes in him should not perish but have eternal life.

1 Corinthians 15:22
For as in Adam all die, so also in Christ shall all be made alive.

John 17:17
Sanctify them in the truth; your word is truth.

Genesis 2:7
Then the Lord God formed the man of dust from the ground and breathed into his nostrils the breath of life, and the man became a living creature.

1 Peter 5:8
Be sober-minded; be watchful. Your adversary the devil prowls around like a roaring lion, seeking someone to devour.

James 5:12
But above all, my brothers, do not swear, either by heaven or by earth or by any other oath, but let your "yes" be yes and your "no" be no, so that you may not fall under condemnation.

Hebrews 2:14
Since therefore the children share in flesh and blood, he himself likewise partook of the same things, that through death he might destroy the one who has the power of death, that is, the devil,

1 Timothy 2:5
For there is one God, and there is one mediator between God and men, the man Christ Jesus,

Mark 9:48
'where their worm does not die and the fire is not quenched.'

Matthew 10:28
And do not fear those who kill the body but cannot kill the soul. Rather fear him who can destroy both soul and body in hell.

Genesis 3:19

By the sweat of your face, you shall eat bread, till you return to the ground, for out of it you were taken; for you are dust, and to dust you shall return."

Revelation 3:21
The one who conquers, I will grant him to sit with me on my throne, as I also conquered and sat down with my Father on his throne.

Revelation 3:20
Behold, I stand at the door and knock. If anyone hears my voice and opens the door, I will come in to him and eat with him, and he with me.

Revelation 2:26
The one who conquers and who keeps my works until the end, to him I will give authority over the nations,

1 John 4:1
Beloved, do not believe every spirit, but test the spirits to see whether they are from God, for many false prophets have gone out into the world.

1 Peter 1:7
So that the tested genuineness of your faith—more precious than gold that perishes though it is tested by fire—may be found to result in praise and glory and honor at the revelation of Jesus Christ.

1 Peter 1:6
In this you rejoice, though now for a little while, if necessary, you have been grieved by various trials,

1 Timothy 6:19
Thus, storing up treasure for themselves as a good foundation for the future, so that they may take hold of that which is truly life.

1 Timothy 6:16
Who alone has immortality, who dwells in unapproachable light,

whom no one has ever seen or can see. To him be honor and eternal dominion. Amen.

1 Timothy 2:4
Who desires all people to be saved and to come to the knowledge of the truth.

Galatians 1:4
Who gave himself for our sins to deliver us from the present evil age, according to the will of our God and Father,

2 Corinthians 5:10
For we must all appear before the Judgement seat of Christ, so that each one may receive what is due for what he has done in the body, whether good or evil.

2 Corinthians 4:4
In their case the god of this world has blinded the minds of the unbelievers, to keep them from seeing the light of the gospel of the glory of Christ, who is the image of God.

1 Corinthians
You are to deliver this man to Satan for the destruction of the flesh, so that his spirit may be saved in the day of the Lord.

Romans 15:4
For whatever was written in former days was written for our instruction, that through endurance and through the encouragement of the Scriptures we might have hope.

Romans 5:8
But God shows his love for us in that while we were still sinners, Christ died for us.

Acts 4:12
And there is salvation in no one else, for there is no other name under heaven given among men by which we must be saved."

Acts 2:38
And Peter said to them, "Repent and be baptized every one of you in the name of Jesus Christ for the forgiveness of your sins, and you will receive the gift of the Holy Spirit.

Acts 2:27
For you will not abandon my soul to Hades, or let your Holy One see corruption.

John 14:6
Jesus said to him, "I am the way, and the truth, and the life. No one comes to the Father except through me.

Ezekiel 18:4
Behold, all souls are mine; the soul of the father as well as the soul of the son is mine: the soul who sins shall die.

Isaiah 26:9
My soul yearns for you in the night; my spirit within me earnestly seeks you. For when your Judgements are in the earth, the inhabitants of the world learn righteousness.

Psalm 16:10
For you will not abandon my soul to Sheol, or let your holy one see corruption.

SECTION 6

(QUANTUM SCIENCE)

CHAPTER 18

Basics of Quantum Science

18.1 Brief (non-mathematical) Introduction of Quantum Science

Quantum Mechanics brings science face-to-face with metaphysics, and that is unpleasant to some of the scientists, considering the manner in which they conduct 21st-century science. However, as we shall see shortly that the concept of quantum physics and love, healing, and happiness is inescapable if we wish appreciate metaphysics and realise the bliss of life in the true sense. So, let us begin introducing quantum mechanics from the point of a layman.

Picture the nucleus of an atom in the centric position of our sun. According to Bohr's model of the atom, the nucleus is positively charged and composed of neutral "particles" called neutrons and positively-charged protons. The neutrons and protons are made up of subatomic "particles" known as quarks, leptons and bosons; however, these subclasses are not immediately pertinent to our discussions here. The positive charge of the protons in the nucleus is balanced to neutrality by an equal number of electrons spinning around the nucleus, much the way the planets in our solar system revolve about our sun.

18.1.1 What is Quantum?

A quantum is a discrete packet of energy, proposed for the first time by Max Planck, in 1900. It denotes that the energy exchange between the two bodies can take place in terms discrete quanta (plural of quantum) of light: one quantum, two quanta, three quanta, but never half quantum and never continuous exchange of energy. One quantum of radiation of energy is one photon. The energy carried by a photon is directly proportional to the frequency associated with it. The electrons revolving about the nucleus of the atom can increase or decrease their energy levels (orbits) by interaction with a variety of forces, including photons of appropriate energy. For example, a low energy electron circumnavigating the nucleus in say a "Mercury" orbit close to the "solar nucleus" can be excited or stimulated by a number of methods with an appropriately energetic photon to "jump" to a higher energy orbit, say the "Jupiter" orbit. Or the reverse can occur, an electron can "jump" from the "Jupiter" orbit down to the lower energy "Mercury" orbit with a consequent emission of energy, usually in the form of a photon. Using this model, often called the "Old Quantum Mechanics," we can derive and describe a number of useful conclusions based on the laws of quantum mechanics, which in more than 100 years have never made a wrong prediction.

But to dig deeply into the metaphysics of quantum theory, we must make the transition to the New Quantum Mechanics, as developed in the mid-1920s by Werner Heisenberg, Erwin Schrödinger, and other astute theoreticians. However, a word of caution and clarity– despite the practical effectiveness of quantum mechanical models, most physicists believe that atoms, electrons, neutrons and protons are not solid particles, as these models might imply. They are more precisely, packets of information and energy. That being said, quantum mechanics can explain numerous properties of what we, with our five senses, perceive to be the stuff of our universe. More important, and perhaps quite surprising, it can provide you with a more accurate perspective of your true reality, and thereby give you specific tools that can significantly enhance your quality of life and well-being. As we shall see, this is by no means any kind of "hocus pocus," but is based on the proven results and implications of experiments and models at the interface of quantum physics and our true reality.

In all that follows, almost no mathematics and only elementary concepts in physics will be used. We will touch on the following *profound phenomena.* They are derived directly from quantum theory:

18.1.2 Quantum Jumps

One of these revolutionaries was Einstein. He was working as a clerk at the patent office in Zurich at the time he published his first research paper on the quantum theory (1905). Challenging the then-popular belief that light is a wave phenomenon, Einstein suggested that light exists as a quantum—a discrete bundle of energy—that we now call a photon. The higher the frequency of the light, the more energy in each bundle.

Even more revolutionary was Danish physicist Niels Bohr, who in 1913 applied the idea of light quanta to suggest that the whole world of the atom is full of quantum jumps. We all have been taught that the atom resembles a tiny solar system, that electrons rotate around a nucleus much as the planets rotate around the sun. It may come as a surprise to learn that this model, originated by the British physicist Ernest Rutherford in 1911, has a crucial flaw that Bohr's work resolved. In an atom, negatively-charged electrons can be considered to be whirling about the atom's positively-charged nucleus, occupying different energy levels or orbits. There are many ways to stimulate an electron to jump from one energy level or orbit to another, either to a higher or lower level. This movement is called a "quantum jump." In the process, the electron is initially present at say lower energy level 1, and then jumps to higher energy level 2. Before and after the jump, it can be observed at each of these respective energy levels. However, during the quantum jump process, it exists nowhere in between. Quantum mechanics forbids its existence between the levels.

18.1.3 Electron's Probability of Location

The electrons around the immediate diameter of an atom spend more than 95 percent of their time within a tight radius about the nucleus. However, there is a small, but finite probability that these electrons can be found anywhere in the universe. Technically speaking, we are all intimately sharing our electrons with each other, and in fact with all matter in the universe. There is a probability of electron contact with everyone from Joe Biden to Narendra Modi in India!

18.1.4 Observer Effect

What you perceive as your reality is actually something you create by your observation of the universe. When you "consciously" observe something under a given set of circumstances, an event occurs and/or an object appears. This event and/or object are directly created by you, the observer. Before your observation, the event and/or object was simply a state of energy vibrating in an infinite domain of potential or possibilities. This includes trees, buildings, and cars, etc. It is your observation that causes the specific possibility to materialize. This effect has been shown experimentally for subatomic particles, atoms, and more recently for large molecules. Quantum mechanics tells us that although it may not be possible to do the same experiments for large objects such as people, since such objects are composed of atoms and molecules, the same conscious creation of these objects is what occurs in what we perceive with our five senses to be reality. In other words, ***you are constantly creating what you perceive.***

18.1.5 Uncertainty Principle

According to Nobel laureate Werner Heisenberg, small or microscopic objects such as electrons and atoms are not "real" in our everyday sense. They exist as "potentialities," and hence what we call the domain of "potentia," where there exist infinite possibilities and one of them is created by the collapse of the wave function to a specific state or set of conditions, as a consequence of our observation. Heisenberg proved mathematically that any observation disturbs things enough to prevent disproval of quantum mechanic's assertion that observation creates the property observed. Stated another way, the more accurately you know the exact position of a moving particle, say an electron, the less accurately you know its velocity, and conversely. This same principle applies to large objects, but the calculated uncertainties are so small as to be immeasurable. Because of this, we need only use Newton's laws or Newtonian mechanics as opposed to quantum mechanics to track spaceships, satellites and planets. Newtonian mechanics is an approximation or simplified form of quantum mechanics.

18.1.6 Infinite Possibilities (Potentialities to Actuality)

What actually exists "out there" is an infinite number of "possibilities," in a domain that physicists refer to as the domain of "potentia." This infinite number of possibilities can be described by a complex mathematical expression called the quantum wave equation or quantum wave function, where you can think of the wave function as "spread out infinitely" over all of the possible outcomes. The probability of you perceiving a given outcome, namely, a certain event or the existence of a specific object under a given set of conditions, can be calculated from the square of the wave function. When you create a certain event by your observation, mathematically speaking, we say that you have caused the **wave function to collapse** from an infinite number of possibilities to a specific possibility or result. The idea that the consciousness collapses the quantum wave function was originally proposed by the mathematician John von Neumann in the 1930s.

In the standard (Copenhagen) interpretation of Quantum Theory, for example, a conscious observer is said to have a central role in getting from multiple quantum possibilities to classical deterministic objects – via the collapse of quantum wavefunction when an observation is made. Quantum Theory has to account for the change from the wavefunction (e.g., Schrodinger equation) in mathematical possibility space to sensory actualities as causally interacting objects in ordinary space. The standard interpretation held that this occurs instantaneously with collapse of the quantum wavefunction upon observation by a conscious observer.

Through the standard Quantum Theory interpretation, there has been important recognition of the role of conscious mind in scientific observations – in comparison to classical physics which basically ignored the issue. But how the mind works, if and where it exists, and what the world is like –indeed, whether it even exists in-between observations – remain in need of a rational explanation. Key assertions including instantaneous wavefunction collapse involving a conscious observer, fundamental randomness at the basis of nature, and the meaninglessness of local causal determinism at the quantum level all contributed to a psychological 'inviolable wall,' within which standard Quantum Theory was held to be complete and no further explanation of nature was even possible.

World-renowned physicist and Nobel laureate, Eugene Wigner speculated that observation and instantaneous collapse of the wave function happens at the very last stage of the observation process, perhaps when awareness occurs. He also speculated that ***human conscious awareness*** might actually "reach out" in some unexplained manner and change the physical state of a system. All we know at this point in time is that somewhere on the scale between subatomic particles, atoms and large molecules, and that of big objects such as cars, buildings and human beings, there is a mysterious unexplained process wherein observation collapses the wave function to a specific possibility and observation. And voilà, there it appears!

18.1.7 History Creation (Travelling Backwards in Time)

For decades, quantum mechanics predicted that your observation not only creates your present reality, but also creates the past history appropriate to that reality, i.e., you actually produce something backwards in time. Most scientists found this difficult to comprehend, much less believe. Quantum cosmologist John Archibald Wheeler suggested what he called a "delayed-choice experiment," which if carried out would determine whether or not one's observation actually could produce something backwards in time. For a long time, this was just conjecture, but in 1987, the experiment was performed and it confirmed that backwards-in-time history is created by the observer.

18.1.8 Duality (Wave and Particle)

Depending on how we measure the properties of an entity such as an electron, a neutron or a photon, they appear as both particles and waves. This attribute applies to big things such as human beings as well, although it is impossible to do the experiment for such large objects to prove this fact. This is the so-called duality of quantum mechanical measurement.

18.1.9 Multiple Places at Once (Probability of locating a particle)

If there is one electron, or photon, or neutron, or atom, or many other entities and two boxes in a given system, there is a calculable probability that the entity will be found in one of the boxes. Before you pick up either box to look inside, the entity is actually present in both boxes, and it is your looking that collapses the wave function and allows you to find it in one of the boxes. In fact, you can calculate from the square of the wave function the precise probability that you will find the entity in one of the boxes. The probability is directly related to the "waviness" of the wave equation. The "wavier" a set of conditions in the wave equation, the higher the probability of you finding a selected object in a chosen place.

18.1.10 Big is Like Small

Even though quantum mechanics is absolutely necessary to describe the state of being for small objects like electrons, neutrons, and photons, it applies to everything–you, me, the planet, the entire universe. In fact, cosmologists struggle with writing a wave equation for our universe. The reason is that the universe is made up of these same entities that obey the laws of quantum mechanics. It is just difficult to see the same profound effects when things get big. However, even with big things, we create our own reality.

18.2 Double-slit experiment with a single electron and Observer Effect

There is an even more subtle, but profound implication that follows from this electron's double-slit experiment, and it provides a glimpse of what lies at the very heart of the difference between classical physics and quantum physics. Consider the following. When a single electron is fired from the electron gun and travels towards the screen containing Slits A and B, through which slit does it pass in order to get to the photographic plate? Suppose it went through Slit A. In that case, Slit B would be unnecessary and we could just as well have closed it. But, with only Slit A open, the electron would not be most likely to arrive at the midpoint of the photographic plate exactly midway between Slits A and B as it does, but instead would end up at the point on the photographic plate exactly opposite Slit A. Since this is not the case, we can conclude that the electrons could not possibly have gone through Slit A. If we make the same argument for Slit B, we see that the single electron could not have gone through Slit B, either! What's happening here? The answer is that the single electron has gone through both slits at the same time! How could this possibly be? Does the electron interfere with itself as light waves do? Physicists decided to do the electron experiment again and this time to put a detector immediately on the other side of the two slits to see which slit the electron was actually going through. However, when they "peeked" by doing this, the experiment returned to the results observed when an electron acted as a particle and a pattern was seen only opposite each of the slits. No interference pattern formed. It was as if the electron "knew" that the experimenter was peeking, and it "decided" to go back to particle-like behaviour.

Our general sense of reality, conditioned by classical physics and our five senses says that this is nonsense, but it isn't. In quantum mechanics, we refer to this phenomenon as the superposition principle, and it makes perfect sense. It means that the state of motion of the electron has a probability of going through Slit A and a probability of going through Slit B, and the final result on the photographic plates is the sum, or in quantum mechanical language, the superposition of these probabilities. It is only by our observation that we "collapse" the wave function describing the system and the probability to a specific result. In essence, there are various probabilities before we observe the system; however, the very act of observing collapses the wave function to a specific possibility. In truth, our observation creates this reality.

In fact, the superposition principle demonstrates **three aspects of quantum mechanics** that appear to most of us to be in the realm of mysticism.

(i) The **first point** is that at our current state of human development and reality perception, it is impossible to form a clear picture in terms of our five senses about what is happening in the course of the physical process. We could not possibly visualize how an individual particle, such as an electron, a photon, or even an atom could simultaneously go through both slits.

(ii) The **second point** is the probabilistic nature of quantum mechanics, in that unlike the perfectly certain world of classical physics, it is no longer possible to predict what will happen when we make an observation, only the probability of what will occur. The deep philosophical and actual point here is that ***classical physics is deterministic and quantum physics is probabilistic.*** In classical physics, if I throw a ball up in the air, knowing all of the forces on the ball, and using Newton's laws, we can tell exactly where the ball will be at any point in time in the future; classical physics is deterministic. Not so in quantum physics. we can only tell the probability of finding the object at a given point at a given time.

(iii) The **third point** is that your observation actually creates your reality! To demonstrate this point, suppose we were to modify the double-slit experiment by putting a photographic plate detector immediately on the other side of Slit A and Slit B, so that we could determine which slit the electron passed through. What we find in this modification of the experiment is that sometimes the electron is detected near Slit A and sometimes it is detected near Slit B. It is impossible to predict which slit the electron will go through, but over a large number of electron firings from the electron gun, we find that the relative probabilities of going through each slit is 50-50. This illustrates that in quantum mechanics, predictions of the results of measurements are always statistical in character and not deterministic as in classical physics. After all, if we were firing a bullet through Slit A, we know that every single time we fire the gun at Slit A, the bullet will exit Slit A. Quantum mechanics deals in probabilities and not in certainties.

A final point concerning this modification of the experiment is the destruction of the interference pattern on the photographic plate. No longer do electrons tend to the midpoint of the photographic plate, but are split evenly between those arriving opposite Slits A and B. This demonstrates that whether we see particle-like or wave-like behaviour, depends on what we look for. **If we ask a particle-like question (which slit is the electron going through?), we get a particle-like answer. If we ask a wave-like question, (What is the final pattern of all of the accumulated electrons?), we get a wave-like answer.** In many respects, the double-split experiment embraces all of the mystery, the essence, and the power of quantum mechanics. In 1926, physicist, Max Born developed the quantitative interpretation of the probabilistic nature of quantum mechanics, for which he received the Nobel Prize 28 years later, in 1954.

18.3 Copenhagen Interpretation of Quantum Mechanics

Copenhagen Interpretation of Quantum Mechanics is based on *three fundamental technical principles*:

(i) Probability–The square of the wave function in a given region of space-time is the probability that the object will be found in that given region. It is important to note that this probability is not where the object is located, but where you will find it. What this means is that the object was not completely there until you observed it. If we consider the presence of a single atom in one of two boxes, quantum mechanics tells us that there is no atom in addition to its wave function. Each box contains the atom's wave function, and therefore, although we appear to be unable to fathom the fact, the atom itself is actually in both boxes until we observe the atom, at which time the wave function collapses and the atom is found in that single box. Indeed, the wave function is the only way to communicate information in quantum mechanics. In all actuality, the wave function is the entire story. Some physicists say that there is no atom in addition to the wave function, and actually the wave function is synonymous with the atom. But the atom is present as an entity of energy and information. The wave function certainly contains information, but not energy. The wave function does not carry specific information as to how a particular entity will behave or a specific event will occur. Rather, it is an expression of potential or statistical probability. This is in stark contrast to classical physics where answers are always exact and specific and the future of a given system is precisely predictable.

(ii) Uncertainty–As discussed above, according to Heisenberg's Uncertainty Principle, if we consider the position and momentum (mass x velocity) of a small particle such as an atom, the more precisely we know about its velocity or momentum, the less precisely we can know its position. The fact is that any observation disturbs things enough to prevent disproval of quantum mechanic's assertion that observation creates the property observed.

(iii) Complementarity between particle- and wave-pictures: The particle-like and wave-like behaviours of a microscopic object are "complementary." A complete description of the object requires that we make use of both behaviours, but never at the same time. This is a statement of the complementarity of Newtonian or classical mechanics and quantum mechanics. The macro world obeys Newtonian mechanics and the micro or quantum world obeys quantum mechanics. If we do a wave-like experiment, we will always get a wave-like answer; if we do a particle-like experiment, we will always get a particle-like answer.

18.4 David Bohm and Quantum Mechanics

Some scientists seek to clarify reality, others to mystify it. David Bohm seemed driven by both impulses. He is renowned for promoting a sensible (according to Einstein and other experts) interpretation of quantum mechanics. But Bohm also asserted that science can never fully explain the world, and his 1980 book, 'Wholeness and the Implicate Order' delved into spirituality. Bohm's interpretation of quantum mechanics has attracted increasing attention lately. He is a hero of Adam Becker's new book 'What Is Real?' In 'The End of Science', Bohm tried to make sense of this paradoxical truth-seeker, who died in 1992 at the age of 74.

Bohm began questioning the Copenhagen interpretation in the late 1940s while writing a book on quantum mechanics. According to the Copenhagen interpretation, a quantum entity such as an electron has no definite existence apart from our observation of it. We cannot say with certainty whether it is either a wave or a particle. The interpretation also rejects the possibility that the seemingly probabilistic behaviour of quantum systems stems from underlying, deterministic mechanisms.

Bohm found this view unacceptable. "The whole idea of science so far has been to say that underlying the phenomenon is some reality which explains things," he explained. "It was not that Bohr denied reality, but he said quantum mechanics implied there was nothing more that could be said about it." Such a view reduced quantum mechanics to "a system of formulas that we use to make predictions or to control things technologically. I said that's not enough. I don't think I would be very interested in science if that were all there was", remarked Bohm.

In 1952 Bohm proposed that particles are indeed particles--and at all times, not just when they are observed in a certain way. Their behavior is determined by a force that Bohm called the "pilot wave." Any effort to observe a particle alters its behavior by disturbing the pilot wave. Bohm thus gave the uncertainty principle a purely physical rather than metaphysical meaning. Niels Bohr had interpreted the uncertainty principle as meaning "not that there is uncertainty, but that there is an inherent ambiguity" in a quantum system, Bohm explained.

Bohm's interpretation gets rid of one quantum paradox, wave/particle duality, but it preserves and even highlights another, nonlocality, the capacity of one particle to influence another instantaneously across vast distances. Einstein had drawn attention to nonlocality in 1935 in an effort to show that quantum mechanics must be flawed. Together with Boris Podolsky and Nathan Rosen, Einstein proposed a thought experiment involving two particles that spring from a common source and fly in opposite directions.

According to the standard model of quantum mechanics, neither particle has fixed properties, such as momentum, before it is measured. But by measuring one particle's momentum, the physicist instantaneously forces the other particle, no matter how distant, to assume a fixed momentum. Deriding this effect as "spooky action at a distance," Einstein argued that quantum mechanics must be flawed or incomplete. But in 1980 French physicists demonstrated spooky action in a laboratory. Bohm never had any doubts about the experiment's outcome. "It would have been a terrific surprise to find out otherwise," he said.

But here is the paradox of Bohm: Although he tried to make the world more sensible with his pilot-wave model, he also argued that complete clarity is impossible. He reached this conclusion after seeing an experiment on television, in which a drop of ink was squeezed onto a cylinder of glycerin. When the cylinder was rotated, the ink diffused through the glycerin in an apparently irreversible fashion. Its order seemed to have disintegrated. But when the direction of rotation was reversed, the ink gathered into a drop again.

The experiment inspired Bohm to write Wholeness and the Implicate Order, published in 1980. He proposed that underlying physical appearances, the "explicate order," there is a deeper, hidden "implicate order." Applying this concept to the quantum realm, Bohm proposed that the implicate order is a field consisting of an infinite number of fluctuating pilot waves. The overlapping of these waves generates what appears to us as particles, which constitute the explicate order. Even space and time might be manifestations of a deeper, implicate order, according to Bohm.

To plumb the implicate order, Bohm said, physicists might need to jettison basic assumptions about nature. During the Enlightenment, thinkers such as Newton and Descartes replaced the ancients' organic concept of order with a mechanistic view. Even after the advent of relativity and quantum mechanics, "the basic idea is still the same," Bohm remarked, "a mechanical order described by coordinates."

Bohm hoped scientists would eventually move beyond mechanistic and even mathematical paradigms. "We have an assumption now that's getting stronger and stronger that mathematics is the only way to deal with reality," Bohm said. "Because it's worked so well for a while, we've assumed that it has to be that way."

Someday, science and art will merge, Bohm predicted. "This division of art and science is temporary," he observed. "It didn't exist in the past, and there's no reason why it should go on in the future." Just as art consists not simply of works of art but of an "attitude, the artistic spirit," so does science consist not in the accumulation of knowledge but in the creation of fresh modes of perception. "The ability to perceive or think differently is more important than the knowledge gained," Bohm explained.

Bohm rejected the claim of physicists such as Hawking and Weinberg that physics can achieve a final "theory of everything" that explains the world. Science is an infinite, "inexhaustible process," he said. "The form of knowledge is to have at any moment something essential, and the appearance can be explained. But then when we look deeper at these essential things they turn out to have some feature of appearances. We're not ever going to get a final essence which isn't also the appearance of something."

Bohm feared that belief in a final theory might become self-fulfilling. "If you have fish in a tank and you put a glass barrier in there, the fish keep away from it," he noted. "And then if you take away the glass barrier they never cross the barrier and they think the whole world is that." He chuckled drily. "So, your thought that this is the end could be the barrier to looking further."

In Wholeness and the Implicate Order Bohm insisted on the importance of "playfulness" in science, and in life, but Bohm, in his writings and in person, was anything but playful. For him, truth-seeking was not a game, it was a dreadful, impossible, necessary task. Bohm was desperate to know, to discover the secret of everything, but he knew it wasn't attainable, not for any mortal being. No one gets out of the fish tank alive.

The quantum theory, as it is now constituted, presents us with a very great challenge, if we are at all interested in such a venture, for in quantum physics there is no consistent notion at all of what the reality may be that underlies the universal constitution and structure of matter. Thus, if we try to use the prevailing world view based on the notions of particles, we discover that the 'particles' (such as electrons) can also manifest as waves, that they move discontinuously, that there are no laws at all that apply in detail to the actual movements of individual particles and that only statistical predictions can be made about large aggregates of such particles. If on the other hand we apply the world view in which the world is regarded as a continuous field, we find that this field must also be discontinuous, as well as particle-like, and that it is as undermined in its actual behaviour as is required in the particle view of relation as a whole, according to David Bohm (1917-1992).

Bohmian mechanics, which is also called the de Broglie-Bohm theory, the pilot-wave model, and the causal interpretation of quantum mechanics, is a version of quantum theory discovered by Louis de Broglie in 1927 and rediscovered by David Bohm in 1952. It is the simplest example of what is often called a hidden variables interpretation of quantum mechanics. In Bohmian mechanics a system of particles is described in part by its wave function, evolving, as usual, according to Schrödinger's equation. However, the wave function provides only a partial description of the system. This description is completed by the specification of the actual positions of the particles. The latter evolve according to the "guiding equation," which expresses the velocities of the particles in terms of the wave function. Thus, in Bohmian mechanics the configuration of a system of particles evolves via a deterministic motion choreographed by the wave function. In particular, when a particle is sent into a two-slit apparatus, the slit through which it passes and where it arrives on the photographic plate are completely determined by its initial position and wave function.

Bohmian mechanics inherits and makes explicit the nonlocality implicit in the notion, common to just about all formulations and interpretations of quantum theory, of a wave function on the configuration space of a many-particle system. It accounts for all of the phenomena governed by nonrelativistic quantum mechanics, from spectral lines and scattering theory to superconductivity, the quantum Hall effect and quantum computing. In particular, the usual measurement postulates of quantum theory, including collapse of the wave function and probabilities given by the absolute square of probability amplitudes, emerge from an analysis of the two equations of motion - Schrödinger's equation and the guiding equation - without the traditional invocation of a special, and somewhat obscure, status for observation.

In relativity, movement is continuous, causally determinate and well defined, while in quantum mechanics it is discontinuous, not causally determinate and not well defined. Each theory is committed to its own notions of essentially static and fragmentary modes of existence (relativity to that of separate events, connectable by signals, and quantum mechanics to a well-defined quantum state). One thus sees that a new kind of theory is needed which drops these basic commitments and at most recovers some essential features of the older theories as abstract forms derived from a deeper reality in which what prevails in unbroken wholeness.

At present quantum physicists tend to avoid the issue by adopting the attitude that our overall views concerning the nature of reality are of little or no importance. All that counts in physical theory is supposed to be the development of mathematical equations that permit us to predict and control the behaviour of large statistical aggregates of particles. Such a goal is not regarded as merely for its pragmatic and technical utility: rather, it has become a presupposition of most work in modern physics that prediction and control of this kind is all that human knowledge is about.

One is led to a new notion of unbroken wholeness which denies the classical idea of analyzability of the world into separately and existing parts … We have reversed the usual classical notion that the independent 'elementary parts' of the world are the fundamental reality, and that the various systems are merely particular contingent forms and arrangements of these parts. Rather, we say that inseparable quantum interconnectedness of the whole universe is the fundamental reality, and that relatively independent behaving parts are merely particular and contingent forms within this whole.

The main problem with modern physics is that quantum mechanics gives only the probability of an experimental result. Neither the decay of an atomic nucleus nor the fact that it decays at one moment and not another can be properly pictured within the theory. It can only enable you to predict statistically the results of various experiments.

Physics has changed from its earlier form, when it tried to explain things and give some physical picture. Now the essence is regarded as mathematical. It's felt the truth is in the formulas. Now they may find an algorithm by which they hope to explain a wider range of experimental results, but it will still have inconsistencies. They hope that they can eventually explain all the results that could be gotten, but that is only a hope.

Younger physicists usually appreciate the implicate order because it makes quantum mechanics easier to grasp. By the time they're through graduate school, they've become dubious about it because they've heard that hidden variables are of no use because they've been refuted. Of course, nobody has really refuted them. At this point, the major issue is mathematics. In supersymmetry theory an interesting piece of mathematics will attract attention, even without any experimental confirmation.

If we supposed that theories gave true knowledge, corresponding to 'reality as it is', then we would have to conclude that Newtonian Mechanics was true until around 1900, after which it suddenly became false, while relativity and quantum theory suddenly became the truth. Such an absurd conclusion does not arise, however, if we say that all theories are insights, which are neither true nor false.

Man is continually developing new forms of insight, which are clear up to a point and then tend to become unclear. In this activity, there is evidently no reason to suppose that there is or will be a final form of insight (corresponding to absolute truth) or even a steady series of approximations to this. Rather, one may expect the unending development of new forms of insight (which will, however assimilate certain key features of the older forms as simplifications, in the way that relativity theory does with Newtonian theory). Bohm's theories are to be regarded primarily as ways of looking at the world as a whole ('world-views') rather than as 'absolute true knowledge of how things are'.

What prevents theoretical insights from going beyond existing limitations and changing to meet new facts is just the belief that theories give true knowledge of reality (which implies, of course, that they never change). Although our modern way of thinking has changed a great deal relative to the ancient one, the two have had one key feature in common: that is. they are both generally 'blinkered' by the notion that theories give true knowledge about 'reality as it is'. Thus, both are led to confuse the forms and shapes induced in our perceptions by theoretical insight with a reality independent of our thought and way of looking. This confusion is of crucial significance, since it leads us to approach nature, society and the individual in terms of more or less fixed and limited forms of thought, and thus, apparently, to keep on confirming the limitations of these forms of thought in experience.

If man thinks of the totality as constituted of independent fragments, then that is how his mind will tend to operate, but if he can include everything coherently and harmoniously in an overall whole that is undivided, unbroken, and without a border then his mind will tend to move in a similar way, and from this will flow an orderly action within the whole.

The notion that all these fragments is separately existent is evidently an illusion, and this illusion cannot do other than lead to endless conflict and confusion. Indeed, the attempt to live according to the notion that the fragments are really separate is, in essence, what has led to the growing series of extremely urgent crises that is confronting us today. Thus, as is now well known, this way of life has brought about pollution, destruction of the balance of nature, over-population, world-wide economic and political disorder and the creation of an overall environment that is neither physically nor mentally healthy for most of the people who live in it. Individually there has developed a widespread feeling of helplessness and despair, in the face of what seems to be an overwhelming mass of disparate social forces, going beyond the control and even the comprehension of the human beings who are caught up in it.

CHAPTER 19

Quantum Entanglement and Connection with Souls

Hiddenly
To each other linked are,
That thou canst not stir a flower
Without troubling of a star.

- *Radin, Dean*

19.1 Introduction to Quantum Entanglement

An entangled system is defined to be one whose quantum state cannot be factored as a product of states of its local constituents; that is to say, they are not individual particles but are an inseparable whole. In entanglement, one constituent cannot be fully described without considering the other(s). The state of a composite system is always expressible as a sum, or superposition, of products of states of local constituents; it is entangled if this sum cannot be written as a single product term.

Quantum entanglement is a physical phenomenon that occurs when pairs or groups of particles are generated such that the quantum state of each particle cannot be described independently of the state of the others, even when the particles are separated by a large distance. Measurements of physical properties such as position, momentum, spin, and polarization, performed on entangled particles are found to be correlated. For example, if a pair of particles is generated in such a way that their total spin is known to be zero, and one particle is found to have clockwise spin on a certain axis, the spin of the other particle, measured on the same axis, will be found to be counterclockwise, as is to be expected due to their entanglement.

Measurements of physical properties such as position, momentum, spin, and polarization performed on entangled particles can, in some cases, be found to be perfectly correlated. For example, if a pair of entangled particles is generated such that their total spin is known to be zero, and one particle is found to have clockwise spin on a first axis, then the spin of the other particle, measured on the same axis, is found to be counterclockwise. However, this behaviour gives rise to seemingly paradoxical effects: any measurement of a particle's properties results in an irreversible wave function collapse of that particle and changes the original quantum state. With entangled particles, such measurements affect the entangled system as a whole.

Such phenomena were the subject of a 1935 paper by Albert Einstein, Boris Podolsky, and Nathan Rosen, and several papers by Erwin Schrödinger shortly thereafter, describing what came to be known as the EPR paradox. Einstein and others considered such behaviour to be impossible, as it violated the local realism view of causality (Einstein referring to it as "spooky action at a distance"). EPR asserted that if such an instant entanglement phenomenon is accepted between the two particles separated by a very large distance; this will violate the maximum limit of the speed of light. Therefore, they argued that the accepted formulation of quantum mechanics must therefore be incomplete. Only after the realization of an experiment suggested by Bell, was the nonlocal nature of quantum mechanics widely accepted.

19.1.1 What is Nonlocality in Quantum Entanglement?

A non-local connection links up one location with another without crossing space, without decay, and without delay. These connections have three identifying characteristics: (i) They are unmediated (no connecting signal is involved, that means it is a signal-less communication), (ii) unmitigated (the strength of the correlations does not fade with increasing distance), and (iii) immediate (they are instantaneous). Basically, the general "principle of locality" requires that "for an action at one point to have an influence at another point, something in the space between the points, such as a field, must mediate the action". In view of the theory of relativity, the speed at which such an action, interaction, or influence can be transmitted between distant points in space cannot exceed the speed of light.

This formulation is also known as "Einstein locality" or "local relativistic causality". It is often stated as "nothing can propagate faster than light, be it energy or merely information" or simply "no spooky action-at-a-distance", as Einstein himself put it.

The phenomenon of entanglement between quantum systems raised the nonlocality problem first noted in the EPR paper: A projective measurement on a quantum system at one space location instantly collapses the state of an entangled counterpart at a distant location. Quantum mechanical nonlocality refers to this apparent entanglement-mediated violation of Einstein locality. Although entanglement correlations are affected instantaneously, they cannot be harnessed for faster-than-light communications. The reason is that the outcome of the local projective measurement is itself statistic and cannot be predicted beforehand.

Nonlocality is subdivided by some physicists into three types. Type I is spatial nonlocality; type II is temporal nonlocality; and type III nonlocality is both spatial and temporal.

19.1.2 What is 'Spatial Nonlocality' in Quantum Entanglement?

Until recently, the two (or more) quantumly entangled objects, satisfying the criterion of non-locality, could be located at any distance apart. This is called the 'Spatial Nonlocality' in Quantum Entanglement. It is to this type of large separation to which Einstein referred to as 'spooky action' because it violated the maximum limit of speed of light.

19.1.3 What is 'Temporal Nonlocality' in Quantum Entanglement?

The non-locality of quantum mechanics, as manifested by entanglement, does not apply only to particles with space-like separation, but also to particles with time-like separation. If the two objects are located at two different times (instead of different points in space) and are entangled, this is called 'temporal nonlocality'. It means that the second object (which was generated at a subsequent time) was entangled with the first object which existed in the past, and vice versa. The future, past, present, and consciousness are entangled within the quantum continuum.

19.2 Happiness is both 'local' and 'nonlocal' temporally

Whether it is a simple shift of committing to treating people with more kindness, and liberating through realization, you are responsible for your own happiness, trying to better make sense of the world. We are called to do it numerous times in a life. There is a beautiful word for this, it's called 'metanoia', and it originates from the Greek word for "changing one's mind or purpose. Metanoia, in other words, is a nonlocal awareness. Happiness is also nonlocal: it is found externally as well as internally. One can thus transcend to the state of happiness through metanoia.

Whereas the nature at its deepest level is quantum mechanical and nonlocal, it appears to our minds in everyday experience as local and classical. Some modern scientists have gone to the extent of asserting that nature is actual nonlocal and it is real. It is our 'spooky mind' that perceives it to be classical and local. The reason behind this spooky mind is that it conceals the ability to perceive the universe in its fundamental, quantum, non-local state by the convenient application of a cognitive filter to perceive it as classical and local.

19.3 Perception of Time and Nonlocality

Time is a concept that spans the human condition. Psychological research shows that just about all of human experience is dependent upon and influenced by how individuals perceive time, localize themselves consciously within space and time and process their temporally-based perceptions and experiences. Classical physics has successfully allowed us to calculate and measure time at the macroscale while relativistic physics demonstrates how time and space are conjugate pairs that manifest in a unified continuum. With the establishment of quantum mechanics, concepts such as entanglement and nonlocality allow us to construct a new cosmological model of time that connects with cognitive perception—one that asserts that time is perceived in a complementary timeful and timeless state. In the timeful state, the mind perceives time in its localized, linear, and causal aspects; while in its timeless state as non-local, symmetrical, and entangled. Many of the spiritual traditions throughout history maintain a similar position of human consciousness as having the capacity to abide within these complementary modes of existence. How time, and conceptions about the past, present or future are therefore illusions, as there is no 'future' or 'past'. However, when considered from the perspective of quantum mechanics, timespace is a continuum, a unity, and time does not exist independent of this continuum, except as an act of perceptual registration by consciousness or mechanical means.

The recognition of the mind's ability to experience both the localized and non-localized complementary aspects of time was the impetus for the ancient Indian mystics to develop advanced mental techniques to master time within the domain of human consciousness. The goal of these disciplines was to liberate from the inherent cognitive filters that limit one's consciousness into the distorted and fragmented perception of time.

The mechanism that reduces human consciousness into experiencing time in its temporally localized state is what is referred to as veiled non-locality. The term implies how consciousness disguises its wholeness and nonlocality in order to produce local processes. This filtering process allows for specific observations and thoughts in a classical world of everyday experience, while keeping quantum and general relativistic processes out of sight.

19.4 Time is Entangled

Time cannot be separate from the continuum except when perceived as such by an observing consciousness or measuring device, thereby inducing a collapse of the wave function of time; experienced as the present, past, or future. Time, be it considered a dimension known as timespace, or as a perceived aspect of the quantum continuum, is also subject to entanglement, as all aspects of time are interconnected and indistinguishable until perceived thereby inducing a collapse of the wave function. "A" future can therefore effect "a" past and change it through entanglement and by influencing the wave function.

The quantum continuum is without dimensions and encompasses space and time in its basic unity of oneness. Everything within the quantum continuum can be influenced by the local effect and distant effects simultaneously at and beyond light speeds. Therefore, the future, and the "present" being part of this continuum can influence the past by effecting the wave function of the past, present, future, and thus, the space-time continuum, as all are entangled. Time-space is interactional, and can contract to near nothingness and then continue to contract in a negative direction such that the time traveler can journey into the past.

19.5 Learning from the Scriptures and Quantum Entanglement on the Perception of Happiness

Thus, the learning of the ancient Hindu scriptures and Quantum Entanglement can be summarized into the following three key points:

(i) There exists a transcendental, infinite, non-local, dimensionless, unchanging reality that is obscured from the limited cognitive perception of the human senses;

(ii) This foundational reality is veiled by means of a cognitive illusion that limits the consciousness into a localized, linear, and dimensionally finite perception of time.

(iii) Advanced mental training needs to be developed and practiced in order to liberate one's consciousness from the illusory cognitive limitations of the mind via a perceptual reframing of time into its fundamental non-local, entangled state.

Turns out, it's probably good for some really important things, and even without knowing how it works, applications of quantum entanglement are already being developed.

19.6 Scaling up of Entanglement for microscopic to macroscopic level

Scientists are now finding that there are ways in which the effects of microscopic entanglements "scale up" into our macroscopic world. Entangled connections between carefully prepared atomic-sized objects can persist over many miles. There are theoretical descriptions showing how tasks can be accomplished by entangled groups without the members of the group communicating with each other in any conventional way. Some scientists suggest that the remarkable degree of coherence displayed in living systems might depend in some fundamental way on quantum effects like entanglement. Others suggest that conscious awareness is caused or related in some important way to entangled particles in the brain. Some even propose that the entire universe is a single, self-entangled object. If these speculations are correct, then what would human experience be like in such an interconnected universe? Would we occasionally have numinous feelings of connectedness with loved ones, even at a distance? Would such experiences evoke a feeling of awe that there's more to reality than common sense implies? Could "entangled minds" be involved when you hear the telephone ring and somehow know—instantly—who's calling? If we did have such experiences, could they be due to real information that somehow bypassed the usual sensory channels? Or are such reports better understood as coincidences or delusions?

The idea of the universe as an interconnected whole is not new; for millennia it's been one of the core assumptions underlying Eastern philosophies. What is new is that Western science is slowly beginning to realize that some elements of that ancient lore might have been correct. Of course, adopting a new ontology is not to be taken lightly.

Cosmologists have learned that we might have accidentally overlooked 96% of the universe. The missing majority of the universe has been dubbed "dark" energy and matter. We know next to nothing about it, and it's spawning whole new concepts about the structure and evolution of the universe. As theories of cosmology are being reconsidered, new light is dawning on astronomical anomalies first observed decades ago.

Molecular biologists, who till recently regarded large segments of the genome as "junk DNA" because no one knew what it was good for, have been astonished to find strong commonalities among DNA base-pairs in humans, chickens, dogs, and fish. It appears that some aspects of DNA have been ultra-conserved for hundreds of millions of years, and that previous assumptions about what is important in DNA were wrong. For a century, neuroscientists believed that neurons in the brain do not regenerate, that once there is a brain injury or as neurons die in the course of aging, normal mental functioning inevitably deteriorates. Now we've learned that the dogma was wrong—brain neurons do regenerate. The plasticity of the brain is much greater than previously expected. This helps shed new light on previous observations that were ignored because they didn't make any sense. In a case study reported in 1980 in the journal 'Science', during a routine examination for a minor medical ailment, a student at Sheffield University in Great Britain was found to have virtually no brain. But that didn't stop him from enjoying an IQ of 126 and graduating with first-class honours in mathematics.

Physicists have been able to entangle ensembles of trillions of atoms in gaseous form, and entanglement has been demonstrated among the atoms of relatively large chunks (centimeter square) of salt. Entangled photons shot through sheets of metal have been shown to remain entangled after punching through to the other side. Photons also remain entangled after being sent through 50 kilometers of optical fiber, and while being transmitted through the open atmosphere. Clusters of four entangled photons have been demonstrated to make quantum computing significantly easier to accomplish than it was previously imagined. And organic molecules, like tetraphenylporphyrin (C44H30N4), have been successfully entangled.

Physicists have even speculated that entanglement extends to everything in the universe, because as far as we know, all energy and all matter emerged out of a single, primordial Big Bang. And thus, everything came out of the chute already entangled. Some further speculate that empty space, the quantum vacuum itself, may be filled with entangled particles. Such proposals suggest that despite everyday appearances, we might be living within a holistic, deeply interconnected reality. To be clear, these speculations are being proposed by traditional physicists, not by starry-eyed new agers or mystics.

19.7 Evidence of Quantumly Entangled Twins: A True Story

Identical twins who grow up separately provide a rare opportunity to study how environment versus heredity influences human development.

Four weeks later, at the now-defunct Knoop Children's Home in Troy, Ohio, the brothers became separated when one of them was adopted by Ernest Springer, a utility-company lineman, and his wife, Sarah, who brought him to their home in Piqua.

The Springers would likely have adopted both boys. But, for reasons still unclear, they were told the other twin had died during birth. In fact, however, the second boy was adopted two weeks later by Jess Lewis, a Lima public-school boilerman, and his wife, Lucille.

When the Lewises completed their adoption papers, one Miami County probate-court official gasped: "That's what [the Springers] named their son, too!"

Jim Springer was in his teens when he was told that his twin brother had died at birth. Jim Lewis, however, learned at age 6 that he was a twin and that his brother had been adopted by another family. His mother, Lucille Lewis, who has since remarried and now goes by the name of Lucille Cheny, began to encourage him even then to look for his lost brother, but procrastinated. Finally, last January, he went to court and started the proceedings. On February 9, the reunion took place.

When identical twins James Arthur Springer and James Edward Lewis were reunited after spending all but the first four weeks of their 39 years apart, they discovered that, despite the long separation, their lives had been astonishingly similar. Aside from sharing a given name. Each married and then divorced a woman named Linda. Their second wives were both named Betty. Springer named his first son James Allan. Lewis named his first son James Alan. Each man grew up with an adopted brother named Larry. During childhood, each owned a dog named Toy. Both twins had law-enforcement training and had worked part time as deputy sheriffs in their Ohio towns 70 miles apart. They shared many common interests, such as mechanical drawing, block lettering and carpentry. Both said their favourite school subject was Maths, their least favorite, spelling. They vacationed at the same, three-block-long beach near St. Petersburg, Fla., both getting there and back in a Chevrolet. Their smoking and drinking patterns were nearly identical.

The twins were tickled. "This is really blowing our minds," said Springer. " Just unbelievable. It's weird. It's downright spooky." "We even use the same slang," Lewis added. "A lot of times, I'll start to say something, and he'll finish it!" (Researchers said when asked about this phenomenon that identical twins are known to have remarkably similar brain waves, which may contribute to the perception that such twins "think alike.") Doctors and scientists were equally surprised by the findings. "If someone else brought this material to me and said: 'This is what I've got,' I'd say I didn't believe it," said psychologist Thomas J. Bouchard Jr., Director of the Minnesota Study of Twins Reared Apart Project, a team that gathered to look into Springer, Lewis and other twins separated in childhood. "The probability of two people independently being given the same name is not that rare. But when you start to compound the coincidences, they become highly unlikely very quickly. In fact, I'm flabbergasted by some of the similarities."

Even more interesting to researchers about twins like Springer and Lewis, however, is the fact that they are a "living laboratory" in which it is possible to examine closely the relative influence of heredity versus environment on the medical and behavioral aspects of human development.

Nearly 20 other such pairs have come to the attention of the University of Minnesota researchers, and at least eight of them have already been enrolled in the study (others are being courted assiduously for their participation). "It could be the most dense volume of data ever gathered on any group of people," said Bouchard. "The University of Minnesota will literally be the world center for the study of twins reared apart. Jim and Jim were undoubtedly the catalysts."

Among the medically significant findings in the study of Springer and Lewis is a form of headache called "mixed headache syndrome," a tension headache that turns into a migraine. It has long been thought to be without genetic basis, but scientists now postulate that heredity may indeed be a factor in this viselike pain caused by muscle contractions, the most common type of headache.

"Springer and Lewis both have peculiar elements to their headaches," said Dr. Leonard Heston, a member of the Minnesota team. "The syndrome began at age 18 for both; each gets it with the same degree of disability and the same frequency — and they used almost identical words to describe it."

Thus, the reunion of Springer and Lewis comes at a time when global interest in the study of twins has definitely been on the upswing. But identical twins reared apart are thought to be a diminishing occurrence, because of more enlightened welfare policies and changing social mores that have removed much of the social disgrace once associated with illegitimacy. When these twins were born slightly premature on Aug. 19, 1939, at the Piqua, Ohio, Memorial Hospital, however, their mother, an unwed, 35-yearold immigrant, immediately put them up for adoption.

The brothers shook hands stiffly, when they saw each other for the first time. Then they hugged and burst into laughter. "I looked into his eyes and saw a reflection of myself," Springer recalled. "I wanted to scream or cry, but all I could do was laugh."

One of the first such experiments was published in 1965 in the journal 'Science'. That study reported that the EEGs of pairs of separated identical twins (two such pairs out of 15 pairs tested) displayed unexpected correspondences. When one twin was asked to close his or her eyes, which causes the brain's alpha rhythms to increase, the distant twin's alpha rhythms were also found to increase. The same effect was not observed in unrelated pairs of people.

19.8 A True Story of Human-Animal Quantum Entanglement

During the 1920s, a two-year-old dog named Bobbie, mostly collie with a bit of English sheep dog, became a national sensation. His owners, Mr. and Mrs. Frank Brazier, restaurant owners in Silverton, Oregon, were vacationing in Indiana when Bobbie got lost. Despite intense efforts to locate the dog, the Braziers finally despaired of finding him. Broken-hearted, they resumed their trip westward, never expecting to see him again. Six months later Bobbie showed up, emaciated, at the family restaurant in Oregon. He ran upstairs to the second-floor living quarters and jumped on the bed, awakening Frank Brazier by licking his face.

No one could believe it. But when the Silverton Appeal published the story, it quickly spread to newspapers across the country, and hundreds of people sent letters to the Braziers claiming they'd seen Bobbie and were able to confirm his identity by several distinguishing marks. Still dubious, the Oregon Humane Society launched an investigation into the Braziers' claims. By interviewing people who claimed to have seen him, they reconstructed the route home, which they estimated was around 2,800 miles, much of which took place in the dead of winter. Bobbie did not follow his owners' route back to Oregon, but travelled an indirect course over land he had never seen nor could have been familiar with. This was no lookalike dog; his owners were able to identify him not only because of his loving behaviour, but also by several unique marks and scars.

19.9 Quantum Entanglement and Love

Love. Quantum physics are completely unrelated, and yet strangely parallel. For one thing, they're both mysterious — we don't really understand how either one of them works. But they share something else — what scientists call "entanglement."

People get entangled with each other when they fall in love, and it can start when they're nowhere near each other, perhaps catching each other's eyes for the first time across a crowded room. And it seems that tiny, subatomic particles — things like electrons or photons — can also get entangled with each other at a great distance, in a way that physicists still don't understand but are already starting to make use of.

It's this really delightful, really strange thing of the phenomenon known as "quantum entanglement." Somehow what happens to one particle can have an impact on what we would expect the second one to do, even if those particles are nowhere near each other.

The experience of falling in love is altogether reminiscent of what in quantum physics is known as entanglement.

In the microscopic realm, once two particles experience a shared state, they are no longer separate entities but exist as one. This remains true even when they are separated by a great distance. The "falling" part of the falling in love process requires a falling away of many individual boundaries as the two people merge significant parts of themselves. The coupling moves the two individuals into an entangled sense of oneness.

All living beings are energy fields manifesting through their physical form. Mere physical attraction to another is based on sensory stimulation, but being in lust is not quite the same as being in love. Falling in love requires that our energies coalesce with one another.

When this occurs, our energy field resonates with our partner's energy field, and our vibrations harmonize with each other's so that two individuals are no longer distinctly separate. This energetic interchange happens simultaneously on physical, emotional, and spiritual levels, and it is what makes falling in love—and staying in love—potentially the most fulfilling experience in life.

Over the course of time, however, many people indicate that although they may still love the other, they no longer feel in love. There's a common belief that as the years pass, falling out of love is natural and to be expected. I'd suggest that it may be ordinary, but that doesn't make it natural. Falling in love and sustaining it requires maintaining a sense of oneness.

In the turmoil that we experience when a relationship becomes adversarial, we need to acknowledge or change something to shift the energy away from separation and back toward entangled wholeness. Making that shift may mean changing our beliefs, our perceptions, or our behaviours or possibly all of these. You might ask yourself, "What is my partner seeing in me that I don't see in myself?"

If you set out to recentre the energy field of the initial romantic entanglement or the caring friendship, you can selflessly try to get in the other's shoes. This is an exercise in empathy. Doing this doesn't mean you are abandoning your position; it simply means loving and validating your partner. If I try to appreciate and care about my upset partner's point of view, I'm invoking a shift of energy.

Connecting empathetically with our partner is the most powerful thing we can do in such troubled moments. It can turn the tide from a competitive, maybe even emotionally and verbally abusive, exchange back into a loving energy field once again entangled with caring. (If you try this approach consistently and with genuine affection, but your partner doesn't reciprocate over time, you might well consider whether the relationship is right for you.)

Another way of shifting the energy of a relationship is to express positive feelings or appreciation for your partner. Once a couple's energy has drifted into separatism and conflict, (called 'decoherence' in quantum entanglement) they may default to unloading critical thoughts and feelings with each other. Negativity then fills the divide they have structured.

Yet there are times in therapy when individuals may share with positive or appreciative feelings they experienced about their partner. When they are asked, "Did you share that with your partner?" I rarely hear a yes. Why would we become acclimatized to sharing the negative, yet feel awkward or reluctant to express approving or positive feelings?

It's because we've gotten stuck in the groove of negativity, which only widens that gap between us. We may be holding back an expression of approval so as not to give the other a stronger hand—a sign that we have set up separate battle stations. So set your intention: When you feel good about the other person, articulate it to him or her. In trying to reset the downward spiral of the relationship cycle, it may be helpful to pause and not be reactive.

Take a moment before criticizing or defending and ask yourself, "Does this really matter?" If it doesn't, you can choose to let it go and create a very different reality. Again, this is an energy shifter. The common expression "You can't change the other person" appears sensible when a relationship is in turmoil. But from the quantum-entanglement point of view of inseparability, if you change some aspect of yourself, it will necessarily affect your partner, because you're both as connected as our quantum particles.

19.9.1 Entangled Families: Monogamy versus Promiscuity

What happens if there are three or more parties in the love game? Technically, we are addressing the complex topic of "multipartite entanglement". In this context, there's a fundamental law: entanglement is monogamous! If our two lovers, traditionally called Alice and Bob, really love each other a lot – they are maximally entangled – there's no way for Alice to be even a little bit in love with a Carlos (or the same for Bob and a Clara). This is maybe a bit controversial, as in our modern culture it's becoming more and more popular to violate monogamy in human relationships...but at least let me say that entanglement, now that we look at it with the eyes of love, is not that bad beast that people (even eminent ones) thought it to be. Are you starting to like it? Be advised though that if the love between Alice and Bob is not total, each of them can share some love with extra parties!!

So back home, be sure that your partner is maximally entangled to you, otherwise, suspicions are legitimate!! Another interesting aspect can arise in multi-party entangled relationships. The above picture (total entanglement excludes third parties) strictly applies to very simple, 'binary' objects (or persons), only capable of answering either yes or no to any question without more structured argumentations (we call them "qubits"). But suppose now that Alice and Bob are more complex characters (we call them "continuous-variable systems"), capable to answer questions providing a series of elaborate motivations. Such kind of more reliable persons, may at some point think to enrich their family life with a baby. Can they love their baby while being monogamous to each other? Yes, they can! In this scenario, the entanglement (love) between any two of them in their family can be arbitrarily strong, and this enhances the genuine entanglement (love) shared by the three of them (mom, dad, and the baby). Isn't it a nice romantic picture? Actually, an alternative description could be in terms of a group of three or more people, which might also be all of the same sex! And this "freedom" that arises if their personality is multifaceted and not binary, is a sort of promiscuity: the more any two of them are attracted by each other, the more they like to stay altogether acting in threesomes and "Entanglement" giving rise to more intricate orgies!

The quantum society, you see, is not that much different from ours after all: we are made of quanta and immersed into them… who's influencing who? Is there a serious quantum impact on our society? These are just funny ways to try to relate the microscopic world (in which entanglement has probably nothing to do with love) to the world in which we are used to live. Everybody may imagine the situation which in his fantasy best applies to this strange quantum realm. Already at the ages of Romans and Greeks, people invented figures (gods) associated to natural events, and pictured them as banqueting and being involved in love affairs. Entanglement is surely one of the mysterious 'gods' of the Book of Nature as we know it today, and "when it comes to entanglement, we've only just discovered the tip of an iceberg".

It is therefore concluded by hinting at what entanglement can really do for us. Apart from its quite interesting social aspects at the microscopic level, the new technological quantum information revolution is taking place, based on entanglement and its properties. In particular, Alice and Bob can send flirting emails to each other with the unconditional security that nobody can eavesdrop, as they encrypt their data via a secret key established from the intrinsic randomness of quantum particles, and protected by the monogamy of entanglement. And this is reality: quantum cryptosystems are plug-and-play devices and you can install on your PC to definitely solve the problem of (quantum) hackers. Similarly, we are working to build quantum computers, which exploit quantum superpositions (wave and particle, dead and alive) to do parallel calculations billions of times faster than current supercomputers!!! And there is much, much more. Like this, there are many others, and remember … we are all entangled!

CHAPTER 20

Quantum Science of Mind-Body Interaction

20.1 Mind-Body Interaction

The mind and body interact in powerful ways that affect a person's health. The digestive system is profoundly controlled by the mind (brain), and anxiety, depression, and fear dramatically affect the function of this system. Social and psychologic stress can trigger or aggravate a wide variety of diseases and disorders, such as diabetes mellitus, high blood pressure, and migraine headache. However, the relative importance of psychologic factors varies widely among different people with the same disorder.

Most people, on the basis of either intuition or personal experience, believe that emotional stress can cause or alter the course of even major physical diseases. How these stressors do this is not clear. Emotions obviously can affect certain body functions, such as heart rate, blood pressure, sweating, sleep patterns, stomach acid secretion, and bowel movements, but other relationships are less obvious. For example, the pathways and mechanisms by which the brain and immune system interact are only beginning to be identified. It is remarkable that the brain can alter the activity of white blood cells and thus an immune response because white blood cells travel through the body in blood or lymph vessels and are not attached to nerves. Nevertheless, research has shown that the brain does communicate with the white blood cells. For example, depression may suppress the immune system and make a person more susceptible to infections such as the common cold.

Stress can cause physical symptoms even though no physical disease may be present because the body responds physiologically to emotional stress. For example, stress can cause anxiety, which then triggers the autonomic nervous system and hormones such as epinephrine to speed up the heart rate and to increase the blood pressure and the amount of sweating. Stress can also cause muscle tension, leading to pain in the neck, back, head, or elsewhere.

The mind-body interaction is a two-way street. Not only can psychological factors contribute to the onset or aggravation of a wide variety of physical disorders, but also physical diseases can affect a person's thinking or mood. People with life-threatening, recurring, or chronic physical disorders commonly become depressed. The depression may worsen the effects of the physical disease and add to a person's misery.

20.2 Mind-Body Interaction and Quantum Mechanics

The American physicist Richard Feynman remarked about Quantum Mechanics once, "I cannot define the real problem therefore, I suspect there's no real problem, but I'm not sure there's no real problem." But he might as well have been talking about the equally knotty problem of consciousness. Some scientists think we already understand what consciousness is, or that it is a mere illusion. But many others feel we have not grasped where consciousness comes from at all.

The perennial puzzle of consciousness has even led some researchers to invoke quantum physics to explain it. That notion has always been met with skepticism, which is not surprising: it does not sound wise to explain one mystery with another. But such ideas are not obviously absurd, and neither are they arbitrary. For one thing, the mind seemed, to the great discomfort of physicists, to force its way into early quantum theory. What's more, quantum computers are predicted to be capable of accomplishing things ordinary computers cannot, which reminds us of how our brains can achieve things that are still beyond artificial intelligence. "Quantum consciousness" is widely derided as mystical woo, but it just will not go away.

Quantum mechanics is the best theory we have for describing the world at the nuts-and-bolts level of atoms and subatomic particles. Perhaps the most renowned of its mysteries is the fact that the outcome of a quantum experiment can change depending on whether or not we choose to measure some property of the particles involved. When this "observer effect" was first noticed by the early pioneers of quantum theory, they were deeply troubled. It seemed to undermine the basic assumption behind all science: that there is an objective world out there, irrespective of us. If the way the world behaves depends on how – or if – we look at it, what can "reality" really mean?

Today some physicists suspect that, whether or not consciousness influences quantum mechanics, it might in fact arise because of it. They think that quantum theory might be needed to fully understand how the brain works. Might it be that, just as quantum objects can apparently be in two places at once, so a quantum brain can hold onto two mutually-exclusive ideas at the same time?

The most famous intrusion of the mind into quantum mechanics comes in the "double-slit experiment". Imagine shining a beam of light at a screen that contains two closely-spaced parallel slits. Some of the light passes through the slits, whereupon it strikes another screen. Light can be thought of as a kind of wave, and when waves emerge from two slits like this they can interfere with each other. If their peaks coincide, they reinforce each other, whereas if a peak and a trough coincide, they cancel out. This wave interference is called diffraction, and it produces a series of alternating bright and dark stripes on the back screen, where the light waves are either reinforced or cancelled out. The implication seems to be that each particle passes simultaneously through both slits

The double slit experiment can also be performed with quantum particles like electrons; tiny charged particles that are components of atoms. In a counter-intuitive twist, these particles can behave like waves. That means they can undergo diffraction when a stream of them passes through the two slits, producing an interference pattern.

Now suppose that the quantum particles are sent through the slits one by one, and their arrival at the screen is likewise seen one by one. Now there is apparently nothing for each particle to interfere with along its route – yet nevertheless the pattern of particle impacts that builds up over time reveals interference bands. The implication seems to be that each particle passes simultaneously through both slits and interferes with itself. This combination of "both paths at once" is known as a superposition state.

But if we place a detector inside or just behind one slit, we can find out whether any given particle goes through it or not. In that case, however, the interference vanishes. Simply by observing a particle's path – even if that observation should not disturb the particle's motion – we change the outcome. If nature seems to be changing its behaviour depending on whether we "look" or not, we could try to trick it into showing its hand. To do so, we could measure which path a particle took through the double slits, but only after it has passed through them. By then, it ought to have "decided" whether to take one path or both. The sheer act of noticing, rather than any physical disturbance caused by measuring, can cause the collapse.

Beginning in the 1980s, the British physicist Roger Penrose suggested that the link might work in the other direction. Whether or not consciousness can affect quantum mechanics, he said, perhaps quantum mechanics is involved in consciousness. What if, Penrose asked, there are molecular structures in our brains that are able to alter their state in response to a single quantum event. Could not these structures then adopt a superposition state, just like the particles in the double slit experiment? And might those quantum superpositions then show up in the ways neurons are triggered to communicate via electrical signals? Maybe, says Penrose, our ability to sustain seemingly incompatible mental states is no quirk of perception, but a real quantum effect. Perhaps quantum mechanics is involved in consciousness.

After all, the human brain seems able to handle cognitive processes that still far exceed the capabilities of digital computers. Perhaps we can even carry out computational tasks that are impossible on ordinary computers, which use classical digital logic.

Other researchers have found evidence for quantum effects in living beings. Quantum effects such as superposition are easily destroyed, because of a process called decoherence. This is caused by the interactions of a quantum object with its surrounding environment, through which the "quantumness" leaks away. Decoherence is expected to be extremely rapid in warm and wet environments like living cells.

In 2016, Adrian Kent of the University of Cambridge in the UK, one of the most respected "quantum philosophers", speculated that consciousness might alter the behaviour of quantum systems in subtle but detectable ways.

Kent is very cautious about this idea. "There is no compelling reason of principle to believe that quantum theory is the right theory in which to try to formulate a theory of consciousness, or that the problems of quantum theory must have anything to do with the problem of consciousness," he admits. He says that it is hard to see how a description of consciousness based purely on pre-quantum physics can account for all the features it seems to have. One particularly puzzling question is how our conscious minds can experience unique sensations, such as the colour red or the smell of frying bacon. With the exception of people with visual impairments, we all know what red is like, but we have no way to communicate the sensation and there is nothing in physics that tells us what it should be like.

Sensations like this are called "qualia". We perceive them as unified properties of the outside world, but in fact they are products of our consciousness – and that is hard to explain. Indeed, in 1995 philosopher David Chalmers dubbed it "the hard problem" of consciousness. "Every line of thought on the relationship of consciousness to physics runs into deep trouble," says Kent.

This has prompted him to suggest that "we could make some progress on understanding the problem of the evolution of consciousness if we supposed that consciousnesses alters (albeit perhaps very slightly and subtly) quantum probabilities." "Quantum consciousness" is widely derided as mystical woo, but it just will not go away.

In other words, the mind could genuinely affect the outcomes of measurements. If that happens, it would transform our ideas about both physics and the mind. That seems a chance worth exploring.

20.3 Application of Bohmian Quantum Theory to Mind-Body Interaction

Mind and brain issues are one of the most challenging issues in the history of science and philosophy. Mind is very different from the matter due to its specific properties, such as unity, integrity and irreducibility to components, and the presence of some special laws and concepts such as perception, specific quality of mental states, thinking, creativity, self-awareness, consciousness, etc. In contrast, matter, especially in classical physics, is known to have properties such as locality in time and space, reducibility to components, atomistic individuality, etc. In this perspective, these two concepts (mind and brain) are so far apart, that it is very difficult to connect them and to explain the modality of their interaction. The developments in physics in the last century, especially in gravity and fundamental particle physics, have led to a new understanding of natural concepts and laws via theories of quantum mechanics and relativity. Relativity changed our understanding of time and the relation between space-time and matter. Quantum mechanics introduced some concepts such as non-reductionism to components, integrity, and wholeness of quantum systems, nonlocality due to quantum entanglement of a system's components, etc. These concepts are very close to the mind concept which is considered to be a nonphysical concept or an illusion concept. Therefore, because of this similarity and our more advanced understanding of nature, the research on the mind-brain interaction and consciousness has begun in physics, by using our modern physical theories. In addition, some attitudes such as top-down causality developed by physicists, some empirical neuroscience results about consciousness and brain activity pattern, relation between a subject's report and brain activity record, and the mathematical and philosophical arguments about non-computational aspects of mind has strengthened the quantum approach to mind-brain interaction and consciousness.

Quantum approach to consciousness has a wide-spread scope, but only some researches have tried to connect the concepts of mind and brain through quantum aspects, and can explain part of mind's features through quantum properties. This has specially occurred in the models of Penrose-Hameroff, Stapp, and Bohm. However, there is no complete and consistent model of mind-brain interaction in which mind is considered as an effective and independent identity. The Orch-OR theory describes some features of mental states in terms of the properties of quantum computing which are claimed to occur in the microtubules of neurons, and it tries to explain some of the experiments in neuroscience and time non-locality of mind effects, in terms of the objective reduction of wave function via quantum gravity effects. But the mechanism and modality of mind-brain interaction is obscure in this theory. In Stapp's model, mental states are recognized as aspects of the wave function reduction process. This process has two aspects; one is the actualization of a pattern of the neural activity at the brain; the other is the creation of a mental state. In this model, the freedom and free will have no place and have no causal effect on the actualization of reality. The free will is not an illusion, but it only affects the state representation before the nature's choice of actualization (wave reduction) and the direct mind-agency on the brain activity is denied. In these models, a realistic physical theory and a philosophical or psychological theory of mind define a model of mind-brain interaction.

In the following we try to show the possibility of the presence of a causal description of mind's effect on the brain. At first, we chose a consistent and appropriate philosophical and psychological framework, and try to describe this model in terms of our modern understanding. To preserve human's free will, we need both causality, which is related to self-agency and refers to "will", and mind's freedom of choice (which refers to "free"). In physics, we chose the Bohmian quantum mechanics, due to its causal description of events.

Recent empirical development in the foundations of quantum mechanics, especially delayed choice style experiments, appear to indicate the non-local feature of nature in time, in addition to its non-locality in space. This intrinsic property of nature is consistent with incorporeity of mind, which leads to its non-temporality. In addition, psychology and parapsychology evidences, especially precognition experiments and neuroscience experiments show the complicated nature of mind-brain interaction, and are in agreement with time non-locality in physics. Therefore, in Bohmian approach we try to explain the mechanism of the non-locality by the use of a modified Bohmian quantum mechanics, obtained via the quantization of Schrödinger wave function.

A quantum delayed choice eraser experiment apparently says that the design of the experimental setup at the final point affects a particle's evolution in the past. More precisely, the choice and design of the experimental setup leads to getting some information about the wave or particle nature of a quantum system. Therefore, due to the entanglement of the system's components, this information, that causes the appearance of particle or wave behavior, affects the determination of the particles' dynamics, occurred in the past at the other side of system. In the delayed choice experiment, there are two path entangled particles, in which the destruction of interference pattern due to the special design of mirror and lens location on one side, leads to getting information about the path of the other particle, due to the nature of entanglement. Because of the quantum nature of system, this information ensures that there is no interference pattern on the other side (second screen) at any time for the partner particles. In fact, two partner particles have the same behavioral characteristics. Therefore, since the detection of second particle has occurred in the past, there is an effect of the future setup on the past result. This can be interpreted as a kind of complicated coordination between the future and the past, which is not like the classical deterministic case. This is due to the nature of quantum mechanics. Although there is no signaling from future to past, but it can be interpreted as a nonlocal influence in time between entangled components, which is the same as space nonlocality in Bell-style experiments. There is the coordination between the future and the past that creates a whole unity. It is a kind of ultimate goal, a kind of novel force, due to the evolution of the whole system that affects the system components in the space-time. It is our Bohmian description, which leads to a non-unitary effect on the pilot wave.

20.4 Quantum Science of Mind-Body Interaction (MBI)

The existence of mind-body interaction (MBI) is a natural common-sense belief. The conceptual tools for describing mind-body interaction are already present in contemporary theoretical physics. The emphasis on mathematical structure is a crucial factor that could lead to theories of MBI that make empirically testable predictions, even if their ontology is vague. As a matter of fact, our current fundamental theory for the microcosm, quantum mechanics, works exactly this way. To quote Dirac:

"When you ask what are electrons and protons I ought to answer that this question is not a profitable one to ask and does not really have a meaning. The important thing about electrons and protons is not what they are but how they behave, how they move. I can describe the situation by comparing it to the game of chess. In chess, we have various chessmen, kings, knights, pawns and so on. If you ask what a chessman is, the answer would be that it is a piece of wood, or a piece of ivory, or perhaps just a sign written on paper, or anything whatever. It does not matter. Each chessman has a characteristic way of moving and this is all that matters about it. The whole game of chess follows from this way of moving the various chessmen."

We find the attitude expressed by Dirac to be very fruitful for the mind-body problem. One should simply substitute the "electrons and protons" in Dirac's quote with thoughts, qualia or any other mental object. We can even expand on Dirac's metaphor. A theory with MBI is analogous to a game that is played with two chessboards, the mental board and the physical board. We should look for a new set of rules that describe how the movements of the pieces on one board are interconnected and affect the movements of the pieces on the other.

There is a huge loss of information when we use classical fields to describe matter. Fundamentally, matter is described by quantum theory; in the Lagrangian field theory (LFT) description, quantum effects are ignored (or averaged out). The treatment of matter as continuous at macroscopic scales also implies that the discrete structure at the atomic level is ignored. The description of matter and geometry in terms of classical fields is suboptimal for both matter and gravity. The field description of geometry contains too much information, the field description of matter contains too little. The LFT formulation of matter-gravity interaction in General Relativity (GR) is a working compromise, and not a perfect fit. Nonetheless, it suffices for a formulation of a theory in which 'spacetime tells matter how to move; matter tells spacetime how to curve'.

20.4.1 Mind-Body Interaction and Quantum State Reduction

The measurement problem in quantum theory is that quantum theory does not explain the emergence of definite properties for physical systems (for example, measurement outcomes). Definite properties are not, in general, compatible with quantum processes. One possible resolution, suggested by the founders of quantum theory, is the use of irreducibly classical concepts for the description of the measurement device. But what constitutes a measuring device? If the particle's position is correlated to the reading of a pointer in an apparatus, should we describe the pointer classically? What if the pointer is recorded by a camera? Should we treat the pointer as a quantum system and the camera as classical? The boundary of the quantum/classical divide appears arbitrary.

The problem is aggravated in interpretations of quantum theory that treat the quantum state as an objective feature of a physical system. In these interpretations, the change of state after measurement (quantum state reduction) is a physical process. Then, the arbitrariness of the quantum/classical split implies an ambiguity in the physical description. Von Neumann and Wigner proposed that the quantum/classical split and the body/mind split coincide: the quantum state is reduced when the result of a measurement enters the observer's consciousness.

In contrast, dynamical state reduction models postulate that there is a tiny probability of reduction for each particle's wavefunction, which adds up to be significant for systems that contain a huge number of particles. This explains why macroscopic measuring apparatuses behave classically. Alternatively, one may postulate irreducibly classical entities that universally interact with quantum systems. Barring consciousness, the main candidate for this role is the gravitational field. The only way to consistently formulate a quantum-classical interaction involves dynamical state reduction for the quantum system; again, this process can cause measurements apparatuses to always behave classically.

20.5 Quantum Physics in Neuroscience of Mind–Brain Interaction

Neuroscientists now have a reasonably good working knowledge of the role of a variety of brain areas in the processing of complex information. In most of the cases, investigators simply assume that measurable-in-principle, properties of the brain are the only factors needed to explain eventually the processing of the psychologically described information that occurs in neuropsychological experiments. This privileging of physically describable brain mechanisms as the core, and indeed final, explanatory vehicle for the processing of every kind of psychologically described data, is the foundational assumption of almost all contemporary biologically based cognitive neuroscience.

To explicate the physics of the interface between mind/consciousness and the physical brain, we shall describe here how the quantum mechanically based causal mechanisms work, and show why it is necessary in principle to advance to the quantum level to achieve an adequate theory of the neurophysiology of volitionally directed activity. The reason, essentially, is that classic physics is an approximation to the more accurate quantum theory, and that this classic approximation eliminates the causal efficacy of our conscious efforts that these experiments empirically manifest.

Quantum dynamics must be used in principle. Furthermore, once the transition to the quantum description is made, the principles of quantum theory must, in order to maintain rational consistency and coherency, be used to link the quantum physical description of the subject's brain to their stream of conscious experiences. The conscious choices by human agents thereby become injected non-trivially into the causal interpretation of neuroscience and neuropsychology experiments. This caveat particularly applies to those experimental paradigms in which human subjects are required to perform decision-making or attention-focusing tasks that require conscious effort.

It is noteworthy that this demand for an entirely brain-based causal mechanism is nullified, in the quantum model developed here, by a specified quantum effect, which will be described below. It might be claimed that the designs and executions of successful clinical practices (and of informative neuropsychological experiments) that depend on the idea of the causal efficacy of conscious effort, and which fit so well into the quantum conceptualization that actually explains the causal efficacy of these efforts, could just as well be carried out within the conceptual framework in which the causal efficacy of willful effort is an illusion, or is something very different from what it intuitively seems to be. But such a claim is not easy to defend.

Although classic physics is unable to account for observable properties that depend sensitively on the behaviors of atoms, molecules and ions, the classic theory is an approximation to a more accurate theory, called quantum theory, which is able to account for these observable macroscopic properties. But if classic physics is unable to account for the moderately complex behavioral properties of most other large systems, then how can it be expected to account for the exquisitely complex behavioral properties of thinking brains?

20.5.1 The Quantum Approach

The key philosophical and scientific achievement of the founders of quantum theory was to forge a rationally coherent and practicable linkage between the two kinds of description that jointly comprise the foundation of science. Descriptions of the first kind are accounts of psychologically experienced empirical findings, expressed in a language that allows us to communicate to our colleagues what we have done and what we have learned. Descriptions of the second kind are specifications of physical properties, which are expressed by assigning mathematical properties to space–time points and formulating laws that determine how these properties evolve over the course of time. Bohr, Heisenberg, Pauli and the other inventors of quantum theory discovered a useful way to connect these two kinds of description by causal laws. Their seminal discovery was extended by John von Neumann from the domain of atomic science to the realm of neuroscience and, in particular, to the problem of understanding and describing the causal connections between the minds and the brains of human beings.

In order to achieve this result, the whole concept of what science is turned inside out. The core idea of classic physics was to describe the 'world out there', with no reference to 'our thoughts in here'. But the core idea of quantum mechanics is to describe both our activities as knowledge-seeking and knowledge-acquiring agents, and the knowledge that we thereby acquire. Thus, quantum theory involves, essentially, what is 'in here', not just what is 'out there'.

How one acts on a system would, in general, be expected to affect it. Nor is it shocking that the effect of the agent's actions upon the system being probed is specified by the quantum mechanical rules. But the essential point not to be overlooked is that the logical structure of the basic physical theory has become fundamentally transformed.

The agent's choice about how to act has been introduced into the scientific description at a basic level and in a way that specifies, mathematically, how his or her choice about how to act affects the physical system being acted upon.

The structure of quantum mechanics is such that, although the effect upon the observed system of the agent's choice about how to act is mathematically specified, the manner in which this choice itself is determined is not specified. This means that, in the treatment of experimental data, the choices made by human agents must be treated as freely chosen input variables, rather than as mechanical consequences of any known laws of nature. Quantum theory thereby converts science's concept of us from that of a mechanical automaton, whose conscious choices are mere cogs in a gigantic mechanical machine, to that of agents whose conscious free choices affect the physically described world in a way specified by the theory. The approximation that reduces quantum theory to classic physics completely eliminates the important element of conscious free choice. Hence, from a physics point of view, trying to understand the connection between mind/consciousness and brain by going to the classic approximation is absurd: it amounts to trying to understand something in an approximation that eliminates the effect we are trying to study.

This original formulation of quantum theory was created primarily at an institute in Copenhagen directed by Niels Bohr and is called 'the Copenhagen interpretation'. Owing to the strangeness of the properties of nature entailed by the new mathematics, the Copenhagen strategy was to refrain from making any ordinary sort of ontological claims, but instead to take an essentially pragmatic stance. Thus, the theory was formulated basically as a set of practical rules for how scientists should go about the tasks of acquiring, manipulating and using knowledge. Claims about 'what the world out there is really like' were considered to lie beyond science.

Copenhagen quantum theory is about how the choices made by conscious human agents affect the knowledge they can and do acquire about the physically described systems upon which these agents act. In order to achieve this re-conceptualization of physics the Copenhagen formulation separates the physical universe into two parts, which are described in two different languages. One part is the observing human agent plus its measuring devices. This extended 'agent', which includes the devices, is described in mental terms—in terms of our instructions to colleagues about how to set up the devices and our reports of what we then 'see', or otherwise consciously experience. The other part of nature is the system that the agent is acting upon. That part is described in physical terms—in terms of mathematical properties assigned to tiny space–time regions. Thus, Copenhagen quantum theory brings 'doing science' into science. In particular, it brings a crucial part of doing science, namely our choices about how we will probe nature, directly into the causal structure. It specifies the effects of these probing actions upon the systems being probed.

This approach works very well in practice. However, the body and brain of the human agent, and also their devices, are composed of atomic constituents. Hence a complete theory ought to be able to describe these systems in physical terms.

The great mathematician and logician John von Neumann formulated quantum theory in a rigorous way that allows the bodies and brains of the agents, along with their measuring devices, to be shifted into the physically described world. This shift is carried out in a series of steps, each of which moves more of what the Copenhagen approach took to be the psychologically described 'observing system' into the physically described 'observed system'. At each step the crucial act of choosing or deciding between possible optional observing actions remains undetermined by the physical observed system. This act of choosing is always ascribed to the observing agent. In the end all that is left of this agent is what von Neumann calls his 'abstract ego'. It is described in psychological terms, and is, in practice, the stream of consciousness of the agent.

At each step the direct effect of the conscious act is upon the part of the physically described world that is closest to the psychologically described world. This means that, in the end, the causal effect of the agent's mental action is on their own brain, or some significant part of their brain.

von Neumann makes the logical structure of quantum theory very clear by identifying two very different processes, which he calls process 1 and process . Process 2 is the analogue in quantum theory of the process in classic physics that takes the state of a system at one time to its state at a later time. This process, like its classic analogue, is local and deterministic. However, process 2 by itself is not the whole story: it generates a host of 'physical worlds', most of which do not agree with our human experience. For example, if process 2 were, from the time of the big bang, the only process in nature, then the quantum state (centre point) of the moon would represent a structure smeared out over a large part of the sky, and each human body–brain would likewise be represented by a structure smeared out continuously over a huge region. Process 2 generates a cloud of possible worlds, instead of the one world we actually experience.

This huge disparity between properties generated by the 'mechanical' process and the properties we actually observe is resolved by invoking process.

Any physical theory must, in order to be complete, specify how the elements of the theory are connected to human experience. In classic physics this connection is part of a metaphysical superstructure: it is not part of the dynamic process. But in quantum theory a linkage of the mathematically described physical state to human experiences is contained in the mathematically specified dynamic. This connection is not passive. It is not a mere witnessing of a physical feature of nature. Instead, it injects into the physical state of the system being acted upon specific properties that depend upon choices made by the agent.

Quantum theory is built upon the practical concept of intentional actions by agents. Each such action is a preparation that is expected or intended to produce an experiential response or feedback. For example, a scientist might act to place a Geiger counter near a radioactive source and expect to see the counter either 'fire' during a certain time-interval or not 'fire' during that interval. The experienced response, 'Yes' or 'No', to the question, 'Does the counter fire during the specified interval?', specifies one bit of information. Quantum theory is thus an information-based theory built upon the preparative actions of information-seeking agents.

The basic building blocks of quantum theory are, then, a set of intentional actions by agents and for each such action an associated collection of possible 'Yes' feedbacks, which are the possible responses that the agent can judge to be in conformity to the criteria associated with that intentional act. For example, the agent is assumed to be able to make the Judgement 'Yes' the Geiger counter clicked, or 'No' the Geiger counter did not click. Science would be difficult to pursue if scientists could make no such Judgements about what they are experiencing.

For each particle's wave function, which adds up to be significant for systems that contain a huge number of particles. This explains why macroscopic measuring apparatuses behave classically. Alternatively, one may postulate irreducibly classical entities that universally interact with quantum systems. Barring consciousness, the main candidate for this role is the gravitational field. The only way to consistently formulate a quantum-classical interaction involves dynamical state reduction for the quantum system; again, this process can cause measurements apparatuses to always behave classically.

CHAPTER 21

Quantum Science of Love, Healing, Happiness, and Bliss

There is no physical world. It's all projection.
The whole thing is a Quantum Soup.
Reality is pulling out from us rather than coming into us.

21.1 Love and Sustainable Behaviour

Sustainability literally means the ability of humankind to sustain itself indefinitely. This definition however addresses only the temporal dimension of sustainability; sustainability over time and bringing justice to future generations. It does not recognize the possibility of an individual, community or a country meeting their needs at the expense of the ability of another individual, community or country to meet theirs. Today's world is so closely interconnected and interdependent that powerful individuals, communities and countries are able to meet their needs at the expense of the ability of their powerless counterparts to meet theirs.

21.1.1 Spirit, Oneness and Separateness

The English term 'spirit' originates from Spiritus, the Latin term denoting 'breath' or that which gives life or vitality to a system. All beings, including ourselves, are living systems. Therefore, if spirit is the source of life of all living systems, what we identify as spirit must be deathless. This brings us to question if there is such a deathless entity within us. In order to find out whether there is, we can look into our body with the help of a powerful microscope. If we do, we will discover an energy that fills each atom of our body. According to physicists, energy cannot be destroyed and is deathless. Therefore, spirit is the energy which fills each and every atom of our body. According to quantum physics, this same energy fills the Universe and the Universe is a mass field of energy. In spite of its vastness, it functions as an inseparable and indivisible single field of energy, or as "a single undivided whole" as described by renowned theoretical physicist, Bohm.

Recent scientific discoveries reveal that the Universe is alive, aware, and conscious. This view of the Universe being conscious, which had been a philosophical concept thus far, is now supported by prominent scientists. The Universe is not dead, but rather uniquely alive. Referring to the consciousness of electrons, the theoretical physicist, Freeman Dyson, "matter in quantum mechanics is not an inert substance but an active agent, constantly making choices between alternative possibilities. It appears that the mind, as manifested by the capacity to make choices, is to some extent inherent in every electron". He considers it reasonable to believe in the existence of a "mental component of the Universe" and uses scientific evidence to show how consciousness is present in molecules consisting of no more than a few simple proteins.

The conscious and living universe is widely called Universal Consciousness. It is our inner reality and what we truly are. It is the part of us which is immortal. It is called by many names; some of which are: Ultimate Reality, Ultimate Truth, Higher Self, Spiritual Self, Infinite Self and Constant Integrated Awareness. This is what is called God in most religions. The Universal Consciousness (God), while remaining as an indivisible and inseparable single entity at the quantum level, manifests itself at the material level in separate forms, e.g., rocks, soils, plants, animals and human beings, creating the material world.

When our senses experience an object, a noise, a smell, a taste or a touch, a group of neurons or neuro-circuits in the brain connected to the relevant sense organ fire and we experience a feeling of awareness. This is pure awareness in which there is no self-other dichotomy, but universal love. If a craving is not involved, our response to the sensation wouldn't be biased towards the self and we would be guided by the hardwired universal love. Our action would be an expression of the universal love; 'universal love in action'.

Such an action is sustainable.

The essence of love is to affectively affirm as well as to unselfishly delight in the well-being of others, and to engage in acts of care and service on their behalf; unlimited love extends to all others without exception, in an enduring and constant way. Widely considered the highest form of virtue, unlimited love often demands a creative presence underlying and integral to all of reality: participation in unlimited love constitutes the fullest experience of spirituality. Unlimited love may result in new relationships, and deep community may emerge around helping behaviour, but this is secondary. Even if connections and relations do not emerge, love endures.

This is the purest form of love which is unselfish, unconditional and unlimited. It is an expression of the oneness of the spirit within. It does not expect anything in return; love for the sake of love. It is different from what we identify as love in our ordinary life; love of a mother toward her child which is affection, love that exists between wife and husband which is infatuation, love shared among friends and relations which is affection, and love toward material objects which is desire. It manifests itself in various forms such as acceptance, forgiveness, compassion, kindness, tolerance, generosity, sharing, empathy, and selfless service. The foundation of love is not our feelings or emotions towards others, but our inner interconnectedness or oneness with others at the quantum level. It is the very nature of humanness and is natural to us. From this perspective, the opposite of love is not hatred but separateness, individuality, and self-centeredness.

21.2 Quantum Love

Quantum Love is the love that results when you consciously take ownership of the energy in your body, heart, and mind and use it to serve your relationship. It's taking quantum physics—the science of how energy works—and applying it to your love life in a way that reveals your hidden power to create exactly the relationship you want.

Quantum Love is a transformation. Once you learn to put the powerful energy of your mind, body, and spirit to work for you, your life and your relationship won't be the same. Quantum Love is also a reclamation. You were born in a perfect state of love, and while your experience may have moved you away from the truth and wisdom of this essential self, it is still there unchanged, bright and perfect. You simply need to move back into it. Quantum Love will show you how.

So, what does this mean for our love lives? Everything! Your mate is in your life because your personal vibrations have pulled you into each other's world. He or she is ultimately in harmony with you (even if it doesn't always feel that way). Each of you has the power to affect the other's energy—and by virtue of affecting each other's energy, you actually affect each other's physical, mental, and emotional frequency. Quantum Love is a state in which you and your partner are in energetic harmony together in your optimal energetic state, as a couple and individually.

A high frequency is key to getting on the path to Quantum Love. It corresponds to higher and happier states of consciousness, like joy, love, and gratitude. A coherent energetic state is great for your body too. It can support your immune system, reduce stress, and keep you feeling really good. And, finally, when you are in a coherent energetic state, you are positively impacting your partner and your relationship. One of the key points is the lesson that you have the power to create or reshape the landscape of your relationship any way you desire, simply by creating the change in yourself first. When you are in an open-hearted, coherent state, you are moving into Quantum Love, and by virtue of quantum physics, you move your partner and your relationship into Quantum Love as well.

The three quantum principles—that we are all energy, we are all connected, and we create our reality—form the basis of Quantum Love. They show us that anything is possible and that we have the power to shape and reshape our lives and our relationships through the power of our personal energy fields and the strength of our energetic connection with our partner.

The universe wants to give you exactly the life and relation-ship you want. It's a friendly place and wants you to succeed at having all your heart desires. Once you want that for yourself as well (and actually believe that you are worthy of all the blessings of the universe) and you direct your body's energy toward Quan-tum Love, amazing things are going to come your way.

Quantum Love comes when we raise and stabilize our body's energetic frequency and stay, as much as possible, in a state of coherence. As we learn how to hone our perception and alter our repetitive thinking patterns—especially the patterns that are based on our early experiences and the beliefs we formed as children—we can start to create new beliefs and new ways of reacting to the world. We can begin to live in our home frequency, rather than in our ego frequency. When you are in the By Me state of consciousness, you are in home frequency. You can see the gifts in this world and how they might serve you. Life is in your service, and you are clear that what is happening is for you and will make sense, even if you can't see it yet. In the By Me zone we can hold a state of wonder in our lives. We have less need to be right in our relationships and in life in general. We are in the Quantum Love zone. The fact is, you are powerful in each of these states because your energy will impact those around you. If the By Me state is moving into Quantum Love, then when you are in a Through Me state you have fully arrived there. When you are in a higher state of consciousness, either a By Me or a Through Me state, you will be able to positively impact others whose own energy will entrain to yours.

If this works exponentially on a global level, imagine what happens in your relationship. When we are in home frequency, our high-vibrating energy can help balance or even raise the frequency of those around us as they entrain to us. This is especially helpful for our purposes in love relationships. One of the key principles of Quantum Love is that you must create in yourself first. When you are in home frequency, a place of fullness, whole-ness, and love, you will move your relationship and your partner up the Quantum Love-map with you.

Just as we move through life outside of our bodies, we all too often move through life outside of our home frequency. We close or constrict our energy channels, partly out of self-defence from this noisy world, and close our heart to others. When we are in that state, we are in ego frequency, and it is not possible to even catch a glimpse of Quantum Love from that place. Opening your heart is how you find home frequency.

Commit yourself to noticing when you are moving from home frequency into ego frequency, and take steps to put yourself back into coherence. After all, your energy and consciousness are creating your reality, including your relationship reality. Commit to doing what it takes to keep both on the path of Quantum Love.

If you are someone who doesn't tend to look on the bright side, especially in your relationship, keep a gratitude journal, either written (maybe in your Quantum Love Journal) or in your smartphone. Keep a list of small and larger things you are grateful for about your partner. Maybe he/she looked really attractive in the outfit he/she was wearing. Perhaps he/she took out the garbage—even though he/she does it every night, you can be grateful that you don't have to. Maybe she/he just put her/his technology down for ten minutes while you were hanging out together. Maybe she/he paid you a compliment. Look for things that you can be grateful for, and keep a running list.

Maybe you don't think you can surrender to whatever is going on in your world. But do you think you can surrender simply to what is in this very moment? Can you surrender just to right now? Quantum Love is found when you really surrender to the moment and only the moment—it doesn't mean that you're making a larger statement about your partner or your relationship or whatever story you might have. If you can surrender to the moment with your mate in love and alignment, it keeps you in home frequency. You're surrendering your ego to your essential self.

Loving detachment plays fundamentally into surrender and our ability to let go of our long-held stories, beliefs, and thought patterns. Most of us have unwittingly woven these stories into the fabric of who we think we are. Loving detachment allows us to stop identifying with our stories. It's also key when we are talking about the art of manifesting because when we really want something, the natural inclination is to cling to it. When we do this, we move into a place of scarcity from which we cannot access Quantum Love. By viewing our well-worn stories or the things we really want through the lens of loving detachment, we can surrender and move back into the By Me and Through Me state from which we can actually create a positive reality.

Honoring your responsibility for your own energy state is one of the most positive and impactful things you can do for yourself, your partner, your relationship, and your life. Whether you are aware of it or not, your energy and consciousness are shaping all of these things every second of every day. You are indeed creating your reality through the resonant frequency you are putting out into the field. As you will learn in the next chapter, the ability to move your relationship into Quantum Love is yours for the taking . . . and it begins with you. This is why it is so important to commit yourself to taking responsibility for the energy you bring into your relationship. Understand what you will create from a place of coherent home frequency versus what will manifest when you are vibrating in ego frequency. Use these techniques to train your awareness, to notice how it feels when you are in home frequency and what it feels like when you are moving into a contraction and looping toward the low-end point. Know what you're transition point is, and use these techniques to steer your energy back onto the path of Quantum Love.

The truth is that every relationship invariably reaches a point of predictability. You feel numb from day-to-day life and the natural conflicts and resentments that can build up over time. You're desperate for a little variety. But the biggest mistake is resigning yourself to the idea that this burnout is love's inevitable conclusion when, in reality, there is a relationship waiting for you that far exceeds the excitement and novelty of the honeymoon phase. The energy in the human body, in its purest potential, has been calculated by physicists to be ten times greater than the energy in a typical hydrogen bomb. This was calculated with Einstein's famous equation E=mc2, using the mass of an average human body (155 pounds or 70 kilograms). If you're willing to claim and use your energy and apply it to this world that is nothing but pure potential, Quantum Love is yours for the taking.

Remember, in Quantum Love, everything starts with you. Quantum Love is a state you must move into within yourself first, and once you do, you don't need your partner to do anything, change anything, or show up in a different way. He or she doesn't even need to know you are reading this book or buy into its concepts. Because when you change, your partner changes. When you harness the power of your body's energy and consciously use it to create Quantum Love, you get everything you are looking for in your relationship.

21.2.1 The Quantum Love: A Spiritual Path

Quantum Love isn't just about your relationship. It's a spiritual path to your truest self. It doesn't start with your partner, the story of your relationship, or even your mutual connection. Quantum Love starts within you alone.

The key difference between love (in its attraction, infatuation, and attachment stages) and Quantum Love is that in the latter you consciously use the energy of your body, heart, and mind to create exactly the kind of love you seek. Your partner doesn't have to do anything differently, but just naturally entrains to your energy, and you mutually create a relationship field that feels joyful, passionate, and fulfilling. In Quantum Love, you are already connected to your essential self and the conscious choice to be with your partner. You accept your partner not only in spite of her or his so-called flaws, but because of them. In infatuation you only see your partner's best self. In Quantum Love you see your partner's whole authentic self and you love him or her for it.

21.3 Quantum Healing

The 21st century materialistic worldview has created living conditions in the world which are based on a rational perspective. The modern world offers little time or incentive to consider the deeper foundations which may exist in the human person, but there have always been philosophers, scientists, theologians, and artists who protest living in a materialist "flatland". Healing practices which involve the whole person, body, mind and spirit, offer an opportunity to consider emotions, sensitivities and deeper foundations to that which is determined only by the material body.

Quantum theory provides a new foundation for reviewing the constitution of the human person as body, mind and spirit. It confirms, with all other living animals, an immaterial being of free-flowing energy. The mechanics of quantum theory offer a blueprint to analyse how individuals comprise body, mind and spirit. This includes what happens when selection and choice is made in the brain, which is now understood to be both the source of subject and object. It proposes that the human person is a part of an energetic universe, where the choices made are beneficial to that universe, if they are not impelled by a conditioned ego response by the person to choose for the self.

The first and most important confirmation to emerge from quantum science is what much of the Eastern world have already surmised: that the world is comprised in its most elementary particles as discrete bundles of energy, or in energy waves. These particles are experienced as energy and seen as light. This process is described as, "The dual nature of light – particle-like or wave-like depending on what one looks for." It follows from this observation that the physical body is a density of energy, as are all other "solid" constructs and natural beings, for without physical bodies there would be no purpose for living in a material world.

This conclusion leads to an awareness that the spaces between people and between objects consist of free-flowing energy. As a corollary to this, the person is actually a porous body, which consistently exchanges energy from the interspace between people and objects, by breathing in and out – an exchange of energy from within the body into the surrounding energy field. When air is seriously blocked or seriously contaminated, an individual may die, or may become sick. Where either positive or negative energy from others is experienced, the receiver also feels a change in his/her internal energy, and may express it in fear, anger, joy or excitement.

To accommodate the benefits of energy for human function, the body has centres of concentrated energy which are called "chakras". This word derives from the Sanskrit *chakrum,* meaning "wheel", recognized in India since between 1,500 and 500 BCE. These energy centres are understood to be connected to the sources of the body's life functions: the claim is that there are seven main chakras, which increase in energy frequency from the base of the spine to the crown. They are seen and felt to spin, and because they are energy vortices, they reflect light. The slowest and most dense vortex emits a red glow at the root or base of the spine; it is directed down towards the earth, and it is understood to establish stability and connectivity with the material world.

The second energy vortex is located in the sacral area, is orange, and is associated with fertility and creativity. It is recognized as the centre of human sexual passion, art, and love. The third, located in the stomach area, is yellow, and is associated with self-expression, or the manifestation of the personal ego to the world. The fourth and central chakra is just to the left of the breastbone; it is called the heart chakra, is green in colour, and is seen to connect the lower three (human oriented) chakras with the upper three (spiritual oriented) chakras. The fifth chakra is located at the throat, is blue in colour, and is associated with verbal expression: changes in speech tone and volume alter the intensity of the blue colour; the sixth is located at the centre of the brow and is often called the 'third eye'; it is said to be the opening of a view into the soul. It is indigo in colour and is associated with inner spiritual vision. The seventh chakra points upward from the crown, is violet in colour, and is understood by many to be the connection with the transcendent, or the full universe.

When all chakras are fully open, the human body is surrounded by a full spectrum of light. This is called the Aura. Those who can see this energy field can determine the health of the individual. The higher the vibration of a healthy individual, open to receiving and exchanging universal energy, the lighter and brighter the blend of colour in the auric field. Various auric fields, in which are identified those in loving, happy relationships with an aura of colours that are light, tinted with pink, purple, and blue; those with little or suppressed energy appear grey or black, and lacking in positive colour. This lack of colour is interpreted as "disease" in the body. The Auric field changes constantly, depending on both the inner disposition the person and the challenging situations which might incite fear, anger, depression, or anxiety.

The chakras are "organizing centres for the reception, assimilation and transmission of life energies [which] form the co-ordinating network of our complicated mind-body system." In a healthy chakra system, a blend of all these colours may be tailored to each person's habitual orientation to life. The existence of these auras has been confirmed many times, and can be captured by an, "advanced kirlian aura capturing system".

The chakra system is well known among alternative treatment practitioners; it is either combined with other treatments, or it can be a healing practice in its own right. Ruth White, a long-time healer from England, suggests the possibility that: "awakening to your chakras heightens and intensifies your spiritual awareness"; as well, she writes that it improves "relationships with family and friends," and also "release blockages associated with material needs".

Chakra healing can also be approached specifically as relating to the "subtle energy system." Colour therapy is also based on the chakra system. Other practitioners suppose that there is "a strong connection between the chakras and the archetypal roles that people play out in their lives." Most energy practitioners also recognize that the human body's energy flow is connected by "meridians"; these are pathways of energy, which interconnect all parts of the body. Eight "supervisory energy channels" are called "extraordinary meridians" which "work continuously to preserve integrity and balance". Each internal organ also has its own meridian: the two main meridians, the governing vessel and the conception vessel form a circular pathway ensuring the flow of Qi, or Chi, around the body. Chi is the "life force" energy within a person, and has different names according to country or origin. Acupoints are positions on the human body with more immediate access to these meridians. Acupuncture and Acupressure treatments, both originated in China, but are now widely used in other parts of the world.

Quantum science indicates that energy is at the very basis of life. As well, the way quanta respond under scientific investigation reveal a much more complicated activity than that originally posed by the behavioural observation of simple Stimulus-Response bonds. The connection of stimulus (what is seen, heard, felt, tasted or touched) to the person's response is not simply an observation of two points intersecting. It may now be seen to involve the need to take account of the wave collapse of options in the choosing of an object, and the ensuing tangled hierarchies, in which the other options remain in the fabric of the quantum field. In quantum observations, the energy wave is not disrupted until an observer pays attention to it, the wave itself consists of particles which move by "jumping", that is, the tiny parcels of quanta are never still and are seen as a wave-like motion. It is the human brain which creates from these energy waves a representation from which to make a choice. In making that choice, the wave collapses, while the discarded alternatives create "loops", which remain in the space-time continuum. These tangled hierarchies have helped develop communication systems, as described in the following:

"If the atoms are separated, information about one is shared, or entangled, in the state of the other. The behaviour is unexplainable except in the language of quantum mechanics. The effects are so surprising that they are the focus of study by a small but active theoretical and experimental community. The issues are not limited to questions of principle, since entanglement can be useful. Entangled states already have been employed in quantum communication systems, and entanglement underlies all proposals for quantum computation."

From these observations, it may be proposed that the "now", which has long been supposed to be connected with past, present and future, cannot be so determined; all this is the work of the brain, its memories and its future predictions. The way in which the brain makes the choice will depend on past experience, and future quests, but it is actually the brain which is continually creating past, present and future in conjunction with others, who are at the same time making their own selections.

It is of course understood that physical damage must be treated by physical, surgical, and other biomedical applications. However, the problems associated with medical treatments using only this approach are:

a) personal and private areas of life experience cannot be easily submitted to biomedical health tests and prognoses;

b) consciousness, intent and conceptual creativity is not well identified through experimental testing;

c) biomedicine does not address full body-mind-spirit healing;

d) repairing separate physical body organs does not necessarily heal the person of disease;

e) a materialistic approach to the universe does not consider its free-flowing, unfolding development towards an unknown future.

The supramental body is the real place where quantum healing can be effective. It is where personal experience extends to recognise the interrelationships which provide the context for mental meaning. It is the domain of consciousness which "contains the laws and archetypal contexts of physical, vital and mental movements".

The bliss body is where the "recovery of wholeness through spiritual healing" is achieved. It is this discovery of wholeness which heals the mind of the problem of ego separation." The ego discovers it has no need to try and support itself out of fear, because it is surrounded by love. This healing of the ego rebalances the mental emotional energies which affect the physical organs of the body.

21.4 Quantum Self-Healing of the Body through Entanglement of Photons

Human body has its own mechanism of healing known as whole body healing. Each healthy cell of human body emits photon, disease is an altered emission of photons. Inside and outside of our body consists of energy. Photons from our cells jump on to others and counter photons may be vibrating at other place in the body, known as quantum entanglement and quantum tunnelling. The matter can be converted in to energy and energy can be converted in to matter proposed by Nobel laureate Hans-Peter Dürr.

Most of all diseases start in mind ends in mind. Mind is nothing but a part of human consciousness, is a canvas, on which our thoughts are projected. It is a holographic presentation of human body. Mind has a blue print of human body. Body tries to rebuild each time, when it oscillate between energy and particle 1044 times in a second. Human body is a holographic projection of human consciousness. With our positive thoughts or consciousness known as quantum thinking, which creates energy, with a genuine intention to heal, known as quantum healing akin to self-healing or auto healing.

Pranic healing, meditation, chi therapy with our positive thoughts, genuine intention to heal known as quantum thinking and healing takes place at spiritual level by producing endorphins. Endorphins are neuropeptides, endogenous morphine produced by pituitary gland and hypothalamus, receptors are present in brain and on immune cells. Endogenous opioids include β-endorphins, enkephalins, and dynorphins, operate via μ-opioid receptor. Beta endorphin is the abundant endorphins secreted and synthesized by anterior pituitary gland; it is a precursor of protein proopiomelanocortin (POMC). It has got immune-stimulatory, stress buster, euphoric, and analgesic activity. Immune- stimulatory due to activation of NK cells and macrophages producing IFN-ϒ, opsonin, granzyme-B, has an antiviral activity.

This activity is due to activation of IFN-ϒ and IL -18band suppressing TNF-α, IL-1, IL-6 pro DmmDtor\ cytokines, suppress free radical release such as ROS, RNS and also suppressing key transcriptional factors NF-KB, STAT-3, which is involved in tumour progression by cell proliferation, cell survival, angiogenesis, immune suppression, genomic instability, invasion, metastasis. Also involved in autoimmune diseases by immune suppression, conversion of H1 type lymphocyte to H2 type, activation of proteolytic enzymes like MMPs (matrix metalloproteases) results in cellular changes, tissue damage, and chronic conditions by activating cytokines such as IL-1, TNF-α, IL-6 . Stress buster activity by reducing cortisol, neuropeptides through HPA axis (hypothalamo-pituitary adrenal axis) and inhibiting activation of sympathetic nervous system and activation of parasympathetic nervous system of autonomic nervous system, which is involved in activity and peripheral immunity. Euphoric activity by inhibiting an inhibitory neurotransmitter GABA and stimulating dopamine release in central nervous system responsible for pleasure, inhibits pain and responsible for tranquility of mind. Analgesic activity by reducing substance P a neurotransmitter of pain in peripheral nervous system. Promotes and prolong human lifespan by lengthening telomeres which shorten with aging. Mindful meditation alters the environment of genes and gene expression. Whole body healing or holistic healing is our future therapeutic approach with inexpensive, preventive, promotive, therapeutic and palliative care of patients without adverse effects Still lot of things need to be understood regarding about quantum healing is at an infant stage. In future, it can be applicable for treating diseases such as autoimmune diseases, cancer, infectious diseases with holistic therapeutic approach.

21.5 Can Quantum Physics Hold the Key to Happiness?

Physicists talk about quantum physics, quantum mechanics, quantum entanglement, quantum computing but what if we could, by analogy, apply the quantum physics theory to our mind and talk about quantum emotions? What if a quantum emotion theory could explain how to get out of depression and into experiencing happiness? Here is how we can get from quantum physics to happiness:

The quantum theory says we can have super positioned elements. The analogy becomes super positioned feelings: We have inside of us at the same time happiness, joy, sadness, anger, fear, disgust, frustration, hope, and many other possible feelings and emotions. But if we choose to focus on one of the feelings, the other ones disappear. If we choose to focus on our sadness, our happiness will disappear, but if we choose to focus on happiness, our sadness will be in the background because we can't focus on both feelings at the same time.

One can make a conscious choice to direct one's neurons and their synapses into happiness and love and in doing so, one's sadness, anger, and fear disappear.

For example, in Quantum Healing, Deepak Chopra describes how a higher level of consciousness and energy (all around the body and not limited to the body) can help healing. As long as we don't make any decision—we have endless possibilities in front of us, but those possibilities disappear once we make a decision to pursue a specific course.

But is it possible, when it comes to the mind, emotions, and behaviors, that quantum physics is much more than an analogy for how our brains work, but actually part of what determines how we think, feel, and behave? Quite possibly.

Recently, neuroscientists and physicists have begun to explore ways that our brains, at least in part, function as quantum machines. For instance, quantum brain, quantum mind, and quantum consciousness are cited in the Stanford Encyclopedia of Philosophy which explains how the quantum physics theory applied to super positioned neurons and synapses could explain consciousness. So, whether or not quantum mechanics is crucial to our thoughts, feelings, and behaviors, we have a decision to make between happiness and sadness, between love and hatred, between joy and depression. For me, I chose happiness, joy, and love.

Energy is required just to experience joy. Energy is required to plan a joyful experience. Energy is required to remember what to do when joy strikes. Energy is required to know when to stop, to know when the joy has passed, and what to do when a state of calm returns. Everything we do requires a discrete amount of energy, and when I say discrete, I mean, that there is a minimum amount of energy that must be expended for consciousness.

Resilience is a quantum of happiness. Everyone has some quantum of happiness. It's there if you look for it and if you work for it. The hard part about happiness is being aware that we are born with the capacity to be happy. The hardest part of being happy is developing the skills required to be happy. Learning the skill of happiness leads to resilience and that, in turn, leads to contentment.

The best part of finding happiness through resilience is that no one can take that away from you. If you have resilience, then happiness is independent of your circumstances. If you make a choice to be happy, people can add to your happiness, but you're not dependent on other people to be happy. When you're resilient, you will know that you can survive a setback. When you have resilience, you begin to see setbacks as challenges, not disappointments. And when you have resilience, the world is your oyster, and your pearl is a quantum of happiness.

21.5.1 The Ground beyond Consciousness according to Bohmian Quantum Physics

The Ground beyond Consciousness is the unmanifested.. But how can we ever know the ground beyond consciousness if it is unmanifested? David Bohm suggests that it is the unmanifested that acts into the manifested, and that action becomes an appearance in Consciousness. And that appearance in Consciousness therefore implies a ground from which it came. So, the reality we encounter unfolds from the deeper unmanifested, non-local, or as Bohm references it, the implicate Order. This also suggests that we may yet get beyond our current understanding of Quantum Theory, implying that there will be a NEW theory from which we will see how quantum theory and the classical world emerges…

It was Bohm's questioning of everything, in physics, in mathematics and in dialogue that provides us with clear direction towards something much more subtle, an awareness of consciousness as something that is beyond name and form, That is why Bohm suggested that mathematics needs to evolve beyond calculations; why science needs to continually go beyond the limits of old formulae; why philosophy needs to go beyond MIND and Religion beyond dogma. Bohm realized that none of these can explain CONSCIOUSNESS.

He continually tried to get some idea of what might be the process which was implied by the mathematics and the science of quantum theory, a process he calls enfoldment, in which the mathematics suggests a movement in which any particular element of space may have a field which unfolds into the whole and the whole folds and enfolds into it. If we get beyond our current understanding of Quantum Theory, we may find common ground in the ancient mystical philosophical views of the EAST, where the relationship of the observer and the observed find each other in both traditions.

This is why the old disciplines only serve to deepen the illusion of manifest reality. Bohm encourages us to look beyond the veil of form and separation which he suggests can put us on the threshold of what is real and deepen our understanding of the nature of Reality. Once realized we encounter wholeness, undivided wholeness - CONSCIOUSNESS itself – The "I" that "I am" which is beyond name and form….

Here we find a potential that empowers us to act positively in the world, to change the world to our needs. To re-imagine and reshape our spiritual, political, social and economic structures so that they can begin to adapt to a new reality? That's where David Bohm's legacy comes to be very, very valuable and puts us "on the edge of something", an appearance in consciousness that is entirely new…

21.6 Quantum Mechanics of Changing Thoughts and Achieving Happiness

Every thought and emotion has its own vibrational frequency or wave frequency. Quantum mechanics has demonstrated how a wave frequency can be altered. The shape of a wave has peaks and valleys. Energy waves are encoders and carriers of information with an infinite capacity for storage. When you overlay an opposite shaped wave on to an original wave, the original wave is straightened. Essentially you cancel out the characteristics of the original wave by overlaying a new exact opposite set of peaks and valleys on top of it. You change the vibrational frequency.

Thoughts are Like Sound Waves:

This has been demonstrated with sound waves where researchers are attempting to create a quiet environment. You can use sound to literally cancel and silence unwanted noises. This technology is used for corporate offices adjacent to noisy businesses or in doctors and counseling offices where voices can be heard between treatment rooms or in the car industry to make engines quieter.

Mechanics of Changing Thoughts:

Let's extend this now to understanding the mechanics of changing thoughts or emotional patterns. Comprehending this is taking into consideration the subatomic causal level of thinking and feeling. If you identify an exact opposite positive thought to counter a negative thought you are using this principle. Take a moment and think about the word 'stress'. Now take a moment and think about the word 'relax'. Think about the word 'fear' and now the word 'safe'. It sounds simple and it is. The trick is you have over 60, 000 thoughts per day to work with. In any case, this is the basic idea and where the positive thinking movement has made a powerful impact in changing lives.

Your Perception Your Reality:

To change your thinking, you must adopt the belief that your perception of the world is what determines your reality. When you discover how to effectively choose your perceptions, you change your ability to cultivate happiness. Because you have far more control over your internal world than your external world, this is the best place to decrease stress and raise your happiness. We are specifically referring to your response to situations via your thoughts, emotions, and actions. When you change your response, you change your experience of the situation. This single factor has the potential to dramatically alter the course of your life journey.

21.6.1 Levels of Internal Control

There are two levels of internal control:

(i) Your Perception

(ii) Your Response

(i) Perception: How you perceive an event impacts the amount of stress you experience. You can choose to view a situation in such a way that validates your reasons for feeling stressed, or you can view it so that you feel motivated and up for the challenge to deal with it. Because every action is preceded by a thought and an emotion, it's a good idea to start with your perception if you plan to rewire your experience of stress.

(ii) Response: You may not be able to control what happens, but you can control how you respond to what happens. Your response includes not only your actions but also the degree of tension you allow in your mind and body. Decreasing mind-body tension requires working with mind-body practices. One of the strategies which is the most helpful on this journey is brain-spotting therapy. It's your response that will either stop your experience of stress or perpetuate and fuel the stress cycle.

"The world we have created is a product of our thinking; it can't be

changed without changing our thinking." — Albert Einstein

Perceptions Are Your Interpretations – Your real mind power

It has been said that we are meaning-make machines overlaying our subjective interpretation onto everything we experience. Why do we do this? This is how we learn and integrate new information in an efficient and economical way. We associate our present experience with our past and make up what it means based on the culmination of our experiences to date on that subject. This allows us to move through our day without relearning how to make breakfast, get dressed, or find our way home. It also enables us to assess our environment and make quick decisions so that we can move through our day with ease and flow. This can be highly useful in these types of basic life situations. However, this can get us into trouble if we aren't conscious of our interpretations. We tend to have the "know-it-all syndrome" where we attempt to figure it all out before allowing ourselves to experience it. You have never been where you are in this moment, now, yet your mind finds a way to make it familiar so that you think it's the same.

Exploring your interpretations is powerful work. It brings you to the empowered place of self-responsibility and gives you real mind power. The key is to realize you are the common denominator in your life. Your perception drives your behavior. You can start with owning your interpretations and navigating your way through other ways of looking at the situation. In doing so, you increase your control over your internal world and raise your happiness potential.

You may think you know or you're certain about your perception. But how can you really be 100% certain? You have the ability to choose your perceptions. As long as you're making it all up, you may as well choose something that moves you in the direction of happiness, well-being, and self-esteem.

The single shift in consciousness regarding the difference between emotions and feelings will save you time and energy by minimizing repetitive stress and unhappiness. It is another key to real mind power. Based on this understanding, the strategy for happiness.

Health Awareness:

You can apply this awareness of the Quantum Mechanics of thoughts and Energy of Emotions to your health. The body has 60 trillion cells. Each cell has its own energetic signature or wave frequency that is highly sensitive to your thoughts and emotions.

21.7 Quantum Happiness through Expansion of Consciousness

What does 'Quantum Science' have to do with happiness? Happiness is about the expansion of consciousness. Quantum science guides you to the expansion of consciousness to its fullest extent.

Enlightenment is a quantumly realized experience where one's ego gets dissolved and the one merges with oneself. So, there is no one to experience this happiness, and hence enlightenment is different than happiness.

Seeking happiness is a positive phenomenon. As stated earlier, it can be done through the expansion of consciousness. Seeking happiness is positive so long as it is not pathological, since in pathological happiness one becomes materialistic. It is like seeking short-lived happiness through drugs or sex. This leads to contraction of consciousness. If you rush too much for achieving happiness through such means, you will ultimately land into misery and depression. In the modern culture, normally it is very difficult to achieve the real happiness.

Dopamine is a chemical found naturally in the human body. It is a neurotransmitter, meaning it sends signals from the body to the brain. Dopamine plays a part in controlling the movements a person makes, as well as their emotional responses. The right balance of dopamine is vital for both physical and mental wellbeing. Vital brain functions that affect mood, sleep, memory, learning, concentration, and motor control are influenced by the levels of dopamine in a person's body. A dopamine deficiency may be related to certain medical conditions, including depression and Parkinson's disease. A dopamine deficiency can be due to a drop in the amount of dopamine made by the body or a problem with the receptors in the brain. Dependence of dopamine may lead to temporary euphoria but it leads to contraction of consciousness of consciousness resulting into depression and unhappiness.

The anterior cingulate cortex (ACC) is a part of the human neocortex. Located dorsal to the corpus callosum, the ACC has many important functions: related to motivation, attention, pain perception and most importantly error detection, monitoring and evaluation. To perform these functions, the ACC needs to be connected directly or indirectly to most of the brain, especially the medial frontal, prefrontal and lateral prefrontal cortices. Some other connections are the basal ganglia, the limbic system and some part of the parietal cortex.

Because the ventral ACC is involved in emotional behaviors, it is part of the limbic system. Connections to other medial limbic areas, such as the hypothalamus, hippocampus and the amygdala among others are well-defined. In addition, these areas are also linked to motivational and affective behaviors. The ACC is also associated with brainstem structures (involved in autonomic control) since one of the functions of the anterior cingulate cortex is to control autonomic behaviors like heart rate and blood pressure. The lateral frontal and parietal areas have connections with the ACC as well. In conclusion, the ACC and amygdala among others decide the degree of happiness in us.

Happiness is a state of 'being'. One of the most effective method for achieving this state is either through breathing (pranayama) or some meditation practice, especially from Hinduism or Buddhism. In the higher happiness level, the positive emotional circuits break to transform to emotional equanimity.

21.8 Principles for Achieving Quantum Bliss

Life is continuous improvement where we learn to balance our powers of mind, body and spirit. Happiness is subjective and we all must build ourselves from the inside out. If we can cultivate self-regard, develop harmony with other people, places and things in our environment, we can operate at a higher order of being.

We all have the opportunity to live a supernatural life in which we have a positive impact and meaning for our family, our community and the world. Our constructive actions can improve the prosperity of generations to come where our legacy as teachers of the quantum mechanics of success will never be forgotten.

The eighth-century Hindu mystic Shankara exuberantly expressed his realization: "I am reality without beginning, without equal. I have no part in the illusion of 'I' and 'you,' 'this' and 'that.' I am Brahman, one without a second, Bliss without end, the eternal, unchanging truth.... I dwell within all beings as the soul, the pure consciousness, the ground of all phenomena, internal and external.

I am both the enjoyer and that which is enjoyed. In the days of my ignorance, I used to think of these as being separate from myself. Now I know that I am All."

The fourteenth-century Kabbalist Moses de Leon, probably the author of the Zohar, which is the primary sourcebook for Kabbalists, wrote: "God ... when he has just decided to launch upon his work of creation is called He. God in the complete unfolding of his Being, Bliss and Love, in which he becomes capable of being perceived by the reasons of the heart ... is called You. But God, in his supreme manifestation, where the fullness of His Being finds its final expression in the last and all-embracing of his attributes, is called *'I'.*"

The 10 Upanishads (Èùá, Kena, Kaûha, Muïãaaka, Mañdükya, Aitereya, Taittirèya, Chandogya, and Brhadaranyaka) forming the wisdom base for which India is known all over the world has the other dimensions of creation presented with such vividity that any scientist would get fascinated about it. The other specialty is that the techniques of Yoga provide the necessary skills to realize the truth or reality or pure consciousness by gaining mastery over the mind. Reality is at the base of all creation and this state of deepest silence of mind is also the supreme bliss, total knowledge, and the power unparalleled. The Taittèreya Upaniúat has promoted this wisdom base through it spaòca koúa viveka—the five layered existence of the whole creation of which the physical world is the grossest. Next to that are the subtle layers unseen by the eyes called práïamaya, Manomaya, and Vijòánamaya Koúás. The causal layer of consciousness is the ánandamaya koúa from where all creation emerges. A schematic of the same is self-explanatory. As a manifest of bliss, as waves in an ocean. The layer of bliss is a state where mind has gone to its deepest levels of silence with all pervasive expanses.

That this whole universe is only in the form of waves but which functions as a solid particle cannot be known by us directly. Vedanta reiterates in each line and each statement that what we see is unreal. Adi Sankaracharya's Vivekachoodamani says that from the point of view of the Self, that is the individuality in all beings, Sarvatman - everything that is seen, heard, tasted, smelt, touched or thought about is only an appearance. It comes and goes. There is no steadiness to it, like waves in the ocean.

In this state of illusion there is no discounting anything. It is a total washout. The whole physical world of matter, the situations happening in our life, the people around us and the day-to-day objects we use have only a momentary existence. More than any ancient book today, particle physics is proving it. Quantum physics says that everything we see around us has a wavy movement at the sub-atomic level. However, when you focus on something, it ceases to function as a wave and behaves like a particle.

In the whole flux of illusion, even the person or the individual that you call "I" is an illusion. There is no person called 'I', actually speaking, even though we are constantly saying, I go, I come, I speak, I feel happy, I feel sad. The going, coming, speaking, happy and sad are all temporary actions and emotions, superimposed on the locus called I all the time. The 'I' has no temporary and changing reality. It is permanent and one consciousness.

That this whole universe is only in the form of waves but which functions as a solid particle cannot be known by us directly. We can only read and listen to what the scientists say and make an attempt to understand it. In the same way the reality that we see around us is only an illusion that cannot be directly seen by us. The masters who explain the words of the Upanishads can speak and write about it or try to explain it. We cannot logically understand it too, but only accept it as we accept the words spoken by someone we love and admire, meditate upon it and realise it.

We keep saying all the time that I know this, I know that. However, actually we know only this and that, but we do not know the 'I'. Why is it so? This word 'I' and mine etc. have only a momentary identification with all the objects known. What is the result of this understanding of the difference between what is permanent and what is temporary? Liberation from limited identification and concepts.

Why should I be liberated?

If that question is asked, it is like a person in prison saying, "Why should I be released from jail?" If we want to help ourselves, we have to seek liberation and that does not come without seeking or asking. Seek the Self within you, be free and experience the bliss of pure existence, or bliss.

21.9 Quantum Physics, Vedanta and Bliss

Toward the end of the 19th century, the Hindu monk and reformer Swami Vivekananda claimed that modern science was inevitably converging towards Advaita Vedanta, an important philosophico-religious system in Hinduism. In the decades that followed, in the midst of the revolution occasioned by the emergence of Einstein's relativity and quantum physics, a growing number of authors claimed to discover striking "parallels" between Advaita Vedanta and modern physics. Such claims of convergence have continued to the present day, especially in relation to quantum physics. Here we examine such claims by engaging a comparative analysis of two concepts: akasa in Advaita Vedanta and vacuum in quantum physics. What is examined is the claim that both concepts would refer to the same reality — an enduring, subtle and all-pervading physical substratum out of which the constituents of the world come into existence and to which they ultimately return. Based on this study, the dissertation argues that comparisons relying on conceptual affinities alone generally fall short of establishing a productive dialogue between Advaita Vedanta and modern physics. Another approach is to bring into focus the epistemological limits respectively encountered by these systems when attempting to define the content of "reality-in-itself" or "ultimate reality." Emphasis is given to epistemology and the problem of reality in Advaita Vedanta, and scientific realism and philosophical implications of non-separability in quantum physics.
In Advaita, Brahman is the one, all-pervasive, unchanging and underlying principle of all being and reality. It is the common essence or substratum that runs through all things but remains beyond them,

not affected by them. Yet, it is not an objective principle of existence, neither a creation of the mind, nor a subjective state of being. It is not a 'He', a personal being; nor is it an 'It', an impersonal concept. Brahman is that state which is when all subject/object distinctions are obliterated. Brahman is beyond the subject-object duality and cannot be predicated with any quality. No positive language can describe adequately Brahman because it would limit or reduce its indescribable (anirvacanıya) reality to conceptual and linguistic categories, and make it an object of knowledge. Still, Advaitins often describe Brahman to be saccidananda, that is, existence (sat), consciousness (chit) and bliss (ananda). As sat, Brahman refers to a state of pure being, undifferentiated, not subject to origination, change, destructions, or relations. As chit, it refers to the principle of pure awareness that informs our real self (atman), a state which is not an object of thought but which illumines every thought. Brahman is the conscious witness (saksin) behind the knower, the known and the knowledge. As to the word 'ananda', it refers to Brahman as the source of all forms of bliss, whether born of sensory experience or from spiritual practices. Brahman is thus described as the anantam brahma, Brahman is truth, knowledge, infinite. Commenting on this passage, Sankara explains that these three terms do not positively describe Brahman but only serve to "differentiate Brahman from other entities that possess opposite qualities." According to Padmapada, these three words, or each of them singly, are not intended to be attributes superadded to Brahman (tatasthalaksana) but only expressions of its essence (svarupalaksana).

In the following, we shall be dealing especially with parallels between Advaita Vedanta and quantum physics. In the view of some authors, quantum physics would advance that there is no separation between subject and object, that reality is essentially of the nature of consciousness, and that human consciousness "creates" physical reality; holism in quantum physics, that is, the idea that the physical universe is an undivided whole in which everything is interconnected. These ideas are recurrent in parallels made with Advaita Vedanta as this system considers the plurality of empirical phenomena to be the expression of a unitive and underlying principle of existence and consciousness called Brahman.

The advent of quantum physics at the beginning of the 20th century radically changed the conception of the physical world which was prevailing in science at that time. Prior to that, and for about three centuries, classical physics constituted the foundation for science as a whole. Classical physics worldview was simple, coherent and agreed with common sense. It made three major assumptions about the universe: 1. realism: the universe embedded in space and time exists apart from the observer; 2. determinism: knowing the initial state of a physical system, it is possible to know with certainty any future state of this system; 3. reductionism: a complex system is nothing but the sum of its parts and its behavior can be known from the behavior of its parts. The classical universe was a huge clockwork mechanism in which physical bodies moved with respect to each other according to precise natural laws. Matter, absolute space and time, and forces between bodies were the basic ingredients of the classical ontology; its epistemology was guided by the principle that an objective representation of the outside world is possible.

Quantum physics put into question these three major assumptions. In only three decades, starting with the pathbreaking work of Max Planck and Niels Bohr, quantum physics shattered the classical picture of the world, revealing classes of phenomena that classical physics could not : 1. the fact that certain physical quantities (ex: energy) are "quantized" in small discrete units; 2. the wave-particle dualism, or the fact that elementary particles behave like particles and waves; 3. the fact, stated in Heisenberg's uncertainty principle, that it is physically impossible to know both the position and momentum of a particle at the same time, implying indeterminism; and 4. non-separability, that is, the phenomenon by which the states of two or more quantum objects are entangled together so that the state of one object is related to the other in some way, whether or not the objects are spatially distant. In contrast with classical physics, quantum physics pays special attention to the process of measurement. Because it deals with small systems (e.g., atoms), interaction between observer and observed system obtains a fundamental importance in this theory. On this basis, some have alleged that classical realism does not hold anymore because of the prominent role played by the observer. Others have merged this idea with non-separability, making the universe an undivided whole in which the observer and the observed are underlain by the same reality, that is, consciousness. Since such ideas are commonly found in Eastern spiritual traditions, it is no surprise that some parallels between the disciplines have been drawn.

Although the Upanishads frequently describe Brahman as such, ′Sankara hesitates to use this word in his own works. Indeed, bliss seems to refer to a temporary pleasant state, having a beginning and an end. As such, it cannot characterize the unchangeable Brahman. However, that the bliss referred to is not an object of consciousness that can be experienced in any empirical way. This bliss, of which our joys and pleasures are only feeble expressions, arises from Brahman being infinite and all-pervasive in nature. According to Swami Dayananda, the word ananda cannot refer to the "experience" of bliss if it refers to the nature (svarupa) of Brahman.

However, if aka′sa is sometimes used as an appropriate symbol for Brahman, under no circumstances can it be identified with it. In fact, despite their similarities, aka′sa and Brahman differ considerably as to their essential nature. Unlike Brahman, whose nature is saccidananda — pure existence, consciousness and bliss — aka′sa has only a relative existence, is insentient and devoid of bliss. Like every other existent, aka′sa is mithya, or sadasadvilaksana: it is neither sat because it is ultimately sublated by the knowledge of Brahman, neither asat because it is actually perceived to be real. It depends upon Brahman for its own existence. From an Advaita perspective, in those instances where aka′sa is identified with the prime matter of the universe (avyakta), it is verily Brahman which is referred to, but Brahman envisaged as the unevolved potential of the world. Brahman is the only creator of the universe. In any case, we must recall that creation for Advaitins — whether mediated through maya, aka′sa or any other primary principle — stands as a valid explanation of the universe from a transactional or conventional standpoint only. From a non-dual standpoint, neither the universe nor the elements do really exist: Brahman alone exists.

To conclude, ay the spirit of the universe bless you and your loved ones as you journey onward with quantum bliss.

BIBLIOGRAPHY

Abbot, Derek; Paul C. W. Davies; Arun K. Pati; " Quantum Aspects of Life" (with foreword by Sir Roger Penrose), Imperial College Press, 2008.

Al-Ghazzali, Imam, "The Alchemy of Happiness", Translated by Clau Field, 1910.
Analayo, "Healing in Early Buddhism", Buddhist Studies Review, BSRV 32.1 (2015) 19–33. doi: 10.1558/bsrv.v32i1.28962.

Anastopoulos, Charis, "Mind–Body Interaction and Modern Physics", https://www.researchgate.net/publication/339946734

Bartmann, Peter; Beate Jakob; Ulrich Laepple; and Dietrich Werner, "Health, Healing and Spirituality: The Future of the Church's Ministry of Healing", The German Institute for Medical Mission (DIFAEM), Tübingen.

Berman, Laura, "Quantum Love", Hay House, 2016.

Bilqies, Shahida. "Understanding the Concept of Islamic Sufism", Journal of Education & Social Policy Vol. 1 No. 1; June 2014.

Bomhard, Allan, " The Original Teachings of the Buddha", https://www.researchgate.net/publication/337707221

Brahm, Ajahn, "Mindfulness, Bliss, and Beyond", Wisdom Publication, 2005.
Brustein, Ram and Yotam Sherf, "Quantum Love", https://www.researchgate.net/publication/343498704

Buddharakkhita, Acharya, "METTâ, The Philosophy & Practice of Universal Love", Buddha Vachana Trust, 2014.

Buddhrakkhita, Acharya, " The Dhammapada: The Buddha's Path of Wisdom", Buddhist Publication Society, 1985.

Bukkyo Dendo Kyokai, "The Teaching of Buddha: Wheel of Dharma", 2005.
Chapter · January 2012 https://www.researchgate.net/publication/278665173

Chopra, Deepak, "Quantum Healing: Exploring the Frontiers of Mind/Body Medicine", Bantan Books, 1989.

Dalai Lama, and Howard C. Cutler, "The Art of Happiness" : A Handbook for Living", 10th Edition, Riverhead Books, 2009.

Dudeja, Jai Paul, "Happiness explained by the ancient Hindu Scriptures and the temporal nonlocality in Quantum Entanglement", https://www.researchgate.net/publication/333817144

Dudeja, Jai Paul. "Scientific Analysis of Mantra-Based Meditation and Its Beneficial Effects: An Overview", International Journal of Advanced Scientific Technologies in Engineering and Management Sciences (IJASTEMS- ISSN: 2454-356X), Vol. 3, Issue 6, June 2017, pp. 21-26.

Dudeja, Prof. (Dr.) Jai Paul, "Quantum Physics of Consciousness and Non-duality in Eastern Philosophy", Blue Rose Publishers, 2021.

Dudeja, Jai Paul, "Emerging Applications of Quantum Entanglement: Quantum Lidar and Unhackable Communication over Large Distances", International Journal of Research and Analytical Reviews (IJRAR), February 2019, Volume 6, Issue 1 www.ijrar.org (E-ISSN 2348-1269, P- ISSN 2349-5138)

Dudeja, Jai Paul, "Chakras Healing and Kundalini Awakening by Yogic Techniques" Chaukhamba Sanskrit Pratishthan, 2021 (in press).

Duquette, Jonathan. "Towards a Philosophical Reconstruction of the Dialogue between Modern Physics and Advaita Vedanta: An Inquiry into the Concepts of akasa, Vacuum and Reality", Ph.D. Thesis. University of Montreal, Sep 2010.

Golkarian, Ghadir, "Divine Love in Rumi Lore and Mysticism", https://www.researchgate.net/publication/330728759.

Goswami, Amit, " The Everything Answer Book: How Quantum Physics explains Love, Death and the meaning of Life", Jaico Publishing House, 2017.

Hall, Howard; Merc S, Micozzi, and Carole A. O'leary. "Sufism and Healing" in the Middle East", Chapter 38, in "Fundamentals of Complementary, Alternative, and Integrative Medicine", Elsevier, 2019.

Hongbao, Ma; Margaret Young; and Yang Yan , "Quantum Entanglement Introduction", Academia Arena 2016;8(7) http://www.sciencepub.net/academia. P. 93-97.

http://what-when-how.com/love-in-world-religions/divine-love-in-christianity/#:~:text=The%20Christian%20experience%20of%20divine,1%20John%204%3A16). https://www.researchgate.net/publication/305703294

John Polis Ministries, "The Complete School of Healing". Issue 6 www.jetir.org (ISSN-2349-5162)

Joshanloo, Mohsen; "A Comparison of Western and Islamic Conceptions of Happiness", J Happiness Stud (2013) 14:1857–1874. DOI 10.1007/s10902-012-9406-7

Kauffman, Stuart, "Mind, Body, Quantum Mechanics", Activitas Nervosa Superior, https://doi.org/10.1007/s41470-019-00045-0

Kern, Dr Peggy L. and Dr Susan D. Benecchi, "Intersections of

Positive Psychology and Christianity", 2019. www.peggykern.org/publications.html

Khanam, Farida, "Sufism: An Introduction", Goodword Books, 2009.

Leigh, Gillian Mary, "Reconceptualising Health: A Conversation between Quantum Science, Energy Medicine and Mystical Theology", Thesis submitted to Atlantic School of Theology, Halifax, Nova Scotia. March 2018.

Lombard, E. B. Joseph, "From Hubb to Ishq: The Development of Love in Early Sufism", J. Islamic Studies, 18:3, 2007, pp 345-385.

Lopez, Donald (Ed.), "Buddhist Scriptures", Penguin Books, 2004.

Lucas, Jacqueline, "Sufism and Curing", ProQuest LLC (2017).

Mentz, George, S. "Quantum Bliss: The Quantum Mechanics of Happiness, Abundance, and Health", Winchester, 2016.

Mihr, Imam Iskender Ali, "Islam Happiness Sufism", The Mihr Publications.

Murphy, Robert E. "Transforming the healing narrative: A pastoral understanding of Christ's healing ministry and the anointing of the sick", eScholarship@BC, Boston College University Libraries, 2014.
Nova Journal of Sufism and Spirituality PII: S236867661400001-2, Vol 2(1), 2014:1-9

Oxenberg, Richard. "Suffering and Bliss in the Heart of God: Steps on the Spiritual Ladder", https://www.researchgate.net/publication/319262710

Prasad, P.V.V. "General Medicine in Atharvaveda with Special Reference to Yaksma (Consumption/Tuberculosis", Bull. Ind. Inst. Hist. Med. Vol. XXXII - 2002. pp 1 to 14.

Pretorius, S.P., 2009, "Is "divine healing" in the 'Faith Movement' founded on the principles of healing in the Bible or based on the power of the mind?', HTS Teologiese Studies/Theological Studies, 65(1), Art. #277, 7 pages. DOI: 10.4102/hts.v65i1.277

Radin, Dean. "Entangled Minds: Extrasensory Experiences in a Quantum Reality ". Pocket Books. Kindle Edition.

Rahman, Farhat Naz; "Spiritual Healing and Sufi Practices", Nova Explore Publications, Nova Journal of Sufism and Spirituality, PII: S236867661400001-2

Rao, Venkoba, A. " Mind in Indian Philosophy" Indian Journal of Psychiatry, 2002,44(4),315-325.

Reynolds, John Warren, "Spiritual and Scientific Healing", https://www.researchgate.net/publication/330810982

Schwartz, Jeffrey M. Henry P. Stapp, and Mario Beauregar, "Quantum physics in neuroscience and psychology: a neurophysical model of mind–brain interaction", Phil. Trans. R. Soc. B (2005) 360, 1309–1327. doi:10.1098/rstb.2004.1598. Published online 29 June 2005

Sharma, Manu, "Ancient Ayurvedic Medical Rituals and Healing Traditions in Vedic Texts", Man in India, June 2016, 96 (4) : 985-993 https://www.researchgate.net/publication/303880633

Sharp, Patricia, "Meditation-induced bliss viewed as release from conditioned neural (thought) patterns that block reward signals in the brain pleasure center", https://www.researchgate.net/publication/259944593

Shaykh Hakim Moinuddin Chishti "The Book of Sufi Healing" Inner Traditions International, 1991.

Shrihari, T. G. "Quantum Healing Approach to New Generation of Holistic Healing", https://www.researchgate.net/publication/322740184

Smith, Katherine; Cindy Crawford; Dawn Bellanti; and Bonnie Sakallaris; "Healing, a Concept Analysis", November 2015, Global Advances in Health and Medicine 4(6):44-50.

Solati, Dr. Bahman, The Concept of Love in Medieval Persian Sufi Poetry", Lecture delivered at the University of California, Berkeley, January 25, 2018.

Sri Swami Sivananda, "All about Hinduism", The Divine Life Society, Sixth Edition, 1997.

Subramanian, Sriram Ganapathi; and Benyamin Ghojogh, "Introduction to the Non-dualism Approach in Hinduism and its Connection to Other Religions and Philosophies", https://www.researchgate.net/publication/342503023

Swami Shantananda Puri, "Infallible Vedic Remedies (Mantras for Common Problems)", Parvathamma C.P. Subbaraju Setty Charitable Trust, 2008.

Thanh, Minh; and P.D. Leigh; "Sutra of the Medicine Buddha", International Buddhist Monistic Institute, 2001.

The Dalai Lama, "The Four Noble Truths", Thorsons, 1997.

Tiliouine, Habib, " Happiness in Islam", January 2014, DOI:10.1007/978-94-007-0753-5_1544. In book: Encyclopedia of Quality of Life and Well-Being Research (pp.2662-2667), Springer Netherlands, Editors: Alex C. Michalos.

Topbas, Osman Nuri, " The Society of the Age of Bliss", Erkam Publications, 2014.

Ulluwishewa, Rohana, "Spirituality, Universal Love and Sustainable Behaviour" , Annal Behav Neurosci, 1(1): 66-76 (2018).

Van der Merwe, Izak Johannes. (2015). Biblical happiness and baptismal identity. Stellenbosch Theological Journal, 1(2), 695-710. https://dx.doi.org/10.17570/STJ.2015.V1N2.A33

Vaughan-Lee, Llewellyn, "Love Is Fire and I Am Wood: Laylâ and Majnûn as a Sufi Allegory of Mystical Love", Sufi Journal, Aug 2011.

Veenhoven, Ruut, "Happiness: Also Known as Life Satisfaction and Subjective Well-Being"

Veeraiah, Chandrasekaran, "The pursuit of happiness: An Advaita Vedanta perspective", https://www.researchgate.net/publication/305703294.

Venerable Master Hsuan Hua, "The Buddha Speaks of Amitabha Sutra" Buddhist Text Translation Society, 2002. Vol 2(1), 2014:1-9, www.novaexplore.com

Warber, Sara L.; Rosalyn L. Bruyere; Ken Weintrub; and Paul Dieppe; "A Consideration of the Perspectives of Healing Practitioners on Research Into Energy Healing", Global Adv Health Med. 2015;4(suppl):72-78. DOI: 10.7453/gahmj.2015.014.suppl

Wood, H., 2016, "A Christian understanding of the significance of love of oneself in loving God and neighbour: Towards an integrated self-love reading", HTS Teologiese Studies/ Theological Studies 72(3), a3401. http://dx.doi.org/10.4102/hts.v72i3.3401
www.novaexplore.com

INDEX

I

J

N

P

W

Y

Z